The Congressional Club Cookbook

The Congressional Club Cookbook

Thirteenth Edition

Compiled and Published by
THE CONGRESSIONAL CLUB
Washington, D.C.

1998

Copyright 1998

by

THE CONGRESSIONAL CLUB
2001 New Hampshire Avenue, N.W.
Washington, D.C. 20009

PRINTED IN THE UNITED STATES OF AMERICA BY
AFFILIATED GRAPHICS
3342 BLADENSBURG ROAD, BRENTWOOD, MARYLAND 20722

Acknowledgements

CONGRESSIONAL CLUB COOKBOOK COMMITTEE

CHAIRMEN

Sharon Archer, *Texas*   Janet Hall, *Ohio*

COMMITTEE

Diana Allen, *Maine*
Laura Bateman, *Virginia*
Lana Bethune, *Arkansas*
Betty Chapman, *Texas*
Mary Clement, *Tennessee*
Nancy Ireland, *Florida*
Jacquelyn Orton, *Utah*
Emilie Shaw, *Florida*
Paula Swift, *Washington*
Carolyn Wolf, *Virginia*

SPECIAL THANKS

Andrew Bradley, *Affiliated Graphics*
Dan Bradley, *Affiliated Graphics*
Alice Duvall, *Affiliated Graphics*
Lydia de La Vina de Foley, *Congressional Club*
Jessie Harris, *Photographer, Washington, DC*
Flo Oxley, *National Wildflower Research Center*
Lady Bird Johnson Wildflower Center, Austin, TX
Marylou Sheils, *Coordinator of the Members and Family Committee*
Lynn Staton, *West Virginia*
Bob Walker, *Affiliated Graphics*

Additional copies of this book are available at:

THE CONGRESSIONAL CLUB
2001 New Hampshire Ave., N.W.
Washington, D.C. 20009
Telephone 202-332-1155

Visa or Mastercard orders by fax only.
Fax: (202) 797-0698

President's Letter

The highlight of the Congressional Club's 90th Anniversary Celebration is the publication of the Congressional Club Cookbook. In this Thirteenth Edition we honor our founders who in 1908 envisioned a Congressional spouses' club that encouraged and nurtured bipartisan friendships.

The Cookbook, first introduced in 1927, is a tradition the Club is proud to continue. The twelve previous editions are important chapters in our history. Our nation's leaders and Congressional spouses have participated throughout the years in this project. It is with pride that we present the 1998 Cookbook as part of our 90th-year celebration.

The inspiration for this Thirteenth Edition of the Cookbook was conceived by Mrs. Bill (Sharon) Archer of Texas and Mrs. Tony (Janet) Hall of Ohio, who have capably led a hardworking committee. It has taken many months of planning and many hours of collecting and editing recipes to accomplish this enormous task, and we are most grateful to them all. The wildflower theme truly captures the spirit of our club. Each flower grows and thrives in its home state just as each member represents the home district and state. When the flowers are arranged into a beautiful bouquet, we are reminded of the many friendships that are made as we share our lives as Congressional spouses and as members of the Congressional Club.

We extend our deep appreciation to the sponsors for their generosity, and to the many persons who have helped in this project.

This new and unique collection of recipes represents the diverse ethnic backgrounds, regional customs and family traditions of our members and their spouses. The book is at home on the coffee table or on the kitchen shelf, as a gift given or a gift received, or whether you like to cook or just collect. This beautiful cookbook is a symbol of the collection of friendships that our members cherish.

The Cookbook Committee and all the members of the Congressional Club hope that you enjoy these delicious recipes, as well as the colorful flowers, and in the company of good friends.

Carolyn Hobson

Mrs. David Hobson, *Ohio*

Table of Contents

The Congressional Club

Celebrating
90 Years

Appetizers & Beverages

The Congressional Club
would like to thank
Diamond Chef Sponsor

Fed Ex

Appetizers & Beverages

WOMEN'S POWER OF PERSUASION

On May 6, 1908, at the very first meeting of the Congressional Club, its founding members voted to ask Congress for a charter. John Sharp Williams, Minority Leader of the House, who opposed women's clubs for keeping women away from hearth and home, announced his opposition. On the day of the vote, May 20, 1908, Mrs. Williams, looking her loveliest, surprised her husband with an invitation to lunch. While they enjoyed an hour in the Representatives Dining Room, the charter resolution passed on the Floor. Since that time the Club has functioned as a self-supporting non-profit organization, thanks to our cookbooks. We hope you enjoy this 13th Edition of The Congressional Club Cookbook issued in honor of our 90th anniversary celebration.

Hot Crab Casserole or Dip

1 pound lump crab meat
1 8-ounce package cream cheese

1 8-ounce container sour cream
1 cup grated sharp yellow cheddar cheese

Soften cream cheese to room temperature. Add sour cream and cheddar cheese. Carefully fold in crab meat. Put into casserole dish. Bake at 350° for 45 minutes or until very bubbly. Serve with crackers or on top of toasted English muffin with country ham slices. Makes a great appetizer or main dish depending on presentation. Lots of servings. (5 minutes preparation time. Suitable for freezing.)

Stan Parris

Stan Parris, *former Representative (Virginia)*

Shrimp Crescents
SERVES 48

1 8-ounce package light Philadelphia Brand Neufchatel Cheese, softened
1 cup finely chopped cooked shrimp
⅓ cup (1½-ounces) Kraft grated Parmesan cheese

1 Tablespoon milk
2 8-ounce cans Pillsbury refrigerated crescent dinner rolls
1 egg, beaten
1 teaspoon water

Combine Neufchatel cheese, shrimp, Parmesan cheese and milk, mixing until well blended. Separate crescent dough into 8 rectangles; press perforations to seal holes. Spread each rectangle evenly with 2 rounded tablespoons of cheese mixture. Cut rectangles into 6 triangles; roll as directed on package. Place on greased cookie sheets; brush with combined egg and water. Bake at 375° for 12 to 15 minutes or until golden brown. Serve warm. Makes about 4 dozen. This is a very fancy appetizer of silver tray quality. (30 minutes preparation time. Not suitable for freezing.)

Martie Parris

Mrs. Stan Parris, *wife of former Representative (Virginia)*

John's Guacamole
SERVES 6

3 avocados, sliced
1 small onion, chopped
1 small tomato, chopped
⅓ cup chopped chilies
2 Tablespoons lemon juice

2 Tablespoons salsa
2 or 3 cloves garlic
2 Tablespoons sugar
hot red pepper sauce to taste

Place all ingredients in a large bowl, mash with potato masher until blended well; do not overdo the mashing. Salt and pepper to taste. Serve with tortilla chips. (Not suitable for freezing.)

John Myers

John Myers, *former Representative (Indiana)*

Monterey Jack Salsa

1 can green chilies (4 ounces), chopped
1 can black olives (3¼ ounces), chopped
4 green onions, chopped
¼ pound Monterey Jack cheese,
  shredded

1 tomato, chopped
½ cup Italian salad dressing
¼ cup chopped fresh cilantro
2 bags tortilla chips for serving

Blend all ingredients and serve with tortilla chips. (15 minutes preparation time. Not suitable for freezing.)

Tyler Lott

Tyler Lott, *daughter of Senator Trent Lott (Mississippi)*

Hot Artichoke Dip
SERVES 6 TO 8

14-ounce can artichoke hearts
1 cup Parmesan cheese
⅔ cup mayonnaise

2 Tablespoons Worcestershire sauce
1 to 2 teaspoons Tabasco sauce
1 teaspoon garlic salt

Drain artichoke hearts well and cut up. Mix all ingredients and bake at 350° for 20 to 30 minutes, until slightly brown on top. Serve with crackers. (10 minutes preparation time. Not suitable for freezing.)

Margaret Anne Morgan

Margaret Anne Morgan, *daughter of former Senator Robert Burren Morgan (North Carolina)*

Dani's Garlic Wowchos Nachos
SERVES 6 TO 10

2 large heads of garlic, separated
   into cloves and peeled
2 Tablespoons olive oil
1 14½-ounce bag of tortilla chips
¼ cup chopped red onion

1 4-ounce can chopped green chilies
⅓ cup pimento-stuffed olives, sliced
1½ cup grated jalapeno jack cheese
¼ cup chopped green onions
¼ cup chopped cilantro

Coat garlic cloves with olive oil and bake at 375° for 30 minutes, until soft and golden. While garlic is roasting prepare other ingredients. Cover a cookie sheet or casserole dish with one layer of tortilla chips. Mash the garlic and sprinkle over the chips. Sprinkle the red onion, green chilies and olives over the chips. Cover with cheese. Broil until the cheese melts. Top with cilantro and green onions. Serve immediately. (45 minutes preparation time. Not suitable for freezing.)

Stacey Rhodes

Stacey Rhodes, *daughter-in-law of former Representative John J. Rhodes III (Arizona)*

Baked Meatballs in Sweet Sour Sauce
SERVES 12

1½ pounds ground chuck
1 can water chestnuts, drained
   and chopped
½ cup rolled oats
½ cup milk
2 eggs

1 teaspoon salt
½ teaspoon onion salt
½ teaspoon garlic salt
1 cup catsup
1 12-ounce jar currant jelly

Combine meat, water chestnuts, oats, milk, eggs and seasonings. Form into small balls. Place in shallow baking pan. In a separate bowl combine catsup and jelly. Pour over meatballs. Bake uncovered at 325° for 1 hour, turning every 15 minutes. Makes 50 small meatballs. (15 minutes preparation time. Suitable for freezing.)

Margaret Grant

Mrs. Robert Grant, *wife of former Representative (Indiana)*

Basil-Parmesan Spread
SERVES 8 TO 10

1 cup chopped spinach leaves

1 cup fresh basil leaves

1 teaspoon minced garlic

¼ cup olive oil

1 cup freshly grated Parmesan

8 ounces cream cheese
  (room temperature)

4 ounces soft, fresh goat cheese
  (room temperature)

¼ cup chopped walnuts

¼ cup thinly sliced, well drained,
  oil packed, sun-dried tomatoes

crackers and bread

Line a 3-cup bowl with plastic wrap, leaving a 4-inch overhang. Combine spinach, basil and garlic in processor and chop finely. Gradually add oil and then Parmesan until smooth. Add salt and pepper. Stir together in a medium bowl cream cheese and goat cheese. Blend well. Spread ⅓ of cream cheese mixture in bottom of prepared bowl. Spread ½ of spinach mixture over cheese. Sprinkle with ½ of walnuts. Arrange ½ of tomatoes over walnuts. Drop ⅓ of cream cheese mixture by spoonfuls over tomatoes. Repeat layering with spinach mixture, walnuts, tomatoes, and cream cheese. Fold plastic overhang over top of spread. Refrigerate overnight. Unfold plastic on top and invert spread onto plate. Remove bowl and plastic wrap. Decorate with basil leaves. Let stand at room temperature and serve with crackers and breads. (Instead of one large container, you can make 3″ × 4″ ramekin or soufflé dishes.) (20 minutes preparation time. Suitable for freezing.)

Adeline P. Rhodes

Adeline Rhodes, *daughter-in-law of former Representative John J. Rhodes III (Arizona)*

Chili Rellenos Squares
SERVES 6-8

3 cups Monterey Jack cheese

1 (3 ounces) can green chilies drained & chopped

4 large eggs, beaten

Preheat oven to 350°. Sprinkle cheese and chilies evenly into the bottom of a greased 8-inch square pan. Pour eggs on top of cheese mixture. Bake for one hour. Allow to cool for 5 minutes. Cut into 1-inch squares. Serve warm or cold. (5 minutes preparation time. Suitable for freezing.)

Elena C. Skelton

Elena C. Skelton, *daughter-in-law of Representative Ike Skelton (Missouri)*

GOLDENROD
(SOLIDAGO SP.)

ALABAMA

An ugly old woman was making her way through a forest. Because she was having a difficult time, she asked the trees to give her one of their branches to use as a walking stick. Every tree refused to help her. As she continued on her way, she came upon a broken stick lying on the path. The stick said, "I'll help you on your journey." She picked it up and together they made their way out of the forest.

Out of the shadow of the trees, the old woman turned into a beautiful fairy. As a reward for its help, she granted the stick's fondest wish: to be loved by all the children of the world. Sprinkling it with gold dust, the fairy turned the stick into the beautiful goldenrod and promised that all children would, forevermore, love the goldenrod.

Clams Casino

SERVES 6 TO 8

¼ cup butter
¼ cup chopped onion
½ cup chopped celery
⅛ teaspoon garlic powder
1 Tablespoon flour
1 teaspoon chili sauce
¾ teaspoon salt
¼ teaspoon pepper

Dash Tabasco sauce
2 cans minced clams and juice
1 egg, beaten
½ cup mashed cracker crumbs
2 Tablespoons parsley
2 Tablespoons butter (melted)
½ cup bread crumbs
paprika

Sauté for 10 minutes butter, onion, celery and garlic powder. Add flour, chili sauce, salt, and pepper, Tabasco, clams and juice, egg, cracker crumbs and parsley. Stir ingredients until blended together. Divide mixture into 6 to 8 baking shells. Melt 2 tablespoons butter and add bread crumbs. Place bread crumbs on top of clam mixture in baking shells. Sprinkle with paprika. Bake at 400° for 10 minutes or until bubbly. (30 minutes preparation time. Suitable for freezing.)

Jean Thompson

Jean Thompson, *daughter of former Representative John H. Terry (New York)*

Warm Blue Cheese Dip with Garlic and Bacon

SERVES 8 TO 10

8 ounces cream cheese, softened
¼ cup heavy cream
4 ounces blue cheese, crumbled
7 slices bacon, cooked crisp and
    crumbled

2 cloves garlic, minced
2 Tablespoons chives, chopped
3 Tablespoons sliced almonds

Beat cream cheese until smooth. Add cream and beat. Stir in remaining ingredients except almonds. Place in baking dish. Top with almonds. Bake at 350° for 20 to 30 minutes. Serve with crackers. (10 minutes preparation time. Not suitable for freezing.)

Clay Shaw

E. Clay Shaw, *Representative (Florida)*

1 cup shelled walnuts or pecans (about 4 ounces)
3 large shallots (2½ ounces total), peeled
2 large garlic cloves, peeled
1 medium onion (4 ounces), peeled and quartered
6 Tablespoons canola oil
2 Granny Smith apples (15 ounces total), peeled, cored and quartered
1 pound chicken livers, trimmed of fat
8 ounces "hot" turkey sausage, casings removed
¼ cup Calvados or Applejack
8 ounces fat-free cream cheese, room temperature
½ package Butter Buds
½ teaspoon dried tarragon
⅛ teaspoon dried thyme
⅛ teaspoon allspice

Lightly oil a 4-cup terrine mold. In a processor with the metal blade process the nuts for 5 seconds and set them aside. With the machine running, drop the shallots and garlic through the feed tube and process until finely minced. Add the onion and turn the machine on and off 12 or 14 times to chop it. In a 9-inch heavy skillet over moderately high heat, heat 3 tablespoons of the oil. Add the shallots, garlic and onion. Stir to prevent scorching. Meanwhile, put the apples in the processor and turn the machine on and off 8 to 10 times to chop them. Add them to the skillet and cook, stirring occasionally until the mixture is soft and transparent. Return the mixture to the processor. Heat the remaining oil in the skillet and sauté the livers and sausage until cooked through. Meanwhile, gently warm the Calvados in a small saucepan. When the meats are done, ignite the Calvados and pour it over them. Let the mixture cool to nearly room temperature. Add it to the processor for about 30 seconds, stopping once to scrape down the bowl. Add the cream cheese, Butter Buds and seasonings and process until smooth. Add the nuts and turn the machine on and off 3 or 4 times to mix them in. Transfer the mixture to the terrine, cover with plastic wrap and chill. Makes approximately 5 cups.

Serving suggestion: Unmold onto thinly sliced apples and surround with sliced cocktail pumpernickel bread. Makes about 5 cups. (45 minutes preparation time. Not suitable for freezing.)

James Corman, *former Representative (California)*

Cranberry Chutney and Baked Brie
SERVES 4

⅔ cup water
⅔ cup sugar
1⅓ cup cranberries
4 teaspoons cider vinegar

⅓ cup raisins
¼ cup chopped walnuts
2 teaspoons brown sugar
¼ teaspoon ginger

Dissolve water and sugar in saucepan. Add remaining ingredients and cook over medium heat until mixture thickens and cranberries pop. This can be refrigerated for several weeks at this point. Makes 4 servings.

To use, cover small round of brie with chutney on a heat-proof dish. Bake for 10 to 12 minutes at 350°. Serve with sliced French bread or crackers. For an 8 to 10 inch round of brie, bake for 15 to 20 minutes and let sit 5 minutes before cutting. (15 minutes preparation time. Not suitable for freezing.)

Patrici M. Tierney

Mrs. John Tierney, *wife of Representative (Massachusetts)*

Crab Stuffed Mushrooms
SERVES 8

24 medium sized fresh mushrooms
2 Tablespoons minced green onion tops
5 Tablespoons butter
1 teaspoon lemon juice
1 cup crabmeat (canned or fresh)

½ cup soft bread crumbs
½ teaspoon dill weed
¾ cup shredded Monterey Jack cheese
¼ cup dry white wine
1 egg, slightly beaten

Remove and chop mushroom stems. Sauté stems with onion tops and 2 tablespoons of butter. Remove above from heat and add lemon juice, crab, bread crumbs, egg, dill weed and ¼ cup of cheese. Melt remaining 3 tablespoons of butter in a 9″ × 13″ baking pan. Spoon filling into mushroom caps and place in pan. Sprinkle with remaining cheese. Pour wine in pan and bake at 400° for 15 minutes. Serve hot. Makes 24 pieces. (30 minutes preparation time. Suitable for freezing.)

Sydna Zeliff

Mrs. Bill Zeliff, *wife of former Representative (New Hampshire)*

Bruschetta
SERVES 6

6 slices crusty Italian bread
3 garlic cloves, peeled and cut in half
2 Tablespoons extra virgin olive oil
1-2 Tablespoons chopped fresh basil
salt and freshly ground pepper to taste
6 plum tomatoes, chopped

Toast or grill the bread. While the bread is still hot, rub garlic over one side of each slice. Drizzle olive oil on the bread. Add the basil, salt and pepper to the tomatoes. Top the bread with a portion of the seasoned tomatoes. Yields 6 servings at 126 calories each. (15 minutes preparation time. Not suitable for freezing.)

Robert N. Giaimo, *former Representative (Connecticut)*

Crab Pizza
SERVES 10

8 ounces light cream cheese
1 Tablespoon lemon juice
1 Tablespoon grated onion
2 teaspoons Worcestershire sauce

2 Tablespoons mayonnaise
½ bottle chili sauce
¼ cup fresh parsley, chopped
6 to 7 ounces crabmeat

Blend the first five ingredients together. Spread on a round serving plate. Top with chili sauce and refrigerate. (This can be made ahead to this point). Just before serving, top with crabmeat and sprinkle with parsley. Serve with crackers. (20 minutes preparation time. Not suitable for freezing.)

Tom Allen, *Representative (Maine)*

Homemade Salsa

7 medium fresh tomatoes, diced
1 3-ounce can of diced mild green chiles
3 green onions, diced
⅓ cup chopped fresh cilantro

1½ Tablespoons fresh lemon juice
2 teaspoons soy sauce
⅛ cup salad oil
2 Tablespoons red wine vinegar

Combine all ingredients in a large bowl and mix well. Cover and chill overnight. Will keep in refrigerator for 1 to 2 weeks. Serve with tortilla chips. (1 hour preparation time. Not suitable for freezing.)

Jeanette Hawkins McCrery

Mrs. James Hawkins McCrery, *wife of Representative (Louisiana)*

Hot Crab Spread
SERVES 8 TO 10

1 8-ounce package cream cheese
1 Tablespoon milk
2 Tablespoons Worcestershire sauce

1 8-ounce container fresh crabmeat
2 Tablespoons chopped green onions
2-3 Tablespoons toasted slivered almonds

Thoroughly combine cream cheese, milk and Worcestershire sauce. Flake crabmeat and add to cream cheese mixture with green onions. Turn into greased 8 inch pie plate or small shallow baking dish. Top with slivered almonds. Bake at 350° for 15 minutes. Serve with melba toast, cocktail bread or crackers. (Note: Better make extra! It disappears quickly at a party.) (10 minutes preparation time. Not suitable for freezing.)

Norma Udall

Mrs. Morris Udall, *wife of former Representative (Arizona)*

80 white pita bouchee (very small round pita bread loaves)
fresh ground parsley
ground red pepper

Shankleesh Cheese Dip

1 pound Shankleesh cheese (mixture of feta cheese, onion, garlic, hot pepper and spices rolled in green thyme),
3 Roma tomatoes
½ purple onion
olive oil

In a large bowl mix cheese, finely chopped Roma tomatoes and finely chopped purple onions with enough olive oil to have a smooth but not runny consistency. 1 pound makes approximately 8 balls.
(Note: Cheese will have to be mashed with a fork.)

Homos Bi Tahini (Chick Peas With Tahini)

2 cans chick peas
6-8 Tablespoons Tahini
    (made from crushed sesame seeds)
juice of 2 lemons, depending on taste

1 clove garlic, mashed
1 teaspoon salt
⅓ to ½ cup water

Rinse and drain chick peas and place in a blender with remaining ingredients. Turn on blender and stir mixture. Garnish with oil, parsley, finely sliced onion, cinnamon or ground red pepper.

Avocado With Tahini Dip

2 large ripe avocados
2 Tablespoons Tahini
    (made from crushed sesame seeds)

1 small clove garlic
juice of 1 lemon
salt to taste

Peel and mash avocado thoroughly. Blend together crushed garlic, lemon juice, salt and Tahini. Mix with avocado.

To assemble hors d'oeuvre: Put a small amount of Shankleesh Cheese Dip, Homos Bi Tahini and Avocado with Tahini Dip on top of white pita bouchee. Garnish with fresh parsley in the center of the three dips and sprinkle ground red pepper on top. (Note: Shankleesh Cheese and Tahini are available from Middle Eastern stores. You probably will not find them in a regular supermarket.)

Spencer Abraham   *Jane Abraham*

Spencer and Jane Abraham, *Senator and Mrs. (Michigan)*

Pesto Cheesecake
SERVES 18

1 Tablespoon sweet butter, room temperature
¼ cup fine dry bread crumbs
½ cup plus 2 Tablespoons Parmesan cheese
2 8-ounce packages lite cream cheese,
    room temperature
1 cup ricotta cheese

⅛ teaspoon cayenne pepper
3 eggs
½ cup pesto
¼ cup pine nuts
basil sprigs
crackers or French bread

Preheat oven to 325°. Rub butter over bottom and sides of a 9" diameter springform pan. Mix bread crumbs with 2 tablespoons of grated Parmesan cheese. Coat pan with crumb mixture. Using electric mixer, beat cream cheese, ricotta, remaining Parmesan and cayenne. Add eggs one at a time, beat well. Transfer half of mixture to medium bowl. Add pesto to remaining half. Pour pesto mixture into prepared pan, smooth top. Carefully spoon plain mixture over pesto, smooth top. Sprinkle with pine nuts. Bake until center no longer moves when pan is shaken, about 45 minutes. Transfer to rack and cool completely. Cover tightly and refrigerate overnight. Run small sharp knife around pan to loosen cheesecake, if necessary. Release pan sides from cheesecake. Transfer to platter. Garnish with fresh basil sprigs. Surround with crackers and serve. (20-30 minutes preparation time. Not suitable for freezing.)

Sally J Patterson

Sally Patterson, *member of Congressional Club (California)*

Fresh Mushroom Spread

½ pound fresh mushrooms, sliced
1 cup butter, soft

3 Tablespoons sherry
¼ teaspoon each of salt and pepper

Sauté sliced mushrooms in ¼ cup butter for about 5 minutes. Pour mushrooms and pan drippings into food processor or blender. Add remaining ingredients and blend until smooth. Serve as a spread for crackers, or over meat. (15 minutes preparation time.)

Ron Paul

Ron Paul, *Representative (Texas)*

Cheese Wafers

2 sticks margarine
2 cups grated sharp cheddar cheese
2 cups flour (plain)

dash of Tabasco sauce or red pepper
1 cup Rice Krispies

Mix 2 sticks margarine and 2 cups grated cheddar cheese with hands. Add 2 cups of flour and a dash of Tabasco. (More Tabasco may be added if you prefer a spicier wafer.) Mix with hands. Add 1 cup Rice Krispies (pack in the cup). Mix with hands. Roll mixture into marble size balls. Place on ungreased cookie sheet. Flatten balls with a fork. Bake at 350° for 15 to 20 minutes. Store in an airtight container when cooled. (Suitable for freezing.)

Roger Wicker

Roger Wicker, *Representative (Mississippi)*

Bacon-Wrapped Scallops

30 small sea scallops or 15 large, halved
10 slices very lean bacon
Bourbon Marinade:
¼ cup Bourbon
¼ cup soy sauce
¼ cup Dijon mustard

¼ cup minced scallion
¼ cup firmly packed
     light brown sugar
1 teaspoon salt
1 teaspoon Worcestershire sauce
pepper to taste

Combine ingredients for marinade and allow scallops to marinate for at least 1 hour, tossing them occasionally. Cut 10 slices of very lean bacon crosswise into thirds. Wrap a piece of the bacon around each scallop, and thread the scallops onto metal skewers, leaving ¼″ between each scallop. Grill the scallops over a bed of glowing coals about 3″ from the heat, turning them twice, for 10 to 15 minutes, or until bacon is crisp. Slide the scallops off the skewers onto a platter. Makes 6 servings. (90 minutes preparation time. Not suitable for freezing.)

Cal Dooley

Cal Dooley, *Representative (California)*

FORGET-ME-NOT
(MYOSOTIS ALPESTRIS)

ALASKA

A member of the Boraginacaea, or borage family, forget-me-not symbolizes loving memory, friendship, and faithfulness.

Two young lovers were walking beside a river when the girl spied a pretty flower on the bank. The young man, leaning down to pick a bloom for his lady love, fell into the river. As he was swept away, he threw the flower to the girl and cried, "Forget me not!".

Almond Chutney Cheese

1 8-ounce package cream cheese
1 cup grated cheddar cheese
2 Tablespoons butter, softened
2 Tablespoons dry sherry

2 teaspoons chives, chopped
1 teaspoon curry powder
½ cup chopped chutney (Major Grey)
⅔ cup slivered almonds, toasted

Combine cream cheese, cheddar cheese, butter, sherry, chives and curry powder in a mixing bowl, food processor or by hand. Process or stir until smooth. Mix in chutney and almonds. Store in covered container in icebox. Serve on crackers. (Not suitable for freezing.)

Virginia Hammerschmidt

Mrs. John Hammerschmidt, *wife of former Representative (Arkansas)*

Goat Cheese Appetizer
SERVES 10 TO 12

1 package goat cheese, chilled
½ cup olive oil
2 cloves garlic, crushed
½ cup chopped black olives
¼ cup sundried tomatoes
2 teaspoons fresh basil, chopped

1½ teaspoon fresh parsley, chopped
1 teaspoon whole peppercorns
½ teaspoon rosemary
½ teaspoon thyme
¼ teaspoon red chili flakes

Slice goat cheese ¼" thick and place in a serving dish, such as a quiche dish or a large bowl with low sides. It will be crumbly. Drizzle the oil over it and add the garlic. Plump the tomatoes in water, drain, chop, and sprinkle over the cheese. Sprinkle on the remaining olives, basil, parsley, peppercorns, rosemary, thyme and chili flakes. Marinate at room temperature 4 to 6 hours. Remove the garlic. Serve with slices of French bread, preferably the small baguette size. (30 minutes preparation time. Not suitable for freezing.)

Diana Allen

Mrs. Tom Allen, *wife of Representative (Maine)*

Will Pliler's Smoked Trout Griddle Cakes
with Black Bean-Corn Salsa
SERVES 8

Bean-Corn Salsa

½ medium red onion, finely diced

2 medium Roma tomatoes, diced

1 clove garlic, chopped

½ medium jalapeno, finely diced

¼ bunch cilantro, chopped

1 medium lime, juice of

1 cup fresh corn kernels

1 can cooked black beans, drained
and rinsed

Bean-Corn Salsa: Place all the salsa ingredients in a bowl. Season with ½ teaspoon salt and toss gently to mix ingredients, being careful not to smash the black beans. Set aside at room temperature.

Chipotle Cream

8 ounces heavy cream

2 Tablespoons Chipotles and sauce

4 ounces chicken broth

Chipotle Cream: Add the ingredients for the Chipotle cream sauce into a medium saucepan. Place over medium heat until it boils rapidly, then lower the heat and simmer until the sauce thickens enough to nap the back of a spoon. Set aside and keep warm.

Mango Sauce

1 cup mango, fresh, packed and drained

1 Tablespoon lime juice

cilantro sprigs for garnish

Mango Sauce: Place the ingredients for the mango sauce into the jar of a blender. Blend for 30 seconds, stopping once or twice to scrape sides of jar as necessary. When completely smooth, place into a squirt bottle and set aside.

Griddle Cakes

2 cups Krusteaz pancake mix

1½ cups water

1 Tablespoon fresh dill, chopped

1 Tablespoon fresh chives, chopped

1 Tablespoon Italian parsley, chopped

6 ounces smoked trout filets, skinless,
broken into bits

Griddle Cakes: Place pancake mix, water and chopped herbs into mixing bowl. Stir just until the larger lumps are gone. Heat a large nonstick skillet or Teflon electric fry pan to medium, just until a little butter dropped onto it sizzles not smokes. Treat the pan with a small amount of Pam spray. Drop the pancake batter onto the pan, 1 tablespoon at a time, making 16 small pancakes. On half the pancakes, sprinkle the broken bits of smoked trout. Do not flip the pancakes. When the pancakes appear to be almost cooked from the underside, turn each of the pancakes that have no smoked trout onto the pancakes with the smoked trout, as if to create a small sandwich.

For the Presentation: Spoon a few tablespoons of the Chipotle cream onto the middle of 8 warm plates making a sauced area approximately 6 inches in diameter. Place 2 of the warm smoked trout cakes in the center, 1 resting slightly on the other. Spoon a couple of tablespoons of the black bean-corn salsa directly onto the center of the cakes (right in the center of the plate). Make some squiggly lines with the mango sauce in the Chipotle sauce, then garnish the salsa with a few cilantro sprigs and finely chopped chives, if desired. (1 hour preparation time. Not suitable for freezing.)

Mrs. Robert Bennett, *wife of Senator (Utah)*

Spinach Dip
SERVES 20

juice of 1 lemon
1 cup Hellman's mayonnaise
8 ounces sour cream
½ cup chopped fresh parsley
½ cup chopped fresh green onions
1 teaspoon dill weed
1 teaspoon salt

½ of a 3-ounce package of cream cheese
1 clove garlic, minced
1 package frozen chopped spinach
    (thaw in microwave for 1 minute
    and squeeze water out thoroughly)
1 round loaf Hawaiian bread

Blend together all ingredients (except Hawaiian bread) in a blender or food processor. Flavors will blend better if refrigerated for an hour before serving or it may be served immediately. Pull out chunks of bread from the top to form a bowl. Fill with dip. Use left-over bread chunks for dipping. (10 minutes preparation time. Not suitable for freezing.)

Mrs. Kika de la Garza, *wife of former Representative (Texas)*

Onion Quesadillas

SERVES 4

1 Tablespoon good olive oil
1 red onion, thinly sliced
4 green onions, sliced
2 cloves garlic, minced
1 teaspoon cumin
½ teaspoon cayenne

¼ teaspoon oregano
1 Tablespoon lime juice
4 10" flour tortillas
2 cups shredded cheese (can mix cheddar, jack and jalapeno cheese)

Garnishes: sour cream, guacamole, salsa and cilantro

Heat oil over medium heat. Saute onions and garlic until very soft and caramelized. Stir in spices. Remove from heat and stir in lime juice. Place 2 tortillas on baking sheet. Spread mixture equally on the 2 tortillas and sprinkle with cheese. Top with remaining tortillas and bake at 400° for about 8 minutes until edges are golden. Let stand out of oven for about 5 minutes and cut into sixths with a pizza cutter. Serve with garnishes. (30 minutes preparation time.)

Steve Horn

Steve Horn, *Representative (California)*

Mexican Corn Relish

SERVES 10

¾ pound sharp cheddar cheese, shredded
½ cup sour cream
½ cup mayonnaise
¼ cup green onion, finely chopped
½ teaspoon salt

2 12-ounce cans mexi-corn, drained
1 4-ounce can green chilies, drained and chopped
1 jalapeno pepper, finely chopped
1 small jar of pimiento, drained and chopped

Mix all ingredients together and chill overnight. Delicious with tortilla chips or blue corn chips. Makes 4 cups. (30 minutes preparation time. Not suitable for freezing.)

Julianne Chambliss

Mrs. Saxby Chambliss, *wife of Representative (Georgia)*

Salsa Surprise
SERVES 4

1 bunch green onions
4 Roma tomatoes
1 yellow bell pepper
4 cloves garlic
2 large jalapeno or 5 serrano peppers
juice of 1 lime

½ green apple
2 teaspoons balsamic vinegar
2 Tablespoons rice wine vinegar
½ ripe mango
1 large carrot

Crush garlic. Dice all ingredients. Combine ingredients in a glass bowl. Add vinegar and lime juice. Toss ingredients. Refrigerate for at least 2 hours. Serve with tortilla chips. It is always fun to have your guests guess the "surprise" ingredients in this salsa. The mango and the apple add a distinct sweetness. (15 minutes preparation time. Not suitable for freezing.)

Angela Green

Angela Green, *daughter of Representative Gene Green (Texas)*

Pizza Rye
SERVES 30

1 pound ground meat
1 pound ground hot sausage
1 pound Velveeta cheese
½ teaspoon garlic powder
½ teaspoon Worcestershire sauce
2 loaves party rye bread

Cook meat and sausage together until it loses pink color. Do not overcook. Drain and return to pan at low heat. Cut Velveeta cheese into chunks and add to meat. Stir until cheese is melted. Add seasonings. Mix thoroughly and let cool. Spread on slices of rye bread. Broil until hot. (45 minutes preparation time.)

Glenda Miller

Mrs. Dan Miller, *wife of Representative (Florida)*

Mexican Rollups
SERVES 15

24 ounces cream cheese, softened
1 pint sour cream
5 jalapeno peppers, finely chopped
(may substitute green chiles, drain well)
½ cup grated cheddar cheese

dash of lime juice
garlic powder and salt to taste
¼ cup chopped green onions
30 flour tortillas

Mix together all ingredients except for tortillas. Warm tortillas to soften. Spread mixture on tortillas. Roll up tortilla and wrap each tortilla individually in a paper towel. Cover tightly and refrigerate overnight. Unwrap and slice into bite size pieces. Serve with salsa. Makes 15 servings. (45 minutes preparation time. Not suitable for freezing.)

Jennifer Chapman

Jennifer Chapman, *daughter of former Representative Jim Chapman (Texas)*

Asparagus Rollups
SERVES 10

20 slices white bread, crusts removed
3 ounces Bleu cheese
1 8-ounce package cream cheese,
    softened

1 egg, beaten
1 14½-ounce can asparagus spears
1 cup butter
wooden toothpicks

Flatten each bread slice with rolling pin. Combine the cream cheese with Bleu cheese and beaten egg. Mix well and spread evenly on bread, covering to the edge. Put one asparagus spear on each slice of bread; roll up and secure with wooden toothpicks. Dip in or brush with melted butter. Place on baking sheet, cover tightly and freeze. When ready to use, partially thaw and slice each rollup into 3 equal pieces. Bake at 375° for 15 minutes or until golden and crispy. You might bake them whole and serve with soup or salad for a luncheon. Makes 10 servings. (30 minutes preparation time. Suitable for freezing.)

Virgil Goode Jr.

Virgil Goode, Jr., *Representative (Virginia)*

ARIZONA

Saguaro cacti grow very slowly and some specimens have been estimated to be 150 - 200 years old. Growing to a height of 50 feet, these majestic giants provide some of life's necessities for Native Americans living in the desert. Preserves can be made from the fruit, which can also be eaten raw. The fermented fruit juice makes an intoxicating drink, and the seeds can be made into a kind of butter.

Humans are not the only ones to benefit from the saguaro cactus. Birds build nests inside dead cacti and a variety of bats, moths, and insects feed on the nectar produced by the flowers.

Large Cheese Ball

1 large package cream cheese
1 wedge sharp Cracker Barrel cheese
8 ounces Velveeta cheese
1 grated green pepper, seeds removed
1 small jar pimento, drained
1 Tablespoon grated onion

½ teaspoon red pepper
⅛ teaspoon granulated garlic
dash of salt
2 Tablespoons Worcestershire sauce
1 cup crushed pecans or more

In an electric mixing bowl soften cream cheese, add grated cheddar and Velveeta cheese. Add all other ingredients and mix until smooth. Roll cheese ball in crushed pecans. Refrigerate 24 hours before serving. Two smaller cheese balls can be made or one large. (30 minutes preparation time. Not suitable for freezing.)

Tom Bliley

Tom Bliley, *Representative (Virginia)*

Käsetoasts mit Welschriesling
SERVES 4

4 slices white bread
Camembert cheese (Gruyère or
    Edam may be substituted)
Gervais (French cream cheese, unsalted)
butter

paprika
Parmesan cheese
greens for salad
bottle of Austrian
    Welschriesling wine

Thickly spread equal parts of Camembert, Gervais and butter over bread, add paprika, grated Parmesan and place under broiler. Broil until cheese melts. Slice toasts into quarters and serve over a salad of greens. Best accompanied by chilled Austrian Welschriesling wine. Makes 4 servings. (10 minutes preparation time. Not suitable for freezing.)

Theana Yatron Kastens

Theana Yatron Kastens, *daughter of former*
Representative Gus Yatron (Pennsylvania)

Hot Artichoke Dip

2 8-ounce cans artichoke hearts
1 cup mayonnaise
1 cup Parmesan cheese

2 cups shredded mozzarella cheese
1 teaspoon garlic powder
paprika

Drain the artichoke hearts and chop into small pieces. Place the chopped artichokes into a medium mixing bowl. Add the mayonnaise, Parmesan cheese, mozzarella cheese and garlic powder. Mix all ingredients together with a large wooden spoon and put into a greased 1-quart casserole dish. Sprinkle with paprika and bake in a 350° oven for 25 to 30 minutes. Serve warm with crackers or Italian bread. Makes 15 servings. (40 minutes preparation time. Not suitable for freezing.)

Donald A Manzullo

Donald Manzullo, *Representative (Illinois)*

Cherry Tomato Salsa

3 cloves garlic, minced
½ cup onion, chopped
2 cups halved, peeled cherry
   tomatoes
½ teaspoon ground cumin
1½ teaspoons chopped lemon thyme

1½ teaspoons chopped fresh dill
½ teaspoon chopped fresh oregano
1½ teaspoons lemon juice
1 Anaheim chili, chopped and seeded
⅓ cup cilantro leaves
salt and pepper to taste

Chop garlic until finely minced. Chop onion to a medium mince. Add to garlic. Set aside. Bring medium sauce pan filled with water to a rapid boil. Drop several whole cherry tomatoes into boiling water and leave for 5 seconds. Remove from water and plunge tomatoes into cold water. (The skins of the tomatoes should easily peel off.) Continue until all tomatoes are peeled and then halve the tomatoes. Add tomatoes, cumin, lemon thyme, dill, oregano and lemon juice. Mix to chunky mixture. (Mix by hand or use a food processor. If using a processor, do not over mix.) Chop Anaheim chili and cilantro by hand and add to tomato mixture. Add salt and pepper to taste. This dish is wonderful served with tortilla chips and is best when made the day before. Drain off excess liquid before serving. Makes 3 cups. (15 minutes preparation time. Not suitable for freezing.)

Danealia Mineta

Mrs. Norman Mineta, *wife of former Representative (California)*

Delicious Cheese Ball

2 8-ounce packages Philadelphia cream cheese
1 Tablespoon Lawry's Seasoned Salt
1 can crushed pineapple (8 ounces), drain well
2 Tablespoons or less of minced onion
1 teaspoon sugar
½ cup chopped pecans
¼ cup diced green pepper

Put all ingredients into a medium sized bowl, stir until well mixed. Make into 1 or 2 balls. Wrap in plastic and store in refrigerator overnight or longer. To serve, roll ball or balls in chopped nuts. Place ball on serving plate. Surround ball with sprigs of parsley and crackers. (30 minutes preparation time. Suitable for freezing.)

Marguerite Nye

Mrs. Gerald Nye, *wife of former Senator (North Dakota)*

Shrimply Superb Dip

1 8-ounce package cream cheese
5 ounces shrimp, steamed, peeled, and coarsely chopped
1 Tablespoon chopped green onion
3 Tablespoons milk
2 teaspoons lemon juice (fresh if possible)
⅛ teaspoon garlic powder

Combine ingredients well and refrigerate for at least 1 hour before serving. Best with "Chicken N a Biskit" crackers. (10 minutes preparation time. Not suitable for freezing.)

Jan S. Berry

Jan Berry, *daughter-in-law of former Representative I.T. Valentine (North Carolina)*

Another World Fish Salad
SERVES 8 TO 12

1 pound wahoo, grouper, king mackerel
   or your favorite fish fillet

mayonnaise

lemon juice

salt, pepper and lemon pepper

3-ounce jar of imported capers

Cook fish in oven or microwave until done. After fish cools, flake with fork in mixing bowl (should be similar to tuna). Add just enough mayonnaise to moisten. Add seasonings to taste (fish needs a lot of lemon). Drain capers and gently fold into salad. Serve as an hors d'oeuvre on melba rounds, wheat thins, Bremer wafers or any bland cracker. Also may be served on lettuce as a salad. (Not suitable for freezing.)

Jack Kingston

Jack Kingston, *Representative (Georgia)*

Ethereal Mushrooms
SERVES 8 TO 10

2 sticks butter or margarine

2 cups Burgundy wine

2 teaspoons Worcestershire sauce

½ teaspoon dill seed

½ teaspoon pepper

1½ teaspoons salt

½ teaspoon garlic powder

1 cup boiling water

2 beef bouillon cubes

2 chicken bouillon cubes

2 pounds fresh mushrooms

Combine all ingredients except mushrooms in a Dutch oven. Bring to a slow boil over medium heat. Add mushrooms. Reduce to simmer. Cook 5 to 6 hours with the pot covered. Remove lid. Mushrooms will shrink and turn very dark. Cook another 3 to 4 hours. Serve as an appetizer in a chafing dish or in ramekins with a meal. Freeze in 1½ to 2 cup quantities and thaw for company. Good for Christmas gifts. Do not be alarmed by the long cooking time. It is well worth the effort. (8-10 hours preparation time. Not suitable for freezing.)

Leslie Howell Sandlin

Mrs. Max Sandlin, *wife of Representative (Texas)*

Mary Lee's Vidalia Onion Dip

SERVES 6 TO 8

1 large Vidalia onion, diced
1 cup mayonnaise
8 ounces shredded Swiss cheese (also good with cheddar or Parmesan)

Mix all ingredients in a small casserole dish. Heat in oven or microwave until cheese bubbles. Serve with spreaders on Triscuits, Wheat Thins or your favorite crackers. (10 minutes preparation time. Suitable for freezing.)

Libby Kingston

Mrs. Jack Kingston, *wife of Representative (Georgia)*

Hot Crabmeat Appetizer

½ cup lemon juice
1 7¾-ounce can Alaskan crabmeat
1 Tablespoon minced onion
2 Tablespoons horseradish
2 Tablespoons real mayonnaise

3½ cups sour cream
8 ounces cream cheese, softened
1 teaspoon chives
1 dash garlic sauce
grated cheddar cheese, longhorn type

Soak crabmeat in lemon juice for one hour; then drain off lemon juice. Mix with other ingredients in one quart casserole and sprinkle with grated cheddar cheese. Bake at 400° until bubbly (about 20 to 25 minutes). Serve with a variety of crackers. (30 minutes preparation time.)

Debbie Dingell

Mrs. John Dingell, *wife of Representative (Michigan)*

Ohio's Big O's

1 17-ounce package Hye Roller Brand soft cracker bread (3 pieces) at room
temperature (or use 5 to 6 large 10" tortillas)
1¼ pounds deli turkey, cut in paper thin slices
1 pound Swiss cheese, cut in paper thin slices
½ pound fresh spinach leaves, rinsed and patted dry
6 ounces oil-packed, sun-dried tomatoes, drained and cut in strips
¾ pound bacon, cooked, crumbled
1 avocado, thinly sliced, drizzled with juice of 1 lemon
1 small red onion, peeled, halved, cut in paper thin slices
⅓ cup toasted, finely chopped walnuts or pine nuts

Horseradish Chive Spread

12 ounces cream cheese, room temperature
2 Tablespoons prepared horseradish
⅛ teaspoon freshly ground black pepper
Pinch salt
1 Tablespoon minced fresh chives
1 Tablespoon minced fresh parsley

Place all the ingredients for the horseradish chive spread into a medium bowl. Cream together until blended. Cover lightly; set aside. Prepare all the remaining ingredients. Spread ⅓ of the horseradish spread evenly over one of the cracker breads. Cover with ⅓ of the sliced turkey and ⅓ of the sliced Swiss cheese. Leave 2 inches of the bread uncovered at the top; the cheese spread will help seal the shaped roll. Scatter ⅓ of each of the remaining ingredients over the turkey and cheese. If bread seems dry, cover with a sheet of waxed paper then a damp tea towel to soften slightly before rolling. Lift the bottom edges of the bread and begin carefully forming a tight roll to enclose ingredients, tuck in any which may escape. Gently press the finished Big O to seal edges. Wrap tightly in plastic wrap. Make 2 more Big O's. Refrigerate at least 3 hours or overnight. To slice a Big O, trim off the ends with a sharp knife. Cut each roll into 12 to 14 pieces. To serve, arrange on a platter, cut sides up. Makes 36 to 42 pieces. Each colorful pinwheel slice is a little cornucopia filled with the bounty of Ohio!

Fran DeWine

Mrs. Mike De Wine, *wife of Senator (Ohio)*

Oysters Rockefeller
SERVES 8 TO 10

1 cup butter
½ cup plain flour
2 cloves garlic, minced
½ teaspoon salt
¼ teaspoon Cayenne pepper
2 packages frozen chopped spinach

1 teaspoon anchovy paste
1 pound bacon, cooked and crumbled
1 pint standard oysters
grated Parmesan cheese
Tabasco sauce

baking shells (Use about 24 small shells for 1 oyster each. May use larger shells for 3 oysters each.)

Cook bacon well; drain and crumble. Melt butter in a skillet. Add flour, stir and cook about 5 minutes until well blended. Blend in oyster water, garlic, salt and cayenne. Place frozen spinach on top of this mixture. Cover and cook over medium heat, stirring every few minutes. Cook until spinach is done, usually about 10 to 15 minutes. This may be done ahead and frozen. Using cookie sheets, cover with crumpled aluminum foil. Place baking shells on foil. The crumpled foil holds the shell in place and makes clean up easy. Place 1 oyster in each shell. Top with a spoon of spinach mixture, 3 drops of Tabasco or any hot sauce, crumbled bacon and then dust with Parmesan cheese. Place in the middle of oven and cook at broil 8 to 10 minutes until bubbly. Serve about 3 as an appetizer. This can be made into a casserole. Also the spinach is delicious as a vegetable. We traditionally have this before Thanksgiving and Christmas dinner. (60 minutes preparation time. Suitable for freezing.)

Gloria Norwood

Mrs. Charlie Norwood, *wife of Representative (Georgia)*

Raspberry Ice
SERVES 8

2 cups water
2 Tablespoons lemon juice

2 cups raspberry juice
½ cup sugar

Combine sugar and water. Heat to a boil. Boil for 5 minutes. Cool. Add raspberry and lemon juices. Freeze as cubes or in an ice ring.

Lucy Carter

Mrs. Steven Carter, *wife of former Representative (Iowa)*

Lanny's Stilton Cheesecake with Pear Onion Jam

Stilton Cheesecake:

1¾ pounds cream cheese, softened
½ pound Stilton cheese
   (can use other blue cheese)

5 whole eggs
½ cup heavy whipping cream
pinch of white pepper

Preheat oven to 350°. Line one 9" or two 6" springform pan(s) with plastic wrap. In a food processor, cream the cheeses together until smooth. Add the eggs, the cream and the seasonings and process to combine. Pour into the pan(s) and bake, uncovered in a water bath halfway up the sides of the pan(s) for 45 minutes for one large pan or 30 minutes for two small pans or until the top is golden and the cake is set. (It should not be too loose.) Cool approximately 1 hour and unmold. Allow to come to room temperature to serve. Can be refrigerated up to 1 week. Serve with crackers and pear onion jam.

Pear Onion Jam:

4 cups yellow onions,
   peeled and sliced thin
olive oil
2 cups Bosc pears, cored and sliced

2½ Tablespoons cider vinegar
pinch cayenne pepper
pinch salt
1 cup brown sugar

Sauté onions in oil over high heat until they begin to take on color. At that point, turn the heat down to medium and continue to cook the onions until they are glazed. The onions should be very dark brown. Add the pears, vinegar, sugar and pinches of cayenne and salt and cook until the pears are tender but still hold their shape. Strain and simmer the juice to reduce it to a thick jam. Mix the jam with the pears and onions and cool. The mixture keeps well under refrigeration, but should come to room temperature before serving.

Janet Hall

Mrs. Tony Hall, *wife of Representative (Ohio)*

1 loaf sliced white bread	1 teaspoon paprika
1 cup mayonnaise	3 Tablespoons parsley flakes
½ stick butter, melted	1 bottle good quality bacon bits
½ teaspoon salt	12-15 cherry tomatoes or Italian tomatoes
½ teaspoon black pepper	1 package bean sprouts

Cut white bread with small circle cutter into 50 circles. Toast for about 30 minutes on cookie sheet at 250°, only until light brown. Mix together all other ingredients except bacon bits, tomatoes and bean sprouts. Chill mixture for several hours. Spread mixture over toasted bread. Top with a slice of cherry tomatoes about ¼" thick. Italian tomatoes can also be used. Be sure the size of the cookie cutter matches the size of the tomato to be used. Sprinkle top of tomato with bacon bits. Arrange on a tray on a bed of bean sprouts. Very pretty presentation and always a hit. (60 minutes preparation time. Not suitable for freezing.)

Gloria Norwood

Mrs. Charlie Norwood, *wife of Representative (Georgia)*

Pacific Salmon

Pacific salmon (smoked)	cream cheese
crackers	capers
chopped onion	

Catch Pacific salmon. Have it smoked and vacuum-packed in individual serving sizes. (These can be frozen up to at least 6 months.) Serve sliced with crackers, chopped onion, cream cheese and capers.

Norm Dicks

Norm Dicks, *Representative (Washington)*

Warm Shrimp Antipasto
SERVES 4

1 pound large shrimp, shelled and deveined, tail section left on
2 medium cloves garlic, minced
3 scallions, white and light green parts only, sliced into ⅛" thick rounds
2 Tablespoons chopped fresh marjoram or oregano

2 Tablespoons balsamic vinegar
6 Tablespoons dry Marsala wine
2 Tablespoons fresh lemon juice
salt and freshly ground pepper to taste
¼ cup olive oil
4 ½" thick slices peasant bread, toasted

Heat broiler. In a medium bowl, combine all the ingredients except shrimp, 1 tablespoon olive oil and the bread. Transfer shrimp to an edged baking sheet, arranging them in a single layer, and pour the sauce over. Broil about 2" from the heat until shrimp are cooked through and browned, about 3 to 4 minutes. Meanwhile, lightly brush 1 side of the bread slices with remaining tablespoon olive oil; sprinkle with salt and pepper. Place a piece of bread on each of 4 plates; divide shrimp among them. Place baking sheet with the sauce on a burner over medium-high heat and stir with a wooden spoon until sauce thickens slightly, 1 to 2 minutes. Drizzle sauce over bread and shrimp, and serve. (Not suitable for freezing.)

Paul Laxalt, *former Senator (Nevada)*

Crab Spread
SERVES 10 TO 15

1 8-ounce package cream cheese, softened
3 teaspoons horseradish
¾ pound imitation crab, chopped in food processor

1-2 Tablespoons lemon juice
1 12-ounce bottle chili sauce
chopped fresh parsley
8 green onions, finely chopped

On a round 12" platter spread cream cheese which has been mixed with horseradish. Mix crab with lemon juice, and spoon over cream cheese. Spread chili sauce over top. Sprinkle with parsley and green onions. Serve with crackers. (15 minutes preparation time. Not suitable for freezing.)

Lori Kerns, *daughter of former Representative John T. Myers (Indiana)*

Pearl of the Sea Mousse

6 hard cooked eggs
1 cup mayonnaise
pepper to taste
2 Tablespoons lemon juice
1 envelope unflavored gelatin
2 Tablespoons water
¼ cup onion, finely minced

1 teaspoon anchovy paste
1 teaspoon Worcestershire sauce
1 4-ounce jar black lumpfish caviar, drained
strips of pimento
black olives for garnish
party rye bread or crackers

Finely chop eggs and add them to mayonnaise. Season with pepper. Do not salt, as caviar and anchovy paste are quite salty. Combine lemon juice, gelatin, water, onion, anchovy paste and Worcestershire sauce. Heat until smooth and liquid. Combine egg mixture with gelatin mixture. Carefully fold in drained caviar. Do not stir too much or the black will run. Decorate bottom of a 1½-quart hollow center mold with strips of pimento. Spoon in mousse mixture. Chill until firm. Unmold to serve and fill center with black olives. Serve with party rye bread or crackers. Yields 1½ quarts. (25 minutes preparation time. Not suitable for freezing.)

Diane N. Lott, *daughter-in-law of Senator Trent Lott (Mississippi)*

Fiesta Hot Bean Dip
S E R V E S   1 2

8 ounces cream cheese
½ pint sour cream
2 cans bean dip
½ package dry taco seasoning

¼ cup chopped green onion
½ cup Monterey Jack cheese, grated
½ cup cheddar cheese, grated
tortilla chips

Mix cream cheese, sour cream, bean dip, taco seasoning and green onions in bowl. Pour into oiled casserole. Top with cheeses. Bake at 350° for 20 minutes, or until it bubbles and is brown on top. Serve with chips. (30 minutes preparation time. Suitable for freezing.)

Bob Riley, *Representative (Alabama)*

Heart Of Tennessee Shrimp Salsa

SERVES 10 TO 14

8 ounces cream cheese (I use lite cream cheese)
2½ cups cocktail sauce
1½ cups grated mozzarella cheese
1 cup chopped green peppers
1 cup chopped tomatoes
1 cup chopped fresh mushrooms
¾ cup sliced black olives
12-16 shrimp (cooked, peeled and sliced lengthwise)

Spread cream cheese on bottom of a 9" dish. Pour cocktail sauce on top. Sprinkle cheese on top of sauce. Layer green peppers, tomatoes, mushrooms and black olives. Top with shrimp and chill. Serve with crackers. This dish is easy and healthy. (30 minutes preparation time. Not suitable for freezing.)

Bill Frist, *Senator (Tennessee)*

Cajun Venison Wraps

SERVES 6 TO 8

1 venison back loin
garlic salt
cayenne pepper
lemon pepper

1 jar jalapeno peppers in liquid
1 pound bacon
toothpicks

Clean venison back loin thoroughly and trim fat. Slice loin horizontally into thin medallions and pound on each side. Season one side of medallions lightly with garlic salt, cayenne pepper and lemon pepper. Slice jalapeno peppers into 3 or 4 pieces. Place one slice of jalapeno pepper on seasoned side of medallion and tightly roll medallion around pepper. Wrap ½ slice of bacon strip around medallion, roll and secure with a toothpick. Grill until bacon is cooked. Serve hot. (15-20 minutes preparation time. Not suitable for freezing.)

Mrs. Billy Tauzin, *wife of Representative (Louisiana)*

**APPLE BLOSSOM
(MALUS PUMILA)**

ARKANSAS

A native of Europe and Asia, apples belong to the rose family (Rosacea). Grown and prized by the ancient Romans who introduced them to Europe, apple farming became popular in England and other parts of Europe. John Endicott, one of the first governors of the Massachusetts Bay Colony, is credited with bringing apples to America.

Fruited Mint Tea

3 cups boiling water
4 regular-size tea bags
12 fresh mint sprigs
1 cup sugar

¼ cup lemon juice
1 cup orange juice
5 cups water
Garnishes: fresh mint sprigs, orange slices

Pour 3 cups boiling water over tea bags and mint, cover and steep for 5 minutes. Remove tea bags and mint, squeezing gently. Stir in sugar, lemon juice, orange juice and 5 cups water. Serve over ice. Garnish if desired. Makes 2½ quarts. (10 minutes preparation time. Not suitable for freezing.)

Lisa Bevill

Lisa Bevill, *stepdaughter of Representative Spencer Bachus (Alabama)*

Nan's Hot Spiced Tea
SERVES 24

3 tea bags
1 quart water
1 quart apple cider
1 quart pineapple juice
1 quart orange juice

1 teaspoon whole cloves
3-4 cinnamon sticks
1 teaspoon whole allspice
1 cup sugar

Boil a quart of water. Add 3 tea bags and allow to steep while you add the other ingredients to a boiler on top of stove. Remove tea bags and add tea to fruit juice mixture. Simmer on low heat for 1 hour. Serve hot. May be stored in refrigerator and reheated. (15 minutes preparation time. Not suitable for freezing.)

Gayle Wicker

Mrs. Roger Wicker, *wife of Representative (Mississippi)*

Mocha Punch
SERVES 60

½ cup instant coffee powder or crystals
2 cups sugar
3 quarts hot water
2 quarts whole milk
1 Tablespoon vanilla extract
1 5½-ounce can Hershey's chocolate syrup
1 gallon vanilla ice cream

Combine coffee powder, sugar and hot water. Stir until dissolved and cool. Add milk, vanilla and chocolate syrup. Chill overnight. Just before serving, add ice cream and stir until blended. This is the most wonderful party punch. . .everyone will ask for the recipe. (Not suitable for freezing.)

Ginny Turner

Mrs. Jim Turner, *wife of Representative (Texas)*

Strawberry Colada Punch

1 16-ounce package frozen strawberries, thawed
1 15-ounce can cream of coconut

3 cups pineapple juice, chilled
3 cups club soda, chilled
2 cups rum (optional)

Combine the strawberries and cream of coconut in a blender. Process until smooth. Pour the mixture into a pitcher. Stir in pineapple juice, club soda and rum. Serve over crushed ice. Makes 2½ quarts. (10 minutes preparation time. Not suitable for freezing.)

Julia Ann Shepard

Julia Ann Shepard, *daughter of former Senator John Sparkman (Alabama)*

Mother's Champagne Punch

16-ounce can frozen orange juice
1 cup lemon juice
1 number 2 can pineapple juice
1 cup sugar
1 bottle ⁴/₅ quart sauterne
2 bottles ⁴/₅ quart champagne
oranges, jar of maraschino cherries or strawberries

Mix together the first 6 ingredients. Garnish with orange slices, maraschino cherries or strawberries. Makes 3-½ quarts. (Not suitable for freezing.)

Mikey Mercer Bilbray

Mrs. James Bilbray, *wife of former Representative (Nevada)*

Bama's Christmas Eggnog

1 egg per person to be served
1 Tablespoon whiskey per person
1 Tablespoon sugar per person
1 small carton whipping cream, whipped

Separate eggs and save whites. Using mixer beat egg yolks until light and fluffy. Continue beating and slowly add whiskey and sugar, alternately, 1 tablespoon at a time. In separate bowl beat egg whites until stiff. Fold into yolk mixture just before serving. Fold in sweetened whipped cream. This recipe needs to be served as soon as it is made. Serve in punch bowl. This recipe was handed down to me by my mother. It was her mother's recipe. (Not suitable for freezing.)

Mary Sessions

Mrs. Jeff Sessions, *wife of Representative (Alabama)*

Soup & Salad

The Congressional Club
would like to thank
Diamond Chef Sponsor

MassMutual

Soup & Salad

THE FIRST LADY'S LUNCHEON HISTORY

A breakfast honoring the First Lady began in 1912 with Mrs. William Howard Taft
as guest of honor. The breakfast was billed as "the most unique and delightful addition to the year's programs."
A tradition was inaugurated that remains unique. In 1979 the breakfast became a luncheon
and to this day the membership plans and executes every detail.
The prophetic words of our first club President, Mrs. Ernest W. Roberts,
"each year we shall find a deep mine of gold and bring to light a gift or talent we might never
have discovered," have become a reality at these annual First Lady's Luncheons.

Carrot Soup
SERVES 4 TO 5

2 pounds peeled carrots, chopped
4 cups chicken stock
1½ teaspoons salt
1 medium chopped potato
1 cup chopped onion
1-2 small cloves crushed garlic
⅓ cup chopped almonds

1 cup milk
2 pinches nutmeg
½ teaspoon dried mint
dash of cinnamon
½ cup toasted nuts
dash of sherry

Bring carrots, stock, salt and potato to a boil. Cover and simmer 12 to 15 minutes. Cool
to room temperature. Sauté in 3 to 4 tablespoons butter, the onion, garlic and almonds
until onions are clear. Salt to taste. Pureé everything together in blender until smooth.
Return pureé to kettle and whisk in milk. Heat very slowly. Season with nutmeg, mint,
cinnamon and sherry. Garnish with toasted nuts. (45 minutes preparation time. Suitable
for freezing.)

Janice H. DeMeritte

Janice DeMeritte, *daughter-in-law of former Supreme Court Justice Hugo L. Black*

Phyllis' Lo Fat Chili
SERVES 12

1 pound ground round steak
2 large green peppers
1 large onion
16 ounces canned mushrooms
4 16-ounce cans seasoned chili beans

1 chili bean can water
1 Tablespoon chili powder
dash cayenne pepper
2-3 bay leaves
4 14-ounce cans tomatoes
1 teaspoon sugar

Brown ground steak, drain off fat and rinse with very hot water. Cut peppers and onion in chunks, put in blender and cover with water. Chop, drain and add to meat. Blend mushrooms with mushroom juice, drain and add to meat mixture. Add remaining ingredients. Simmer until vegetables are soft and flavors are well blended. (Suitable for freezing.)

Bea Smith

Mrs. Neal Smith, *wife of former Representative (Iowa)*

Tomato-Carrot Bisque
SERVES 6

3 medium carrots, sliced
1 large onion, chopped
2 cloves garlic, minced
¼ teaspoon each of basil, thyme, rosemary, pepper
2 Tablespoons butter

2 cups chicken stock or broth
1 28-ounce can whole tomatoes, undrained
1 cup grated sharp cheddar cheese
1 cup half and half
Tabasco

Sauté carrots, onion, garlic and spices in butter for approximately 10 minutes in large soup pot. Add stock/broth and tomatoes. Cook, covered, over low heat for 15 minutes. Turn off heat and purée mixture with hand blender. Add cheese and half and half. Stir slowly until cheese melts. Add Tabasco to taste. (45 minutes preparation time. Suitable for freezing.)

Jane Portman

Mrs. Rob Portman, *wife of Representative (Ohio)*

Bean, Ham and Escarole Soup

SERVES 6

1 Tablespoon olive oil
½ cup chopped onion
1 garlic clove, crushed through a press
2 19-ounce cans cannellini (white kidney beans), liquid reserved
4 cups unsalted or reduced-sodium chicken broth
1 carrot, peeled and thinly sliced
¼ cup slivered baked ham (about 2 ounces)
1 bay leaf
2 cups packed coarsely chopped fresh escarole, kale or spinach
salt and freshly ground black pepper

Heat the olive oil in a large heavy saucepan. Add the onion and cook over low heat, stirring occasionally, until tender, about 5 minutes. Add the garlic and cook 1 minute longer. Add the beans with their liquid, the chicken broth, carrot, ham, bay leaf and 2 cups water. Bring to a boil, stirring occasionally. Cover and simmer over low heat 10 minutes. Add the greens and cook, covered, until tender, about 12 minutes for escarole or kale, 3 to 5 minutes for spinach. Because the beans are salty, taste the soup before seasoning with salt and pepper. (20 minutes preparation time. Not suitable for freezing.)

Patricia LaFalce

Mrs. John LaFalce, wife of *Representative (New York)*

CALIFORNIA

The state flower of California covers hillsides in a carpet of gold from February to September. The flowers, which close at night and on cloudy days, emit a spicy fragrance which attracts beetles, their primary pollinators. The genus name Eschscholztia, honors Russian botanist Dr. Johann F. Eschscholtz, a surgeon and naturalist who traveled the Pacific Coast during the early 1800s.

Called Copa del Ora by early Spanish settlers, the flowers' orange petals were believed to fill the soil with gold. California's Native Americans used different parts of the plant to treat head lice, toothaches, headaches, and consumption.

Greek Egg-Lemon Soup
SERVES 8

8 cups chicken broth
1 cup rice or orzo

3 eggs, separated
juice of 2 lemons

Using a large saucepan bring broth to a boil. Add rice and simmer for about 20 minutes. Remove from burner. With electric mixer, beat egg whites until fluffy. Slowly add yolks and continue beating. Slowly add lemon juice. Still beating, slowly add 2 cups of hot broth to egg-lemon mixture in the mixing bowl. Pour mixture in the mixing bowl slowly into the remaining broth and rice, stirring constantly until well mixed. Serve hot with Greek or Italian bread. (Not suitable for freezing.)

Mrs. Michael Bilirakis, wife of Representative (Florida)

Santa Fe Soup

2 pounds ground turkey or beef
1 onion, chopped
1-ounce package ranch-style dressing mix
2 1¼-ounce packages taco seasoning mix
1 16-ounce can black beans, undrained
1 16-ounce can kidney beans, undrained
1 16-ounce can pinto beans, undrained
1 16-ounce can diced tomatoes with chilies, undrained
1 16-ounce can tomato wedges, undrained
2 16-ounce cans white corn, undrained
2 cups water
Garnish: sour cream, shredded cheddar cheese, sliced green onions

Cook meat and onion together until meat is browned. Stir ranch-style dressing mix and taco seasoning mix into meat. Add remaining ingredients with juices from all. Add water. Simmer for 2 hours. If mixture is too thick, add additional water. Garnish each serving with sour cream, shredded cheddar cheese and sliced green onions, if desired. Serve with tortilla chips. Makes 4 Quarts. (Suitable for freezing.)

Mrs. Spencer Bachus, wife of Representative (Alabama)

Scholastic Stew

1-2 pounds chuck or arm roast cut into cubes
2 Irish potatoes, cut into big chunks (not necessary to peel unless you want to)
1 pound carrots, cut into large chunks
1 onion, coarsely chopped
1 regular can green beans, drained
1 regular can corn, drained
1 green pepper, cut into strips
5 large stalks celery, cut into 1" pieces
1½ cups beef broth
1 bottle beer
2-4 bay leaves
½ teaspoon peppercorns
1 Tablespoon dried parsley
1 teaspoon cilantro

Early in the morning, put all ingredients into a slow cooker in the order listed, checking liquid level. It should come up almost to the top. If not, add a little more broth or water. Cook all day. Serve with French bread or cornbread, and, of course, good beer. This relatively inexpensive and very filling dinner is said to have originated on the campus of the University of Missouri/Columbia. It is good warmed up the next day, and can be frozen. You can leave out or add any other vegetables you desire. (30 minutes preparation time. Suitable for freezing.)

Barbara H. Burlison

Barbara Burlison, *member of Congressional Club (Missouri)*

Mushroom and Chive Bisque
SERVES 4

1½ pounds mushrooms
½ cup butter
¼ cup flour
¼ teaspoon dry mustard
2 cups chicken broth

2 cups light cream
⅓ cup minced chives
¼ cup sherry
1 teaspoon salt
¼ cup heavy cream

Clean and finely chop mushrooms, stems and all. In a large saucepan melt butter and sauté mushrooms until soft. Add flour and mustard, stirring for a minute. Add chicken broth and cook until thickened, blending with a whisk. Add light cream and chives, reserving some of the chives for garnish. Flavor with sherry and salt to taste. (15 minutes preparation time.)

Sharon Archer

Mrs. Bill Archer, *wife of Representative (Texas)*

Chilled Avocado Soup
SERVES 6

2 ripe avocados
3 cups light cream (half and half)
1 10½-ounce can condensed
   cream of chicken soup
1 teaspoon Worcestershire sauce

½ teaspoon salt
¼ teaspoon pepper
¼ teaspoon nutmeg
dash pepper sauce (Tabasco),
   optional

In a blender, mix all ingredients except the avocados. Place in refrigerator, covered, and chill for at least 3 hours. One hour before serving; peel and seed the avocados. Halve the avocados and place in the refrigerator in a covered container with 1 of the seeds (prevents discoloration). Just before serving; process the avocados (without the seed) until smooth. Add the remaining ingredients and serve garnished with chopped chives. (30 minutes preparation time. Not suitable for freezing.)

Annie Rhodes

Mrs. John Rhodes III, *wife of former Representative (Arizona)*

Cheeseburger Soup

1 pound ground beef
4 Tablespoons margarine
¾ cup chopped onion
¾ cup shredded carrots
¾ cup diced celery
1 teaspoon dried basil
1 teaspoon dried parsley flakes
3 cups chicken broth

4 cups diced peeled potatoes
¼ cup flour
2 cups cubed processed American cheese
1½ cups milk
¾ teaspoon salt
¼ teaspoon pepper
¼ cup sour cream

In a large saucepan, brown beef, drain and set aside. In the same pan, melt 1 tablespoon of margarine and sauté onion, carrots, celery, basil and parsley for 10 minutes. Add beef, broth and potatoes; bring to a boil. Reduce heat, cover and simmer for 12 minutes or until potatoes are tender. In a small skillet, melt remaining butter. Add flour and cook for 3 minutes or until bubbly. Add to soup. Bring to a boil; cook and stir for 2 minutes. Reduce heat to low. Add cheese, milk, salt and pepper. Cook and stir until cheese melts. Remove from heat. Blend in sour cream. (90 minutes preparation time. Not suitable for freezing.)

Carolyn Snowbarger

Mrs. Vince Snowbarger, *wife of Representative (Kansas)*

White Chili

SERVES 6 TO 8

1 can chicken broth
4 cans great northern beans
2 cans chopped green chilies
2 large cans white chicken meat
1 small chopped onion

1 teaspoon ground cumin
1 teaspoon oregano
1 teaspoon chopped garlic or
substitute garlic powder

Combine all ingredients in a crockpot. Cook on low heat for 6 hours. This recipe can be cooked overnight. Makes lots and freezes well. (6 hours preparation time. Suitable for freezing.)

Ed Bryant

Ed Bryant, *Representative (Tennessee)*

Vegetable Soup

SERVES 8

3 pounds short ribs
1 can tomatoes, large
1 can tomato soup
2 large potatoes
¼ head cabbage, sliced
4 carrots, sliced
2 large onions, sliced
2 Tablespoons Worcestershire sauce

1 can peas, with liquid
1 can cream style corn
1 can okra, sliced
1 can green beans
5 stalks celery, sliced
½ cup parsley, cut
2 garlic cloves
2 bay leaves

Cover the meat generously with water, include bones for additional flavor. Simmer for 2½ to 3 hours (until meat is tender). Cool, strain. Let liquid get cold enough for fat to form on top and then remove fat. Trim fat from meat. Pull meat from bones, cut into bite size pieces. Place back in pot with all reserved soup stock. Add all remaining ingredients. Cook slowly on top of stove until all vegetables are tender. Add salt and pepper to taste. This soup makes a delicious base for jambalaya. (30 minutes preparation time. Suitable for freezing.)

Yvonne Rousselot

Mrs. John Rousselot, *wife of former Representative (California)*

DeWine Chili

SERVES 6

1 pound ground beef
2 onions, chopped
2 cloves garlic, chopped
1 quart tomatoes, chopped
2 Tablespoons chili powder
1 teaspoon cinnamon

1 Tablespoon cocoa powder
1 15-ounce can kidney beans or
  pork and beans
1 pound spaghetti, cooked
½ pound cheddar cheese, shredded
1 chopped onion

Sauté beef, onion and garlic. Drain off fat. Add tomatoes, seasoning and beans. Simmer about 30 to 60 minutes. Serve over spaghetti and garnish with cheddar cheese and onions. This is our version of "Cincinnati-style" chili. We like it "5-way" with beef, beans, spaghetti, cheese and onions. (45 to 60 minutes preparation time. Suitable for freezing.)

Michael DeWine, *Senator (Ohio)*

Tortellini Soup

SERVES 6

2 14½-ounce cans chicken broth
1 16-ounce can whole tomatoes, undrained and chopped
1 16-ounce can chickpeas, rinsed and drained
2 medium garlic cloves, pressed
1 teaspoon dried basil, crushed
1 9-ounce package refrigerated cheese tortellini, uncooked
2 Tablespoons chopped fresh parsley
2 Tablespoons grated Parmesan cheese

Bring first 5 ingredients to a boil in a large saucepan. Stir in tortellini and return to a boil. Reduce heat and simmer 3 minutes. Stir in parsley, and sprinkle with Parmesan cheese. Serve immediately. (15 minutes preparation time. Not suitable for freezing.)

Carol Myers, *daughter of former Representative John T. Myers (Indiana)*

Minestrone with White Beans and Pasta
SERVES 12

1 19-ounce can cannellini beans, drained and rinsed
2 Tablespoons olive oil
1 clove garlic
1 onion, finely chopped
5 cups meat stock
1 can (1 pound) plum tomatoes with juice
1 large carrot, coarsely chopped
1 zucchini, coarsely chopped

1 cup savory cabbage, cut in shreds
½ Tablespoon dried basil
½ Tablespoon dried oregano
½ Tablespoon sugar
1 bay leaf
⅓ cup dried small elbow macaroni
2 Tablespoons balsamic vinegar
salt and pepper to taste
2 Tablespoons chopped parsley
⅔ cup freshly grated Parmesan cheese

Heat oil in a large pan, add onion and garlic. Sauté until translucent. Add the stock, tomatoes (coarsely breaking them up with a wooden spoon), carrot, zucchini, cabbage, basil, oregano, sugar and bay leaf. Cover partially and simmer until the vegetables are tender and crisp, about 20 minutes. Add the macaroni and cook, uncovered until al dente, 8 to 10 minutes. Add the beans and balsamic vinegar. Season to taste with salt and pepper. Serve in warmed bowls. Top with toasted Italian bread sliced and sprinkled with Parmesan cheese. (45 minutes preparation time. Suitable for freezing.)

Mary C. Bunning

Mrs. Jim Bunning, *wife of Representative (Kentucky)*

Creamy Crab Bisque

SERVES 6

½ cup chopped onions
1 Tablespoon olive oil
2 14½-ounce cans chicken broth
1 14½-ounce can Italian-style tomatoes,
    with basil, garlic and oregano,
    undrained
2 cups frozen hash brown potatoes, thawed

1 bay leaf
1 2.75-ounce package country gravy
    mix
1 8-ounce package crabmeat
    (imitation may be substituted)
1 can evaporated milk

In a large saucepan, cook and stir onions in oil until onions are translucent. Reserve ½ cup chicken broth and set aside. Add remaining broth, tomatoes, potatoes and bay leaf to onions. Heat to a boil. Cook, covered, over medium heat for 15 minutes or until potatoes are soft. Dissolve gravy mix in reserved chicken broth. Stir into tomato mixture until thickened. Stir in crabmeat and evaporated milk; heat through. Remove bay leaf before serving. (25 minutes preparation time. Not suitable for freezing.)

Kylene White, *daughter of former Representative Richard H. Ichord (Missouri)*

Gazpacho Rose

SERVES 7

6 cups peeled and chopped ripe
    tomatoes
½ cup chopped bell pepper
½ cup chopped cucumber
2 cups tomato juice
1 clove minced garlic

1 chopped onion
2 Tablespoons olive oil
¼ cup vinegar
coarse ground pepper and
    salt to taste
garlic croutons for garnish

In a blender or food processor, purée tomatoes, onion, bell pepper and cucumber. Add tomato juice, garlic and pepper. Blend thoroughly. Pour into container, cover and refrigerate. Garnish with garlic croutons. (30 minutes preparation time. Not suitable for freezing.)

Charlie Rose, *former Representative (North Carolina)*

Tomato "Ancho Chili" Soup
SERVES 6 TO 8

2 Tablespoons canola oil
1 medium onion, chopped
3 cloves garlic, mashed
2 medium bell peppers, chopped
1 16-ounce can red kidney beans, rinsed, drained
1 cup chopped fresh or canned tomatoes (reserve juice)
5 cups vegetable broth
1 6-ounce can tomato paste
2 large ancho chilies, seeded, cut into thin strips
   (Ancho chile is dark reddish brown and has a smoky, hot flavor.)
1 teaspoon dried oregano
½ teaspoon black pepper
1 cup shredded cheddar cheese
2 cups coarsely crushed tortilla chips
½ cup sour cream

In a large soup pot, heat oil. Add onion, garlic and peppers. Sauté just until onion begins to brown, about 7 minutes. Pureé beans and tomatoes together in a food processor. If necessary, add reserved juice a teaspoon or 2 at a time. Add purée, broth, tomato paste, chilies, oregano and black pepper to bell pepper mixture in soup pot. Cover and cook over low heat for 45 minutes, stirring occasionally. To serve, place 2 tablespoons cheese in each soup bowl. Ladle in hot soup over cheese, and garnish with tortilla chips and a dollop of sour cream. (60 minutes preparation time. Suitable for freezing.)

Nancy Ireland

Mrs. Andy Ireland, *wife of former Representative (Florida)*

Penny's Denver Soup
SERVES 6

1 onion
3 stalks celery
2 zucchini
3 carrots
3-4 cloves of garlic
optional: green beans, peas
3 diced tomatoes or 2 medium cans diced tomatoes
1 can garbanzo beans
1 heaping Tablespoon of ketchup
6-8 cans of chicken broth or substitute with chicken bouillon
1 head chopped cabbage (you may want to use less)
optional: spinach can be added at the last. Add only the amount wanted
for that meal. Spinach does not freeze well.
1 teaspoon basil
1 teaspoon parsley
1 teaspoon thyme
1 teaspoon marjoram
1 teaspoon oregano
fresh Parmesan cheese (grated)

Sauté in small amount of olive oil: 1 onion, 3 stalks of celery, 2 zucchini, 2 carrots and 3 to 4 cloves of garlic. In saucepan add 3 diced tomatoes (or 2 medium cans of tomatoes), 1 can garbanzo beans, 1 heaping tablespoon of ketchup, 6 to 8 cups of chicken broth and 1 head chopped cabbage. Add the seasoning: 1 teaspoon basil, 1 teaspoon parsley, 1 teaspoon thyme, 1 teaspoon marjoram and 1 teaspoon oregano. Cook on medium heat about 30 minutes. Add spinach in last 10 minutes. Top off each serving with a little Parmesan cheese. Try penne pasta on the side. (Suitable for freezing.)

Cyndi L. Bryant

Mrs. Ed Bryant, *wife of Representative (Tennessee)*

ROCKY MOUNTAIN COLUMBINE
(AQUILEGIA CAERULEA)

COLORADO

A distinctive feature of the Rocky Mountain columbine is the hanging or horizontal flowers whose five petals have long tubes, or "spurs," extending upward or backward and are typically 1-1/2 inches long. Often cultivated in gardens, Rocky Mountain columbines bloom from mid-June to mid-August.

The Rocky Mountain columbine grows at elevations of 6,000 to 12,000 feet; those found at higher elevations are often more colorful that those at lower elevations. The genus name, Aquilegia, comes from the Latin word "aquila" which means eagle and refers to the spurred petals that many believe resemble an eagle's talons.

Fresh "Mintpea" Soup
SERVES 8

2 cups chicken stock or 3 chicken bouillon cubes dissolved in 2 cups water, add a liberal dash of dried leaf tarragon and "fine herbs" or "bouquet garni" to chicken stock.

1½ pounds frozen peas
1 medium onion, sliced thin
1 small carrot, sliced thin
2 lettuce leaves, tear apart
3-4 fresh mint leaves or
   ½ teaspoon dried mint to taste

1 teaspoon sugar
3 Tablespoons butter
1 cup heavy cream or evaporated milk
2 teaspoons salt
pepper to taste

If you use fresh mint, when it becomes tender from cooking in the broth, discard. Simmer first 7 ingredients in the stock until tender. Purée all, gradually, in blender. Pour purée batches into saucepan. Add remaining 4 ingredients and stir to melt butter. Then chill. To serve, reheat soup to "hot". Do not let it boil or it will curdle! Garnish each bowl with croutons or chopped green onions. (25 minutes preparation time.)

Mildred Curtis

Mrs. Carl T. Curtis, *wife of former Senator (Nebraska)*

Potato Soup
SERVES 6

½ cup chopped onion
2 Tablespoons butter
4 medium potatoes, diced
¼ cup flour

1½ teaspoons paprika
1 cup sour cream
2½ cups milk

Cook onion in butter until tender. Add potatoes, salt and 1 cup of water. Cover and cook for 15 minutes or until tender. Blend flour, paprika and sour cream until smooth. Stir into potato mixture. Add milk and heat until boiling, stirring. Cook 1 minute and season to taste. Garnish with a sprinkle of cheese. (25 minutes preparation time. Not suitable for freezing.)

Karen Shimkus

Mrs. John Shimkus, *wife of Representative (Illinois)*

2 large onions, chopped (about 4 cups)
¼ cup olive oil
4 garlic cloves, minced
6 ribs celery, chopped (about 2½ cups)
3 carrots, chopped coarse (about 1¼ cups)
1 teaspoon curry powder
1 teaspoon ground cumin
1 teaspoon salt
1 teaspoon pepper
½ teaspoon dried thyme; crumbled

5 cups chicken broth
5 cups water
2 bay leaves
2 teaspoons dark brown sugar
2 Tablespoons ketchup
3 cups coarsely chopped, canned
    plum tomatoes
2 cups lentils, rinsed
½ cup dry sherry

In a kettle cook the onions in the oil over moderate heat, stirring occasionally, until they are softened. Add the garlic, celery and carrots. Cook the vegetables, stirring occasionally, for 10 to 15 minutes, or until they are softened. Add the curry powder, cumin, salt, pepper, thyme, water, broth, bay leaves, brown sugar, ketchup, tomatoes, lentils and sherry. Simmer the soup for 2 hours, or until the lentils are tender. Discard the bay leaves. Makes about 10 cups. (2½ hours preparation time. Suitable for freezing.)

Karen Minge

Mrs. David Minge, *wife of Representative (Minnesota)*

Tortilla Soup

1 Tablespoon vegetable oil
1 onion, minced
1 large garlic clove, minced
2 medium tomatoes, peeled,
   seeded and chopped
½ teaspoon salt

Garnish
4 corn tortillas
oil for frying

2 quarts chicken stock
1 carrot, diced
1 small zucchini, diced
1 skinless, boneless chicken breast half,
   cooked and shredded
¼ cup canned green chilies, chopped

1 small ripe avocado
2 scallions chopped
chopped fresh cilantro
shredded Monterey Jack cheese, optional

Heat the oil in a saucepan. Add the onion and garlic. Cook over medium heat until just softened, 5 to 8 minutes. Add the tomatoes and salt and cook 5 minutes more. Stir in the stock. Bring to a boil, then lower the heat and simmer, covered about 15 minutes. Add the carrot to the soup. Cook, covered, 10 minutes. Add the zucchini, chicken and chilies and continue cooking, uncovered, until the vegetables are just tender, about 5 minutes more.

Garnish: Put a ½" layer of oil in a skillet and heat until hot but not smoking. Trim the tortillas into squares and then strips. Add the tortilla strips in batches and fry until just beginning to brown. Remove and drain on paper towels. Peel and pit the avocado. Chop into a fine dice. Ladle the soup into bowls. Add some tortilla strips, sprinkle with chopped avocado. Scatter scallions and cilantro on top. Serve immediately, adding shredded cheese if desired. (45 minutes preparation time. Not suitable for freezing.)

Silvestre Reyes, *Representative (Texas)*

California Comfort Chicken Soup

1 pound boneless, skinless chicken breasts

1 Tablespoon olive oil

2 medium, yellow onions, chopped

3 garlic cloves, finely minced

¼ teaspoon cayenne pepper

1 Tablespoon paprika

½ teaspoon coriander

2 teaspoons ground cumin

1 red bell pepper, seeded and diced

2 Tablespoons fresh lemon juice

½ small butternut squash, peeled and diced

1 zucchini, finely diced

1 carrot, coarsely chopped

1 small potato, peeled and diced

6 cups chicken broth

Cut chicken breasts into ½" strips. Toss chicken strips with 1 tablespoon combined mixture of paprika, cumin and coriander. Set aside. In a Dutch oven or large, heavy pot, heat olive oil to medium heat. Add spiced chicken and cook for 3 minutes. Transfer to a plate and set aside. Add garlic, onions and red bell pepper to heated oil in pot. Cook until softened, about 5 minutes. Add cayenne pepper and remaining spice mixture to pot; cook over medium low heat, stirring for 1 minute. Add broth, reserved chicken and vegetables. Bring to a boil. Reduce heat to low and simmer uncovered until vegetables are fork tender. Add lemon juice and let simmer for an additional 7 minutes. Ladle into bowls and garnish with fresh dill. Serve with crusty sour dough bread. (50 minutes preparation time. Suitable for freezing.)

Norman Mineta, *former Representative (California)*

Manhattan Clam Chowder - No Fat!

SERVES 8

2 Tablespoons oil
3 onions, chopped
1 28-ounce can crushed tomatoes
4 carrots, diced
2 small potatoes, peeled and diced
2 celery stalks, chopped
1 teaspoon thyme

½ teaspoon salt
¼ teaspoon pepper
1 bay leaf
3 6½-ounce cans minced clams
¼ teaspoon minced parsley
6 drops hot pepper sauce

In a Dutch oven heat oil. Add onions and cook, stirring until softened, about 5 minutes. Add tomatoes, carrots, potatoes, celery, thyme, salt, pepper, bay leaf and 2 cups water. Bring to a boil. Cover, reduce heat and simmer; stirring as needed, until vegetables are tender, about 20 minutes. Discard bay leaf. Stir in clams and liquid. Add parsley and hot pepper sauce until heated throughout; about 3 minutes. If desired, you can add a can of whole kernel corn and a can of mushroom soup. Also, you can add a can of chicken broth if too thick. (20 minutes preparation time. Suitable for freezing.)

Henry and Rose Nowak, *former Representative and Mrs. (New York)*

My Crock Pot Chili

SERVES 10 TO 12

2 large onions
2 pounds lean, ground beef
2 #303 cans stewed tomatoes
2 tall cans of Dennison chili without beans
2 #2½ cans kidney beans
1 can garbanzo beans

3 large cans Hunts small red beans
1 large can Ortega chilies, chopped
1 package Lipton onion soup
1 teaspoon ground ginger
3 beef bouillon cubes
1 Tablespoon sugar

Brown onions. Add meat, crumble and cook to brown. Add remaining ingredients in order. Makes a large crock pot full. (3 hours preparation time. Not suitable for freezing.)

Mrs. Ron Packard, *wife of Representative (California)*

Wild Rice Autumn Soup

SERVES 6 TO 8

1 large onion, chopped
2 cloves garlic, chopped
1 leek, white part only, chopped
½ pound mushrooms, sliced
½ cup celery, sliced
¼ cup butter
½ cup flour
6 cups chicken broth,
    preferably homemade

2 cups cooked wild rice
½ teaspoon curry powder
½ teaspoon dried chervil
1 teaspoon dry mustard
salt and white pepper to taste
2 cups half and half cream
¼ cup good dry sherry,
    not cooking sherry
chopped chives, parsley, or carrot curls

Sauté onions, garlic, leeks, mushrooms and celery in butter. Stir in flour and slowly add broth while stirring constantly. Continue to stir until mixture is slightly thickened. Add wild rice and seasonings. Reduce heat and stir in cream and sherry. Adjust seasonings and reheat, being careful not to boil. Beautiful served in scooped out pumpkins, eggplants, gourds or various kinds of squashes. Garnish with chives, parsley or carrot curls. Like any soup, this tastes better the second or third day. (1 hour preparation time. Not suitable for freezing.)

John Bryant

John W. Bryant, *former Representative (Texas)*

MOUNTAIN LAUREL
(KALMIA LATIFOLIA)

CONNECTICUT

Mountain laurel is a large evergreen shrub with showy clusters of pinkish-white flowers, which begins blooming in late May and continues through mid-July. Often used in ornamental plantings, it is shade-tolerant and provides showy color during the early summer and an evergreen accent during the winter months.

Cincinnati Chili Cockaigne

SERVES 6

1 quart water
2 pounds ground chuck
2 medium onions, finely chopped
5-6 crushed garlic cloves
1 15-ounce can tomato sauce
2 Tablespoons cider vinegar
1 Tablespoon Worcestershire sauce
10 peppercorns, ground
8 whole allspice, ground
8 whole cloves, ground

1 large bay leaf
2 teaspoons salt
2 teaspoons ground cinnamon
1½ teaspoons ground cayenne pepper
1 teaspoon ground cumin
½ ounce unsweetened chocolate, grated
cooked spaghetti
Optional: grated mild cheddar cheese,
   chopped onion, kidney beans, oyster
   crackers

Bring water to a boil in a 4 to 6-quart pot and add ground chuck. Stir until beef separates and reduce to simmer. Add chopped onions, garlic, tomato sauce, vinegar and Worcestershire sauce. Add spices, salt and chocolate and bring back to a boil. Reduce heat and simmer for 2½ hours. Remove bay leaf, cook, uncovered and refrigerate overnight. Before reheating, skim fat. Serve hot chili over spaghetti with optional shredded cheddar cheese, chopped onion, beans and oyster crackers. (30 minutes preparation time.)

John Boehner, *Representative (Ohio)*

Pumpkin Soup

SERVES 6 TO 8

1 large onion, finely chopped
¼ cup butter
¾ teaspoon curry powder
2 cups canned pumpkin

2½ cups chicken stock (I use Wyler's instant)
¼ teaspoon white pepper
2 cups heavy cream
sour cream and fresh dill or parsley for garnish

Sauté onion in butter in large kettle until clarified and soft. Sprinkle with curry powder and sauté a few minutes more. Add pumpkin and chicken stock; heat slowly, but do not boil. Blend in pepper and cream. Continue heating, but avoid boiling. Garnish with sour cream, parsley or dill. (10 to 15 minutes preparation time. Suitable for freezing.)

Mrs. Jim Slattery, *wife of former Representative (Kansas)*

Seafood Gumbo
SERVES 8 TO 10

⅔ cup vegetable oil

⅔ cup flour

1 large, white onion, chopped

½ cup green onions, chopped

3 garlic cloves, minced

¼ cup bell pepper, chopped

½ cup celery, chopped

1 1-pound can chopped tomatoes, undrained

1½ pounds frozen okra or equivalent of fresh

oil for frying okra

2 quarts seafood or chicken stock

1 Tablespoon salt

¾ teaspoon red pepper

1 large bay leaf

¼ teaspoon thyme

8-10 allspice berries

few grains of crushed red pepper

2 pounds headless medium raw shrimp

1 pound jumbo lump crabmeat

1 pint oysters (optional)

½ cup chopped parsley

Tabasco sauce

filé powder

First, you make a roux. Use a heavy black iron pot. Heat oil over medium heat, add flour slowly and stir constantly until the roux is <u>very dark</u> brown. Add white onions, green onions, garlic cloves, bell pepper and celery and stir until the vegetables are wilted. Add tomatoes and cook on low heat (about 30 minutes) stirring frequently. In a separate skillet, fry the okra in oil on moderately high heat, stirring constantly until the okra is no longer stringy. Add okra to the other mixture, stir and simmer about 10 minutes. Add seafood or chicken stock, salt and pepper. Simmer partially covered for 45 minutes. Add other seasonings and simmer an additional 20 minutes. Add shrimp; simmer 15 minutes. Add crabmeat and simmer for 10 minutes. If using oysters, add to gumbo the last 5 minutes of cooking. Taste carefully for seasonings, adding more if necessary. Remove from the fire. Stir in parsley. Gumbo is best served over mounds of hot Louisiana rice in a large flat soup bowl. Let each person add filé and Tabasco to his own taste. A long process, but worth the effort. (3 hours preparation time. Suitable for freezing.)

Ann Cooksey

Mrs. John Cooksey, *wife of Representative (Louisiana)*

Chicken Soup

SERVES 6

1 chicken cut up, skinned, preferably stewing chicken, approximately 3 pounds
6 cups water
½ pound carrots, sliced (use whole rather than precut)
1-2 celery stalks, cut into bite size pieces
1 large onion, peeled
1 green pepper, cut in large pieces
3 plum tomatoes, quartered
½-1 parsnip
1 turnip
1 leek
¼ cup fresh dill
½ small bunch of parsley tied
1 bay leaf
peppercorns
parsley root, if available
salt to taste

Put chicken in soup pot and cover with water. Bring to a boil. Simmer on medium low, skim and add vegetables. Cook at least 2 hours covered on low heat. Remove parsley when finished. Skim off fat and check seasonings. (Suitable for freezing.)

Janet F Waxman

Mrs. Henry Waxman, *wife of Representative (California)*

Duck Gumbo

1 cup butter
1½ cups flour
4 onions, chopped
1 green pepper, seeded and chopped
1 cup chopped celery
3 cloves minced garlic
1 gallon water (or substitute broth for a portion)
4 ducklings, skinned
2 pounds smoked sausage, cut into ½ inch pieces
salt, pepper, red pepper to taste
½ cup chopped green onions
⅓ cup chopped fresh parsley
2 Tablespoons file powder

Cook melted butter and flour in a large stockpot over medium heat, stirring constantly, until flour is a dark mahogany color. (This takes about 45 minutes). Add onion, garlic, green pepper and celery and continue cooking until all vegetables are tender. Gradually add water and stir until well blended. Add ducks, sausage and spices. Simmer uncovered for 2 hours or until meat is tender and falling off bones. Cool, cover and refrigerate overnight. Skim solidified fat from surface of soup and discard. Take ducks out and remove meat from bones. Cut duck meat into small pieces and return to soup. Heat gumbo and add remaining onions, parsley, seasonings and port or sherry to taste. Use filé powder (or substitute fresh okra) to thicken gumbo to your liking. Serve with rice. This is a delicious way to cook and serve ducks that accumulate in the freezer during the winter months. Makes about 5 quarts. (3 hours-overnight preparation time. Suitable for freezing.)

Marshall (Mark) Sanford, *Representative (South Carolina)*

Carrot and Cilantro Soup

SERVES 4 TO 6

1 pound carrots	1 garlic clove, crushed
2 Tablespoons olive oil	3¾ cups chicken stock
1 teaspoon ground coriander	1 small onion, chopped
1 Tablespoon fresh cilantro	salt and pepper to taste

Chop carrots. Heat oil in a large sauce pan. Gently cook chopped carrots, onion and garlic in oil for 10 minutes. Stir in coriander and cook for 1 minute. Pour in chicken stock. Cover, then bring to a simmer and cook 15 minutes or until carrots are tender. In food processor fitted with a metal blade or a blender, process mixture to a pureé. Season with salt and pepper. Reheat gently. Stir in chopped cilantro. Serve with homemade croutons. (25 minutes preparation time.)

Liz McEwen

Mrs. Bob McEwen, *wife of former Representative (Ohio)*

Crab Salad

SERVES 4 TO 6

1 pound crabmeat
1 small sweet onion, soaked for 2 hours in white vinegar
½ bell pepper, diced
1 cucumber, peeled, seeded and cubed
enough mayonnaise or salad dressing to bind mixture

Mix all ingredients and serve chilled in lettuce cups. (10 minutes preparation time. Not suitable for freezing.)

Evelyn P. Burnside

Mrs. Maurice Burnside, *wife of former Representative (West Virginia)*

Julie's Corn Salad
SERVES 6 TO 8

2 boxes frozen shoepeg white corn
(no sauce)

1 medium green pepper, chopped

1 small (or medium) onion, chopped

1¼ cup celery, chopped

red and/or yellow peppers, chopped
(optional for extra color, as much as desired)

Sauce:

½ cup mayonnaise

1 teaspoon dry mustard

½ teaspoon salt

⅛ teaspoon pepper

1 Tablespoon lemon juice

Defrost corn, do not cook, drain and pat dry. Mix sauce ingredients. Combine corn and other vegetables with as much sauce as needed. There will probably be some left over. Chill. The flavor improves as it marinates. (20 minutes preparation time. Not suitable for freezing.)

Mrs. David Hobson, *wife of Representative (Ohio)*

Watergate Salad

1 box instant pistachio Jello pudding

1 8-ounce can crushed pineapple, drained

1 12-ounce container Cool-Whip

1 small package of frozen coconut

½ cup pecans

Add pistachio pudding to Cool-Whip and mix well. Add drained pineapple, coconut and pecans. Mix well. Place in refrigerator until ready to serve. Serve on lettuce. (Not suitable for freezing.)

Mrs. L. H. Fountain, *wife of former Representative (North Carolina)*

**PEACH BLOSSOM
(PRUNUS PERSICA)**

DELAWARE

Blooming in the spring, peach trees are used as ornamentals in parks, gardens, and along streets. Peaches and nectarines are really the same fruit, the main difference being that peaches have fuzzy skin, nectarines do not.

Easy Potato Salad
SERVES 6

12-15 small, red, new potatoes
3 Tablespoons chives
3 Tablespoons parsley (fresh if possible)

1½-2 sticks butter
  or butter substitute
salt and pepper to taste

Boil potatoes with skins on until done. Drain. Finely chop parsley and chives and add to potatoes. Add butter, salt and pepper and serve warm. Great with steaks. (45 minutes preparation time. Not suitable for freezing.)

Cindy Stenholm

Mrs. Charles Stenholm, *wife of Representative (Texas)*

Raspberry Jello Salad
SERVES 15

1 6-ounce package raspberry Jello
1 10-ounce package frozen raspberries
1 small carton sour cream
2 cups boiling water

1½ cups cold water
½ cup chopped walnuts
1 small carton of whipping cream
  or Cool Whip

Dissolve Jello in boiling water. Add frozen raspberries, 1½ cups cold water and nuts. Let sit until raspberries thaw. Stir well and pour ½ mixture in a 9″ × 13″ glass dish. Refrigerate until Jello sets. Top with sour cream and refrigerate again. After about ½ hour pour remaining Jello over sour cream and refrigerate again. Right before serving top with either whipping cream or Cool Whip. (Not suitable for freezing.)

Kathy Latham

Mrs. Tom Latham, *wife of Representative (Iowa)*

Kansas Christmas Cranberry Salad

SERVES 12

1 package of cranberries, ground
2 cups sugar
2 packages raspberry Jello
3 cups water, boiling

2 cups red grapes, quartered
1 cup pecans, chopped
1 cup whipped cream

Grind cranberries and add sugar. Refrigerate overnight. Dissolve Jello in only 3 cups of boiling water. Cool. When Jello starts to thicken add grapes and pecans. Fold in whipped cream. Refrigerate until firm. (60 minutes preparation time. Not suitable for freezing.)

Vicki Tiahrt

Mrs. Todd Tiahrt, *wife of Representative (Kansas)*

Mandarin Lettuce Salad

SERVES 12

Dressing:
½ teaspoon salt
dash of pepper
2 Tablespoons sugar

2 Tablespoons vinegar
¼ cup oil
dash of Tabasco sauce

Combine and shake:
¼ cup sliced almonds

1 Tablespoon and 1 teaspoon sugar

Stir almond and sugar mixture over low heat in a nonstick pan until caramelized. Pour onto waxed paper until cool. Mix dressing ingredients and set aside.

Mix:
¼ head lettuce
¼ head Romaine lettuce
1 cup chopped celery

2 green onions, chopped
1 11-ounce can Mandarin oranges, drained

Pour dressing over salad at last minute. Sprinkle carmelized almonds on top. Serve. (Not suitable for freezing.)

Judy Lee Istook

Mrs. Ernest Istook, *wife of Representative (Oklahoma)*

Black Bean Salad
SERVES 8

2 16-ounce cans black beans,
   drained and rinsed
1 cup corn, cooked fresh
   or thawed frozen
1½ cups chopped seeded tomatoes
¾ cup thinly sliced scallions

⅓ cup minced fresh coriander
   (cilantro) leaves
½ cup olive oil
½ cup lemon juice
2 teaspoons salt

Combine first 5 ingredients. Whisk together oil, lemon juice and salt. Pour over vegetable mixture. Cover and refrigerate overnight if possible. May be served either chilled or at room temperature. (20 minutes preparation time plus overnite. Not suitable for freezing.)

Diane Bradley

Diane Bradley, *daughter of former Representative R. James Harvey (Michigan)*

Carolyn Becker's Chicken Salad
SERVES 8

1 whole frying chicken, baked, cut into cubes
1 large red apple, crisp, peel on, cubed
1 small can crushed pineapple with juice
1 small bag slivered almonds
2-3 stalks celery
½ cup Hellmann's mayonnaise with 2 Tablespoons sugar
½ cup halved seedless grapes (optional)

Toss all ingredients with mayonnaise. Serve on lettuce. Garnish with grape bunches or red-skin apple slices dipped in lemon juice or vinegar-water to retain color. (90 minutes preparation time. Not suitable for freezing.)

Betty Ann Tanner

Mrs. John Tanner, *wife of Representative (Tennessee)*

Dressing:
½ cup vegetable oil
¼ cup cider vinegar
¼ cup sugar
2 Tablespoons finely chopped parsley
1 teaspoon salt
¼ teaspoon hot pepper sauce

Salad:
1 cup sliced almonds
⅓ cup sugar
1 large head iceberg lettuce, cored and torn in bite-size pieces
1 large head Romaine lettuce, cored and torn
2 cups chopped celery
2 11-ounce cans Mandarin oranges, drained
1 cup thinly sliced red onion

Shake all dressing ingredients in a jar. Store in refrigerator. Stir almonds and sugar in small pan over medium heat until sugar melts and starts to caramelize and almonds are very lightly toasted. Cool to room temperature. Just before serving, put lettuces in a large bowl. Add celery, onions, oranges and almonds. Shake dressing well. Pour over salad and toss to mix and coat. (20 minutes preparation time. Not suitable for freezing.)

Tawni Kind

Mrs. Ron Kind, *wife of Representative (Wisconsin)*

Wilted Spinach Salad with Bacon Dressing

SERVES 4

1 pound young spinach
6 green onions
1 Tablespoon olive oil
½ clove garlic

3 slices bacon
1 egg
1 Tablespoon sugar
1 Tablespoon each tarragon vinegar and
  red wine vinegar
salt and pepper

Cut roots and tough stems from spinach. Wash thoroughly in cold water being careful to remove all sand. Drain to remove all moisture; blot dry with paper towels. Tear leaves into bite size pieces. Mince green onions. Mix with spinach leaves in large wooden bowl. Mash ½ clove garlic and cover with 1 tablespoon oil. Let stand for about 30 minutes. Discard the garlic. Trickle the tablespoon of garlic oil over the spinach and let stand. Bacon dressing: Sauté 3 slices of bacon until crisp. Remove from pan and drain on absorbent paper. Reserve bacon fat. Beat together the egg, sugar, and vinegars. Pour slowly into warm bacon fat, stirring constantly, until mixture has thickened slightly. Season with salt and pepper to taste. (It will not need much salt.) Pour over the spinach mixture and toss well.

Presentation: Crumble bacon strips over salad. Serve immediately. (40 minutes preparation time. Not suitable for freezing.)

Wes and Rosemary Cooley, *former Representative and Mrs. (Oregon)*

Crippen Salad

1 large bunch of watercress
toasted sliced almonds

hearts of palm
vinaigrette dressing

Wash the watercress and discard tough stems. Toast almonds on cookie sheet in 350° oven tossing several times. Slice heart of palm in bite size circles. Toss the watercress with a vinaigrette dressing. Sprinkle the toasted almonds and heart of palm on top. Serve.

Mariel Goss

Mrs. Porter Goss, *wife of Representative (Florida)*

Broccoli Salad - "They'll come back for more"
SERVES 8

2 heads of broccoli
12 slices of bacon, crumbled
1 medium onion, chopped
2 cups cheddar cheese, grated

1 cup raisins
1 cup mayonnaise (Hellmann's)
¾ cup sugar
2 Tablespoons white vinegar

Mix broccoli, bacon, onion and cheese in one large bowl. Mix raisins, mayonnaise, sugar and vinegar together. Pour over broccoli mixture and stir. Cover and refrigerate overnight. (Not suitable for freezing.)

Susan Hobson Nunner

Susan Nunner, *daughter of Representative David Hobson (Ohio)*

Fruity Chicken Salad
SERVES 8 TO 10

1 15½-ounce can pineapple tidbits, undrained
1 11-ounce can Mandarin oranges, drained
4 cups chopped cooked chicken
1 8-ounce can sliced water chestnuts, drained
1 cup chopped celery

1 cup seedless grapes, halved
1½ cups mayonnaise
1 Tablespoon soy sauce
1 teaspoon curry powder
1 2½-ounce package sliced almonds, toasted
1 3-ounce can chow mein noodles
lettuce leaves (optional)

Drain pineapple, reserving 2 tablespoons juice. Combine with chicken, oranges, celery, grapes and water chestnuts; mix well. Combine 2 tablespoons pineapple juice with mayonnaise, soy sauce and curry powder. Stir well and add to chicken mixture. Chill. Stir in almonds and noodles just before serving on lettuce leaves if desired. (Not suitable for freezing.)

Julie W. Collins

Mrs. Mac Collins, *wife of Representative (Georgia)*

Heavenly Fruit Salad
SERVES 12

½ can Eagle Brand condensed milk
1 can Comstock cherry pie filling
1 large can fruit cocktail
1 large can crushed pineapple

1-2 cups of Cool Whip
½ cup sour cream
nuts
coconut

Mix together well. Thickens as it sets, so it is best when made a few hours in advance or even the day before it is to be served. (15 minutes preparation time. Not suitable for freezing.)

Helen Green

Mrs. Gene Green, *wife of Representative (Texas)*

Spiral Salad for Summer
SERVES 8

1 pound corkscrew pasta
1 cup celery, cut up
½ cup chopped onion
grated carrot, for color (optional)
1 cup sugar
1 cup water

¾ cup vinegar
½ teaspoon turmeric
1 teaspoon celery salt
2 cups mayonnaise (may use
    Lite Hellmann's and may use less)

Cook pasta and drain. Add cut up celery, onion and carrot (if desired). Mix together sugar with water, vinegar, turmeric, celery salt and mayonnaise. Add to cooled pasta. Refrigerate overnight or longer. Stir occasionally. Great with ham. (30 minutes preparation time. Not suitable for freezing.)

Joyce M. Murtha

Mrs. John Murtha, *wife of Representative (Pennsylvania)*

Mixed-Vegetable Salad
SERVES 12

2 cucumbers, cut in half lengthwise,
    then into chunks
4 ribs celery, cut into chunks
1 medium red onion, cut into wedges
½ cup Caesar style salad dressing

3 ripe avocados
1 3¼-ounce can pitted ripe olives,
    drained
1 pint cherry tomatoes

In large bowl mix cucumber pieces, celery and red onion. Add dressing and toss to coat vegetables evenly. Cover and refrigerate until about 1 hour before serving. Just before serving, cut avocados in half and remove seeds. Scoop flesh from peel. Cut flesh into ½" pieces. Add to salad with olives and tomatoes; toss lightly. Serve at room temperature. (30 minutes preparation time. Not suitable for freezing.)

Dorothy Mathews

Dorothy Mathews, *daughter of former Representative Claude A. Fuller (Arkansas)*

ORANGE BLOSSOM
(CITRUS AURANTIUM)

FLORIDA

Oranges were first brought to the United States in 1518 by Spanish and Portuguese settlers. There are three main orange growing regions in the United States: Florida, the California-Arizona region and Texas.

Artichoke Salad
SERVES 8 TO 10

1 package chicken Rice-A-Roni
½ green pepper, chopped
½ red pepper, chopped
2 green onions, chopped
1 small can sliced black olives

2 6-ounce jars marinated artichoke hearts (drain and save marinade)
½ teaspoon curry powder
⅓ cup mayonnaise

Cook rice according to package directions. Mix drained marinade with mayonnaise and curry powder. Add to cooked rice. Combine remaining ingredients with rice and refrigerate. (30 minutes preparation time. Not suitable for freezing.)

Anne Burhans

Anne Burhans, *daughter of former Representative John C. Mackie (Michigan)*

Iowa Pea Salad
SERVES 8 TO 10

1 16-ounce package frozen peas (thawed)
2 stalks celery (sliced)
4-5 ounces cubed cheddar cheese or Velveeta cheese
2 Tablespoons pickle relish
3 hard-cooked eggs (chopped)
½ teaspoon salt
½ onion (chopped) or 2 bunches green onions (chopped)
½ cup Miracle Whip salad dressing

Mix all ingredients together and chill for several hours or overnight. (Not suitable for freezing.)

Cathryn O. Greigg

Mrs. Stanley Greigg, *wife of former Representative (Iowa)*

Greek Village Salad

2 red tomatoes, cut into wedges
2 cucumbers, peeled and sliced
4 scallions, chopped
¼ pound Feta cheese,
   cut into small chunks

1 green pepper, sliced
1 small can anchovies (optional)
juice of 1 lemon
½ cup olive oil (extra virgin)
salt, pepper, and oregano to taste

Combine all ingredients, except seasonings, in salad bowl. Mix lemon and oil and pour over ingredients in bowl. Sprinkle with salt, pepper and oregano. Toss ingredients until all are well coated. Serve with fresh Italian bread and do not be afraid to dunk.
(20 minutes preparation time. Not suitable for freezing.)

Evelyn M. Bilirakis

Mrs. Michael Bilirakis, *wife of Representative (Florida)*

Wild Rice Salad

SERVES 6

1 box wild rice
¾ cup tomatoes, chopped
1 cup corn, fresh or canned

⅓ cup red onion, chopped
2 Tablespoons chives, chopped

Dressing:
1 Tablespoon Dijon mustard
1 Tablespoon honey

⅓ cup cider vinegar
¼ cup olive oil

Cook wild rice as directed; place in serving bowl. On top of the rice spread the tomatoes, corn, onion and chives. Mix dressing ingredients and pour over salad. Toss, season with salt, and marinate at room temperature for 1 hour. (20 minutes preparation time. Not suitable for freezing.)

Diana Allen

Mrs. Tom Allen, *wife of Representative (Maine)*

Curry Chicken Salad
SERVES 8

2 cups mayonnaise

2 Tablespoons lemon juice

2½ Tablespoons Chinese soy sauce

1 Tablespoon curry powder

1 Tablespoon onion juice

1 Tablespoon chutney, chopped

3 cups diced white meat of chicken

1½ cups chopped celery

1 6-ounce can water chestnuts,
    drained and sliced

2 cups seedless white grapes

½ cup slivered almonds, toasted

Combine mayonnaise, lemon juice, soy sauce, curry powder, onion juice and chutney. Toss with remaining ingredients, except almonds. Refrigerate overnight. Sprinkle with almonds. Fill papaya or pineapple half with salad. (30 minutes preparation time. Not suitable for freezing.)

Sharon Archer

Mrs. Bill Archer, *wife of Representative (Texas)*

Hot Chicken Salad
SERVES 8 TO 10

4 cups cooked, diced chicken
(approximately 5 breasts)

2 Tablespoons lemon juice

⅔ cup slivered almonds (may be toasted)

¾ cup mayonnaise

2 cups finely chopped celery

1 cup cream of chicken soup

1 teaspoon minced onion

1 cup grated cheddar cheese

1½ cups crushed potato chips
    or corn flakes

Toast almonds on cookie sheet in a 350° oven for 5 to 7 minutes (watch carefully). Mix all ingredients except cheese and potato chips. Add cheese, then chips to top of mixture. Bake at 400° for 20 minutes. (60 minutes preparation time. Suitable for freezing.)

Joyce M. Bennett

Mrs. Robert F. Bennett, *wife of Senator (Utah)*

Corn Bread Salad

1 box Jiffy Corn Bread Mix (8½ ounces)
1 cup Miracle Whip
2 Tablespoons prepared mustard
3 Tablespoons salad oil
¾ cup chopped onion (purple)

1 cup chopped green pepper
1 cup chopped celery
1 cup chopped tomatoes
1 8-ounce can whole kernel corn, (drained)

Cook corn bread according to box directions and let cool. Crumble cooled corn bread in a mixing bowl. Add onions, peppers, celery, tomatoes and corn. Mix Miracle Whip, mustard and oil. Add mixture to corn bread/vegetable mixture. TOSS. DO NOT STIR.

Bill K. Brewster

Bill Brewster, *former Representative (Oklahoma)*

Grandma Richard's Cranberry Salad
SERVES 12 TO 15

2 6-ounce boxes of strawberry Jello with Nutrasweet (lowers calorie count)
1 package fresh cranberries
4 medium apples, chopped
1 cup sugar
1 #20-can crushed pineapple with juice
4 cups hot water
½ cup celery
½ cup chopped walnuts
1 cup chopped seedless red grapes

Combine Jello, cranberries and apples in food processor while adding sugar slowly. To this mixture, add 1 #20-can crushed pineapple with juice and 4 cups hot water. Add at least ½ cup each of the following: chopped celery, chopped nuts, seedless red grapes. The amount should make the salad chunky. Place in a 9″ × 13″ dish. Chill and serve. (20 minutes preparation time. Not suitable for freezing.)

Joyce Eldridge Brown

Mrs. Clarence Brown, Jr., *wife of former Representative (Ohio)*

Napa Salad

1 large head of Napa cabbage
(also called Chinese celery)

6 green onions

2 packages of Ramen noodles
(remove flavor packet)

4 ounces slivered almonds

4 ounces unsalted sunflower seeds

1 stick (½ cup) butter or margarine

2 Tablespoons soy sauce

1 cup sugar

½ cup tarragon vinegar

1 cup sunflower oil

Dice cabbage and onions. Mix together then refrigerate for at least 2 hours. Break apart Ramen noodles. Put noodles, almonds, sunflower seeds and butter in skillet and sauté until slightly brown. Refrigerate. Combine cabbage mixture and noodle mixture 2 hours before serving.

Dressing: Mix together soy sauce, sugar, vinegar and oil. Pour over salad 15 minutes before serving. Stir. Serve. (30 minutes preparation time. Not suitable for freezing.)

Sam Brownback, *Senator (Kansas)*

Holiday Cranberry-Raspberry Mold

3 ounces raspberry Jello

3 ounces lemon Jello

1½ cups boiling water

10 ounces frozen raspberries

14 ounces cranberry orange relish

7 ounces or 1 cup lemon-lime drink

Dissolve the Jello in the boiling water. In a large mixing bowl add the frozen raspberries immediately while the water is hot. Stir until the berries are completely thawed. Add the cranberry orange relish and stir. Place the bowl in the refrigerator and chill until cold but not set. Remove from the refrigerator and add the lemon-lime drink, stirring gently. Put into a Jello mold and chill until set. (20 minutes preparation time. Not suitable for freezing.)

Mrs. Donald Manzullo, *wife of Representative (Illinois)*

Mandarin Salad

¼ cup sliced almonds or walnuts
3 Tablespoons sugar
½ head iceberg lettuce
½ head Romaine lettuce

1 cup chopped celery
2 green onions (chopped)
1 11½-ounce can Mandarin oranges
(drained)

Dressing:
½ teaspoon salt
pepper
¼ cup vegetable oil

1 Tablespoon chopped parsley
2 Tablespoons sugar
2 Tablespoons vinegar

Mix dressing in a jar, shake to mix and chill. Mix almonds or walnuts in the sugar and cook on stove in a small amount of butter, or cover nuts with sugar and put in microwave for 30 seconds. Cool almonds/walnuts and set aside. Mix lettuces, celery and onion; add almonds/walnuts and oranges. Toss with dressing before serving. (30 minutes preparation time. Not suitable for freezing.)

Cyndi L. Bryant

Mrs. Ed Bryant, *wife of Representative (Tennessee)*

Easy Tomato Aspic

1 3-ounce package lemon gelatin
1 cup boiling water
1 8-ounce can tomato sauce

1 Tablespoon horseradish
1 Tablespoon apple cider vinegar
2 teaspoons grated onion

Dissolve gelatin in 1 cup boiling water. Stir until completely dissolved. Add remaining ingredients and stir. Refrigerate until firm. Serve over lettuce with mayonnaise. (10 minutes preparation time. Not suitable for freezing.)

Annie Ben Kornegay

Mrs. Horace R. Kornegay, *wife of former Representative (North Carolina)*

Club's 7 Grain Salad with Greens

Grain mixture:

1 cup uncooked wild rice prepared according to directions. Use chicken broth in place of water and add 1 Tablespoon oil and extra salt

1 package Tabbauleh mix prepared according to directions. Omit the oil, cucumber and tomatoes

1 package chicken flavored Rice-A-Roni prepared according to directions

1 cup each of dried cranberries, dried golden currants, wheat berries, enoli beans, pine nuts and pumpkin seeds

Greens mixture:

6-8 cups mixed mesclun greens

1 small bunch cilantro, chopped

1-2 cups sprouted alfalfa beans

2 heads Bibb lettuce torn into bite size pieces

1 head red leaf lettuce torn into bite size pieces

Dressing:

2 Tablespoons peanut oil

2 Tablespoons light soy sauce

juice of 2 large limes

¼ cup white vinegar

½ cup sugar

¾ cup vegetable oil (not olive oil)

Prepare first 3 grains and cool before adding the next 6 ingredients. Wash, mix and crisp various greens. Combine all the dressing ingredients and whip in food processor or blender until thickened. Refrigerate dressing and whip again just before tossing with greens. To serve: place dressed greens on chilled plate and top with desired amount of chilled grain mixture. Serve with crusty sourdough bread for a luncheon entree or smaller portions for dinner salad course. (60 minutes preparation time. Not suitable for freezing.)

Janet Bryant

Mrs. John W. Bryant, *wife of former Representative (Texas)*

Pretzel Salad

1 cup crushed pretzels
1 stick butter
½ cup sugar
1 8-ounce package softened
   cream cheese
1 8-ounce carton Cool Whip

½ cup sugar
2 Tablespoons cornstarch
¼ cup sugar
1 20-ounce can crushed pineapple
   Drain and reserve liquid

Mix pretzels, butter and sugar together and spread into a 8″ × 12″ dish. Bake crust 5 minutes at 350°. Let cool. Mix cream cheese, Cool Whip and sugar. Spread over first layer. Mix cornstarch, sugar and pineapple juice drained from the can of crushed pineapple. Cook on stove over medium heat until thick. Let cool. Stir in crushed pineapple. Spread over second layer. Top with Cool Whip. Chill (Not suitable for freezing.)

Mrs. Chet Edwards, *wife of Representative (Texas)*

Black Bean Salad

4 16-ounce cans black beans
1 large red onion
1 large red pepper
1 large yellow pepper
1 bunch fresh parsley
3 Tablespoons fresh cilantro

1 Tablespoon ground cumin
¼ cup fresh lemon juice
½ cup olive oil
½ teaspoon Tabasco
salt and pepper

Drain and rinse black beans. Finely chop red onion, red and yellow peppers, fresh parsley and cilantro. Toss all ingredients together. Add salt and pepper to taste. Refrigerate for 1 hour to blend flavors. May be served at room temperature. (20 minutes preparation time. Not suitable for freezing.)

Mrs. Daniel Mica, *wife of former Representative (Florida)*

Pistachio Whip
SERVES 8

1 3.4 ounce pistachio instant pudding mix
1 20-ounce can crushed pineapple, drain and reserve liquid
1 8-ounce container Cool Whip

Empty pistachio pudding mix into a mixing bowl. Add reserved pineapple liquid. Using a large spoon mix well. Add drained pineapple and mix well. Add Cool Whip and blend well. Salad will thicken as it stands. Chill. Good side dish with baked ham. (15 minutes preparation time. Not suitable for freezing.)

Janeen M. Morse

Janeen Morse, *daughter of former Representative Walter H. Moeller (Ohio)*

Easy Spinach Salad
SERVES 6

1 15½-ounce can dark red kidney beans
4-6 green onions, sliced thinly
¾ cup sliced green pepper
¾ cup diced celery
4 cups washed and drained baby spinach
bottled Italian Wish Bone dressing
cherry tomatoes (optional)
fresh ground pepper

In a salad bowl combine drained kidney beans, sliced onions, sliced green pepper and diced celery. Toss with enough Italian dressing to moisten. Place spinach on top. Refrigerate. Before serving toss with additional Italian dressing to taste. Season with freshly ground pepper. As an option, garnish with cherry tomatoes. Can be made early in the day and tossed with final dressing at the last minute. (Not suitable for freezing.)

Peggy Nedzi

Mrs. Lucien N. Nedzi, *wife of former Representative (Michigan)*

Chicken Salad Quesadilla
SERVES 5

3 cups cooked chicken, chopped
½ cup chopped tomatoes
½ cup shredded carrots
½ cup finely chopped celery
½ cup finely chopped onion
¼ cup minced pecans
¾ cup mayonnaise (low fat)
1 Tablespoon chili powder
1 teaspoon pepper
dash of lemon juice
10 flour tortillas
2 cups shredded cheddar cheese (Mexican blend can be used)
softened butter or margarine
salsa

Mix first 10 ingredients and toss lightly. Set aside. Coat a large pan with cooking spray and preheat to medium. Generously spread butter or margarine on 1 side of 2 tortillas. Place 1 tortilla, buttered side down, in heated pan. Spread enough chicken mixture on tortilla to cover. Sprinkle with cheese. Top with second tortilla, buttered side up. Grill. When bottom tortilla is browned and crisp, flip over quesadilla. Top with cheese, salsa and onions, if desired. Continue grilling until bottom tortilla is crisp. Repeat procedure for additional quesadillas. (30 minutes preparation time. Not suitable for freezing.)

Connie Quinlivan

Margaret Quinlivan, *daughter of former Representative John R. Foley (Maryland)*

CHEROKEE ROSE
(ROSA LAEVIGATA)

GEORGIA

The Cherokee rose was introduced to the United States from China. The fragrant white flowers can be up to 3-1/2 inches across and produce orange, pear-shaped fruits called "hips."

Fruit Salad Dressing

1 cup sugar
2 teaspoons salt
2 teaspoons mustard
    (dry or prepared)

2 teaspoons paprika
½ teaspoon grated onion
2 cups salad oil
½ cup cider vinegar

Mix onion and dry ingredients, then 1 tablespoon oil to moisten. Alternate 1 tablespoon oil and vinegar on slow mixer. Will be thick and keeps in refrigerator indefinitely. (10 minutes preparation time. Not suitable for freezing.)

Betty Rhodes

Mrs. John J. Rhodes, *wife of former Representative (Arizona)*

Baked Hot Chicken Salad
SERVES 6

4 cups diced cooked chicken
2 cups chopped celery (with leaves)
1½ cups Miracle Whip
1-2 ounces toasted almonds
4 diced hard-cooked eggs

1 teaspoon Accent
2 Tablespoons minced onions
1 small jar chopped pimiento
1 10-ounce package frozen peas
2 cups grated cheese

Combine above ingredients. Place in a 9″ × 13″ Pyrex dish, lightly greased with Miracle Whip. Refrigerate overnight or 5 hours. Bake at 350° for 25 minutes. Top with grated cheese before baking (may use potato chips). Very delicious. (60 minutes preparation time. Not suitable for freezing.)

Marie Porter Royce

Mrs. Ed Royce, *wife of Representative (California)*

Strawberry and Brie Salad
SERVES 10

2 heads of Romaine lettuce, washed and torn in bite size pieces
2 pints strawberries, sliced
1 small sized wheel of Brie (not double cream) cut up in pieces
3 packages sliced almonds sugarized
½-¾ cup sugar

Dressing

1½ teaspoons poppy seeds	½ cup oil
1 teaspoon dry mustard	⅓ cup apple cider vinegar
a little minced onion	½ cup sugar

Make dressing ahead. Mix all ingredients together and chill. To sugarize almonds, place sugar in saucepan and add almonds. Over medium heat, stir constantly for about 10 minutes so the sugar will melt and almonds will start to toast. Let all melt together and then put on aluminum foil to cool. Spread apart while hot. Break in pieces when cooled. To make salad: Layer Romaine, strawberries, brie and almonds. Dress and toss. Serve immediately. (30 minutes preparation time. Not suitable for freezing.)

Emilie Shaw

Mrs. Clay Shaw, *wife of Representative (Florida)*

Mother's Ruby Salad

1 cup diced beets and juice	½ cup vinegar
1 envelope unflavored gelatin	½ teaspoon salt
¼ cup cold water	1 teaspoon horseradish
½ cup sugar	

Soften gelatin in cold water. Drain beets. Heat juice in saucepan with sugar, vinegar and salt. Add gelatin and stir until dissolved. Chill until slightly thickened. Fold in beets. Chill until firm.

Jan Shepard

Jan Shepard, *daughter of former Senator John Sparkman (Alabama)*

Chicken and Rice Salad
SERVES 8 TO 10

5 cups diced cooked chicken
2 Tablespoons canola oil
2 Tablespoons orange juice
1 Tablespoon vinegar
½ teaspoon salt
3 cups cooked rice

1 cup pineapple tidbits
1 can Mandarin oranges
1 cup toasted almond slivers
1½ cups chopped celery
1 cup seedless grapes
1½ cups mayonnaise, reduced fat

Marinate diced, cooked chicken overnight (or several hours) in the oil, orange juice, vinegar and salt. Mix together the chicken and all other ingredients. Refrigerate and serve when chilled. (Not suitable for freezing.)

Carolyn S. Wolf

Mrs. Frank Wolf, *wife of Representative (Virginia)*

Fantasy Fruit Salad
SERVES 8

1 small can (about 5½ ounces)
   Mandarin oranges
1 small can pineapple tidbits
1 small can fruit cocktail
1 cup creamy cottage cheese
1 box lime Jello gelatin

1 cup shredded coconut
1 small package of Funmallows
   (miniature flavored marshmallows)
1 cup Cool Whip
½ cup broken walnuts or pecans

Place the first 8 ingredients in a large bowl including the juices from the cans of fruit. Toss to mix all ingredients (do not stir). Save a tablespoon of walnuts for garnish. Chill overnight and serve on a bed of lettuce. (10 minutes preparation time. Not suitable for freezing.)

Vera D. Davis

Mrs. Danny Davis, *wife of Representative (Illinois)*

Apricot Chicken Salad
SERVES 8 TO 10

4 cups chopped chicken breast
2 cups chopped celery
2 cups red seedless grapes, halved
¼ cup chopped onion
8 ounces apricot preserves

1½ cups pecan halves
1 cup mayonnaise
1 cup sour cream
2 Tablespoons sugar

Make a dressing of mayonnaise, sour cream and sugar. Combine the chicken breast, celery, grapes, chopped onion, apricot preserves and pecan halves. Toss thoroughly with chicken mixture. Refrigerate overnight. (25 minutes preparation time.)

Ted Strickland

Ted Strickland, *Representative (Ohio)*

Jay's Jeweled Flank Steak Salad
SERVES 6 TO 8

Rub:
1¾ pound flank steak
1 Tablespoon dried oregano
¾ teaspoon salt

2 Tablespoons chili powder
2 Tablespoons ground cumin
¼ teaspoon cinnamon

Salad:
3 bell peppers, yellow, green and
  red, finely sliced

1 Bermuda onion, finely sliced
1 Tablespoon cilantro, chopped

Dressing:
⅓-½ cup red wine vinegar
1 shallot, minced
1 cup extra virgin olive oil (Add in a slow steady stream, whisking constantly.)

1 teaspoon Dijon mustard
salt and ground black pepper to taste

After preparing rub, score and pat approximately 2 tablespoons on each side of steak. Grill or broil steak to medium, 8 to 10 minutes. Cool, and slice thinly. Mix with sliced peppers and onions. Toss with vinaigrette to taste. Add cilantro just before serving. (30 minutes preparation time. Not suitable for freezing.)

Jay Rhodes

Jay Rhodes, *former Representative (Arizona)*

Garden Salad with Pears and Roquefort Croutons
SERVES 6 TO 8

Vinaigrette:
2½ Tablespoons red wine vinegar
1 shallot, minced
1 Tablespoon walnut or other nut oil
3 Tablespoons olive oil
¼ cup extra virgin olive oil
salt and freshly ground pepper

Croutons:
3 Tablespoons butter, at room temperature
4 ounces Roquefort cheese, at room temperature
2 ounces cream cheese, at room temperature
1 Tablespoon chopped fresh parsley
2 scallions, white and green, thinly sliced
2 Tablespoons finely chopped walnuts, toasted
6 large slices rustic country-style bread, cut in half on the diagonal and lightly toasted

Salad:
2-3 small heads of salad greens (oak leaf lettuce, frisée, mizuna, radicchio, arugula and watercress)
2 pears or apples, peeled and thinly sliced
⅓ cup walnuts or pecans, toasted

To make the vinaigrette, place the vinegar and shallots in a small bowl and let sit 10 minutes. Combine the oils and whisk into the vinegar. Season with salt and pepper and set aside. Preheat the oven to 400°. In a bowl, mash the butter, Roquefort cheese, cream cheese, parsley, scallions and walnuts together or place in a food processor and pulse until the ingredients are mixed. Season with salt and pepper. Spread the mixture on the toasted bread. Place the bread on a baking sheet and toast on the top shelf of the oven until golden around the edges, 30 to 45 seconds. Trim the heads of the salad greens. Discard any outside leaves that may be damaged. Tear the leaves into the appropriate size for a salad, wash them and spin dry. Season the greens with salt and pepper. Toss the greens, pears and walnuts with the vinaigrette. Divide among 6 plates. Garnish each salad with 2 croutons. Serve immediately. (30 minutes preparation time. Not suitable for freezing.)

Franki Roberts

Mrs. Pat Roberts, *wife of Senator (Kansas)*

Oriental Spinach Salad
SERVES 2 TO 3

Dressing:

1 cup oil

¼ cup vinegar

⅓ cup ketchup

2 Tablespoons Worcestershire sauce

¾ cup sugar

½ teaspoon salt

¾ onion, grated

Salad:

1 8-ounce bag of fresh spinach

1 8-ounce can sliced water chestnuts, drained

8 strips crisp bacon, crumbled

3 hard cooked eggs, chopped

Combine dressing ingredients in a large jar. Shake well and refrigerate overnight. This dressing will stay fresh for 3 weeks. Wash spinach. Toss salad ingredients. Add dressing when ready to serve. (30 minutes preparation time. Not suitable for freezing.)

Karyn Frist

Mrs. Bill Frist, *wife of Senator (Tennessee)*

Cheery Cherry Salad
SERVES 9

1 3-ounce package raspberry Jello

1 can cherry pie filling

1 cup whipping cream

1 can crushed pineapple

1 cup tiny marshmallows

1 3-ounce package cream cheese

1 3-ounce package lemon Jello

chopped walnuts

Add 1 cup boiling water to raspberry Jello. Fold in pie filling and let set in an 8″ × 8″ pan. Whip whipping cream, and set aside. Add 1 cup boiling water to lemon Jello. Stir in drained pineapple and softened cream cheese. Fold in whipped cream and marshmallows. Spread on top of raspberry-cherry mixture. Sprinkle with nuts. Chill. (20 minutes preparation time. Not suitable for freezing.)

Paul E. Gillmor

Paul Gillmor, *Representative (Ohio)*

Greek Salad

4-5 cups salad greens (optional) (i.e. lettuce, chicory, escarole, or other greens)

2-3 tomatoes, cut into wedges

1-2 red or green peppers, cored, seeded and cut into thin rings or strips

1-2 cucumbers, sliced

1 onion, peeled and cut into thin rings or strips (use according to taste)

10-12 Kalamata or other black olives

½-1 pound of feta cheese, cut into small pieces

1 Tablespoon dried oregano or ½ cup fresh oregano leaves torn into small pieces

1 Tablespoon dried dill or ½ cup fresh dill torn into small pieces

salt to taste (optional)

2-4 Tablespoons fresh lemon juice or wine vinegar

½ cup virgin olive oil

Use a large salad bowl. If using salad greens, wash and dry greens and tear into small pieces. If omitting greens, begin with tomatoes. Prepare and combine tomatoes, peppers, cucumbers, onion, Kalamata olives and feta cheese. Toss lightly. Add oregano, dill and salt to taste. Again toss lightly. Sprinkle lemon juice or wine vinegar and olive oil. Toss again, this time thoroughly. Add more lemon juice or wine vinegar and olive oil to taste. Serve immediately. (20 minutes preparation time. Not suitable for freezing.)

George W. Gekas

George W. Gekas, *Representative (Pennsylvania)*

Garden Egg and Potato Salad
SERVES 5 TO 7

5 medium potatoes
3 dill pickles (any brand)
1 large onion
1 can diced carrots (drained)
1 can sweet peas (drained)
5 eggs (hard boiled)

1 teaspoon pepper
1 teaspoon salt
1 Tablespoon original
    Grey Poupon mustard
1 cup mayonnaise

MA'O HAU HELE
(HIBISCUS BRACKENRIDGEI SSP. MOKULEIANUS)
SPECIES SENT: HIBISCUS COULTERII

HAWAII

Endemic to the islands of Kauai and Oahu, ma'o hau hele was adopted as Hawaii's state flower in 1988. It produces large numbers of bright yellow flowers during the summer and then blooms sparingly during the rest of the year. Unlike most hibiscus, ma'o hau hele has broad smooth leaves with coarsely serrated margins.

Wash potatoes, leave on skin and boil until soft. Set aside to cool completely; then peel. Dice the potatoes to small cubes; cover and set aside. Hard-boil eggs. Set aside to cool. Peel and dice into very small cubes (eggs must be completely cold to prevent them from falling apart when diced), cover; set aside. Dice pickles into very small cubes. Cover and set aside. Dice onion into very small cubes. Cover and set aside. Combine potatoes, carrots and peas. Mix well. Add eggs, pickles and onions. Mix well, avoid crushing ingredients. Add mayonnaise and mustard. Mix well. Add salt and pepper as desired. Refrigerate for 1 hour. Salad is best when served chilled. Enjoy! (45 minutes preparation time. Not suitable for freezing.)

Lynne Hunter

Mrs. Duncan Hunter, *wife of Representative (California)*

Artichoke Rice-A-Roni Salad
SERVES 8

1 6-ounce package of Rice-A-Roni, chicken flavored
4 green onions, sliced
½ green pepper, chopped
12 (or more) green olives with pimientos, sliced
½ cup mayonnaise
¼-½ teaspoon curry powder
2 6-ounce jars marinated artichokes, cut in halves or smaller

Cook rice according to package, let cool. Add green onions, peppers and olives. Drain artichokes, reserving marinade. Whisk marinade, mayonaise and curry powder in blender. Add artichokes to rice. Pour dressing over everything and refrigerate. Can prepare 2 days ahead. (20 minutes preparation time. Not suitable for freezing.)

Caroline Aderholt

Mrs. Robert Aderholt, *wife of Representative (Alabama)*

Raspberry-Walnut Vinaigrette Salad

3 Tablespoons walnut oil
1 Tablespoon orange juice
1 Tablespoon raspberry wine vinegar
finely grated zest of ½ orange
pinch of nutmeg
salt and cayenne pepper to taste
1 head of leaf lettuce, clean and dry

½ cup diced apple or pear
¼ small red onion, thinly sliced
½ cup walnut pieces lightly toasted
¼ cup crumbled feta cheese

In a small bowl whisk oil, juice, vinegar and zest. Add nutmeg, salt, cayenne and refrigerate. Break lettuce into bite size pieces. Toss with onion, nuts, cheese and apples or pears. Add dressing immediately. Sprinkle evenly over lettuce and serve. (Not suitable for freezing.)

Kathleen Schweiker

Mrs. Malcolm Schweiker, *daughter-in-law of former Cabinet Secretary and former Senator Richard Schweiker (Pennsylvania)*

Mediterranean Salad
SERVES 8

1 8-ounce package of spaghetti, uncooked
1 6-ounce jar marinated artichoke hearts, drained and chopped
1 4-ounce can ripe olives, sliced and drained
1 medium red pepper, chopped
1 small zucchini, chopped
½ small purple onion, thinly sliced
½ cup fresh grated Parmesan cheese
½ cup mayonnaise
½ cup Italian dressing
1 teaspoon dried parsley flakes
½ teaspoon dried dillweed
½ teaspoon coarsely ground pepper

Cook spaghetti and rinse. Combine artichokes with next 6 ingredients in a large bowl. Add spaghetti and stir well. In separate bowl combine mayonnaise with remaining ingredients, stirring well with wire whisk. Add to spaghetti mixture and stir well. Cover and chill. (40 minutes preparation time. Not suitable for freezing.)

Mrs. Robert Aderholt, *wife of Representative (Alabama)*

Champagne Salad
SERVES 20

1 8-ounce package cream cheese
¾ cup sugar
12 ounces frozen strawberries, thawed (or fresh)

1 large can crushed pineapple, drained
½ cup pecans, chopped
2 bananas, diced
1 10-ounce container Cool Whip

Cream together the cream cheese and sugar. Add strawberries, pineapple, nuts and bananas. Fold in the Cool Whip. Store in the freezer. Remove from the freezer 30 minutes before serving. Can add other fruit to taste. (15 minutes preparation time. Suitable for freezing.)

John E. Ensign, *Representative (Nevada)*

Layered Chicken Salad
SERVES 8

Salad :

3 cups chopped, cooked
  chicken, divided
2 cups torn lettuce
1 cup cooked, long-grain rice
1 10-ounce package frozen
  green peas, thawed

¼ cup chopped fresh parsley
2 large tomatoes, seeded and chopped
1 cup thinly sliced cucumber
1 small sweet, red pepper, chopped
1 small green pepper, chopped
red pepper rings for garnish

Dressing:

1 cup mayonnaise
½ cup sour cream
½ cup raisins
½ cup finely chopped onion
¼ cup sweet pickle relish

2 Tablespoons milk
½ teaspoon celery seeds
½ teaspoon dill seeds
½ teaspoon dry mustard
½ teaspoon garlic salt

Salad: Layer 1½ cups chicken and lettuce in a 3-quart bowl. Combine rice, peas and parsley; spoon evenly over lettuce. Layer tomatoes, cucumber, chopped red pepper, green pepper and remaining 1½ cups chicken. Spoon dressing evenly over top of salad, sealing to edge of bowl. Top with red pepper rings. Cover and chill 8 hours. Toss before serving. Dressing: Combine all ingredients, stir well. (25 minutes preparation time. Not suitable for freezing.)

Ginny Pitts

Mrs. Joseph Pitts, *wife of Representative (Pennsylvania)*

Cucumber-Roast Beef Salad
SERVES 4

1 medium cucumber, sliced
1 cup (4 ounces) cubed cheddar cheese
1 cup cubed, cooked roast beef
½ cup sliced green onions
⅔ cup commercial creamy cucumber salad dressing
½ Tablespoon white vinegar
1 Tablespoon prepared horseradish
½ Tablespoon chopped fresh dill
1 avocado
1 large tomato, cut into wedges
lettuce leaves

Combine the first 4 ingredients in a bowl. Mix together cucumber dressing and next 3 ingredients. Combine with beef mixture, tossing well; cover and chill. Just before serving, peel and slice avocado. Arrange beef mixture, tomato and avocado on a lettuce-lined platter. (20 minutes preparation time. Not suitable for freezing.)

Ginny Pitts

Mrs. Joseph Pitts, *wife of Representative (Pennsylvania)*

Broccoli Salad

1 bunch fresh broccoli florets
½-1 cup chopped red onion
1 cup chopped celery
2 carrots, shredded
1-1½ cups golden raisins
1 cup sunflower seeds (kernels)

8 slices bacon, crumbled

Dressing:
1 cup salad dressing or mayonnaise
¼ cup cider vinegar
2 Tablespoons sugar (or to taste)

Mix vegetables. (Also peel and chop the tender parts of the stem, if you wish.) Mix dressing. Add to salad and add bacon just before serving. Keeps for several days in the refrigerator, if it lasts that long.

Chuck Grassley

Chuck Grassley, *Senator (Iowa)*

Southwest Potato Salad (From Ohio)

SERVES 8

10-14 red skinned potatoes (about 2 pounds) washed and unpeeled
2 cups mayonnaise or salad dressing
1 medium, ripe tomato, chopped
½ cup chopped onion
½ green bell pepper, chopped
2 green onions, tops and bottoms, chopped
2 cloves garlic, minced
2 Tablespoons chopped fresh cilantro
1 Tablespoon Dijon mustard
2 Tablespoons lime juice
1 teaspoon salt
½ teaspoon black pepper
½ teaspoon cayenne pepper, or more to taste
Optional: hard boiled eggs, 1 pound fried, chopped bacon

Place potatoes in pot and add cold water to cover by about 2″. Bring to a boil and cook for 20 to 25 minutes, until potatoes are done. While potatoes are cooking, combine mayonnaise with remaining ingredients in a large bowl. After potatoes are done, allow to cool enough to handle. Cut into sixths or eighths and add to dressing while still warm. Toss gently to coat. Let stand at room temperature for 30 minutes before serving, or refrigerate up to 2 days. (40 minutes preparation time.)

Deborah Boehner

Mrs. John Boehner, *wife of Representative (Ohio)*

Broccoli Salad

Salad:
4-5 cups broccoli flowerets
½ cup purple onion, chopped
1 cup raisins
10 slices bacon, crumbled
½ cup nuts (sunflower seeds,
  pecans, peanuts)

Dressing:
¾ cup mayonnaise
3 Tablespoons sugar
1 Tablespoon vinegar

Toss salad with dressing. Serve.

Shirley Johnson

Mrs. Sam Johnson, *wife of Representative (Texas)*

Fluffy Orange Salad
SERVES 8

1 3-ounce package cream cheese
1 5-ounce jar Neufchatel cheese spread with pimento
1 16-ounce can sliced peaches
1 16-ounce can Mandarin orange sections, drained
1 13½-ounce can pineapple tidbits, drained
1 cup tiny marshmallows
1 cup whipping cream

Beat together cream cheese and cheese spread. Drain and cut up peaches; reserving ¼ cup syrup. Beat reserved peach syrup into cheese mixture. Fold in fruits and marshmallows. Whip cream and fold into fruit mixture. Chill. (20 minutes preparation time. Not suitable for freezing.)

Karen L. Gillmor

Mrs. Paul Gillmor, *wife of Representative (Ohio)*

Italian Bread Salad (Pansanella)

SERVES 4

3 cups ½″ cubes of toasted stale Italian or French bread
2 large, fresh tomatoes, cut into ½″ cubes
1 cucumber, peeled, quartered, cut into ½″ cubes
½ cup finely chopped red onion
1 cup fresh basil leaves, chopped
1 garlic clove, minced
¼ cup red wine vinegar
½ cup olive oil of good quality

Combine bread, tomatoes, cucumber and onion. Add salt and pepper to taste. Toss well. In blender or food processor combine the rest of the ingredients until basil is pureed. Pour onto and toss salad. If you wish a crunchy texture, salad may be served now. The longer it stands, the softer it becomes as the bread absorbs the juices. Better served at room temperature. (20 minutes preparation time. Not suitable for freezing.)

Nini Horn

Mrs. Steve Horn, *wife of Representative (California)*

Debbie Rissitto's Layered Salad

SERVES 10 TO 12

Salad:
1 medium sized head of lettuce
½ cup thinly sliced green onions
1 cup thinly sliced celery

1 8-ounce can sliced water chestnuts, drained
1 10-ounce package frozen peas

Dressing:
2 cups mayonnaise
½ cup Parmesan cheese
¼ teaspoon garlic powder

Garnish:
3 grated hard boiled eggs
1 pound bacon, cooked and crumbled
2 to 3 tomatoes, cut in wedges

Layer salad ingredients in the order listed above. Top with dressing mixture. Cover and chill up to 24 hours. Garnish before serving. (25 minutes preparation time. Not suitable for freezing.)

Pamela C. Herger

Mrs. Wally Herger, *wife of Representative (California)*

Main Dishes & Casseroles

The Congressional Club
would like to thank
Diamond Chef Sponsor

National Restaurant Association

Main Dishes & Casseroles

CONSTRUCTION OF THE CONGRESSIONAL CLUBHOUSE

The first Congressional Club was a historic residence located at 1432 K St. After 6 years, Mrs. John B. Henderson very generously donated the land to build a new clubhouse at its present location of 2001 New Hampshire Ave., and signed a $30,000 note for its construction and furnishings. Mrs. Fletcher, the Club President, and Mrs. Towner, the Recording Secretary, took on the responsibility of overseeing the construction in 1914. They spent the summer and autumn in Washington at their own expense, consulting on all the details as the building progressed. Mrs. Towner spent days searching for just the right shade of green tiles for the dining alcove hearth. She returned one day just in time to see the finishing touches on the tiles being painted white, which they are to this day.

Bailey House Apple French Toast
SERVES 4 TO 6

1 cup packed brown sugar	3 eggs
½ cup butter	1 cup milk
2 Tablespoons light corn syrup	1 Tablespoon vanilla
5 apples	1 loaf French bread, sliced into thick slices

Cook brown sugar, butter and corn syrup in saucepan 4 to 5 minutes until thick. Then pour into a 9″ × 12″ baking pan. Peel and slice apples and put apple slices on top of syrup in pan. Beat 3 eggs slightly. Add milk and vanilla to eggs. Dip thick slices of French bread into egg mixture for 15 seconds each. Place soaked bread slices on top of apples in pan. Cover and refrigerate overnight. Bake in 350° oven for 35 minutes uncovered. The Bailey House is a bed and breakfast across from President Grant's boyhood home. (10 minutes preparation time. Not suitable for freezing.)

Fran DeWine

Mrs. Michael DeWine, *wife of Senator (Ohio)*

Breakfast Casserole
SERVES 6 TO 8

¼ cup butter
¼ cup flour
1 cup cream
1 cup milk
¼ teaspoon thyme
¼ teaspoon marjoram

¼ teaspoon basil
1 pound cheddar cheese
1½ dozen hard boiled eggs, sliced
½ pound bacon, cooked until crisp
½ pound link sausage, cooked
¼ cup finely chopped parsley

Melt butter, blend in flour. Add cream and milk gradually. Cook, stirring until thick. Add herbs, then cheese to sauce. Stir until melted. Place layer of eggs in greased casserole, then bacon, sausage and parsley, then cheese sauce. Repeat 2 times. Sprinkle with buttered bread crumbs. Bake uncovered at 350° for 30 minutes. (30 minutes preparation time. Not suitable for freezing.)

Mrs. John Linder, *wife of Representative (Georgia)*

John's Huevos Ranchero
SERVES 4 TO 6

6 slices bacon
1 small onion, minced
1 10-ounce can Ro-Tel (diced tomatoes and green chilies)
1 pound grated Velveeta cheese
4-6 eggs

Cook bacon until crisp. Remove and drain. Sauté onion in bacon grease until soft. Add Ro-Tel and grated cheese. Stir until cheese is melted. Drop eggs in cheese sauce. Crumble bacon on top of eggs. Cover and cook until eggs are done. (20 minutes preparation time. Not suitable for freezing.)

John Linder, *Representative (Georgia)*

Apple Pancake
SERVES 4

3 Gala or McIntosh apples,
  peeled, cored and sliced
2 Tablespoons lemon juice
¼ teaspoon cinnamon
5 Tablespoons confectioners' sugar
4 Tablespoons canola oil

3 eggs, at room temperature
⅛ teaspoon salt
½ package Butter Buds
½ cup all-purpose flour
½ cup nonfat milk, at room temperature

Put the apple slices in a large bowl with the lemon juice. Stir the cinnamon into the sugar and sprinkle the sugar mixture over the apple slices. Toss to mix. Heat the oil in the skillet at medium. Add the apples and cook, stirring often, for about 3 to 4 minutes, or until the apples are tender but still hold their shape. Meanwhile, in a separate bowl, combine the eggs, salt, flour, milk and Butter Buds. Beat until smooth. Spread the apples evenly over the bottom of the skillet and pour the batter on top. Place skillet in the center of a pre-heated 425° oven. Bake for about 20 minutes, or until golden and puffy. Turn immediately onto a warm platter so the apples are on top. Dust with a little confectioners' sugar. Serve at once. (40 minutes preparation time. Not suitable for freezing.)

Nancy Malone

Mrs. James C. Corman, *wife of former Representative (California)*

Baked Eggs with Three Cheeses
SERVES 12

7 eggs
1 cup milk
2 teaspoons sugar
1 pound shredded Monterey Jack
  or Muenster cheese

4 ounces cream cheese, cubed
1 pound small curd cottage cheese
⅔ cup butter or margarine, melted
½ cup flour
1 teaspoon baking powder

Beat together eggs, milk and sugar. Add cheeses and melted butter. Mix well. Mix in flour and baking powder then pour into a 3-quart baking dish sprayed with non-stick pan coating. Bake for 45 to 50 minutes in a 350° oven or until knife inserted in center comes out clean. May be prepared in advance and refrigerated, covered. If put in oven directly from refrigerator, uncover and bake up to 60 minutes. Cut into rectangles to serve. (1¼ hours preparation time.)

John Tanner, *Representative (Tennessee)*

Ham and Egg Casserole
SERVES 10

16 slices Pepperidge Farm bread
  (crusts removed)
4 Tablespoons softened butter
2 Tablespoons prepared mustard
2 cups grated Cheddar cheese
2 cups chopped ham

4 eggs
3 cups whole milk or milk and
  part half and half
½ teaspoon salt
1 teaspoon Worcestershire sauce

Place 8 slices of buttered bread in well greased 9″ × 13″ dish buttered side up. Cover with 1 cup cheese and 1 cup ham. Top with buttered bread slices buttered side down. Add remaining cheese and meat. Beat 4 eggs, 3 cups whole milk or part milk and part half and half, 1 teaspoon salt and 1 teaspoon pepper. Pour over casserole. Cover tightly with foil. Store in refrigerator overnight. Bake for 1 hour at 350°. (30 minutes preparation time. Suitable for freezing.)

Jean Terry

Mrs. John Terry, *wife of former Representative (New York)*

Breakfast Casserole
SERVES 8

6 slices bread, trimmed and cubed
1½ pounds sausage, cooked, drained
  and crumbled
2 cups cheddar cheese, shredded

2½ cups milk
4 eggs, beaten
1 large jar sliced mushrooms
1 can cream of mushroom soup

Combine all ingredients and pour into a 3-quart greased casserole dish. Bake at 325° for 1½ hours. May be made the day before and baked 1 hour. Complete cooking when ready to serve. This is a wonderful casserole for breakfast or brunch. (1½ hours preparation time.)

Ronnie G. Flippo

Ronnie G. Flippo, *former Representative (Alabama)*

Kathy Canfield's Dutch Babies
SERVES 3

Pan size	Butter	Eggs	Milk and Flour	Servings
2-3 quarts	¼ cup	3	¾ cup each	3
3-4 quarts	⅓ cup	4	1 cup each	4
4-5 quarts	½ cup	5	1¼ cups each	5

Select the recipe portion to fit your pan (oven-proof glass casserole). Place the butter into the pan and set it into a 425° oven, then mix the batter quickly while the butter melts. Place eggs in the blender and whirl at high speed for 1 minute. With the motor running, gradually pour in the milk, then slowly add the flour. Continue whirling for 30 seconds. Remove the hot pan from the oven and pour the batter into the hot melted butter. Return to oven and bake until puffy and well-browned (20 to 25 minutes depending on the pan). Dust with ground nutmeg, if you wish, and cut into individual servings. The puffing will deflate. Serve at once with any of the toppings below.

Classic: Shake powdered sugar and squeeze fresh lemon wedges on top.

Syrups: Pass warm honey, maple, or fruit syrups.

Fresh Fruit: Strawberries, kiwi, and bananas.

Hot Fruit: Sauté apple or pear slices in butter until tender. Sweeten with sugar or honey.

Larry LaRocco, *former Representative (Idaho)*

SYRINGA
(PHILADELPHUS LEWISII)

IDAHO

When Idaho's state flower is in full bloom, the flowers fill the air with a scent similar to that of orange blossoms. The genus name, Philadelphus, pays homage to the Egyptian king Ptolemy Philadelphus, while the species name, lewisii, honors explorer Meriwether Lewis who first collected it during his exploration of the Louisiana Purchase.

Also known as mock orange and Indian arrowhead, Native Americans made arrows using the plant's straight stems.

Eggs Andouille Casserole
SERVES 10 TO 12

16 slices white bread (crusts removed)
3½ cups grated cheddar cheese
1½ pounds andouille sausage,
    (cooked, drained and chopped)
¼ cup green peppers, chopped
6 eggs
2 teaspoons Worcestershire sauce

½ teaspoon salt
dash of pepper
dash of paprika
1 teaspoon dry mustard
3 cups milk
dash of nutmeg

Place 8 slices bread in a 9″ × 13″ greased baking dish. Place sausage on each slice. Sprinkle green pepper over all. Place 8 slices bread over this. Mix eggs and beat in rest of ingredients except butter. Pour over bread and refrigerate overnight. Melt butter and drizzle over top. Bake at 350° for 1 hour. (1½ hours preparation time. Not suitable for freezing.)

Jeane Chappell

Mrs. William Chappell, *wife of former Representative (Florida)*

Bacon Cheese Soufflé for Brunch
SERVES 8

10 slices whole wheat bread, crusts cut off
8 ounces grated sharp cheese
2½ Tablespoons melted butter
4 eggs, beaten slightly
2 cups milk
1 teaspoon salt
½ teaspoon dry mustard
½ pound of cooked bacon, finely chopped
½ cup chopped green onion
pinch white pepper

Cube bread. Mix all ingredients in large bowl until well blended. Pour into greased low baking dish. Bake at 350° for just under an hour, or until golden brown. Can be assembled the night before and baked the next morning.

Barbara Morris-Lent

Mrs. Norman Lent, *wife of former Representative (New York)*

Sausage Squares

SERVES 8

2 cups Bisquick
¾ cup milk
2 eggs
2-3 Tablespoons poppy seeds
1 pound sausage

1 large onion
¾ Tablespoon salt
1½ cups sour cream
paprika
grated cheddar cheese

Mix together Bisquick, milk and 1 egg. Spread in 9″ × 13″ greased baking dish. Sprinkle with poppy seeds. Brown sausage and onion and drain well. Add salt. Spread sausage mixture over Bisquick mixture. Beat 1 egg in sour cream until well blended. Spread over sausage. Sprinkle with paprika and top with grated cheese if desired. Bake at 350° for 25 to 30 minutes. Let stand for 5 minutes and cut into squares. (30 minutes preparation time. Not suitable for freezing.)

Zach Wamp

Zach Wamp, *Representative (Tennessee)*

Fat Man Shrimp

SERVES 6

2 packages frozen chopped spinach (cook and drain well)
1 cup sour cream
2 cans undiluted cream of mushroom soup
6 8-ounce cans of browned sliced mushrooms (drained)
2 cups cooked shrimp (1½ pounds, medium size)
bread crumbs for topping

Preheat oven to 350°. Mix sour cream, soup and mushrooms. Heat the shrimp separately. Layer in casserole pan, spinach, shrimp and then sauce. Repeat the layers once more. Sprinkle bread crumbs on top. Cook uncovered for ½ hour. (25 minutes preparation time. Not suitable for freezing.)

Charles Vanik

Charles Vanik, *former Representative (Ohio)*

Italian Sausage and Tortellini Soup

SERVES 6

1 pound sweet Italian sausage, casings removed
1 cup chopped onion
2 large garlic cloves, sliced
5 cups beef broth
2 cups chopped tomatoes
1 8-ounce can tomato sauce
1 large zucchini, sliced
1 large carrot, thinly sliced
1 medium-size green bell pepper, diced
½ cup dry red wine
2 Tablespoons dried basil
2 Tablespoons dried oregano
8-10 ounces fresh tortellini
freshly grated Parmesan cheese

Sauté Italian sausage in heavy pot over medium-high heat until cooked through, crumbling with back of spoon, about 10 minutes. Using slotted spoon, transfer sausage to large bowl. Pour off all but 1 tablespoon of drippings from pot. Add onion and garlic to pot and sauté until translucent, about 5 minutes. Return sausage to pot. Add beef broth, tomatoes, tomato sauce, zucchini, carrot, bell pepper, wine, basil and oregano. Simmer until vegetables are tender, about 40 minutes. (Can be prepared 2 days ahead. Cover and refrigerate. Bring to a simmer before continuing.) Add tortellini to soup and cook until tender, about 8 minutes. Season soup to taste with salt and pepper. Ladle into bowls and sprinkle with Parmesan and serve. (30 minutes preparation time. Not suitable for freezing.)

Linda Dooley

Mrs. Calvin Dooley, *wife of Representative (California)*

Cheese Grits

SERVES 8

1 cup quick grits
1 teaspoon salt
4 cups water
1 roll garlic cheese, cut up

½ cup margarine
½ cup milk
2 eggs, beaten
grated cheddar cheese

Cook grits slowly in 4 cups salted water. Remove from heat. Add garlic cheese and margarine. Stir until melted. Add milk and beaten eggs. Mix well. Pour into greased 9″ × 13″ casserole and bake at 350° for 40 minutes. Remove from oven, top with grated cheese and cook an additional 5 minutes. Good with fried fish for dinner or sausage and biscuits for brunch. (30 minutes preparation time. Not suitable for freezing.)

Mary Sessions

Mrs. Jeff Sessions, *wife of Representative (Alabama)*

Sour Cream Enchiladas

SERVES 12

2 pints sour cream
2 cans cream of chicken soup
1 4-ounce can diced green chiles
2 bunches green onions sliced (about 12)
1 dozen corn tortillas
1 whole chicken, cooked and boned, sliced into strips or chunks

¾ pound sharp cheddar cheese (or ½ cheddar and ½ Monterey Jack), grated
Parmesan cheese
paprika

Mix sour cream, soup, chiles and onion together. Warm tortillas slightly in microwave or oven so they are pliable. Spread some of the soup mixture down the middle of a tortilla. Put a few chunks of chicken and a sprinkling of cheese on top of the soup mixture. Roll up the tortilla and place in a 9″ × 13″ glass pan. Repeat for all tortillas. Cover the tortillas with the remaining soup mix. Sprinkle with grated Parmesan cheese and a little paprika. Bake until sauce is bubbling, about 35 minutes. (25 minutes preparation time. Suitable for freezing.)

Lois C. Bramblett

Mrs. Ernest Bramblett, *wife of former Representative (California)*

Chicken Green Bean Casserole
SERVES 6 TO 8

1 package Pepperidge Farm Dressing
¼ cup chopped celery
¼ cup chopped onion
¼ cup chopped green pepper
2 packages cut green beans, cooked
4 double chicken breasts, cooked (microwave is fine), cut into bite size pieces

1 can cream of chicken soup
1 cup chicken broth
buttered casserole dish
optional: slivered almonds

Combine dressing, celery, onion and pepper. Layer ½ dressing mix on bottom. Next layer is the green beans, third layer is the chicken, fourth layer, the soup and broth mix. Lastly, layer the balance of the dressing. Salt and pepper to taste. Bake at 325° for 45 minutes. Add slivered almonds if desired. (15 minutes preparation time. Suitable for freezing.)

Bob McEwen, *former Representative (Ohio)*

Crab Bake
SERVES 6

4 Tablespoons melted butter
1½ cups plain bread crumbs
1½ cups real mayonnaise
2 Tablespoons lemon juice
1 Tablespoon lemon zest
1 Tablespoon horseradish
1 Tablespoon soy sauce

3 drops Tabasco
1 small onion, grated
1 teaspoon celery salt
1 pound crabmeat (pick through for any shells, fresh lump crabmeat is best)

Mix bread crumbs with melted butter and set aside. Mix together the mayonnaise, lemon juice, lemon zest, horseradish, soy sauce, Tabasco, grated onion and celery salt. Fold in the crabmeat and 2 tablespoons of the buttered bread crumbs. Place a few buttered bread crumbs in the bottom of an ovenproof casserole dish and add the crab mixture. Sprinkle the remaining buttered bread crumbs on top. Bake at 375° for 15 to 20 minutes. (15 minutes preparation time. Not suitable for freezing.)

Mrs. Ernest Hollings, *wife of Senator (South Carolina)*

Marjoram Meat Balls and Spaghetti Sauce

Marjoram Meat Balls:

½ cup fine dry bread crumbs
¼ cup milk
1 pound ground beef
1 teaspoon Season-All
½ teaspoon onion powder
½ teaspoon ground marjoram
¼ teaspoon ground thyme
¼ teaspoon black pepper
⅛ teaspoon MSG
dash mace
3 Tablespoons oil
1 teaspoon beef flavor base
¼ cup hot water
½ cup wine, optional

Soak crumbs in milk, then combine with ground beef, Season-All, onion powder, marjoram, thyme, pepper, MSG and mace. Shape into 30 to 36 small balls, using a rounded teaspoonful for each. Brown on all sides in hot oil. Dissolve beef flavor base in hot water; pour over meat balls. Cover and simmer 20 minutes. For extra zest, add ½ cup wine to these miniature meat balls before simmering. Serve plain or with your favorite sauce. Makes 3 dozen. This recipe is so good! Be sure to use the wine with the meat balls. Yum-yum!

Spaghetti Sauce:

3½ cups plum tomatoes (28-ounce can)
1 6-ounce can tomato paste
3 cups water
2 Tablespoons instant minced onion
½ teaspoon garlic powder
½ teaspoon oregano leaves
1 teaspoon Bon Appétit
1 bay leaf
1½ teaspoons salt
¼ teaspoon black pepper
1 teaspoon sugar
¼ teaspoon MSG
¼ teaspoon crushed red pepper
2 Tablespoons olive oil or salad oil
1 Tablespoon arrowroot, optional

Force tomatoes through a coarse sieve to puree and remove seeds. Combine the tomato puree and remaining ingredients, except arrowroot, in glass or stainless steel saucepan. Bring to boil; reduce heat and simmer, uncovered, 1 hour. Remove bay leaf. For a thicker sauce, simmer 20 minutes longer; or thicken by making a thin, smooth paste of the arrowroot and an equal amount of water. Stir into sauce and cook, continuing to stir, until thickened. Serve over cooked spaghetti topped with grated Parmesan cheese. Meat balls, sautéed chicken livers, clams or calamari (very small whole squid) may be added to the sauce or served on the side. Makes 5 cups sauce or enough for 1 pound spaghetti.

Mary Hayworth

Mrs. J. D. Hayworth, *wife of Representative (Arizona)*

Chicken, Cheese and Sour Cream Enchiladas

SERVES 4 TO 6

1 whole chicken
2 cans green chili enchilada sauce
1 can cream of onion soup
1 package corn tortillas

grated cheddar cheese
1 onion, chopped
1 pint sour cream

Cook one whole chicken, de-bone and cut up or shred. Make a mixture of 2 cans green chili enchilada sauce and 1 can cream of onion soup. Dip raw corn tortillas in sauce and fill with grated cheddar cheese, chopped onions and shredded chicken. Roll up and lay in baking dish. Pour remaining sauce over the top of all the enchiladas. Bake for 30 minutes at 375°. Spread with sour cream and top with grated cheese. Put back in the oven until cheese bubbles. (Not suitable for freezing.)

J.D. Hayworth, *Representative (Arizona)*

One-Dish Chicken and Pasta with Vegetables

SERVES 4

1 pound skinless, boneless chicken breasts, cut up
1 teaspoon salt, optional
1 teaspoon vegetable oil
1 10¾-ounce can Campbell's mushroom soup (can be fat-free)

2¼ cups water
½ teaspoon dried basil
2 cups frozen vegetables (broccoli, cauliflower, carrot combination)
2 cups uncooked corkscrew pasta

In skillet brown chicken in hot oil. Salt. Remove and set chicken aside. To skillet add soup, water, basil and vegetables. Heat to a boil. Add uncooked pasta. Cook over medium heat 10 minutes, stirring often. The pasta cooks right in the soup! Add browned chicken. Cook 5 minutes, or until pasta is done, stirring often. Sprinkle with Parmesan cheese, if desired. (10 minutes preparation time. Not suitable for freezing.)

Mrs. John Murtha, *wife of Representative (Pennsylvania)*

Donald's Chicken Divan
SERVES 6

3 whole chicken breasts
2 cans cream of chicken soup
¾ cup mayonnaise

6 Tablespoons fresh lemon juice
1 pound fresh asparagus
grated Parmesan cheese

Cut boneless chicken breasts in half to make 6 servings. Parboil for 20 minutes. Mix together thoroughly, the chicken soup, mayonnaise and lemon juice. Arrange chicken breasts and asparagus in an oven-to-table serving dish. Add the prepared sauce over all. Sprinkle the cheese to cover. Bake at 325° for 1 hour. (1 hour and 20 minutes preparation time. Not suitable for freezing.)

Rita S. Hanley

Mrs. James Hanley, *wife of former Representative (New York)*

"Roast in a Crock"
SERVES 6 TO 8

crock pot
pot roast

1 24-ounce jar Pace picante sauce (mild)
sourdough rolls

Put roast in crock pot. Add 1 jar Pace picante sauce (mild). Cover crock pot. Start crock pot in early morning and cook on low until evening. Put meat between sourdough rolls. (All day preparation time. Suitable for freezing.)

Carolyn Condit

Mrs. Gary Condit, *wife of Representative (California)*

Glazed Tenderloin of Pork
with Carrot-Stuffed Potatoes

1 cup honey
2 Tablespoons balsamic vinegar
4 teaspoons Dijon-style mustard
2 whole pork tenderloins (12 ounces each)
3 baking potatoes
1 teaspoon salt
½ teaspoon pepper
8 ounces carrots, peeled and coarsely shredded
½ cup low-fat milk (1%)
1 Tablespoon butter
¾ teaspoon ground ginger
1 13¾-ounce can reduced sodium beef broth
2 Tablespoons all purpose flour (might need more)

Whisk honey, vinegar and mustard in bowl. Place tenderloin in plastic bag; add honey mixture; seal. Refrigerate overnight. Turn occasionally to coat. Scrub potatoes; pierce with fork almost to center. Place on side of oven rack. Bake potatoes in preheated oven at 375° for 50 minutes or until tender. Remove pork from bag. Brush with honey mixture. Sprinkle each roast with ½ teaspoon salt and ¼ teaspoon pepper. Roast pork in preheated oven (375°) with potatoes. Brush occasionally with honey mixture. Bake for 35 to 40 minutes until internal temperature registers 160°. Meanwhile, cook carrots in ½" boiling water in saucepan about 5 minutes or until tender. Remove tenderloins to warm platter, cover and let stand 20 minutes. Reserve baking pan with drippings. Remove potatoes from oven; cut in half lengthwise. Reserve. Increase oven temperature to 450°. Combine milk, butter and ginger in saucepan. Heat just to boiling. Carefully scoop out potato, being careful not to break skins. Add potato to milk mixture in saucepan along with ½ teaspoon salt and ¼ teaspoon pepper. Mash until smooth. Fold in carrots. Spoon into potato shells. Place on pie plate. Bake stuffed potatoes in 450° oven 10 minutes. Add water to beef broth to make 2 cups. Whisk in flour until smooth. Skim any fat from drippings in pan. Stir broth mixture into drippings. Cook, stirring, until mixture thickens. Slice tenderloins. Serve with potatoes and gravy.

Alta Leath

Alta Leath, *member of Congressional Club (Texas)*

Atlanta Casserole

4 whole (or 8 half) chicken breasts, cooked, boned and cubed
1½ pounds shrimp, cooked and shelled
1 can artichoke hearts, drained and quartered
1½ pounds mushrooms, sautéed
4 cups white sauce made with half and half (can use skim milk)
½ cup sherry
1 Tablespoon Worcestershire sauce
¼ cup freshly grated Parmesan
1 box Uncle Ben's long grain and wild rice

White Sauce:
1 cup half and half or skim milk
2 Tablespoons margarine
2 Tablespoons flour

Melt margarine; add flour and cook until bubbly. Slowly add half and half or skim milk. Chicken broth and salt may be added if you desire.

Prepare rice according to package directions and spread in the bottom of a large casserole dish. Mix white sauce, sherry and Worcestershire gently. Stir in first 4 ingredients and pour mixture over rice. Top with Parmesan. Bake, uncovered, at 350° until hot, about 30 to 40 minutes. May be prepared ahead and refrigerated until baking.

Hardie Knollenberg

Mrs. Joe Knollenberg, *wife of Representative (Michigan)*

Venison (or Chicken) Stir Fry

Marinade:

¼ cup soy sauce

¼ cup sesame oil (Chinese section at grocery store)

1 Tablespoon ginger root, peeled and minced

2 large cloves garlic, peeled and minced

3-4 venison steaks or boneless chicken breasts, cut into 1" pieces

Vegetables:

1 Tablespoon oil

1 small green pepper sliced into strips

1 small red pepper sliced into strips

5 scallions, sliced

1 cup snow peas, rinsed and strings removed

4 Tablespoons Hoisin sauce (Chinese section at grocery store)

Combine soy sauce, sesame oil, ginger root and garlic in a shallow dish and whisk until well blended. Add the meat and let stand at room temperature for at least 30 minutes, turning often in the marinade. While the meat is marinating, prepare the vegetables. In a wok or large sauté pan, heat the oil over medium high heat. Add the peppers, scallions, and snow peas and cook, stirring constantly until crisp-tender (about 3 to 5 minutes). Remove the vegetables from the pan and set aside. Remove the meat from the marinade and drain slightly. Add more oil to pan, if needed. Add meat and stir constantly until just cooked through (8 to 10 minutes). Add cooked vegetables and Hoisin sauce to the pan and stir until well combined and just heated through. Serve with steamed white rice. (45 minutes preparation time. Suitable for freezing.)

Vicki Barcia

Mrs. Jim Barcia, *wife of Representative (Michigan)*

Sunday Chicken
SERVES 4

whole chicken
1 large bag whole baby carrots
rosemary (2 bunches, fresh)
salt to taste

seasoned pepper to taste
1 chicken bouillon dissolved in one cup water
1 cup orange juice

Wash whole chicken, vegetables and herbs. Salt and pepper interior cavity of chicken. Stuff with herbs. Place on rack in roasting pan. Fill bottom of pan with whole baby carrots. Bake at 300° for 30 minutes per pound. Baste frequently alternating chicken broth and orange juice. Carve chicken and serve on platter surrounded by carrots. Good served with rice with mushrooms and scallions. (Not suitable for freezing.)

Debi Alexander

Mrs. Bill Alexander, *wife of former Representative (Arkansas)*

Easy Beef Stew
SERVES 6

2 pounds beef stew meat, cubed
2 medium onions, chopped
2 stalks celery, cut in chunks
6 small-medium carrots, cut in chunks
3 potatoes, quartered
2 teaspoons salt (or less)

¼ teaspoon pepper
2 Tablespoons tapioca
1 Tablespoon sugar
1 11½ ounce can tomato juice
   (can substitute part red wine)

Place meat in large casserole. Arrange vegetables on top of meat. Combine salt, pepper, tapioca and sugar; sprinkle over vegetables. Add tomato juice and cover tightly. Bake at 275° for 3 to 4 hours. DO NOT PEEK! (20 minutes preparation time. Suitable for freezing.)

Ruth Fawell

Mrs. Harris Fawell, *wife of Representative (Illinois)*

Venison Stroganoff
S E R V E S   6

2-3 pounds venison cut into 1″ pieces
6 Tablespoons butter or margarine
1½ cups sliced fresh mushrooms
2 Tablespoons minced onion
3 Tablespoons flour
1 cup chicken broth or ¼ cup dry wine

1 Tablespoon tomato paste
½ teaspoon Worcestershire
1 cup sour cream
1 Tablespoon chopped parsley
salt to taste
steamed white rice or noodles

Melt 3 tablespoons of butter in large skillet. Add venison and cook, turning, 8 to 10 minutes until done. Remove and keep warm. In same skillet, melt remaining butter. Add mushrooms and sauté for 2 minutes. Add onion and garlic; sauté until tender, not browned. Add a tablespoon more butter if needed. Stir in flour, then stir in broth or wine and cook, stirring, until thickened. Stir in tomato paste and Worcestershire sauce; remove from heat and quickly blend in sour cream and parsley. Season to taste. Stir venison into mixture. Serve on hot, fluffy rice or noodles. (60 minutes preparation time. Suitable for freezing.)

Jim Barcia, *Representative (Michigan)*

No Peek Chicken
S E R V E S   8

1 Tablespoon diced parsley
¾ cup uncooked minute rice
1 can cream of mushroom soup
1 can cream of celery soup

1 package dried onion soup mix
1 cup water
8 chicken breasts, skinned and de-boned

Mix all ingredients together and pour into a large, greased Pyrex 11″ × 7″ × 2″ dish. Place chicken breasts on top. Cover with foil. Bake 2 hours at 350°. Do not peek. (Not suitable for freezing.)

Scotty Baesler, *Representative (Kentucky)*

Artichoke Chicken
SERVES 4

16 ounces desired pasta, boiled
1½ pounds boneless, skinless chicken
    breasts, cut into bite size pieces
2 Tablespoons butter
4 cloves of garlic, minced
1 11-ounce can cream of chicken soup

8 ounces sour cream
½ cup mozzarella cheese, grated
⅛ cup dry white wine
2 Tablespoons Parmesan cheese
12-16 ounces canned or frozen artichoke
    hearts, drained and chopped

In 12" skillet, cook garlic in butter, add chicken and cook until done. In a mixing bowl, stir together soup, sour cream, mozzarella cheese, wine, Parmesan cheese and artichoke hearts. Add to skillet, cover and simmer for 15 minutes. Serve over cooked pasta. (Not suitable for freezing.)

Shannon M. Breslow

Shannon Breslow, *daughter of Representative Elton Gallegly (California)*

Lost Tree's Chicken Broccoli Casserole
SERVES 6

4 chicken breasts
1 10¾ ounce can cream of
    chicken soup
½ cup mayonnaise
½ teaspoon lemon juice
½ teaspoon curry powder

2 10-ounce boxes chopped broccoli
½ cup grated mild cheddar cheese
¼ cup grated sharp cheddar cheese
1 Tablespoon melted margarine
    or butter
½ cup corn flakes or bread crumbs

Boil chicken for 1 hour, then shred or cube. Combine soup, mayonnaise, lemon juice and curry to make a sauce. Salt and pepper to taste. Line the bottom of a casserole dish with one layer of broccoli. Follow with a layer of sauce and a layer of chicken. Continue to layer in sequence until chicken, broccoli and sauce are combined in layers. Top with cheese and buttered corn flakes or bread crumbs. Bake covered for 20 minutes at 350°. (1½ hours preparation time. Suitable for freezing.)

James T. Broyhill

James T. Broyhill, *former Senator (North Carolina)*

PEONY
(PAEONIA SP.)

INDIANA

Peonies are some of the most popular flowers in American gardens. Hardy, peonies bloom in the spring and early summer and thrive in any kind of soil.

Peonies are named for Paeon, the physician to the Greek gods.

Steak 'n Shake Chili
SERVES 4 TO 8

2 pounds ground round
14 ounces beef broth
2 cans water
6 ounces tomato paste
1 teaspoon chocolate syrup
3 #3-cans red kidney beans, undrained

½ teaspoon instant coffee
1 Tablespoon chili powder
2 teaspoons cumin
¼ teaspoon oregano
½ teaspoon seasoned salt

In a large pot brown ground meat. Drain off fat. Add remaining ingredients and stir thoroughly. Heat to boiling. Reduce heat and simmer 30 to 60 minutes, stirring occasionally. (10 to 15 minutes preparation time. Suitable for freezing.)

Janice H. Burlison

Janice H. Burlison, *daughter-in-law of former Representative Bill Burlison (Missouri)*

Gwen's Breast of Turkey Artichoke
SERVES 10

3 packages frozen artichoke hearts
½ cup butter
½ pound mushrooms, quartered
6-8 cups cooked turkey breast
   in large cubes
½ cup flour
3 cups rich chicken stock

4 cups grated cheddar cheese
⅛ teaspoon thyme
dash nutmeg
¼ teaspoon Worcestershire sauce
dash Tabasco sauce
salt and freshly ground pepper to taste
½ cup bread crumbs

Preheat oven to 350°. Cook artichokes according to package directions, drain and place in an 11″ × 13″ baking dish. In a skillet melt butter and gently sauté mushrooms until soft. Remove mushrooms and add to baking dish. Add cubed turkey to butter in skillet. Add flour, stir and cook for 3 minutes until well blended. Add chicken stock, stir and cook until thickened. Add 3 cups of the cheese and stir until melted and blended. Add thyme, nutmeg, Worcestershire, Tabasco, salt and pepper. Pour sauce over turkey mixture in baking dish. Sprinkle top with bread crumbs. Cover with remaining cup of grated cheese and bake uncovered for 30 minutes until bubbling, hot and browned. (35 minutes preparation time. Not suitable for freezing.)

Marguerite Cederberg

Mrs. Al Cederberg, *wife of former Representative (Michigan)*

Al's Mini Meat Loaf

SERVES 4

1 pound lean ground sirloin
  or ground round
3 Tablespoons ketchup
3 Tablespoons light mayonnaise
⅓ cup red wine, or ¼ cup if too moist

salt and pepper to taste
1 Tablespoon finely chopped onion,
  optional
4 Tablespoons grated Parmesan cheese
additional ketchup for topping to taste

Mix first 5 ingredients until thoroughly blended. Shape into 2 separate loaf shaped sections; about 8″ × 2-2½″. Place in a small greased baking dish which will accommodate them without crowding. Spread tops with Parmesan cheese and additional ketchup to taste. Bake at 350° for 35 to 40 minutes. (30 minutes preparation time. Suitable for freezing.)

Al Cederberg

Al Cederberg, *former Representative (Michigan)*

Chicken Squares

SERVES 8

6 ounces softened cream cheese
5 Tablespoons melted butter
4 cups cubed, cooked chicken or turkey
¼ cup milk
½ teaspoon salt
Sauce:
1 can cream of mushroom soup

¼ teaspoon pepper
¾ cup chopped green onions
¾ cup chopped celery
2 cans refrigerated crescent rolls
¾ cup seasoned bread crumbs

¼ cup milk

In medium bowl, blend cream cheese and 4 tablespoons butter until smooth. Add chicken, milk, salt, pepper, onions and celery; mix well. Separate crescent dough into 8 rectangles; firmly press perforations to seal. Spoon ½ cup chicken mixture on to center of each rectangle. Pull 4 corners of dough to top center of filling and twist firmly. Place on ungreased cookie sheet. Brush with reserved butter. Sprinkle with bread crumbs. Bake in preheated 350° oven for 20 to 30 minutes until golden brown. For sauce, combine soup with milk and heat, stirring occasionally. Serve over squares. Unbaked squares may be refrigerated overnight. (30 minutes preparation time. Not suitable for freezing.)

Joyce Chandler

Mrs. Rod Chandler, *wife of former Representative (Washington)*

Basque Halibut and Potatoes
SERVES 5 TO 6

¼ cup olive oil
1 small onion, chopped
4-6 cloves garlic, minced
2 Tablespoons flour
1 jar whole pimientos

½ cup chopped parsley
1½ pounds fresh halibut
12 small red potatoes, cut in 1" chunks
salt and pepper

In a large frying pan, fry the onion and garlic in the olive oil until lightly browned. Stir in the flour, then add the halibut and potatoes. Salt and pepper to taste. Cover the fish with pimientos and sprinkle the entire dish with parsley. Gently add boiling water to the height of the fish. Simmer on low or transfer to a shallow baking dish; cover and bake until the fish is flaky and the potatoes are soft. Serve with tossed salad and sourdough bread. (60 minutes preparation time. Not suitable for freezing.)

Christine B. LaRocco

Mrs. Larry LaRocco, *wife of former Representative (Idaho)*

Montelle's Meal-in-One Casserole
SERVES 6 TO 8

1 pound veal or steak (tender meat)
1 cup rice (minute)
2 large onions
1 bunch celery chopped
1 small can pimentos

1 can mushrooms drained
1 can mushroom soup plus 1 can water
1 can chicken rice soup plus 1 can water
¼ pound slivered almonds

Cook rice according to directions. Cut veal or steak into small squares. Brown meat with celery, onions and mushrooms (drained) in butter. Combine remaining ingredients in large bowl; add meat and vegetables. Put in buttered casserole dish. Bake 1½ hours at 350°. Great served with a cold fruit compote of your choice. (20 minutes preparation time.)

Mary Clement

Mrs. Bob Clement, *wife of Representative (Tennessee)*

Absolutely Delicious Turkey Hash

3-4 Tablespoons turkey fat or margarine
1 medium onion, chopped
½ cup red pepper
3-4 cups diced potatoes
1½ cups sliced mushrooms
1 clove garlic, minced
¼ cup chopped parsley

5 cups diced cooked turkey
4 cups leftover turkey stuffing
1 cup or more turkey gravy
1½ cups half and half
1 teaspoon ground nutmeg
freshly ground pepper to taste
3 Tablespoons grated Swiss cheese

Heat fat in a 12″ skillet over medium heat. Add onion, red pepper, potatoes and sauté for 5 minutes until softened. Add mushrooms and garlic; sauté until softened. Add turkey and stuffing. Cook until heated through. Stir in 1 cup of half and half, gravy, parsley, nutmeg and pepper. Increase heat to medium high. Cook for 5 minutes. Transfer into casserole dish and pour the remaining ½ cup of cream around the dish, shaking the dish so that the cream flows under the hash. Bake at 350° for 25 to 30 minutes. Sprinkle the top of dish with the cheese and broil it until the cheese is melted and lightly browned (about 2 minutes). The hash can be made in advance and reheated in oven (or frozen). Add more milk or gravy to keep it moist. Serve as a supper dish with red cabbage or baked tomatoes; or for brunch with eggs or quiche. (Suitable for freezing.)

Christiane English

Mrs. Philip English, *wife of Representative (Pennsylvania)*

Linda's Mexican Chicken
SERVES 8

4 chicken breasts
1 cup chicken broth
1 can cream of mushroom soup
1 can cream of chicken soup

1 can Ro-Tel green chilies and tomatoes
1 package taco flavored Doritos
½ cup cheddar cheese, grated
small amount finely chopped onion

Cook chicken; save 1 cup broth. Mix both soups, broth, canned chilies and tomatoes. In ovenproof casserole, layer Doritos, cut up chicken and soup mixture. Sprinkle with grated cheddar cheese and onion. Bake at 350° approximately 20 minutes or until casserole bubbles. (20 minutes preparation time. Suitable for freezing.)

Joan M. Cole

Joan Cole, *daughter-in-law of former Representative Sterling Cole (New York)*

June's Oyster Spaghetti
SERVES 4

3 Tablespoons olive oil
1 large onion, chopped
2 ribs celery, chopped
3 cloves of garlic, finely chopped
2 Tablespoons parsley, finely chopped
1 12-ounce can tomato paste

2 cups water
2 bay leaves
3 dozen fresh oysters
oyster water and tap water to make 2 cups
salt and pepper to taste
1 pound thin spaghetti

My mother, June Menard, has carried on an old Christmas Eve family tradition and served this delicious and easy recipe. In the olive oil, sauté onion, celery, garlic and parsley for 2 minutes. Add tomato paste and stir constantly to prevent burning. Stir in 2 cups of water and bay leaves. Cook for 10 minutes. Add oysters, water, salt and pepper to taste. Cover, simmer on medium heat for 30 minutes. Serve over spaghetti. (30 minutes preparation time.)

Jeanne Livingston

Jeanne Livingston, *daughter-in-law of Representative Bob Livingston (Louisiana)*

Chicken Taquitos
SERVES 25

2 cups shredded or chopped
  cooked chicken
¼ cup sliced green onion
⅔ cup salsa
¾ teaspoon ground cumin
vegetable oil

25 corn tortillas
2 cups shredded cheddar cheese or
  Monterey Jack cheese
salsa, sour cream, guacamole,
  fresh diced tomatoes for garnish

Combine chicken, salsa, green onion and cumin in small bowl. Heat oil in skillet until hot but not smoking. Quickly fry each tortilla until just soft, about 10 seconds on each side. Drain on paper towels. Spoon 1 to 2 tablespoons of chicken mixture and about 1 tablespoon cheese down center of tortilla. Roll tightly into thin taquitos and place seam-side down in a glass baking dish. (May be frozen at this point.) Bake in 400° oven for about 20 minutes or until crisp. Serve with salsa, sour cream, guacamole and fresh chopped tomatoes if desired. (30 minutes preparation time. Suitable for freezing.)

Kristy Gavin

Kristy Gavin, *daughter of Senator Jon Kyl (Arizona)*

Baked Spaghetti
SERVES 4

1 pound lean ground beef
8 ounces spaghetti, cooked
1 14-ounce can tomatoes

1 medium onion
salt and pepper to taste
4 ounces mozzarella cheese

Brown and drain ground beef. In casserole dish layer ½ of the spaghetti, ½ of the ground beef, ½ can of tomatoes (slice or dice), ½ of the remaining onion separated into rings, salt and pepper. Repeat with remaining ingredients, except cheese. Bake for 30 minutes at 350°. Add cheese (sliced) and bake 10 minutes more or until cheese melts. (20 minutes preparation time. Suitable for freezing.)

Nancy Hamilton

Mrs. Lee Hamilton, *wife of Representative (Indiana)*

Pasta Chicken Salad
SERVES 6 TO 8

8 ounces angel hair pasta
1 pound boneless chicken breasts
¾ cup plus 2 Tablespoons
   Italian dressing
¾ cup sliced green onions
2 Tablespoons finely chopped
   fresh ginger
½ cup finely chopped cilantro

2 Tablespoons peanut butter
1 Tablespoon brown sugar
1 Tablespoon soy sauce
1 Tablespoon dry sherry
¼ teaspoon crushed red pepper
2 medium onions, sliced
1 medium red pepper, chopped
2 carrots, grated

Cook pasta. Drain and rinse with cold water. Brush chicken with 2 tablespoons dressing and broil 5 to 6 minutes or until lightly browned. Turn once. Let cool, slice diagonally. In large skillet, heat the remaining dressing and cook the onions and ginger over medium heat. Stir in cilantro, peanut butter, sugar, soy sauce, sherry and red pepper. In large bowl, toss the pasta with green onion mixture, carrots and red pepper. Just before serving, add chicken and toss lightly. (30 to 40 minutes preparation time.)

Nini Horn

Mrs. Steve Horn, *wife of Representative (California)*

Red Clam Sauce
SERVES 6

2 Tablespoons olive oil
3 cloves garlic, chopped
1 medium onion, chopped
2 stalks celery, chopped
½ teaspoon oregano
1 teaspoon dried basil
salt and pepper to taste

2 cups canned tomatoes
1 can tomato paste
1 cup water
2 cups bottled clam juice
2 cups minced clams
½ cup chopped parsley
1 pound cooked linguine

Heat oil and add garlic, onion and celery; cooking until onion is transparent. Add herbs, seasonings, tomatoes, tomato paste and water. Bring to boil. Reduce heat and simmer uncovered ½ hour. Add clam juice. Simmer 20 minutes. Just before serving add clams. Cook 3 minutes and add parsley. Heat thoroughly. Serve with linguine. (60 minutes preparation time.)

Marlene Howard-Lazzaro

Mrs. James J. Howard-Lazzaro, *wife of former Representative (New Jersey)*

Beef Stroganoff
SERVES 4

sirloin steak, cut into cubes
¼ pound butter
1 onion, minced
1 green pepper, diced
salt and pepper to taste
1 Tablespoon Worcestershire sauce

1 Tablespoon garlic powder
1 cup sliced mushrooms
dash of Tabasco
2 Tablespoons red wine vinegar
1 cup heavy cream
1 pint sour cream

Cook steak cubes in butter. Add onion and green pepper, cook until soft. Add remaining ingredients. Cover and simmer 1 to 2 hours. Serve on rice cooked in beef bouillon. (30 minutes preparation time. Not suitable for freezing.)

Lynne Linder

Mrs. John Linder, *wife of Representative (Georgia)*

Boo's Oyster Dressing
SERVES 12

2 quarts of oysters with oyster water
1 loaf day-old French bread or
    equivalent of regular bread
2 onions, chopped
2 ribs celery, chopped
4 cloves of garlic, chopped
½ stick butter

½ stick margarine
1 cup shallots, chopped
½ cup parsley, chopped
1 teaspoon sage
1 teaspoon poultry seasoning
salt
pepper (red and black) to taste

My mother's oyster dressing is the best I have ever tasted! First, drain oysters and reserve water. Boil this water for 3 minutes. Remove any foam and discard. Toast bread in oven and break into bite size pieces. Pour some of the oyster water on bread and allow to soak in. In another pan, melt butter and sauté onions, celery and garlic for 3 or 4 minutes. Now, add margarine, shallots and parsley. Sauté for 3 or 4 minutes. Stir in oysters and remaining oyster water; along with sage, poultry seasoning, salt and peppers. Now put bread into this mixture and mix thoroughly. Put in casserole; sprinkle with bread crumbs and bake in 325° oven for 25 minutes. Fantastic! And even better the next day. (25 minutes preparation time. Suitable for freezing.)

Bonnie and Bob Livingston

Bob and Bonnie Livingston, *Representative and Mrs. (Louisiana)*

WILD ROSE
(ROSA SETIGERA)

IOWA

The wild rose grows along streams and roads or in areas with good drainage. Easily identified by its thorns, reddish bark, and pink flowers which fade to white, it ranges from Ontario to Kansas and south to Florida and Texas. The buds and flowers can be brewed into a sweet tea and the flowers can be eaten alone or added to soups. The fruits, called "hips," can also be brewed into a tea.

Shrimp and Fettucine
SERVES 4

8 Tablespoons (1 stick) butter
2 cloves garlic, minced
4 teaspoons minced parsley
½ onion, diced
4 fresh mushrooms, sliced
4 Tablespoons fresh tomato, peeled, seeded and chopped

½ cup chopped green onions
2 teaspoons Creole seafood seasoning
¼ cup shrimp stock
2 cups cooked fettucine noodles (12 ounces dry pasta)
24 medium shrimp, peeled and deveined
½ cup dry white wine

Melt half the butter in a large saucepan and sauté the garlic, parsley, onions and seafood seasoning for 30 seconds; stirring gently. Add stock and simmer until onions are transparent. Add the cooked fettucine, shrimp and wine and simmer until liquid is almost evaporated. Remove pan from heat. Add remaining butter and stir gently until butter is melted and sauce is creamy. Serve immediately. (45 minutes preparation time. Not suitable for freezing.)

James McCrery, *Representative (Louisiana)*

Italian Chicken
SERVES 4

4 chicken breasts
4 chicken thighs
2 green peppers, sliced
1 red pepper, sliced
2 onions, cut into wedges

4 large potatoes, cut in wedges (do not peel)
¼ cup olive oil
garlic salt
pepper
oregano

Preheat oven to 350°. Place chicken, peppers, onions and potatoes in large baking pan. Pour oil over all and sprinkle with seasonings to taste. Toss, making sure all ingredients are coated well. Cover pan with foil and bake for 30 minutes. Uncover and bake for an additional 15 minutes or until chicken and potatoes are browned. (30 minutes preparation time. Not suitable for freezing.)

John L. Mica, *Representative (Florida)*

Creole Shrimp Pasta

2 pounds large shrimp, peeled and deveined
1 package of crab boil or seafood seasoning
½ cup oil
½ cup sugar
½ cup brown Creole mustard or spicy coarse grained mustard
½ chopped onion
¼ cup tarragon vinegar or red wine vinegar
2 teaspoons seasoned salt
2 teaspoons paprika
2 cloves garlic, crushed
¾ teaspoon ground red pepper
½ cup sliced green onion
½ cup sliced ripe olives
10-12 ounces vermicelli or capellini

In a large 6-quart stockpot combine 3 quarts water and crab boil or similar seasoning. Boil and add shrimp. Cook uncovered for 1 to 3 minutes or until shrimp turns pink. Remove shrimp from stock and cut in half crosswise. For sauce, in a blender or processor combine oil, mustard, onion, vinegar, salt, paprika, red pepper and garlic. Cover and blend or process until smooth. Add green onion and blend 2 seconds more. In the same 6-quart stockpot, cook pasta in 3½ quarts of boiling, salted water 4 to 7 minutes (tender, but firm). Drain well and return to pot. Top with sauce. Add shrimp and olives. Mix well. Cook over low heat until thoroughly heated. This can be served hot or cold. (30 to 40 minutes preparation time. Suitable for freezing.)

W. Henson Moore, *former Representative (Louisiana)*

Pork and Apple Casserole
SERVES 4

4 pork loin chops
1½ teaspoons Kitchen Bouquet
1 Tablespoon cooking oil
½ teaspoon salt
1 quart diced tart red apples
½ cup seedless raisins

2 Tablespoons brown sugar
½ teaspoon basil
⅛ teaspoon ground cloves
3 Tablespoons lemon juice
3 Tablespoons water

Brush entire surface of pork chops with Kitchen Bouquet. Brown in oil in heavy skillet over moderate heat; sprinkle with salt. Place diced apples and raisins in mixing bowl. Sprinkle with sugar and spices, tossing lightly. Sprinkle with lemon juice and toss again. Place in well-greased 6″ × 10″ × 2″ baking dish. Remove pork chops from pan. Add water to pork chop drippings and pour over apples. Top with pork chops. Cover with foil. Bake at 350° for 30 minutes; uncover and bake for 1 hour longer. (Suitable for freezing.)

Kimberly Puckett

Kimberly Puckett, *daughter of former Representative George E. Sangmeister (Illinois)*

Crested Butte White Chili
SERVES 10

1 pound white beans
   (rinsed and soaked overnight)
6 cups chicken broth
2 onions, chopped
1 Tablespoon oil
6-8 cloves minced garlic
3 ounces diced green chilies

4 teaspoons ground cumin
2 teaspoons dried oregano
4 teaspoons cayenne pepper
4 cups cooked diced chicken
1 cup sour cream
3 cups shredded Monterey Jack cheese

Combine beans and broth in large pot. Simmer for 2 hours. Sauté onions in oil until golden. Add everything else to bean mixture except last 2 ingredients and simmer for 2 more hours. Add sour cream and cheese at the end. Heat until sour cream and cheese melt. Serve. You may garnish with chopped cilantro, green onions, tomatoes and cheese. (4 hours preparation time. Not suitable for freezing.)

Mary Morgan Reeves

Mary Reeves, *daughter of former Senator Robert B. Morgan (North Carolina)*

Cheese Fondue
SERVES 4

½ pound Gruyere cheese
½ pound Swiss Emmenthaler cheese
3 Tablespoons flour
1 garlic clove
2 cups good white wine (dry)

1 generous Tablespoon Kirsch
(if desired)
1 loaf French bread
2 crisp apples

Grate cheese in large bowl. Add flour and mix. Rub fondue pot with garlic clove, then add wine. Bring to boil and slowly add cheese until melted and bubbly. Stir in Kirsch. Place pot over flame. Serve with French bread and sliced apples cut into bite size pieces. (Not suitable for freezing.)

Victoria Beall Muth

Victoria Muth, *daughter of former Representative J. Glenn Beall, Jr. (Maryland)*

Swedish Meatballs
SERVES 6 TO 8

1 pound ground chuck
½ pound lean ground pork sausage
½ cup minced onion
1 egg
½ cup milk
¾ cup bread crumbs

1 Tablespoon parsley
½ teaspoon salt
¼ teaspoon pepper
½ teaspoon allspice
1 teaspoon Worcestershire sauce

Sauce:
¼ cup flour
2 Tablespoons melted butter
2 cups milk
¾ cup sour cream

½ teaspoon dill weed
½ teaspoon salt
⅛ teaspoon pepper

Mix first 11 ingredients together and refrigerate 2 hours. Shape into 1½" balls. Bake in a 9" × 13" pan (lined with foil) at 325° for 45 minutes or until done. Drain off drippings. To make sauce, melt butter and stir in flour. Add milk and stir until thick. Reduce heat and add sour cream, dill weed, salt and pepper. Add meatballs to sauce and serve over mashed potatoes. (20 minutes preparation time. Not suitable for freezing.)

Sue Neumann

Mrs. Mark W. Neumann, *wife of Representative (Wisconsin)*

Chicken Broccoli Casserole
SERVES 4 TO 6

4 chicken breasts
  (boil 1 hour in water, bone)
1 10-ounce can chicken soup
½ cup Hellmann's mayonnaise
½ teaspoon lemon juice
½ teaspoon curry powder

2 packages broccoli (frozen) cooked
½ cup grated American cheese
¼ cup grated sharp cheese
1 Tablespoon melted butter
¼ cup bread crumbs or ½ cup corn
  flake crumbs

Combine chicken soup, mayonnaise, lemon juice and curry powder to make sauce. Heat a little to combine flavors. Line bottom of casserole dish with broccoli. Add cooked chicken breasts as next layer. Add sauce. Top with grated cheeses. Sprinkle on bread crumbs browned in butter or corn flake crumbs. Bake at 350° for 20 minutes. (1½ hours preparation time. Suitable for freezing.)

Mary A. Regula

Mrs. Ralph Regula, *wife of Representative (Ohio)*

Easy Beef Stew
SERVES 6 TO 8

2 pounds beef stew meat (no fat)
6 carrots (cut up)
1 cup chopped celery
2 onions (cut up)
2-3 potatoes

1½ cups tomato juice or V-8 juice
3 Tablespoons tapioca
1 Tablespoon sugar
salt and pepper to taste

Mix above ingredients together and put in covered casserole dish and bake at 275° for 5 hours. (Suitable for freezing.)

Doris Sangmeister

Mrs. George Sangmeister, *wife of former Representative (Illinois)*

Wild Rice and Barley Casserole
SERVES 6

¼ cup butter
½ cup chopped onion
1 cup sliced fresh mushrooms

3 cups chicken broth
½ cup uncooked wild rice
½ cup uncooked barley

Melt butter in skillet. Add chopped onion and sliced mushrooms. Stir until onion and mushrooms are cooked. Combine mushroom and onion mixture to remaining ingredients in a 2-quart casserole, blending well. Cover and bake at 325° for 1½ hours or until tender. (1½ hours preparation time. Suitable for freezing.)

Susan Sikorski

Mrs. Gerry Sikorski, *wife of former Representative (Minnesota)*

Jeanne's Penne with Fresh Tomato-Basil Sauce
SERVES 6

2 large fresh tomatoes, cut into bite size pieces
¼-½ cup fresh basil, chopped
½ cup olive oil
2 cloves garlic, crushed
½-¾ cup fresh mozzarella cheese, cut into bite size pieces
plenty of salt and pepper
¾ pound penne pasta

Combine all ingredients except pasta. Cover mixture and marinate at room temperature for at least 6 hours. Once marinade is ready, cook pasta according to package directions, drain and return to pot. Add marinade to pasta, cover and let sit for a few minutes before serving to allow cheese to melt. (Not suitable for freezing.)

Lani Schweiker Shelton

Lani Shelton, *daughter of former Senator and former Cabinet Secretary Richard Schweiker (Pennsylvania)*

Glazed Buffalo Medallions
SERVES 8

2 pounds buffalo tenderloins, trimmed of all fat
2 Tablespoons cornstarch
½ cup cold water
⅔ cup rice vinegar

½ cup dry sherry
2 Tablespoons apple juice concentrate
2 cloves garlic, minced
2 Tablespoons low sodium soy sauce
½ cup sugar-free apricot preserves

Slice buffalo tenderloin crosswise, against the grain, into ¼" slices and set aside. In small bowl, dissolve the cornstarch in cold water. Add the vinegar, sherry, apple juice concentrate, garlic, soy sauce and preserves. Spray a large nonstick skillet lightly with food release (i.e. Pam). Over moderately high heat, brown the buffalo slices on both sides, 2 or 3 minutes per side. Do them in 2 or more batches if necessary. Remove to a platter and keep warm. Add the preserve mixture to the skillet and cook 3 to 5 minutes over medium heat, or until thickened, shiny and somewhat transparent. Add buffalo medallions to the skillet and turn to coat them in the glaze mixture. Cook over low heat until the buffalo is fully cooked and heated through. Serve as an appetizer if cut into bite size and use kabob skewers or serve sliced buffalo over rice or another grain of your choice. Makes 8 servings. Each portion contains 1 protein serving, 1 fruit serving and approximately 230 calories. (Suitable for freezing.)

Harriet Pressler

Mrs. Larry Pressler, *wife of former Senator (South Dakota)*

Boot Hill Beans

SERVES 12

2 cups brown beans
5 cups water
8-12 ounces picante sauce

½ small onion, diced
1-2 pound pork roast with bone in
salt and pepper

Trim fat from pork roast. Put all ingredients in crock pot. Cook on low for 16 to 18 hours. Add water if needed. Before serving remove bone and shred pork. (Not suitable for freezing.)

Todd Tiahrt

Todd Tiahrt, *Representative (Kansas)*

Chicken Creole

SERVES 8

3 Tablespoons margarine
2 Tablespoons finely chopped onion
2 Tablespoons finely chopped
   green bell pepper
3 Tablespoons flour
¼ teaspoon salt
¼ teaspoon paprika

½ can canned tomato purée
1 cup chicken broth
½ teaspoon horseradish
1 teaspoon lemon juice
1 can Campbell's Golden Mushroom
   soup (not cream of mushroom)
2 cups cooked, diced chicken

Sauté onion and green pepper in margarine. Add flour, salt, paprika, tomato purée and chicken broth; stirring until bubbly. Add remaining ingredients. Stir until blended and serve over rice. This is a Turner family favorite! (30 minutes preparation time. Suitable for freezing.)

Ginny Turner

Mrs. Jim Turner, *wife of Representative (Texas)*

SUNFLOWER
(HELIANTHUS ANNUUS)

KANSAS

The sunflower was an all purpose plant for early American settlers. They planted sunflowers near their homes in the belief that the plants would protect them from malaria. The leaves and stems were used to feed cattle and horses. Fibers from the stems were used to make cloth. The leaves were dried and smoked as a substitute for tobacco. Sunflower seed oil was used for cooking and to make soap, while the shells were ground up and used to make a "pseudo" coffee. A very pretty yellow dye was extracted from the ray flowers.

Arrowhead Ranch Enchiladas
SERVES 8

2 dozen corn tortillas
1½ lbs. hamburger meat
1 medium onion
1 Lowry's Enchilada Sauce packet

½ green pepper
your own chili or 2 cans Wolf Brand chili
16 oz. extra sharp cheddar cheese
salt and pepper

Warm tortillas in oven (covered with aluminum foil) so that they will not break when rolled. Chop onion into small pieces, slice ½ green pepper into large pieces, combine with meat, and sauté until browned. Stir in enchilada sauce (dry from the packet) and salt and pepper. Discard green pepper. Line buttered 9" x 12" casserole with flat tortillas. To stuff tortillas, place enough meat and cheese in each tortilla so that it will close well, with seam side down in pan. When stuffed tortillas (about 16) are in place, cover with chili, then grated cheese. Bake at 350° from 45 to 60 minutes…depends on how crusty you like your enchiladas.

Ken E. and Tamra Bentsen, Jr., *Representative and Mrs. (Texas)*

Corn Pudding
SERVES 4

2 eggs
1 small can of evaporated milk
1 teaspoon salt
pepper to taste
cream

½ teaspoon dry mustard
¼ cup grated onion
2 cups corn (cream style)
¼ cup cracker crumbs

Take 2 eggs and small can of milk. Add cream to make 1 cup. Beat. Add salt and pepper to taste. Add dry mustard, onion, corn and cracker crumbs. Mix well. Bake in buttered casserole for 1 hour at 350°. (60 minutes preparation time. Not suitable for freezing.)

Mrs. Olin Teague, *wife of former Representative (Texas)*

Black Bean Chili
SERVES 4 TO 5

2 cups black turtle beans
4 Tablespoons cumin seeds
canola oil
4 teaspoons oregano leaves
4 teaspoons paprika
1/16-1/8 teaspoon cayenne pepper or chili powder
3 medium onions
5 carrots
5 ribs of celery
1-4 cloves garlic, to taste
½ teaspoon salt
1½ pounds peeled, seeded, chopped, canned tomatoes and juice
1 Tablespoon rice vinegar or lemon juice
chopped fresh cilantro, stems removed
sour cream with 1 lime squeezed in

Soak beans overnight. Drain. Put in a pot and cover with water. Boil. Simmer 1 hour. In heavy skillet, toast cumin seeds over medium heat in a small amount of canola oil until a tiny bit golden, probably less than 1 minute. Add oregano leaves, after first rubbing them for a moment in the palm of your hand. Remove from heat. Add paprika (rubbing first in hands) and cayenne pepper (or chili powder). Using the same pan, sauté diced onions plus diced carrots. Cook over low heat until the onions are clear. Add and sauté diced celery ribs and cloves of garlic, chopped. Cook 5 to 10 minutes. Add to the pot of beans. Add ½ teaspoon salt. Simmer over low heat 1 hour or so. Add tomatoes, plus the juice. Add rice vinegar, or lemon juice to bring out a more flavorful taste in the beans. Garnish with stemmed, chopped cilantro. Squeeze a fresh lime into the sour cream. Serve with chili.

Janet F Waxman

Mrs. Henry Waxman, *wife of Representative (California)*

Bulgur-Stuffed Eggplant

SERVES 2

1 small eggplant (1 pound)
2 teaspoons olive or vegetable oil
¼ cup chopped onion
1 garlic clove, minced
½ cup uncooked bulgur
1 teaspoon vegetable flavor
   instant bouillon

¼ teaspoon salt
¼ teaspoon dried Italian seasoning
⅛ teaspoon pepper
1 cup water
1 medium tomato, seeded, chopped (⅔ cup)
2 Tablespoons shredded fresh Parmesan cheese
2 Tablespoons chopped fresh parsley

Heat oven to 375°. Cut eggplant in half lengthwise. Scoop out pulp, leaving ¼" thick shells. Coarsely chop pulp; set aside. Place shells, cut side down in a 12" × 8" (2-quart) baking dish. Pour about ¼ cup water into dish and cover with foil. Bake at 375° for 15 minutes. Meanwhile, heat oil in medium pan over medium-high heat until hot. Add onion, garlic and eggplant pulp. Cook 1 to 2 minutes or until garlic just begins to brown; stirring constantly. Add bulgur, bouillon, salt, Italian seasoning, pepper and water. Mix well. Bring to a boil. Reduce heat. Cover and simmer about 15 minutes or until bulgur is tender and liquid is absorbed. Stir cooked bulgur mixture. Stir in tomato, cheese and parsley. Spoon mixture into eggplant shells. Bake at 375° for 10 to 15 minutes or until shells are tender and bulgur mixture is thoroughly heated. If desired, add salt and pepper to taste and sprinkle with additional cheese. (30 minutes preparation time. Not suitable for freezing.)

Patricia Oxley

Mrs. Michael Oxley, *wife of Representative (Ohio)*

Crab Quiche

½ cup finely chopped onion
1 Tablespoon butter
4 eggs, slightly beaten
2 cups half and half
1 teaspoon salt

½ pound Swiss cheese, finely grated
dash of nutmeg
dash of cayenne
1 6½-ounce can lump crabmeat
9" pie shell

Sauté onions in butter until transparent, about 5 minutes. Set aside. Combine next 6 ingredients, mixing well. Add onions and crabmeat. Pour into pie shell and bake 10 minutes at 450°. Reduce heat to 325° and cook until done, 20 to 25 minutes.

John R. Foley, *former Representative (Maryland)*

Texas Chili
SERVES 6 TO 8

3 pounds cubed or ground meat, well-browned and drained
1 medium onion, chopped
2 28-ounce cans tomatoes
1 15-ounce can tomato puree
1 package REAL TEXAS Chile Mix

Brown meat. Add onions, tomatoes, puree, and chile mix. Simmer at least 1 hour for best flavor. (1 hour 30 minutes preparation time.)

Nick Smith, *Representative (Michigan)*

Caramelized Onion and Goat Cheese Soufflé
SERVES 6 TO 8

3 Tablespoons olive oil
3 medium onions (1½ pounds), thinly sliced
salt and freshly ground pepper
1 teaspoon chopped fresh thyme
6 Tablespoons plus 2 teaspoons butter
6 Tablespoons all-purpose flour
1 cup milk
1 cup heavy cream
5 egg yolks
1¼ cups or 5 ounces crumbled goat cheese
6 egg whites
½ cup grated Parmesan cheese

Heat the olive oil in a skillet and add the onions, salt, pepper and ½ teaspoon thyme. Sauté the onions over medium-low heat, covered, stirring occasionally, for 30 minutes. Uncover and sauté until very soft and light golden, 30 minutes. Remove the onions with a slotted spoon and place them in a strainer set over a bowl to drain. Reserve. Butter a large 10″ × 18″ oval oven-proof platter with 2 teaspoons butter. Preheat the oven to 450°. Meanwhile, melt the remaining 6 tablespoons butter in a saucepan over low heat and add the flour. Stir with a whisk to combine and let the mixture bubble for 2 minutes. Add the milk and cream to the flour-butter mixture, stirring rapidly with a whisk. Cook for 2 to 3 minutes, until very thick and smooth. Transfer to a bowl and add the drained onions. Mix well. Add the yolks, one at a time, stirring well after each addition. Add the goat cheese and mix well. Season with salt and pepper. Beat the whites until stiff. Add half of them to the base and fold well. Fold in the remaining whites. Pour this onto the prepared platter. Sprinkle with the Parmesan cheese and the remaining ½ teaspoon thyme and bake on the top shelf of the oven for 10 to 14 minutes, until well browned. Serve immediately. This soufflé base is like any other and can be made ahead up to the point of whipping the egg whites to stiff peaks. What makes it different is that it is baked on a large oven-proof platter on the top shelf of a hot oven, resulting in a soufflé that is about 2″ high. (40 minutes preparation time. Not suitable for freezing.)

Franki Roberts

Mrs. Pat Roberts, *wife of Senator (Kansas)*

Italian Casserole

SERVES 8 TO 12

2 packages of egg noodles
1 pound of hamburger
4 Tablespoons of oil or bacon fat
2 large onions, chopped
2 cups canned tomatoes
1 small can corn
1 small can chopped black olives

1 package of grated sharp cheese
salt
pepper
paprika
garlic salt
pinch rosemary

Cook the noodles in salted boiling water; about 15 minutes. Drain and rinse in fresh hot water; drain again. Fry hamburger in extra fat until all the red is out of the meat; drain. Use some of the fat to fry the onion to a soft yellow. Add hamburger to onion and season as highly as you wish. Combine with noodles, corn, tomatoes and chopped olives. Spread in a large shallow pan. Cover top with grated cheese and bake for at least 30 minutes at 350°. (20 minutes preparation time. Suitable for freezing.)

Marilyn Burnside Weaver

Marilyn Burnside-Weaver, *daughter of former Representative Maurice Burnside (West Virginia)*

Apricot Pork Medallions

SERVES 4

1 pound pork tenderloin
1 Tablespoon butter
1 teaspoon butter
2 sliced green onions

½ cup apricot jam
¼ teaspoon dried mustard
1 Tablespoon cider vinegar

Cut pork into 1" slices. Flatten each piece slightly. Heat 1 tablespoon butter over medium high heat in a skillet and sauté pork about 2 minutes on each side. Remove from pan. To pan juices add 1 teaspoon butter, jam, sliced green onions and cider vinegar. Cover and simmer 3 to 4 minutes. Add pork to heat thoroughly. Serve with buttered noodles and a green salad. (20 minutes preparation time.)

Marjorie Wylie

Mrs. Marjorie Wylie, *wife of former Representative (Ohio)*

KENTUCKY

Growing throughout the United States and Canada, goldenrod can be found in meadows and open woodlands. The yellow flowers bloom during the late summer - early fall. Goldenrod often gets the blame for hay fever during its blooming season. But, the real culprit is ragweed, an inconspicuous plant which blooms at the same time.

Steak and Onion Salad
SERVES 6

1 beef flank steak (about 1½ pounds)
¼ cup soy sauce
1 Tablespoon honey
1 teaspoon cornstarch
¼ teaspoon ground ginger
2 large onions (1½ pounds)
4 Tablespoons salad oil
½ teaspoon salt
8 cups loosely packed assorted salad greens

About 40 minutes before serving or early in the day, trim fat from steak. Cut steak lengthwise into 1½" strips; then cut each strip into 1½" chunks. In bowl, toss steak chunks with soy sauce, honey, cornstarch and ginger; set aside. Slice onions into 1" thick slices. In a 12" skillet heat 3 tablespoons salad oil until hot. Cook onions with salt, stirring occasionally, until very tender. With slotted spoon, remove onions to bowl. Meanwhile, arrange salad greens on large platter. Add 1 tablespoon salad oil to oil remaining in skillet. Over high heat, cook steak chunks until medium-rare, stirring quickly and constantly. Return onions to skillet; toss gently to mix with steak. Top salad greens with hot steak mixture. Serve immediately, or refrigerate to serve chilled later. (45 minutes preparation time. Not suitable for freezing.)

Anthony Beilenson, *former Representative (California)*

Kathryn's Potato Casserole
SERVES 10

8 ounces sour cream
1 can cream of chicken soup
1 stick margarine
1 2-pound bag frozen hash brown potatoes, thawed
1 cup shredded cheddar cheese
½ cup diced onion
1 cup Corn Flake crumbs

Mix sour cream, soup and margarine. Add potatoes, cheese, salt, pepper and onion. Place in a 9″ × 13″ buttered pan. Sprinkle Corn Flakes on top. Bake at 325° for 1 hour. (10 minutes preparation time. Suitable for freezing.)

Kathryn Sellers Howell

Mrs. Evan Howell, *wife of former Representative (Illinois)*

Cottage Cheese Loaf
SERVES 8 TO 10

1 stick margarine, melted
4 eggs, beaten a little
5 cups Special K cereal
2 cups cottage cheese
½ cup milk
¾ cup walnuts or pecans, chopped
2 envelopes G. Washington broth
1 big onion, chopped

Mix all ingredients thoroughly and bake in a 13″ × 9″ buttered pan for 45 minutes at 350°. (5 minutes preparation time. Suitable for freezing.)

Ellen Bartlett

Mrs. Roscoe Bartlett, *wife of Representative (Maryland)*

Chicken or Turkey Seafood Gumbo
SERVES 12+

Gumbo:
4-6 quarts water
1 chicken, cut up or 2-3 pounds
   turkey parts (legs and wings
   preferred)
1 large onion, chopped
1 large clove garlic, chopped fine
3 Tablespoons salt (may substitute
   soy sauce)
pepper
1½ cups sifted flour
vegetable oil or olive oil (preferred)
4 ounces dried shrimp (optional)
2-3 pounds shrimp or prawns
   peeled, deveined

1 dozen crab legs (optional)
2 cups oysters (optional)
1 pound sausage, in ¼″ slices
   (andouille, linguisa or smoked sausage)
curry powder
2 bay leaves
poultry seasoning
thyme seasoning
sage seasoning
1 fresh hot pepper (or 1 teaspoon
   hot sauce)
1-2 bunches parsley (remove stems)
gumbo filé

Roux:
1½ cups sifted flour
vegetable oil or olive oil

Okra:
2 pounds fresh okra
1 small tomato sauce (approximately 8½ ounces)
2 cups chopped green onion
4 Tablespoons Worcestershire sauce
1 small tomato paste (approximately 8½ ounces)
3 cups chopped bell pepper
2 Tablespoons cayenne pepper

Prepare a broth by placing chicken or turkey, onion and garlic into a large pan of water. Bring to a boil and cook about 45 minutes. Add salt and pepper. Soak dried shrimp in water (retain water). Prepare the roux by adding oil to heavy skillet and browning flour as if preparing a gravy, stirring constantly over low heat. Continue to stir and cook flour slowly for about 45 minutes. Brown deeply but do not burn (get rid of flour taste and maintain a uniform color) then add to boiling broth. Add remaining seasonings except filé. Reduce heat and add pre-soaked dry shrimp, washed shrimp or prawns, crabs and oysters to broth. Add cooked sliced sausage. Add water from dried shrimp and parsley. Continue to season to taste. Serve over rice. Sprinkle filé on top.

Okra Gumbo: When making okra gumbo use tomato paste and sauce in place of roux. Prepare broth the same as in chicken and turkey seafood gumbo. Wash and dry okra. Slice into small pieces. In large skillet heat oil, add okra, diced onion, garlic and bell pepper. Fry until most of sticky substance is gone. Add tomato sauce and tomato paste to ingredients in skillet. Add pre-soaked dry shrimp and shrimp water to cooking broth. Add fresh shrimp, prawns and oysters to broth. Put ingredients in skillet into broth. Add seasoning. Add sliced sausage to broth. Cook down to taste. Serve over rice, sprinkle gumbo filé on top to taste. (2 hours preparation time. Suitable for freezing.)

Roscoe Higgs Dellums, *member of Congressional Club (California)*

Sausage-Apple Casserole
SERVES 4 TO 6

2 pounds pork sausage, lightly browned and drained (links or
   formed in balls or patties)
5 cups tart apples, peeled and cut in eighths
1 cup brown sugar
¼ cup Minute tapioca

Arrange apples and sausage in casserole in layers. Blend sugar and tapioca and sprinkle over top. Bake covered for ½ hour or until mixture begins to cook, then uncovered for 45 minutes at 350°. Nick and the kids loved this on a chilly Michigan fall evening on the farm after they had been picking corn or "filling silo". Serve with baked potatoes. (30 minutes preparation time. Not suitable for freezing.)

Mrs. Nick Smith, *wife of Representative (Michigan)*

Savory Cheesecake

¾ cup toasted fine bread crumbs

3 Tablespoons melted butter

3 8-ounce packages cream cheese

¼ cup whipping cream

½ teaspoon salt

¼ teaspoon nutmeg

¼ teaspoon pepper

4 eggs

1½ cup shredded Gruyere cheese

1 package spinach, thawed and
    squeezed dry

3 Tablespoons minced onions

½-¾ pound mushrooms

4 Tablespoons butter

salt and pepper

Preheat oven to 350°. Grease or butter a 10″ spring form pan. Combine butter (3 tablespoons) and bread crumbs. Press mixture in bottom and onto sides of pan. Bake 8 to 10 minutes. Set aside to cool. Reduce oven to 325°. Beat cream cheese, cream, salt, nutmeg and pepper until smooth. Add eggs one at a time. Divide mixture between bowls. Stir Gruyere in one. Stir spinach and onions in other. Pour spinach into cooled crust. Melt butter in skillet or wok. Stir and sauté mushrooms until moisture evaporates. Season. Spread mushrooms over spinach. Pour cheese mixture over mushrooms. Set pan in oven for 1 hour. Turn off oven. Cool cheesecake in oven for 1 hour with door ajar. May be served hot or at room temperature. (30 minutes preparation time. Not suitable for freezing.)

Kimberly Hood-Jacobs

Mrs. Andrew Jacobs, Jr., *wife of former Representative (Indiana)*

Quick and Easy Jambalaya

1 large onion, diced
1 large green bell pepper, diced
1 pound smoked sausage, cut into ¼" slices
1 Tablespoon olive oil
4 cups chopped cooked chicken
3 cups uncooked long-grain rice

2 10½-ounce cans French onion soup, undiluted
1 14½-ounce can chicken broth
1 14½-ounce can beef broth
2-3 teaspoons Creole seasoning
2-3 teaspoons hot sauce

Sauté first 3 ingredients in hot oil in a Dutch oven for 4 to 5 minutes or until sausage is browned. Stir in chicken and next 6 ingredients. Bake, covered, at 350°F for 40 minutes; stirring after 30 minutes. (15 minutes preparation time. Not suitable for freezing.)

Barbara Everett

Mrs. Terry Everett, *wife of Representative (Alabama)*

Alabama Garlic Cheese Grits

SERVES 8

1 cup instant grits, cook as directed on package
1 roll of garlic cheese
½ cup butter
½ cup milk
2 eggs, beaten
2 cups cheddar cheese, grated

Cook grits as directed on package, then add 1 roll of garlic cheese, butter and milk. Stir in eggs and 1 cup of grated cheddar cheese. Cook for 40 minutes at 350°. Take out and cover with 1 cup of cheese and bake 5 more minutes. (30 minutes preparation time. Not suitable for freezing.)

Robert B. Aderholt

Robert Aderholt, *Representative (Alabama)*

Chicken Acapulco
SERVES 6

1 medium onion, chopped
1 Tablespoon butter
3 cups chopped cooked chicken
1 can cream of chicken soup
1 8-ounce carton sour cream
1 4½-ounce jar sliced mushrooms, drained
1 4-ounce can chopped green chiles, drained

½ teaspoon dried whole oregano
¼ teaspoon salt
⅛ teaspoon pepper
10 7" flour tortillas
1 10¾-ounce can cream of chicken soup
1 cup (4 ounces) shredded sharp cheddar cheese
⅓ cup milk

Sauté onion in butter in a large saucepan until tender. Stir in the next 9 ingredients, mixing well. Spoon about ½ cup chicken mixture in center of each tortilla; roll up and place, seam side down, in a lightly greased 13" × 9" × 2" baking dish. Combine remaining ingredients; spoon over tortillas. Bake uncovered at 350° for 35 minutes. (20 minutes preparation time. Not suitable for freezing.)

John Thune, *Representative (South Dakota)*

Enchilada Casserole
SERVES 6

1½ pounds hamburger
1 small onion
1 small can enchilada sauce
1 small can chile peppers
1 can cream of mushroom soup
1 can cream of chicken soup

1 cup milk
1 can pitted black olives
1 dozen corn tortillas
2 cups cheddar cheese, grated
3 Tablespoons salad or olive oil

Brown meat and onion in 3 tablespoons oil. Add no seasoning. Add remaining ingredients, except tortillas and cheese. Layer meat and tortillas in 9" × 13" baking dish. Sprinkle cheese on top. Cover with foil. Cook for 1 hour at 350°. Uncover and cook for 10 minutes. (20 minutes preparation time. Not suitable for freezing.)

Mrs. John Thune, *wife of Representative (South Dakota)*

Pork Pie
SERVES 6

1 pound bulk pork sausage
1 cup cubed fully cooked ham
½ teaspoon ground sage
½ teaspoon pepper
1 medium green pepper, chopped
 (about 1 cup)
1 medium onion, chopped
 (about ½ cup)

1 medium stalk celery, thinly sliced
 (about ½ cup)
1 10¾-ounce can condensed cream
 of chicken soup
1 apple, sliced
Parmesan cheese, grated
1 pie crust

Cook and stir sausage in a 10″ skillet until done, about 10 minutes; drain. Stir in ham, sage, pepper, green pepper, onion, celery and soup and place in ungreased deep dish pie plate or quiche pan. Place sliced apples on top of mixture and sprinkle with Parmesan cheese. Cover with pie crust and seal. Prick pie crust and dot with butter or margarine. Bake in a 375° oven until crust is brown, 30 to 45 minutes. (1 hour preparation time. Suitable for freezing.)

John Shimkus, *Representative (Illinois)*

Dennis W's Salmon 7 Layer Surprise
SERVES 6 TO 8

1 medium onion, sliced
2 medium potatoes, sliced and
 peeled
1 16-ounce can flaked salmon
½ cup uncooked rice

½ cup chopped celery
1 16-ounce can peas
1 16-ounce can tomatoes, diced
 (can be spiced)
shredded cheddar cheese

Layer in the order above in a 10″ × 13″ casserole. Cover with foil. Bake at 350° for 2 hours. Top with shredded cheddar cheese. Bake for 5 minutes more uncovered. Serve. (15 minutes preparation time. Suitable for freezing.)

Clarence Brown, Jr., *former Representative (Ohio)*

LOUISIANA

Magnolias epitomize the American South. Often described as an "aristo-crat" of American trees, magnolias enjoy world-wide popularity because of their shiny evergreen leaves, and large, fra-grant, flowers. Relatively easy to grow, magnolias enjoy full sun and moist, well-drained, acidic soils rich with organic matter. Flower color ranges from white to different shades of pink, purple, and even yellow.

Ham, Broccoli and Pineapple Au Gratin
SERVES 4 TO 6

4-8 slices cooked ham
1 bag frozen broccoli
1 can mushrooms, drained

1 can crushed pineapple
1 teaspoon dark brown sugar

Sauce:
1 Tablespoon flour
1 Tablespoon butter, melted
¼ teaspoon dry mustard
½ cup milk
1 Tablespoon shredded cheddar cheese
salt and pepper

Topping:
¼ cup dry seasoned bread crumbs

Cook broccoli according to package directions, drain. Mix in mushrooms and set aside. Stir together butter, flour, mustard, salt and pepper. Add milk gradually and cook to boiling, stirring constantly until thick. Arrange broccoli mixture on center of ham slices. Roll ham around vegetables and place seam side down in casserole. Arrange pineapple around ham rolls and sprinkle with brown sugar. Coat the cheese sauce over the broccoli and ham rolls and top with bread crumbs. Microwave on medium for 3 to 4 minutes or until hot. Serve immediately. (30 minutes preparation time. Not suitable for freezing.)

Mrs. John Shimkus, *wife of Representative (Illinois)*

Green Chili Casserole

¾ pound hamburger
1 small onion, chopped
salt and pepper to taste
1 small can diced green chilies
6 tortillas (or use crumbled tortilla
chips, about ⅓ of a small bag)

1 can cream of chicken soup
½ cup longhorn cheese
1 small can tomato sauce
1 teaspoon chili powder
1 teaspoon cumin

Brown hamburger and onion together with salt and pepper. Add chilies and soup and blend together. Dip 6 tortillas into hot grease (or use crumbled tortilla chips, about ⅓ of a small bag). Put 3 tortillas or ½ chips in a 2-quart casserole. Pour ½ meat mixture on top. Repeat. Grate about ½ cup of longhorn cheese on top. Bake for 30 minutes in a 300° oven. Top with sauce, made from tomato sauce, chili powder and cumin, which have been heated together.

Scott McInnis, **Representative (Colorado)**

Hot Chicken Salad Casserole
SERVES 8

5-6 chicken breasts, cooked and
    cut into chunks
2 Tablespoons minced onion
½ cup chopped celery
2 cans cream of chicken soup
2½ cups Minute rice

½-¾ cup chicken broth
1 cup Hellmann's mayonnaise
salt and pepper to taste
Pepperidge Farm herb-seasoned
    stuffing mix

Mix all ingredients except stuffing together and spread in a 9″ × 13″ glass pan (or next size smaller). Bake at 350° for 15 to 20 minutes; then sprinkle stuffing mix on top and bake 10 to 15 minutes longer. (45 minutes preparation time. Suitable for freezing.)

Mrs. Jerry Moran, *wife of Representative (Kansas)*

Grandma Anna's Verenika

Filling:
2 cups dry cottage cheese
Note: If you cannot find dry cottage
 cheese, place cottage cheese in
 strainer and rinse liquid off. Drain.
½ teaspoon salt
1 Tablespoon sour cream
2 egg yolks, beaten

Onion Gravy:
2 large onions
3 Tablespoons bacon or ham drippings
cream

Dough:
2 cups flour
1 Tablespoon shortening, cut in
½ teaspoon salt
½ cup milk

Mix all filling ingredients together. Set aside. Mix thoroughly all dough ingredients. Turn out onto a floured pastry board. Knead until smooth. Roll out to ½" thickness. Cut out circles using large round cookie cutter. Put a rounded tablespoon of cottage cheese mixture in each circle. Fold in half and pinch the edges together. Boil in salted water for 15 minutes. Drain. Place a little oil in a skillet and fry until light brown on both sides. Serve with melted butter and syrup or onion gravy.

For Onion Gravy: Fry onions in bacon or ham drippings. Add cream needed to make desired amount of gravy. Sour cream can also be added.

Janet Hall

Mrs. Tony Hall, *wife of Representative (Ohio)*

Leigh's Shrimp and Grits Casserole
SERVES 6

Cheese Grits:
3 cups water
¾ cup quick grits
¼ teaspoon salt
1 egg, beaten
1 roll garlic cheese
2 Tablespoons butter
seasoning salt to taste

Shrimp:
6 slices bacon
1 medium onion, sliced
1 garlic clove, chopped
8 ounces sliced mushrooms
1 pound raw shrimp, peeled
¼ lemon

Grits: Bring water to boil in saucepan. Stir in grits and salt. Reduce heat and cook for 5 to 7 minutes or until thick, all the while stirring. Add small amount of grits to beaten egg and return to grits pot. Add cheese and butter in pieces and stir until melted. Add seasoning salt to taste. Bake for 30 to 40 minutes at 350° in a greased 1½-quart casserole. This portion may be assembled a day ahead, baking right before use.

Shrimp: Cook bacon, remove from heat and crumble. In bacon fat sauté onion, garlic and mushrooms. Add shrimp and quickly sauté until shrimp are pink and cooked through, (about 3 minutes). Add lemon juice and season to taste with seasoning salt. Pour shrimp mixture on top of grits and top with crumbled bacon. This is a wonderful dish for brunch. (30 minutes preparation time. Not suitable for freezing.)

Horace R. Kornegay, *former Representative (North Carolina)*

Beef Stroganoff Home Style
SERVES 4

1 Tablespoon butter
10 fresh mushrooms, sliced
2 Tablespoons sherry wine
salt and pepper to taste
1 can cream of mushroom soup
1 pound steak (tenderloin, sirloin or rump, cut into narrow strips about 2" long and ½" thick)

¼ cup sour cream
1 Tablespoon chopped shallots or white onion
1 Tablespoon dry white wine
½ teaspoon paprika
1 cup light cream
1½ Tablespoons vegetable oil

In a saucepan melt butter and sauté shallots and mushrooms for a few minutes. Add white wine, sherry, paprika, salt, pepper, cream and mushroom soup. Simmer for 5 minutes. In a separate pan heat oil and add the meat, salt and pepper. Brown meat quickly on both sides. Remove the meat from the pan. Add the meat to the sauce. DO NOT let the sauce and the meat boil. Simmer until the meat is tender. Add the sour cream and mix thoroughly.

Deane C. Walsh

Mrs. James Walsh, *wife of Representative (New York)*

Polish Sausage Stew

1 can cream of celery soup
⅓ cup light brown sugar
1 quart sauerkraut, drained
1½-2 pounds Polish sausage, cut in chunks
4 medium potatoes, peeled and cubed
1 cup chopped onion
1 cup shredded Monterey Jack cheese (optional)

Combine soup and sugar; add sauerkraut, potatoes, sausage and onion. Put in 3-quart crock pot. Cook on low for 8 hours or high for 4 hours. Skim off fat, and stir in cheese if desired.

Barbara Ann Grassley

Mrs. Charles Grassley, *wife of Senator (Iowa)*

One Dish Meal
SERVES 6

1 pound hamburger
1 pound hot Italian sausage
½ cup chopped onion
2 8-ounce cans mushrooms
2 cups shredded mozzarella cheese
1 quart spaghetti sauce
8-ounce package shell macaroni, cooked
1 teaspoon Italian seasoning
grated Parmesan cheese (optional)

Brown hamburger and sausage. Add onion and cook until clear. Drain fat. Add spaghetti sauce, seasoning and cooked macaroni. Heat and add mozzarella cheese and stir until melted and blended. You may sprinkle with Parmesan when serving, if you wish.

Barbara Ann Grassley

Mrs. Charles Grassley, *wife of Senator (Iowa)*

Hot Chicken Salad
SERVES 8

2 cups chicken
1 cup celery
½ cup bell pepper
1 cup water chestnuts (sliced)

1 can cream of chicken soup
½ cup mayonnaise
1 Tablespoon lemon juice

Mix all of the ingredients together and put in a casserole dish. Top with grated cheese and bread crumbs. Bake at 400° for 20 minutes uncovered. (45 minutes preparation time. Suitable for freezing.)

Shirley Shadegg

Mrs. John Shadegg, *wife of Representative (Arizona)*

WHITE PINE CONE AND TASSEL
(PINUS STROBUS)

MAINE

White pine is one of the most important timber trees in the Northeast. The wood is light, soft, straight-grained, and not as resinous as other species of pine. Native Americans used the bark of the white pine as a food source and different parts of the tree have medicinal value.

Gold Cup Chili-Chicken Picnic Rolls

SERVES 4

6 single chicken breasts, boned and skinned
2 teaspoons salt
2 teaspoons chili powder
1 teaspoon basil, crumbled
2 teaspoons cornstarch
1 Tablespoon oil
1 Tablespoon butter

¾ cup Chablis or other white dinner wine
1 8-ounce can tomato sauce with bits
¼ cup finely chopped green pepper
¼ cup finely chopped green onion
¼ cup finely chopped celery
1 Tablespoon finely chopped parsley
4 Savory or Kaiser rolls

Bone and skin the chicken breasts. Cut meat into small cubes. Toss with salt, chili powder, basil and cornstarch. Sauté in heated butter and oil to a rich brown. Add wine and tomato sauce. Continue to cook, stirring now and then, until the sauce thickens, about 10 to 15 minutes. Add green pepper, onion, celery and parsley. Pile on Savory rolls. Wrap and tuck in picnic box. (30 minutes preparation time.)

Tess McDade

Mrs. Tess McDade, *member of the Congressional Club (Pennsylvania)*

Meats, Seafood & Poultry

The Congressional Club
would like to thank
Diamond Chef Sponsor

Oxxford Clothes

Meats, Seafood & Poultry

CONGRESSIONAL CLUB COOKBOOK IN THE 20TH CENTURY

The early 20's brought a period of discussion about how the support of the Congressional Club should continue. A cookbook with wonderful recipes from each of the Congressional families seemed to be a great idea. The ladies set to work and in 1927 published the first cookbook. This book, described as "an adventure in the art of cooking," proved to be exactly the fund-raising vehicle the Club needed. The Club's financial needs have been met since that time by the sale of the last twelve editions, each unique in design and content and each a great, time-consuming labor of love by the Cookbook Committee. This Thirteenth Edition will complete this century of wonderful memories and history. We know that the new millennium will only add many more special events to remember.

Crawfish Étouffée

2 pounds peeled crawfish
2 sticks butter
1 onion, chopped
½ large bell pepper, chopped
½ cup celery, chopped
4 cloves garlic, minced

1 can golden cream of mushroom soup
(½ can of water)
salt to taste
¼ cup green onions, chopped
¼ cup parsley, chopped
red pepper to taste

Sauté onions, bell pepper, celery, garlic and red pepper in butter until tender and clear. Add mushroom soup, water and blend. Cook for 5 minutes. Add crawfish and salt. Cook for 10 minutes. Sprinkle with parsley and green onions. Serve over hot rice. (5 minutes preparation time. Not suitable for freezing.)

Beth Breaux Shepherdson

Beth Breaux Shepherdson, *daughter of Senator John Breaux (Louisiana)*

Pork Roast in Mustard Sauce
SERVES 12 TO 14

4-pound boneless pork loin
½ teaspoon salt
¼ teaspoon garlic powder
2 Tablespoons Dijon mustard
⅓ cup vinegar

freshly ground pepper
2 cups cream
⅓ cup Dijon mustard
2 Tablespoons cold butter
salt to taste

Trim excess fat from roast. Sprinkle roast with salt, pepper and garlic powder. Spread ⅓ cup mustard over roast and place in large Dutch oven. Cover and bake for 3 hours at 325° or until meat thermometer reads 170°. Remove roast and set aside to keep warm. Add vinegar and freshly ground pepper to pan. Boil mixture, scraping bottom of pan. Cook mixture until it is reduced in volume by half. Stir in cream; simmer for 5 minutes. Remove from heat; stir in 2 tablespoons mustard, remaining butter and salt to taste. Spoon half of hot sauce over sliced pork roast and serve with remaining sauce. Note: I usually prepare half of this recipe when serving my family. It is very easy, very tender and leftovers reheat well. (3½ hours preparation time. Not suitable for freezing.)

Jon Kyl, *Senator (Arizona)*

Teriyaki Marinade

4 Tablespoons brown sugar
4 Tablespoons soy sauce
2 Tablespoons lemon juice

1 Tablespoon vegetable oil
¼ teaspoon ginger
¼ teaspoon garlic powder

Mix all ingredients together and marinate your meat or seafood for ½ to 1 hour. Good with beef, pork, chicken, or seafood.

Tom Latham, *Representative (Iowa)*

Hal's Wild Ducks

SERVES 10

5 wild ducks, halved
salt and pepper
onions
carrots
celery
1¼ cups red port wine,
(¼ cup per duck)

Sauce:
1 can beef gravy
1 jar red currant jelly

Garnish:
watercress
Tokay grapes, seedless

Clean and scissor-trim duck halves. Soak in salt water overnight. Dry ducks. Salt and pepper both sides and lay on a bed of onions, carrots and celery in a roasting pan. Cover and bake in a preheated oven at 450° for 1 hour. Remove pan and pour red wine over the ducks. Re-cover and return to the oven quickly. Turn off oven and leave ducks there for 1 hour. Sauce: Heat both gravy and jelly. Serve duck with sauce and garnish with watercress and seedless Tokay grapes. (1½ hours preparation time. Suitable for freezing.)

Marcia S. Sawyer

Mrs. Harold Sawyer, *wife of former Representative (Michigan)*

Dilled Salmon

SERVES 2

10 ounces salmon fillet
2 Tablespoons chopped dill
1 Tablespoon lime juice
¼ teaspoon grated lime zest
¼ pound Kirby cucumbers (2 small)

4 Tablespoons nonfat yogurt
2 Tablespoons low-fat sour cream
½ teaspoon olive oil
nonstick pan spray

Wash and dry the salmon. Wash and chop the dill and combine 1 tablespoon with the lime juice in a small pot. Add the salmon and coat on both sides, leaving the skin side up. Allow to marinate until it is time to cook. Wash, trim and chop the unpeeled cucumbers into ½" chunks. In a serving bowl combine the yogurt, sour cream, oil and remaining dill. Mix well. Grate the lime zest and add to bowl. Stir in the cucumbers. Grill the salmon on a stove-top grill, starting skin side up, following the Canadian rule: measure the salmon at thickest part and cook 8 to 10 minutes to the inch. Turn once. Serve with cucumber mixture on the side or on top. (30 minutes preparation time. Not suitable for freezing.)

Mrs. Mark Hatfield (Antoinette)

Mrs. Mark Hatfield, *wife of former Senator (Oregon)*

Leg of Lamb with Sauce
SERVES 12

6 stalks celery, diced
4 medium-size carrots, sliced
4 medium-size onions, sliced

1 cup water
1 leg of lamb (6 or 7 lbs.)
salt and pepper

Sauce:
⅓ cup butter or margarine
1¼ cups water
1½ cups red currant jelly

1 Tablespoon vinegar
1 cup flour
1½ pints sour cream

Place vegetables and water in roasting pan. Put meat on top with the skin side up. Roast in a 450° oven for 25 minutes or until brown. Turn fat side up. Season to taste. Lower temperature to 350° and roast for 30 minutes per pound. Put meat on heated platter. Keep warm. Strain liquid from roasting pan. Skim off excess fat. Use liquid to make sauce. For sauce, melt butter in double boiler; add water, currant jelly, vinegar and strained liquid from roasting pan. Mix well. Sprinkle flour over mixture. Beat with rotary beater until blended. Stir over hot water until mixture is thickened. Fold in sour cream. Cook 2 minutes longer. Serve hot with roast lamb. (45 minutes preparation time. Not suitable for freezing.)

Ron Klink, *Representative (Pennsylvania)*

Not Just the Same Old Chicken
SERVES 8 TO 10

2 chickens, cut into pieces
1 bottle Russian salad dressing

1 10-ounce jar apricot-pineapple jam
1 envelope dried Lipton onion soup

Place the chicken pieces in a baking dish. Mix the Russian dressing, apricot-pineapple jam and the onion soup mix together and pour over the chicken. Bake about 1 hour at 350°. Do not cover unless browning too fast. (1¼ hours preparation time. Suitable for freezing.)

Robert F. Bennett, *Senator (Utah)*

Southern Shrimp Creole
SERVES 4 TO 6

3 Tablespoons olive oil
1 medium onion, chopped
4 stalks celery, chopped
1 small green pepper, chopped
1 large can tomato sauce
2 teaspoons salt

1 teaspoon black pepper
hot seasonings to taste
  (e.g. Tabasco or red pepper flakes)
¼ pound fresh bean sprouts
½-1 pound deveined and peeled shrimp
1 cup cooked rice

Sauté onion, celery and green pepper in olive oil until transparent. Add tomato sauce, salt, pepper and hot seasonings. Simmer for 20 to 30 minutes. Add fresh bean sprouts and simmer for 15 minutes. Add shrimp. Continue to simmer until shrimp turns pink. Do not over-cook. Serve over rice. (30 minutes preparation time. Suitable for freezing.)

Nancy Fuqua

Mrs. Don Fuqua, *wife of former Representative (Florida)*

Fried Trout
SERVES 6

6 pounds (6) pan-ready trout
¼ cup milk
1 teaspoon salt
⅛ teaspoon pepper

½ cup flour
½ cup cornmeal
½ teaspoon rosemary
12 bacon slices

Wash fish and pat dry with paper towel. Mix milk, salt and pepper. Mix flour, cornmeal and rosemary. Dip fish in milk; then coat with flour mixture. In a large skillet fry bacon until cooked but not crisp. Drain. Place 2 slices inside each fish. Drain most of bacon fat from skillet. Fry fish in remaining fat 4 or 5 minutes per side, or until fish is brown and flakes easily when tested with a fork. (20 minutes preparation time. Not suitable for freezing.)

Carl T. Curtis

Carl T. Curtis, *former Senator (Nebraska)*

BLACK-EYED SUSAN
(RUDBECKIA HIRTA)

MARYLAND

The genus name, Rudbeckia, honors Swedish botanist Olaf Rudbeck who taught Caroleus Linnaeus, the "father of modern botany." The species name, hirta, means hairy and refers to the many tiny barbs that cover the stems. The barbs discourage unwanted insect visitors, such as ants, from crawling up the stem to the pretty yellow flowers.

Shrimp Creole
SERVES 10

¼ cup flour
¼ cup bacon drippings
1 cup chopped celery
1 cup chopped bell pepper
1 cup chopped green onions
1½ cups chopped white onions
3 cloves garlic, minced
1 6-ounce can tomato paste
1 16-ounce can chopped tomatoes
 with liquid
1 8-ounce can tomato sauce
¾ cup water

5 teaspoons salt
1 teaspoon pepper
½ teaspoon red pepper
Tabasco sauce to taste
2 bay leaves
1 Tablespoon lemon juice
1 teaspoon sugar
1 teaspoon Worcestershire sauce
4 pounds, peeled deveined raw shrimp
½ cup fresh parsley
3 cups cooked rice

In a large, heavy iron pot, make a dark brown roux of flour and bacon drippings. Add celery, bell pepper, green onions, white onions and garlic. Sauté until soft. Add tomato paste and mix this well with vegetables. Add tomatoes and tomato sauce, water, salt, pepper, red pepper, Tabasco sauce, bay leaves, lemon juice, sugar and Worcestershire sauce. Simmer very slowly for 1 hour, covered, stirring occasionally. Add shrimp and cook until done, about 10 to 15 minutes. This is much better made the day before. If made the day before, reheat but do not boil. (2½ hours preparation time. Suitable for freezing.)

Ann Cooksey

Mrs. John Cooksey, *wife of Representative (Louisiana)*

Blackened Fish

Fresh fish   Redfish, Black Drum, Tuna or any other heavy fish
(Note: trout, turbot and other light fish can be blackened,
but are best grilled)

Blackened Seasoning (commercially available through Chef Hans at
P.O. Box 3252, Monroe, LA 71217-3252), or from
Paul Prudhomme (New Orleans)

Olive or vegetable oil
Lemon juice

Rinse fish in tap water and generously season with Blackened Seasoning. Pour olive or vegetable oil over fish, do not pour oil directly onto skillet.

Use a dry iron skillet over a fire so hot that the inside of the skillet is white hot. You must have an extremely hot fire, usually outside over a propane jet burner. Place the seasoned fish into the skillet and cook for two minutes or less on each side. Turn with a large spatula one time to blacken the other side of the filet of fish. (2 minutes preparation time. Not suitable for freezing.)

Squeeze lemon juice over the fish before serving. Bon appetite!

John Cooksey

John Cooksey, *Representative (Louisiana)*

Golden Pork Chops
SERVES 4

4 thick pork chops   1 10¾-ounce can golden mushroom soup
lemon pepper   white wine
cooking oil   fresh mushrooms

Sprinkle pork chops with lemon pepper, then brown slightly in oil. Put chops in covered casserole. Cover with golden mushroom soup and a little white wine. Top with sliced fresh mushrooms. Bake at 300° for 3 hours or longer. (25 minutes preparation time. Suitable for freezing.)

Luella Rowland

Mrs. Roy Rowland, *wife of former Representative (Georgia)*

Pork Roast with Coconut

SERVES 6

1 2½-pound lean, boneless pork roast
salt and freshly ground black pepper
2 Tablespoons peanut, vegetable or corn oil
½ cup finely chopped onion
3 Tablespoons finely minced garlic
2 Tablespoons finely minced fresh ginger
1 Tablespoon sambal oelek (see note), or ¾ teaspoon crushed hot red-pepper
   flakes
1 cup ketjap benteng manis (see note), or use an equal amount of soy sauce plus
   1 Tablespoon sugar
1 cup coconut milk (see instructions for making coconut milk)

Sprinkle the pork with salt and pepper to taste. Heat the oil in a heavy Dutch oven or casserole and add the pork. Cook, turning often, until nicely browned all over, about ½ hour. Pour off most of the oil from the Dutch oven. Combine the onion, garlic, ginger and sambal oelek in the container of a blender, food processor or use a mortar and pestle. Grind as finely as possible. Add this to the fat remaining in the Dutch oven. Cook, stirring briefly. Add the ketjap benteng manis (or soy sauce and sugar) and coconut milk. Cover and bring to a boil. Simmer slowly until quite tender; about 1½ hours. Serve sliced with fluffy rice.

Note: Ketjap benteng manis and sambal oelek are widely available in food specialty stores that deal in fine imported products.

Coconut Milk: You can "create" coconut milk by combining 1¼ cups of very hot tap water with 1½ cups coconut flakes. Let sit for 10 minutes. Strain to use the "coconut milk". (1 hour preparation time. Not suitable for freezing.)

Carol Sarpalius

Mrs. Bill Sarpalius, *wife of former Representative (Texas)*

Chicken a la King
SERVES 6

¼ cup sliced mushrooms
¼ cup chopped green pepper
¼ cup melted butter
¼ cup flour
1 teaspoon salt
½ teaspoon white pepper

1 cup half-and-half
1 cup chicken broth
1 cup cooked, diced chicken
2 Tablespoons chopped pimento
6 baked patty shells

Sauté mushrooms and green pepper in butter until tender. Add flour, salt and pepper, stirring until smooth. Cook for 1 minute. Gradually add half-and-half and chicken broth, stirring constantly until thickened. Stir in chicken and pimento and cook until hot. Spoon into patty shells. (30 minutes preparation time. Not suitable for freezing.)

Mrs. Terry Everett, wife of Representative (Alabama)

Charcoaled Beef Tenderloin with Mushroom Sauce
SERVES 6

3-4 pounds beef tenderloin
garlic powder
¼ cup olive oil
1 medium onion, minced

½ cup butter, melted
1 large can sliced mushrooms (with liquid)
Worcestershire sauce
salt and pepper

Rub whole tenderloin with garlic powder and coat thoroughly with olive oil. Allow to marinate and come to room temperature. Sauté onion in butter. Add mushrooms. Add Worcestershire sauce, salt and pepper to taste. Place tenderloin on large sheet of foil and turn up edges enough to keep sauce from running out. When mushroom sauce has been added, fold up and seal foil around tenderloin. Cook over hot coals 45 minutes for rare, longer for medium or well done, turning constantly. Unwrap foil and fold into funnel to pour sauce in a dish to keep warm. Now place meat (without foil) on grill and char on all sides. Slice to desired thickness and serve with the mushroom sauce. Beef consommé may be added to sauce if additional sauce is needed. (15 minutes preparation time. Suitable for freezing.)

Terry Everett, Representative (Alabama)

Pork Tenderloin in Bourbon Marinade
with Mustard Sauce
SERVES 8

¼ cup soy sauce
¼ cup bourbon
3 Tablespoons brown sugar
2 (1 to 1½-pound) packages pork tenderloins
Mustard Sauce:
⅔ cup sour cream
⅔ cup mayonnaise
2 Tablespoons dry mustard
3-4 green onions, finely chopped

Combine first 3 ingredients in an 11″ × 7″ × 1½″ baking dish; add tenderloins. Cover and refrigerate at least 2 hours, turning occasionally. Overnight is even better. Remove from marinade; discard marinade. Place on a rack in a shallow roasting pan. Bake at 325° for 45 minutes or until a meat thermometer inserted into thickest portion registers 160°. Serve with mustard sauce.

Mustard Sauce: Combine all ingredients; cover and chill. Yields 1⅓ cups.

(3 hours preparation time. Suitable for freezing.)

Tara Sherer

Mrs. Jack Sherer, *daughter of former Representative William L. Dickinson (Alabama)*

Chicken Breasts with Tarragon

SERVES 6 TO 7

3 whole chicken breasts, boned
  and halved
salt and freshly ground pepper
½ cup flour
¼ cup butter
1 Tablespoon chopped shallots
  or onions

¼-½ cup white Bordeaux wine
1 teaspoon freshly chopped tarragon
  or ½ teaspoon dried tarragon
½ cup chicken broth
¼-½ cup heavy cream

Skin the chicken breasts. Between 2 sheets of wax paper, pound to a thickness of approximately ¼". Sprinkle with salt and pepper and dredge with the flour. Reserve the remaining flour. In a large skillet heat 3 tablespoons of butter, add the chicken and brown on both sides. Transfer to a heated platter. Add the shallots to the skillet and sauté briefly. Add the wine. Cook the liquid over high heat until it is nearly evaporated, while scraping loose all the brown particles. Add the reserved flour and stir to make a thick paste. Sprinkle with the tarragon and stir in the chicken broth. Return the chicken to the skillet, cover and cook over low heat until tender, about 25 minutes. Transfer the chicken to a heated serving platter and keep hot. Add the remaining butter and the cream to the skillet; heat, stirring, and pour the sauce over the chicken. Serve with rice. (45-60 minutes preparation time. Not suitable for freezing.)

Mrs. Glenn English, wife of former Representative (Oklahoma)

Alaska Marinated Grilled Salmon

SERVES 15

1 cup liquid brown sugar
1 cup soy sauce
3 cloves garlic, diced

1 cup dry white wine
1 onion, sliced
1 9-pound salmon, butterflied
  (backbone removed)

Combine all ingredients. Pour over fish. Refrigerate at least 3 hours, turning occasionally. Place salmon on aluminum foil on a grill, skin side down; over medium-hot charcoal or mesquite. Test frequently for doneness. Cooking should take about 30 minutes - until the salmon loses its translucence. (3½ hours preparation time. Not suitable for freezing.)

Mrs. Ted Stevens, wife of Senator (Alaska)

Bob and Jeannie Penney's Kenai Salmon
SERVES 10

1 20-ounce bottle Kikkoman teriyaki sauce
1 20-ounce bottle water (you can just refill the Kikkoman bottle)
¼ pound butter
1 large lemon
1 handful chopped parsley or chives or onion
5 pounds salmon, filleted and cut into serving pieces (pieces should be 6 to 8 ounces and not over 1½" to 2" in thickness)

While frozen or "fresh frozen" salmon will certainly do well for this recipe, fresh fish is even better. If you do get fresh, make sure the fish has been put on ice as quickly as possible after catching. Whether you get fresh or frozen, however, try to get Reds, Silvers or Kings. Filet the fish so that no bone is retained with the meat. Salmon is one of the most delicate foods and will quickly take on any offensive odors when cooked, such as those contained in fat and skin that lies next to the meat. Combine the teriyaki sauce and water. Marinate the filets in this solution for 45 minutes. Make sure the marinade covers the fish. If it does not, add more water and teriyaki maintaining the 50/50 ratio. While the fish is marinating, prepare the grill. Allow the fish to air dry or pat it lightly with paper towels before grilling. Place the fish directly onto the grill and cook 3 to 5 minutes per side. DO NOT OVER-COOK THE FISH. Salmon is very tender and, if anything, it should be undercooked since it will continue to cook after it has been removed from the grill. Some charring of the flesh will occur during the cooking process, but it is the same thing as searing a steak - it enhances and adds flavor to the fish. While the fish is cooking, prepare a chafing dish of butter and lemon juice. To this mixture add the parsley, chives or onions. (You can also add some garlic if you like.) Remove the fish from the grill and place it in the lemon solution. Turn it over once and then drain. Serve immediately. We can promise this will be as good as any salmon you have ever tasted if properly done. The thing we like about this family recipe is it does not have that normal "salmon" flavor. It has a different taste and one that allows you to eat salmon 2 or 3 times a week and not become tired of it. We hope you will enjoy it as much as our family does. (1 hour preparation time. Not suitable for freezing.)

Senator Ted Stevens

Ted Stevens, *Senator (Alaska)*

Grilled Catfish
SERVES 4

2 Tablespoons White Wine
  Worcestershire sauce
1 stick melted butter
1 Tablespoon fresh dill or
  ½ teaspoon dried dill

2 Tablespoons Allegro marinade
salt and pepper
3 pounds fresh catfish
Golden Dipt lemon butter dill sauce

Combine first 4 ingredients to make a marinade. Lightly salt and pepper catfish before coating with marinade. Brush catfish with marinade to coat before grilling. Baste while grilling and grill until flaky. Coat with Golden Dipt sauce during last 2 minutes on grill. (30 minutes preparation time. Not suitable for freezing.)

Mike and Dee McIntyre, *Representative and Mrs. (North Carolina)*

Roast Beef Tenderloin with Red Pepper Sauce
SERVES 8 TO 10

2 Tablespoons butter or margarine
2 garlic cloves, crushed
4 cups diced red peppers (about 5)
½ teaspoon thyme
½ teaspoon salt
½ cup crème fraîche, whipped

pinch ground red pepper
1 beef tenderloin, trimmed
  (about 4 pounds)
1 teaspoon salt
2 Tablespoons coarsely ground black pepper
2 Tablespoons olive oil

Sauce: Melt butter in medium skillet over low heat. Add remaining ingredients except crème fraîche. Cover and cook, stirring occasionally, until very tender, about 30 minutes. Purée in food processor; strain into small bowl. Refrigerate. Fold crème fraîche into purée. Refrigerate until ready to use. Makes 2 cups. Can be made ahead, and frozen up to 1 week. Thaw in refrigerator overnight.

Meat: Preheat oven to 450°. Smooth oil over entire tenderloin. Sprinkle salt and pepper. Place on rack in roasting pan. Roast 1 hour for pink medium rare. Serve at room temperature with sauce. (1 hour preparation time. Not suitable for freezing.)

Richard S. Schweiker, *former Senator and former Cabinet Secretary (Pennsylvania)*

Baked Garlic Chicken

SERVES 4

1 chicken, cut into pieces
garlic salt
¼ cup flour
½ teaspoon paprika

1 teaspoon salt
¼ teaspoon pepper
1 cup bouillon

Rinse chicken in cold water and dry. Sprinkle each piece with garlic salt. Combine flour, paprika, salt and pepper and dust chicken pieces with the mixture. In a shallow baking dish, place ½ cup bouillon and place chicken skin side down in the bouillon. Bake for 30 minutes in a 400° oven. Turn chicken. Add remaining bouillon and bake another 30 minutes, or until tender. (1 hour preparation time. Suitable for freezing.)

Dolores Beilenson

Mrs. Anthony Beilenson, *wife of former Representative (California)*

Spicy Shrimp Antigua

2 pounds medium to large shrimp
4 spring onions
3 cloves garlic
6 Tablespoons oil

3 Tablespoons chili relish (see note)
2 Tablespoons balsamic vinegar

Peel and devein shrimp, leaving tails on. Place shrimp in 1 layer in 1 or 2 baking dishes. Finely chop garlic cloves and thinly slice spring onions. Place into a bowl and add oil, chili relish and balsamic vinegar. Stir until well blended. Pour sauce over shrimp and broil approximately 8 minutes. Turn shrimp over and broil for about 2 to 3 minutes longer. Excellent served with rice. (Note: Chili relish is available in large grocery and oriental stores, also called chili purée, sometimes flavored with garlic.) (20 minutes preparation time. Not suitable for freezing.)

Gisela Hages Blatnik

Mrs. John Blatnik, *wife of former Representative (Minnesota)*

Venison Pot Roast

SERVES 6

3-4 pounds venison roast, thawed
2 cups vinegar
4 cups water
1 onion, sliced
1 clove of garlic
2 teaspoons salt
2 teaspoons black pepper

1 bay leaf
5 carrots, whole
5 potatoes, whole
5 onions, whole
¼ cup celery, chopped
more water if needed

Place venison in container with lid. Mix vinegar, water, onion, salt, pepper and bay leaf. Pour over venison and cover. Place in refrigerator to marinate 2 to 3 days; turning each day. When ready to cook roast, remove, rinse and dry. Dredge meat in flour and brown in a skillet with hot fat or shortening. When golden brown, add a small amount of water; cover, lower heat and simmer 2 to 3 hours. When meat is tender, add carrots, potatoes, onions, celery and more water if needed. Cover and cook until vegetables are tender. Arrange on a warmed platter. Make a gravy of the liquid in the skillet and pour over venison and vegetables. (Not suitable for freezing.)

Georgeanne Price

Mrs. Jack Price, *daughter of former Representative William L. Jenkins (Tennessee)*

Spinach in Phyllo Dough

SERVES 16

2-4 pieces phyllo dough (to make 2 rolls)
10 ounces frozen spinach or substitute
   with 2 bags of fresh spinach
2 breasts of chicken, chopped finely
1 small onion, diced

1 cup cheddar cheese, grated
1 Tablespoon Parmesan cheese
¼ cup melted butter
salt and pepper to taste

Mix all of the above ingredients except the phyllo dough. Brush 1 sheet of the phyllo dough with butter, layering a total of 4 sheets at a time. Place spinach-chicken mixture onto center of phyllo dough. Starting at the edge with the mixture, roll up the dough like a jelly roll. Brush the roll with leftover butter. With seam side down on baking sheet, partially slice it diagonally in 1" slices. Repeat the procedure on the second roll. Bake at 400° for 20 minutes or until it is golden brown. (20 minutes preparation time. Suitable for freezing.)

Lydia de La Viña de Foley

Mrs. John Foley, *daughter-in-law of former Representative John R. Foley (Maryland)*

MASSACHUSETTS

The mayflower actually is a member of the lily family and is also called wild lily-of-the-valley. Blooming from May through June, it can be found growing in upland woods and clearings from New England, Pennsylvania, and Delaware, to the mountains of Georgia and Tennessee, and west to Iowa. It spreads by underground stems called rhizomes and often forms dense stands on the woodland floor.

Sesame Chicken
SERVES 6

2 pounds of chicken breasts (I use chicken tenders)
1 egg
2 Tablespoons flour
2 Tablespoons cornstarch
2 Tablespoons water
1 teaspoon salt
2 teaspoons vegetable oil
¼ teaspoon baking soda
¼ teaspoon white pepper
½ cup water
¼ cup cornstarch

1 cup sugar
1 cup chicken broth
¾ cup rice vinegar
2 teaspoons soy sauce
2 teaspoons chili paste (I use less)
1 teaspoon vegetable oil
1 clove garlic, finely chopped
2 Tablespoons toasted sesame seeds
(for a variation fruit may be added to sauce)

Cut chicken into 2½" strips. Mix next 8 ingredients and stir chicken into mixture. Cover and refrigerate 20 minutes. Mix water and cornstarch and set aside. Heat last 7 ingredients and cook to boiling. Stir in the cornstarch mixture. Cook and stir until thickened. Remove from heat, but keep warm. Heat 1½" oil to 350°. Fry chicken, adding 1 at a time for 3 minutes, or until light brown. Remove chicken with a slotted spoon and drain on paper towels. Increase temperature of oil to 375°. Again fry ⅓ of chicken for 1 minute more or until golden brown. Remove and drain on paper towel. Place chicken on heated platter. Heat sauce to boiling and pour over chicken. Sprinkle with sesame seeds. Serve with white rice. This is so yummy and my kids love it! (1 hour preparation time. Not suitable for freezing.)

Darlene Ensign

Mrs. John Ensign, *wife of Representative (Nevada)*

Barbecued Ribs
SERVES 6

5 pounds of pork or beef ribs

10 fluid ounces of lemon juice

2 teaspoons dry mustard

½ cup diced onion

5 Tablespoons brown sugar

24 ounces chili sauce

16 ounces puréed apricots

5 Tablespoons Worcestershire sauce

5 shakes of Tabasco sauce

5 Tablespoons vinegar

Place ribs in a 9″ × 13″ pan. Pour the lemon juice over the ribs. Cover with clear wrap and let sit 4 hours at room temperature. Mix all the other ingredients in a blender until puréed and blended. Cook the ribs in a microwave on high for 10 minutes. Grill the ribs, basting with the barbecue sauce, generously. Cooking time on the grill is approximately 20 minutes. (45 minutes preparation time. Suitable for freezing.)

Rebecca M. Yates

Mrs. Richard Yates, *daughter of former Representative Wilbur D. Mills (Arkansas)*

Sautéd Steaks with Vinegar Sauce
SERVES 4

1½ pounds boneless, tender steak, such as filet mignon

2 teaspoons paprika

salt and pepper

2 Tablespoons butter

¼ cup red wine vinegar

1 cup heavy cream (or fat reduced sour cream)

2 Tablespoons finely minced shallots

If filet mignon is used, have it cut into 8 pieces. Sprinkle each side with paprika, and salt and pepper to taste. Heat the butter in a skillet. When it is very hot and almost brown, add the pieces of steak in 1 layer. Cook about 2 minutes on one side; turn and cook about 2 minutes, or until golden brown on the other side. Remove the steaks from the skillet and keep warm. Pour off the fat from the skillet. Add the vinegar, stirring to dissolve the brown particles that cling to the bottom and the sides of the skillet. Cook until the vinegar has almost evaporated. Add the cream or sour cream. Cook, stirring, over high heat until reduced by almost half. Add any juices that have accumulated around the meat. Add salt and pepper to taste. Return the steaks to the skillet and turn in the sauce. Add the shallots and heat briefly. (15 minutes preparation time. Not suitable for freezing.)

Sandra L Lamb

Mrs. Gordon Lamb, *daughter of former Representative Harold Lovre (South Dakota)*

Chuletas De Cerdo Adobado
(Seasoned Pork Chops - Low Cal)

SERVES 4

4 1"-thick pork chops
salt and pepper
2 cloves garlic, minced
2 Tablespoons parsley, minced
3 Tablespoons onion, minced

2 Tablespoons fresh thyme, minced
1½ teaspoons paprika
½ teaspoon red pepper, crushed
2 Tablespoons dry red wine
1 Tablespoon sherry

Trim fat from chops; salt and pepper both sides, and set aside. Mix together the following ingredients: garlic, parsley, onion, thyme, paprika, red pepper, red wine and sherry. Coat one side of chops with half of the above mixture, grill for 5 minutes on high. Coat other side with remaining mixture; turn chops and grill for 5 minutes. Lower heat to medium, grill 5 to 10 minutes, turning chops twice. Serve immediately. (25 minutes preparation time. Suitable for freezing.)

David McIntosh, *Representative (Indiana)*

Crispy Halibut

SERVES 4

2 pounds of halibut filets
¼ cup lemon juice
½ cup mayonnaise
½ cup Parmesan cheese
2½ cups potato chips, crushed

Dip halibut first in plain lemon juice, then in mixture of lemon juice and mayonnaise. Mix the Parmesan cheese and potato chips together. Dip the halibut in this mixture, then place in baking dish and bake for 20 minutes at 375°. (30 minutes preparation time. Not suitable for freezing.)

Mrs. Elton Gallegly, *wife of Representative (California)*

Charles' Orange-Grilled Pork Tenderloin
SERVES 8 TO 10

1 3 to 4-pound boneless pork tenderloin roast

Marinade:

¼ cup soy sauce

1 cup orange juice

1 teaspoon grated orange rind

2 Tablespoons brown sugar

¼ cup vegetable oil

Combine marinade ingredients in a large zip-top bag. Reserve ½ cup of the mixture in refrigerator for basting during grilling. Place the roast in the marinade; seal bag and refrigerate for 6 to 8 hours, turning bag occasionally. Remove the pork from marinade, discarding marinade. Coat a grill rack with cooking spray and place over medium-hot grill (350-400°). Place pork on the rack. Cook covered with the grill lid approximately 35 minutes, turning and basting with reserved marinade after 20 minutes. (1 hour plus marinating preparation time. Suitable for freezing.)

Charles T. Canady signature

Charles T. Canady, *Representative (Florida)*

Famous Maryland Crab Cakes
SERVES 7

1 pound crabmeat

2 slices of white bread without crusts

1 teaspoon dry mustard

2 Tablespoons Old Bay Seasoning

1 egg, slightly beaten

2 Tablespoons parsley flakes

1-2 Tablespoons mayonnaise

Combine all ingredients in a large mixing bowl. Shape into 7 crab cakes. Place crab cakes in refrigerator at least 2 hours prior to broiling. Place crab cakes on greased cookie sheet on middle rack. Broil for 10 minutes or until golden brown and hot. (15 minutes plus 2 hours refrigeration preparation time. Not suitable for freezing.)

Robert L. Ehrlich signature

Robert L. Ehrlich, Jr., *Representative (Maryland)*

½ pound raw shrimp, medium size
1 teaspoon dried thyme
½ teaspoon dried lavender flowers
½ teaspoon candied lovage seeds or anise seeds
3 white peppercorns
3 Tablespoons butter, softened
1½ Tablespoon flour
1 teaspoon powdered milk
10½-ounce can chicken broth
½ teaspoon salt
1 teaspoon basil wine vinegar
2 Tablespoons Pernod or anise liquor
1 teaspoon cornstarch
1 Tablespoon fresh parsley

Wash, peel and devein shrimp; set aside. Crush the following herbs: thyme, lavender, lovage/anise seeds and peppercorns; set aside. Cream butter, flour and powdered milk; set aside. Bring chicken broth to boil. Add salt and vinegar. Stir in herb mixture and reduce by a quarter. Drop shrimp into boiling broth. Cook shrimp only 1½ to 2 minutes until they begin to turn pink. Remove shrimp and set aside. Add Pernod and butter mixture to broth, stir, and bring to a boil. Remove ¼ cup. Reduce heat to warm and add shrimp. Add cornstarch to ¼ cup reserved broth. Stir well to remove all lumps. Add this mixture to shrimp broth. Stir well, and sprinkle with fresh parsley. Optional: Serve over white rice. (25 minutes preparation time. Not suitable for freezing.)

Mrs. David McIntosh, *wife of Representative (Indiana)*

Ted's Grilled Pork Tenderloin
on Spaghetti Squash
SERVES 4

Knorr Swiss Bernaise mix
1 spaghetti squash
4 ounces maple syrup
2 Tablespoons butter
salt and pepper
2 pork tenderloins, about 1 pound each

Prepare bernaise sauce and allow to cool. Cut spaghetti squash in half and seed. Fill with 1 tablespoon butter and 1 to 2 ounces of maple syrup. Salt and pepper to suit. Place in deep pan with a little water and cover with foil. Bake in 400° oven about 1 hour, before you start to grill tenderloins. Grill tenderloin about 30 minutes a side until just pink in the center. Let stand a few minutes. While waiting for meat to set, scoop out the squash onto serving platter. Slice the meat and place on top of squash and top with bernaise sauce. (1 hour preparation time. Not suitable for freezing.)

Freda Solomon

Mrs. Jerry Solomon, *wife of Representative (New York)*

Chinese Pork Tenderloin
SERVES 6 TO 8

2 pork tenderloins
½ cup soy sauce
½ cup chicken broth
1 cup honey
½ cup sherry

2 cloves garlic, crushed
1 teaspoon dried ginger
1 teaspoon Dijon mustard
1 teaspoon paprika

Put pork tenderloin in a glass baking dish. Mix together all other ingredients and simmer over medium heat until ingredients are all blended. Let cool slightly and then pour over tenderloins. Marinate in refrigerator for about 3 hours, turning every 30 minutes. Place dish in oven as is and bake uncovered in preheated 350° oven for approximately 1½ hours. Time may vary. Baste every 15 to 20 minutes until done. (5 hours preparation time. Not suitable for freezing.)

Johnette Hawkins McCrery

Mrs. James O. McCrery, *wife of Representative (Louisiana)*

Salmon Riesling
SERVES 2 TO 4

1 pound salmon filets (4 4-ounce
    pieces, skin removed)
9 Tablespoons flour
2 teaspoons Old Bay Seasoning
½ medium onion, chopped - optional
1 Tablespoon dried parsley - optional
1 Tablespoon dried cilantro - optional

Johnny's Seasoning to taste - optional
salt to taste
white pepper to taste
3 Tablespoons butter
½ cup white Riesling wine
½ cup heavy cream

Mix dry ingredients in a plastic, ziplock bag. As some of the ingredients are optional, you can add all or only some of the ingredients depending on your taste. Toss salmon in the dry ingredients until evenly coated. Heat the butter in a pan over medium-high heat. Place the coated salmon in the pan and brown lightly on both sides. Add the wine. Cover the pan and reduce heat to a slow simmer. Poach salmon gently for 10 minutes until it flakes easily. Remove the salmon from the pan and place on a serving platter. Add heavy cream to the pan and raise the heat to high. Cook rapidly until sauce has thickened and reduced to ¾ to 1 cup. Pour the sauce over the fish and serve at once. (20 to 25 minutes preparation time. Not suitable for freezing.)

Sara R. Smith

Mrs. Adam Smith, *wife of Representative (Washington)*

Pork Tenderloin and Apple Filling
SERVES 4 TO 6

2 pork tenderloins (1½ pounds)
¾ cup apple jelly
¼ cup lemon juice concentrate
¼ cup soy sauce
¼ cup olive oil
1 Tablespoon ginger root, grated

1 cup chopped apple
1 cup fresh bread crumbs
¼ cup chopped celery
¼ cup chopped pecans
apple wedges
parsley sprigs

Slit tenderloins lengthwise, being careful not to cut all of the way through. In small saucepan, combine jelly, lemon juice, soy sauce, oil and ginger root. Cook and stir until jelly melts, reserving 3 tablespoons. Place tenderloins in zippered plastic bag. Pour jelly mixture over tenderloins and seal bag. Refrigerate overnight. At cooking time, combine apple, bread crumbs, celery, pecans and reserved jelly mixture. Place tenderloins in baking dish. Spoon apple mixture into the slits of the tenderloins. Bake at 350° for 30 minutes. Loosely cover and bake 10 minutes longer (until meat thermometer reaches 160°). Garnish with apple wedges and parsley. (60 minutes preparation time. Not suitable for freezing.)

Mrs. Ike Skelton, *wife of Representative (Missouri)*

Grilled Flank Steak
SERVES 6

1 teaspoon minced garlic
3 Tablespoons soy sauce
fresh ground pepper
2½ pounds flank steak

Score both sides of steak with diagonal slices ½" thick and 2" apart. Mix garlic and soy sauce. Rub mixture into both sides of steak. Season with fresh pepper. Wrap in foil. Marinate for 1 hour or longer, even overnight. Preheat grill. Grill each side as desired. Slice along the diagonal. Serve slices as is or wrap up in fajitas. (10 minutes preparation time. Suitable for freezing.)

Chris Smith, *Representative (New Jersey)*

Ted's Rosemary Garlic Steak

1 large sirloin or individual steaks

Marinade:

1 cup olive oil

¼ cup soy sauce

2 Tablespoons chopped garlic

2 Tablespoons chopped fresh rosemary

salt and pepper to taste

Marinate steak 1 hour or longer. Reserve marinade and heat to serve with grilled steak. Grill steak using your favorite method.

Jerry Solomon

Jerry Solomon, *Representative (New York)*

Shrimp Lisbon
SERVES 4

4 Tablespoons extra virgin olive oil

4 cloves garlic, chopped

1 onion, chopped

2-3 tomatoes, chopped

1 pound large shrimp or ½ pound shrimp and ½ pound bay scallops

½ cup dry white wine

2 cups water

1 cup white basmati rice

fresh coriander/cilantro

Heat olive oil in a large skillet (with top). Add the garlic, onions and tomatoes and cook over medium heat. Add the shrimp and scallops. Cook, stirring often for 3 to 5 minutes until shrimp turn pink. Remove the seafood and keep warm. Add ½ cup wine, 2 cups water, 1 cup rice to the skillet. Cover and simmer 20 minutes until the rice is done. Return the seafood and add lots of fresh chopped coriander. This dish should be runny - do not let it dry out. You should wait for the rice; not have the rice wait for you. Serve with a dash of hot pepper oil if desired. (30-45 minutes preparation time.)

Marisol Goss

Mrs. Porter Goss, *wife of Representative (Florida)*

APPLE BLOSSOM
(MALUS PUMILA)

MICHIGAN

Apples were spread westward from the east coast of America by Native Americans who planted apple seeds near their homes in the wilderness. John Chapman, known as Johnny Appleseed, also helped increase their distribution. Carrying apple seeds with him as he traveled across America, he planted them wherever he stopped. Today, more than 7,000 varieties of apples are grown in the United States.

Kitty's Crab Cakes
SERVES 4 TO 6

2 slices bread, crusts removed
1 pound flaked crabmeat
1 teaspoon mayonnaise
1 Tablespoon Worcestershire sauce
1 Tablespoon chopped parsley

1 Tablespoon baking powder
2 eggs, beaten
⅔ Tablespoon Old Bay Seasoning
1 teaspoon paprika
1 teaspoon onion flakes

Crumble bread slices and combine with remaining ingredients. Shape into 8 large or 12 small patties. Let stand for several hours in refrigerator. (Easier to shape and handle.) May be dipped in beaten eggs, then flour, to be fried in 4 to 5 tablespoons vegetable oil or broiled. (15 minutes preparation time. Not suitable for freezing.)

Betty M. Vanik

Mrs. Charles A. Vanik, *wife of former Representative (Ohio)*

Italian Sausage

pork
1 teaspoon salt for every pound of pork
1 teaspoon pepper for every pound of pork
1 teaspoon sage for every pound of pork
1 teaspoon MSG for every pound of pork (optional)
1½ teaspoons fennel for every pound of pork
sausage casings

Grind and stuff to desired size. Cook in skillet with small amount of water for 30 minutes or until done.

Susan Lampson

Mrs. Nicholas V. Lampson, *wife of Representative (Texas)*

Chuck "No Peek"
SERVES 6 TO 8

3-4 pounds cubed chuck roast
1 can cream of mushroom soup
1 8-ounce can drained mushrooms
½ cup wine
1 package onion soup mix

Mix meat with cream of mushroom soup, mushrooms, wine and onion soup mix. Place in covered casserole. Bake 3 hours at 300°. (30 minutes preparation time. Suitable for freezing.)

Keely Burns

Keely Burns, *daughter of Senator Conrad Burns (Montana)*

Sautéed Chicken in Red Wine Vinegar
SERVES 4

¼ cup butter (or less)
⅓ cup diced onion
4 whole chicken breasts, skinned, boned and halved
½ cup red wine vinegar
1 cup whipping cream
hot rice

Melt butter on medium heat in a heavy, large skillet. Sauté onions until very soft. Remove with slotted spoon. Increase the heat to medium-high. Add chicken. Cook until golden or juices run clear when pierced. Remove chicken. Add vinegar. Boil until reduced by ⅔ (3 to 5 minutes). Add cream. Boil until thickened. Return onion and chicken to skillet. Heat through. Serve over hot rice. (20 minutes preparation time. Not suitable for freezing.)

Chris M. Rhodes

Mrs. Tom Rhodes, *daughter-in-law of former Representative John J. Rhodes (Arizona)*

Claudia's Wonderful Chili
SERVES 8

4 pounds boneless beef chuck steak
¼ cup vegetable oil
1 cup chopped onion
2 cloves crushed garlic
2 28-ounce cans tomatoes
2 6-ounce cans tomato paste
2 cups water

½ cup chili powder
¼ cup sugar
1 Tablespoon salt
2 teaspoons oregano leaves
¾ teaspoon cracked pepper
½ cup shredded Monterey Jack cheese

Two hours before serving cut steak into 1″ cubes. Heat vegetable oil in Dutch oven and brown meat, ⅓ at a time. Remove, set aside. Reserve ¼ cup onion. Add remaining onions and garlic to Dutch oven. Over medium heat, cook and stir for 10 minutes. Return meat to Dutch oven. Add tomatoes with their liquid and remaining ingredients except cheese and reserved onions. Cook over high heat until boiling. Reduce heat to low. Cover and simmer 1½ hours, stirring occasionally. Remove cover if necessary to reduce liquid. Serve with cheese and reserved onions. (2½ hours preparation time. Suitable for freezing.)

Elizabeth Rhodes Reich

Mrs. Frank Reich, *daughter of former Representative John J. Rhodes (Arizona)*

Pork with Broccoli and Hoisin Sauce
SERVES 4

1 pound lean pork, thinly sliced against the grain
1 teaspoon soy sauce
1 teaspoon honey
2 teaspoons orange juice

2 teaspoons cornstarch
2 teaspoons peanut oil
1 cup chopped fresh or frozen broccoli
3 scallions, chopped
2 Tablespoons hoisin sauce

In a medium bowl, mix pork, soy sauce, honey, orange juice and cornstarch. Marinate pork for about 1 hour. In a wok or non-stick skillet, heat oil over medium heat. Add pork and stir-fry over high heat for about 3 minutes. Add broccoli and scallions, stir-fry for about 2 minutes more. Stir in hoisin sauce, toss until meat and vegetables are coated with sauce and cooked. Serve hot with rice. (35 minutes preparation time. Not suitable for freezing.)

Charles B. Rangel, *Representative (New York)*

Nana McCarthy's Lobster Stew
SERVES 4

1 pound lobster meat cut into bite size pieces - frozen is fine
1 quart milk
1 can Carnation milk (not sweetened)
2 Tablespoons paprika
2 Tablespoons butter

A quick, elegant stew prepared the day before. Sauté lobster lightly in butter and paprika. Combine 2 milks and add to lobster. Bring to a quick boil. Remove and refrigerate overnight. This allows for flavors to combine. Heat and serve the following day. (20 minutes preparation time. Not suitable for freezing.)

Mrs. Fred Upton, *wife of Representative (Michigan)*

Lamb Curry
SERVES 6

2 pounds boneless lamb, cut
  into ¾" pieces
olive oil
2 Tablespoons curry powder
1 quart chicken stock
2 teaspoons salt
1 large onion, chopped
2 cups diced apples
¼ cup seedless raisins
1 egg yolk

2 Tablespoons cream
bananas
dash of red pepper
cooked rice
chopped nuts
chopped sweet pickles
chopped boiled egg
chopped onion
chutney

Brown lamb in oil and add curry powder. Add stock, salt, onion, apples and raisins; simmer until lamb is tender. Thicken liquid with mixture of egg yolk and cream. Do not boil. Cook bananas in butter; sprinkle with red pepper. Serve curry in depression in mound of rice; garnish with bananas. Serve nuts, pickles, eggs, onion and chutney as condiments. (Not suitable for freezing.)

Mrs. Guy Vander Jagt, *wife of former Representative (Michigan)*

Northwest Salmon with Brazilian Flavor
SERVES 4

4 salmon filets, 5-6 ounces each
juice of ½ large orange
juice of ½ large lemon
salt and pepper to taste
zest of 1 orange

2 Tablespoons brown sugar
½-1 Tablespoons chili powder
1 large garlic clove, minced
2 Tablespoons butter, melted

In a shallow glass dish large enough to hold salmon; combine the juices, salt and pepper. Add the salmon, turning to coat with the marinade. Let soak in marinade at room temperature for 20 minutes, turning the filets once. Preheat the oven to 425°. Line a shallow baking pan with aluminum foil and grease with a little of the melted butter. In a small dish, combine the orange zest, brown sugar, chili powder and minced garlic. Rub the marinated salmon with the brown sugar mixture. Place in the pan and drizzle with the remaining melted butter. Bake for 8 to 12 minutes. (Serve with mix of brown and wild rice and steamed green vegetables.) (45 minutes preparation time. Not suitable for freezing.)

Mrs. Don Bonker, *wife of former Representative (Washington)*

Bob and Sally's Favorite Chicken
SERVES 6

2 10-ounce packages frozen chopped spinach (thawed)
4 whole chicken breasts, cut in half
1 cup mayonnaise
2 cans cream of chicken soup
1 Tablespoon lemon juice
1 teaspoon curry powder
½ cup grated sharp cheddar cheese
½ cup buttered bread crumbs

Squeeze liquid out of spinach and spread in bottom of a 9″ × 13″ greased baking dish. Add chicken. Mix mayonnaise, soup, lemon juice and curry powder together and spread on chicken. Sprinkle with cheese and top with bread crumbs. Bake at 350° for 1 to 1¼ hours. Can be made ahead of time and reheated. (15 minutes preparation time. Not suitable for freezing.)

Jennette Prouty

Mrs. Winston Prouty, *wife of former Senator (Vermont)*

Chicken Breasts with Fresh Fruit
SERVES 8

8 chicken breasts, boned and skinned
1½ Tablespoons curry powder
vegetable cooking spray
¾ cup mango chutney
¼ cup fresh lime juice

1 cup coarsely chopped apples
1 cup coarsely chopped pears
1 cup sliced kiwi fruit
1 cup fresh or frozen cranberries
¼-½ cup sherry

Cook chicken with curry powder and cooking spray in oiled baking dish for 10 minutes at 350°. Combine chutney and lime juice and pour ¾ of the mixture over chicken. Bake 10 minutes. (This can be done ahead of time.) Arrange all fruit over chicken, add sherry and the rest of the chutney mixture and bake 10 to 15 minutes or until done. This is a very pretty dish and low in fat too. (30 minutes preparation time. Not suitable for freezing.)

Andy Ireland

Andy Ireland, *former Representative (Florida)*

Cajun Barbecued Redfish (Rockfish)
SERVES 6 TO 8

1 large redfish or rockfish
¼ pound lump crabmeat
¼ pound peeled shrimp
cayenne pepper
black pepper
salt

1 stick butter
½ cup of Italian salad dressing
3-4 Tablespoons Worcestershire sauce
dash of meat sauce
1 large lemon

Clean and prepare fish by removing backbone and head leaving the scales on and saving as much of the throat as possible. This can be accomplished by opening the fish along each side of the backbone, in effect butterflying the fish, and then thoroughly cleaning the body cavity. Slice the meat of the fish along its thickest parts and, using the crabmeat and shrimp, stuff the openings. Season the fish well using salt, cayenne and black pepper or your favorite fish seasonings. Prepare the basting sauce by melting a stick of butter with a ½ cup of Italian salad dressing along with 3 to 4 tablespoons of Worcestershire sauce and a healthy dash of your favorite meat sauce. Cut and squeeze a large lemon into the sauce and then slice the lemon into small slices and drop into the sauce. Stir the sauce over low heat until well blended. Apply the sauce liberally over the fish after it is placed on the grill or in the oven at 450° and add as needed during the cooking process. Cook until the fish is cooked through to the scales and the crabmeat and shrimp are also cooked to taste. (15 to 20 minutes preparation time. Not suitable for freezing.)

Billy Tauzin

W. J. Billy Tauzin, *Representative (Louisiana)*

MINNESOTA

The tallest and most beautiful of our native orchids, the pink and white lady's slipper grows in the acidic soils of bogs and damp woods, and ranges from Newfoundland to Manitoba, and south to the eastern United States. The flowers bloom from May to August. Like many orchids, lady's slippers are becoming rare due to loss of habitat and overcollection.

Smothered Round Steak with Onions

1-3 pounds round steak; cut in pieces. Try to buy a steak with the bone in. It makes the gravy much better.

flour

4 Tablespoons cooking oil

2 medium size onions, chopped

1-2 stalks celery, chopped

1 medium bell pepper, chopped

½ green onions or shallots, chopped

2 cups water (more or less)

Tony Chachere's Creole seasoning (you may substitute your favorite creole seasoning or make your own using salt, pepper, and garlic powder to your own taste)

Season steak with seasoning. Drench or pat each piece of steak in flour. In a large skillet, brown steak in oil on all sides. Remove from pan. Sauté onions, celery and bell pepper in pan drippings until clear (about 5 minutes). Add back the browned round steak pieces. Add 1 to 2 cups of water (just enough to barely cover steak). Bring to a boil, cover and reduce heat to simmer for about 45 minutes to 1 hour. Check occasionally. Stir and add water if needed. Gravy will thicken as it cooks, but do not allow it to stick to the bottom of the pan. Last 10 minutes of cooking add green onions. Serve steak with gravy over a bed of cooked rice or mashed potatoes. This is a staple of Cajun Country.

Lois Breaux

Mrs. John Breaux, *wife of Senator (Louisiana)*

Marinated Pork Chops
SERVES 4

4 pork chops

½ cup vegetable oil

½ cup soy sauce

2 Tablespoons brown sugar

1 teaspoon mustard

1 teaspoon garlic powder

Place pork chops in large plastic bag. Combine all other ingredients and pour over chops. Marinate all day or overnight in the refrigerator. Turn several times. Grill chops 7 to 9 minutes on each side. Do not add salt. (25 minutes preparation time. Not suitable for freezing.)

Vince Snowbarger

Vince Snowbarger, *Representative (Kansas)*

Lemon Barbecued Meat Loaves

SERVES 6

1½ pounds ground chuck
4 slices stale bread, cubed
¼ cup lemon juice
¼ cup onion, minced
1 egg, slightly beaten
2 teaspoons seasoned salt

½ cup ketchup
⅓ cup brown sugar
1 teaspoon dry mustard
¼ teaspoon allspice
¼ teaspoon ground cloves
6 thin lemon slices

Preheat oven to 350°. In bowl, combine ground chuck, bread, lemon juice, onion, egg and salt. Mix well and shape into 6 individual loaves. Place in a greased 9″ × 13″ baking dish. Bake 15 minutes. In small bowl, combine remaining ingredients except lemon slices. Cover loaves with sauce and top each with a lemon slice. Bake 30 minutes longer; basting occasionally with sauce from pan. (1 hour 15 minutes preparation time. Not suitable for freezing.)

Mary Bateman

Mrs. Bert Bateman, *daughter-in-law of Representative Herbert Bateman (Virginia)*

Stuffed Green Peppers

SERVES 4

4 green peppers
½ teaspoon salt

⅛ teaspoon pepper

Filling:

1 pound ground veal or hamburger
⅔ cup finely chopped onion
½ teaspoon salt
¼ teaspoon oregano

⅛ teaspoon pepper
1 cup tomato sauce
½ cup beef consommé
1 Tablespoon chopped parsley

Cut out the tops, seeds, and white membranes of the peppers. Simmer peppers in salted water for about 5 minutes. Remove, drain and salt and pepper the insides. Brown the meat. Drain and add chopped onions. Cook until tender. Season with salt, oregano and pepper. Add ½ cup tomato sauce and consommé. Simmer gently for 5 to 7 minutes. Add parsley and stuff the peppers. Pour 2 tablespoons tomato sauce over each. Place in baking dish and cover with aluminum foil. Bake at 350° until heated through, about 15 to 20 minutes. (45 minutes preparation time. Suitable for freezing.)

Sylvia Sabo

Mrs. Martin Sabo, *wife of Representative (Minnesota)*

Crab Cakes Diane
SERVES 6 TO 7

1½ pounds crabmeat (I like lump meat)
1 cup Italian seasoned bread crumbs
   or herb seasoned stuffing
1 large egg or 2 small eggs
about ¼ cup mayonnaise
⅓ cup chopped green onions

½ teaspoon salt
¼ teaspoon pepper
1 teaspoon Worcestershire sauce
1 teaspoon dry mustard
few drops Tabasco
margarine or butter or oil for frying

Remove cartilage from crabmeat. In a bowl mix crumbs, egg, mayonnaise and seasonings. Add crabmeat and gently mix well. If mixture is too dry, you may add a little more mayonnaise. Shape into 6 or 7 cakes. Brown cakes in fry pan in enough fat to prevent sticking, about 5 minutes on each side. Great with salad and French bread. (30 minutes preparation time. Not suitable for freezing.)

Tricia Lott

Mrs. Trent Lott, *wife of Senator (Mississippi)*

Currant Jelly Glazed Veal
SERVES 4

1½ pounds veal, cut in bite size cubes
¼ cup flour
salt and pepper to taste
1½ teaspoons dry mustard

3 Tablespoons oil for browning
¼ cup currant jelly
1 Tablespoon Worcestershire sauce
4 Tablespoons lemon juice

Season flour with salt, pepper and mustard in a bag. Shake veal until covered. Brown in hot oil, cover and cook slowly for 20 minutes. Turn meat often. Add other ingredients and continue cooking and stirring until veal is coated and glazed with jelly. (30 minutes preparation time. Suitable for freezing.)

Shirley H. Wilson

Mrs. Bob Wilson, *wife of former Representative (California)*

Pork Medallions in Mustard Sauce

SERVES 4

3 Tablespoons vegetable oil
1 Tablespoon coarse-grained mustard
½ teaspoon salt
½ teaspoon pepper

2 ¾-pound pork tenderloins
¼ cup dry white wine
fresh basil, as garnish

Mustard Seed Sauce:
1¾ cups whipping cream
¼ cup coarse-grained mustard

¼ teaspoon salt
⅛ teaspoon white pepper

Pork Medallion: Combine first 4 ingredients, stirring well. Rub mixture over pork; place in a plastic bag; refrigerate 8 hours. Place tenderloins on rack in a shallow roasting pan. Insert meat thermometer into thickest part of meat. Bake at 375° for 25 minutes or until meat thermometer registers 160°. Baste every 10 minutes with wine. Slice tenderloins into ¾" slices and arrange 4 slices on each dinner plate. Spoon mustard seed sauce around pork on each plate.

Mustard Seed Sauce: Heat whipping cream in a heavy saucepan until reduced to 1¼ cups (about 15 minutes). Do not boil. Stir in remaining ingredients, and heat for 1 minute. Yields 1¼ cups. (25 minutes preparation time. Not suitable for freezing.)

Becky Rogers

Mrs. Paul Rogers, *wife of former Representative (Florida)*

Baked Fish in Browned Butter

SERVES 4

2 pounds fish filets
seasoned salt
¼ pound butter
lemon juice

2 Tablespoons white wine
paprika (prefer imported)
Parmesan cheese

Heat oven to 450°. Brown butter in shallow baking dish. This takes about 10 minutes and is critical. Do not burn, but let it get dark brown. Watch butter carefully and stir or shake occasionally while browning. Cut fish filets into serving pieces and season with seasoned salt on both sides. Place fish filets in browned butter and bake 10 to 15 minutes depending on thickness of fish. Turn fish with spatula and baste with browned butter. Sprinkle fish with white wine, lemon juice, Parmesan cheese and paprika. Return to oven about 5 minutes until done. Fish is done when it flakes apart. Do not overcook. Baste with butter sauce from dish and serve hot. (45 minutes preparation time.)

Glenda Miller

Mrs. Dan Miller, *wife of Representative (Florida)*

Kathie Lee Chicken

SERVES 4

1 bottle Russian dressing
1 jar apricot preserves
1 package dry onion soup mix

1 4-ounce can pineapple slices or chunks
4 chicken breasts

Combine Russian dressing, onion soup mix and apricot preserves in mixing bowl. Stir and add to chicken in Pyrex dish. Cover and cook for 1 hour at 350°. Uncover and cook ½ hour after adding pineapple and juice. (10 minutes preparation time. Not suitable for freezing.)

Mary Laughlin

Mary Laughlin, *daughter of former Representative Greg Laughlin (Texas)*

Chicken for Company
SERVES 6

1-ounce jar dried beef
6 slices thick-sliced bacon
6 chicken breasts, skinned
    and boned

1 8-ounce container sour cream
1 10½-ounce can cream
    of mushroom soup

Line a shallow glass baking dish (9″ × 9″) with layer of dried beef slices. Wrap chicken breasts with a slice of bacon and place upon the beef layer. Mix the sour cream and mushroom soup together and pour over the chicken. Bake in a preheated 325° oven for 2½ hours. (Suitable for freezing.)

Diana Enzi

Mrs. Mike Enzi, *wife of Senator (Wyoming)*

Giovanni's Pollo Marinato
SERVES 6

1 pound chicken breasts
    (boneless and skinned)
6 ounces good white wine
6 ounces olive oil
1 lemon for juice
1 teaspoon salt
½ teaspoon pepper
fresh basil

tarragon
dill
3 cups whipping cream
3 ounces porcini mushrooms
3 ounces sundried tomatoes
12 ounces penne pasta
grated Parmesan cheese to taste

Marinate chicken breasts in wine, olive oil, lemon juice and spices for 2 hours. Boil water for pasta and cook approximately 15 minutes. Slice chicken into thin strips and cook in the whipping cream. When chicken appears almost done add mushrooms, sundried tomatoes, and salt and pepper to taste. Toss with penne pasta and serve with grated Parmesan cheese on top. This recipe is compliments of our favorite restaurant, "Pastabilities". (2½ hours preparation time. Not suitable for freezing.)

Elton Gallegly, *Representative (California)*

Shrimp Scampi
S E R V E S   2

12 shrimp in shell
¾ stick butter (melted)
1 lemon

⅓ cup chopped garlic
⅓ cup corn oil
black pepper

Arrange shrimp (not touching) in a metal or glass oven-proof pan (8½″ × 11″). Pour melted butter over shrimp. Squeeze lemon over shrimp into butter; add oil and garlic; cover shrimp with black pepper. Broil about 10 minutes. Serve with French bread. (25 minutes preparation time. Not suitable for freezing.)

Christine DeLay

Mrs. Tom DeLay, *wife of Representative (Texas)*

California Chicken
S E R V E S   6

3 chicken breasts, halved
2 cups sour cream
1 can cream of mushroom soup
½ cup dry white wine

2 cups cheddar cheese, grated
1 3½-ounce can French fried
  onion rings

Place breasts, skin side up in buttered baking dish. Mix together sour cream, mushroom soup and wine. Spread over chicken. Sprinkle grated cheese over all. Top with onion rings. Bake for 1 hour at 325°. Can be prepared in advance, refrigerated, and then baked when you are ready.

Bonnie Bryan

Mrs. Richard Bryan, *wife of Senator (Nevada)*

Alaska Salmon Surprise
SERVES 6

6 red potatoes, scrubbed but not peeled
1 1-pound can salmon
1½ cups milk
3 Tablespoons butter
3 Tablespoons flour
1 teaspoon dried dill

dash cayenne pepper
salt and pepper to taste
1 cup frozen peas, thawed
¾ cup mayonnaise
¾ cup grated sharp cheddar cheese
1 teaspoon mustard
1 teaspoon Worcestershire sauce

Boil potatoes until easily pierced by fork (about 20 minutes). Drain well, cool, and cut into thin slices. Drain and flake salmon reserving liquid. Pour liquid into measuring cup and add milk to make 2 cups. Melt butter and blend in flour. Gradually blend in liquid and cook, stirring until thick and smooth. Add dill, cayenne, salt and pepper. Layer ⅓ of the potatoes in casserole. Add a layer of ½ the salmon, and then a layer of ½ the peas. Spoon ⅓ of sauce over it and repeat layers. Top with remaining ⅓ of sauce. Combine mayonnaise, cheese, mustard and Worcestershire sauce. Spread over top of casserole. Bake in 375° oven for 30 minutes until bubbly. (45 minutes preparation time. Not suitable for freezing.)

Laurie C. Battle

Laurie C. Battle, *former Representative (Alabama)*

MAGNOLIA
(MAGNOLIA GRANDIFLORA)

MISSISSIPPI

Flowering plants first appeared about 120 million years ago. Most botanists agree the first flowers resemble the magnolia flowers we enjoy in our gardens today. If we look at the arrangement of the floral parts, sepals, petals, stamens, and pistils, in modern day magnolia flowers, we can see their arrangement closely resembles that of flowers that bloomed 120 million years ago.

Fried Shrimp Batter

1 cup sifted flour
1 teaspoon salt
1 teaspoon baking powder

1 cup whole milk
1 egg (beaten)
bread or cracker crumbs

Sift dry ingredients together. Add milk and egg. Stir until mixed, do not over stir. Dip peeled and deveined shrimp in batter. Roll in bread or cracker crumbs and fry in hot grease about 3 minutes each side or until golden brown. (5 minutes preparation time. Not suitable for freezing.)

Christine DeLay

Mrs. Tom DeLay, *wife of Representative (Texas)*

Colonial Pot Roast
SERVES 6 TO 8

3-4 pounds beef blade pot roast
¼ cup flour
1½ teaspoons salt
⅛ teaspoon pepper
3 Tablespoons cooking fat
¼ cup water

2 medium onions, cut in quarters
1 beef bouillon cube
⅓ cup hot water
1 acorn squash, cut in twelfths and pared
2 medium tart apples, quartered
   and cored

Combine flour, salt and pepper. Dredge meat in seasoned flour. Reserve leftover flour. Brown meat in cooking fat. Pour off drippings. Add ¼ cup water and onions. Cover tightly and cook slowly for 2½ hours. Dissolve bouillon cube in ⅓ cup hot water. Add bouillon, squash, and apples to meat. Cover tightly and cook for 30 to 35 minutes or until meat and vegetables are tender. Remove meat and vegetables to heated platter. Thicken cooking liquid with reserved flour dissolved in water. (Suitable for freezing.)

Conrad Burns, *Senator (Montana)*

Chicken Cacciatore
SERVES 4

1 medium bottle Italian dressing
2 cups Corn Flakes
4 chicken breasts, boneless, skinless

1 30-ounce jar spaghetti sauce
1 cup mozzarella cheese
2 cups cooked spaghetti

Marinate the chicken in Italian dressing. In plastic bag, coat the chicken with Corn Flakes. Arrange chicken in baking dish and cover with spaghetti sauce. Cover and bake at 375°for 35 minutes. Remove and cover with cheese. Bake uncovered for 5 minutes or until cheese melts. Serve over ¼ cup of spaghetti. (45 minutes preparation time. Not suitable for freezing.)

Beth Valentine Dollar

Mrs. Steven Dollar, *daughter of former Representative Tim Valentine (North Carolina)*

Trudy's Marinated Flank Steak
SERVES 4

½ cup vegetable oil
¼ cup soy sauce
¼ cup red wine vinegar

2 teaspoons Worcestershire sauce
1 teaspoon minced garlic (1 clove)
1⅓ pounds flank steak

Mix first 5 ingredients for marinade. Put flank steak in a freezer bag, pour marinade over it, seal bag and refrigerate overnight. When ready, broil steak 10 to 12 minutes per side, 8" from heat of barbecue or grill. Cut steak across the grain at slanted angle into thin slices. (10 minutes preparation time. Suitable for freezing.)

Cynthia L.B. Rice

Cynthia Rice, *daughter of former Representative Laurie C. Battle (Alabama)*

Wisconsin Grilled Bratwurst
SERVES 4

4 bratwurst
cooking oil
1½ cups chopped onion
1 12-ounce can beer
2 Tablespoons butter

½ teaspoon onion salt
4 large hot dog buns
½ cup grated sharp cheddar cheese
4 slices cooked bacon, crumbled

Brown bratwurst over medium heat in oil. Add onions and beer. Simmer uncovered for 25 minutes. Mix butter and onion salt together and spread on buns. Make a lengthwise cut in each bratwurst to within ½" of each end. Spoon on drained onions and sprinkle with cheese. Place in a foil "boat", leaving side open. Broil 4" from heat for 2 minutes if using oven. Top with crumbled bacon. (This recipe can be done ahead except for the final heating.) Then, if using a grill, put bratwurst on a baking sheet and cover grill a few minutes. Watch so bratwurst does not burn on the bottom. Serve with German potato salad. (Not suitable for freezing.)

Mrs. F. James Sensenbrenner, wife of Representative (Wisconsin)

Helene's Stuffed Fish
SERVES 6 TO 8

1 rockfish (or other firm-fleshed fish)
½ carrot, sliced
½ small onion, sliced
1 sprig parsley, chopped

½ cup white wine
1 small sliver lemon rind
salt and pepper
2 cups water

Stuffing:
1 can red salmon
juice of ½ large lemon
2 Tablespoons mayonnaise

1 stalk celery, finely chopped
4 sprigs minced parsley

For stuffing, blend together all ingredients until smooth. For fish, simmer vegetables in water until tender. Remove vegetables and lay whole fish, boned, in the liquid. Cover and simmer just 10 minutes. Gently remove fish from pan. While still warm, remove skin. Cool to room temperature, and fill fish with stuffing. Cover with a thin layer of mayonnaise and decorate as desired (cucumber slices for scales, etc.). Chill. Present on a bed of watercress and garnish with tomato wedges. Beautiful and delicious. (30 minutes preparation time. Suitable for freezing.)

Mrs. Tom Bevill, wife of former Representative (Alabama)

Bulgogi - Korean Barbecue

2 pounds rib eye beef or tenderloin beef
¾ cup soy sauce
¼ cup rice wine or red wine
3 Tablespoons finely chopped
   green onion
2-3 teaspoons crushed garlic

2 teaspoons minced fresh ginger
½ teaspoon black pepper
1½ Tablespoons sugar
2 Tablespoons sesame seed,
   roasted (optional)
2 Tablespoons sesame oil

Slice beef into very thin slices, and set aside. Mix all remaining ingredients. Add beef to the mixture, and stir thoroughly. Cover and marinate for 30 minutes or so. Preheat table top broiler (griller), protecting the table top with aluminum foil or other suitable heat shield. Each diner, or the host/hostess, places a portion of meat on the grill and cooks it quickly on both sides. Serve with boiled rice and fresh salads. Can be cooked on Jenn-Air broiler. Put aluminum foil on the grill and place meat. (1 to 2 minutes preparation time. Suitable for freezing.)

Cindy Daub-Han

Cindy Daub-Han, *member of Congressional Club (Nebraska)*

Long Island Peconic Bay Scallops Supreme

SERVES 4

⅓-½ cup butter or margarine
1 cup soft bread crumbs, freshly
   made in blender from
   4 slices of bread
1 teaspoon instant minced onion
1 teaspoon parsley flakes

¼ teaspoon crumbled tarragon
⅛ teaspoon black pepper
2 teaspoons lemon juice
1 pint bay scallops (or sea scallops
   cut in quarters)

Melt butter or margarine. Place soft bread crumbs in a bowl and spoon on 3 tablespoons of melted butter. Toss well to coat. Measure remaining ingredients (except scallops) into remaining butter in skillet. Simmer over very low heat for 5 minutes. Arrange scallops in 4 to 5 individual greased shells or shallow individual baking dishes. Spoon herbed butter over scallops. Spread buttered crumbs over this. Bake until nicely browned, about 5 minutes at 400°. (25 minutes preparation time. Not suitable for freezing.)

Carol Ann Hochbrueckner

Mrs. George Hochbrueckner, *wife of former Representative (New York)*

Barbecue Meat Balls

1½-2 pounds ground beef or mixed
   with pork and veal
1 egg slightly beaten
1 large grated onion

salt to taste (1 teaspoon per pound)
1 12-ounce bottle chili sauce
juice of 1 lemon
8 ounces grape jelly

Combine ground meat with beaten egg, onion and salt. Mix and shape into small balls (smaller than walnuts). Drop into sauce made of chili sauce, lemon juice and grape jelly. Simmer balls until cooked and browned a little. Serve in a chafing dish or reheat a day or two later, or freeze. Makes about 60 meat balls. (1½ hours preparation time. Suitable for freezing.)

Glen Kleppe

Mrs. Tom Kleppe, *wife of former Representative (North Dakota)*

¼ cup margarine or butter
¼ cup flour
3 Tablespoons ketchup
½ teaspoon salt
dash of paprika

½ teaspoon curry
1½ cups half and half
¼ cup sherry
2 cups cooked rice
1 pound medium shrimp (cooked)

Melt margarine in a pan on low heat. Add flour and seasonings. Cook on low heat until blended. Stir in warm half and half. Add ketchup, sherry and shrimp. Cook until well heated. (20 minutes preparation time. Suitable for freezing.)

Nancy S Beall

Mrs. J. Glenn Beall, Jr., *wife of former Representative (Maryland)*

Flank Steak Marinade

¼ cup soy sauce
3 Tablespoons honey
2 Tablespoons vinegar
1 teaspoon garlic powder
1 teaspoon ground ginger
¾ cup salad oil
1 green onion, chopped

Combine all ingredients in a jar. To marinate, pour mixture over meat and marinate all day. Grill 5 to 10 minutes per side. Slice diagonally. (Makes enough marinade for 2-3 pounds flank steak or London broil).

Richard R. Chrysler   *Katie Chrysler*

Richard and Katie Chrysler, *former Representative and Mrs. (Michigan)*

MISSOURI

People have used haw-
thorns for food and medi-
cine for centuries and the
flowers and fruits provide
food for wildlife. The
genus name, Crataegus, is
derived from the Greek
word kratos which means
"strong" and refers to the
hardness of the wood.
Hawthorns are hardy,
long-lived plants, making
them perfect for use in
the home garden and
landscape.

Mustard Baked Chops with Brie
SERVES 4

½ cup Italian seasoned bread crumbs
2 Tablespoons chopped parsley
2 Tablespoons butter, melted
2 garlic cloves, minced
¼ teaspoon dried thyme, crushed
⅓ cup all purpose flour
½ teaspoon salt

¼ teaspoon ground coriander
¼ teaspoon pepper
4 boneless pork chops (1″ thick)
2 Tablespoons Dijon style mustard
2 Tablespoons olive oil
1 4½-ounce container Brie cheese,
  halved crosswise

Preheat oven to 400°. Combine bread crumbs, parsley, butter, garlic and thyme in
a small bowl. Combine flour, salt, coriander and pepper in a wide shallow bowl.
Evenly coat both sides of the chops with mustard and then flour mixture. Heat
oil in a large skillet over medium-high heat. Add chops and brown on both sides.
Place chops in a 13″ × 9″ × 2″ baking dish. Cut each piece of Brie in half horizontally to form in thin half circles. Place a half-circle on each chop. Spoon
crumb mixture on top of chops. Bake uncovered for 20 to 30 minutes, or until
chops are faintly pink in the center and bread crumbs are golden brown. (40 minutes preparation time. Not suitable for freezing.)

Lynne Hobson Foran

Mrs. Jay Foran, *daughter of Representative David L. Hobson (Ohio)*

Duck and Wild Rice Casserole
SERVES 6

2 medium ducks (3 cups meat)
3 stalks celery
1 onion, halved
salt and pepper
½ cup margarine
½ cup chopped onion
¼ cup flour

4 ounces sliced mushrooms
1½ cups half and half cream
1 Tablespoon parsley
1 6-ounce package wild rice and
    long grain rice
slivered almonds

Boil ducks for 1 hour in water with celery, onion halves, salt and pepper. Remove meat and cube. Reserve broth. Cook rice according to package directions. Melt margarine, sauté onions, and stir in flour. Drain mushrooms reserving broth. Add mushrooms to the onion mixture. Add enough duck broth to the mushroom broth to make 1½ cups of liquid. Stir this into the onion mixture. Add other ingredients plus 1½ teaspoons salt and ¼ teaspoon pepper. Put into greased 2-quart casserole dish. Sprinkle almonds on top. Bake covered at 350° for 15 to 20 minutes. Uncover and bake for 5 to 10 minutes more. Chicken substituted for duck also makes a tasty dish. (20 minutes preparation time. Suitable for freezing.)

Mrs. Marion Berry, *wife of Representative (Arkansas)*

Southern Shrimp Scampi

1 pound whole large shrimp
½ cup melted butter
½ teaspoon salt
6 cloves crushed garlic

2 Tablespoons chopped parsley
1 Tablespoon lemon juice
1 teaspoon grated lemon rind

Peel and devein shrimp. Combine next 4 ingredients. Place in 9″ × 13″ baking dish with shrimp on top. Bake at 400° for 8 minutes. Turn, sprinkle with lemon juice and lemon rind. Bake for another 8 minutes.

Jim Bilbray, *former Representative (Nevada)*

Beef Tenderloin with Mushroom Sauce

SERVES 12

1 cup bourbon
1 cup water
juice of 1 lemon
2 teaspoons Worcestershire sauce
2 teaspoons Pickapeppa sauce
1 teaspoon onion salt
1 teaspoon lemon-pepper seasoning
1 teaspoon paprika
1 5-pound beef tenderloin, trimmed
2 slices bacon
1 cup water
1½ teaspoon beef-flavored bouillon granules
2 teaspoons browning-and-seasoning sauce
2 Tablespoons cornstarch
¼ cup water
lettuce (optional)
tomato rose (optional)

Combine first 8 ingredients; stir well. Spear tenderloin in several places. Place tenderloin and marinade in a zip top heavy-duty plastic bag; seal tightly. Refrigerate 8 hours. Drain and reserve marinade. Place tenderloin on rack of broiler pan; place bacon lengthwise over tenderloin. Insert meat thermometer, making sure it does not touch fat. Bake at 425° for 45 to 60 minutes or until thermometer registers 140° (rare) or 150° (medium). Baste occasionally with marinade while baking. Remove to a serving platter. Reserve remaining marinade. Pour remaining marinade in a saucepan; cook over medium heat until reduced to ½ cup. Add mushrooms, 1 cup water, bouillon granules and browning-and-seasoning sauce. Cook until mushrooms are tender. Combine cornstarch and ¼ cup water; stir into mushroom mixture. Bring mixture to a boil. Cook 1 minute or until thickened and bubbly, stirring constantly. Brush tenderloin with mushroom sauce. Slice tenderloin, and serve with sauce. If desired, garnish with lettuce and tomato rose. (45 to 60 minutes preparation time. Not suitable for freezing.)

Sharon Combest

Mrs. Larry Combest, *wife of Representative (Texas)*

Sautéed Shad Roe

SERVES 2

6 fried bacon strips
2 sets shad roe
1 quart salt water
4 sheets of wax paper

2 teaspoons lemon juice
salt and pepper to taste
2 Tablespoons bacon fat

Soak shad roe in salt water for 15 minutes. Drain. Place each set of shad roe on a square of wax paper. Season each with 1 tablespoon lemon juice, seasonings, and 1 teaspoon bacon fat. Wrap sandwich style. Keep folded ends tucked underneath. Grease heavy skillet with remaining fat. Place wrapped roe in pan, edges tucked under; fry over medium heat for 10 to 15 minutes on each side, until roe browns. (Browning can be seen through paper.) Unwrap and serve with bacon strips on top. Note: Allow one medium roe set per person. "No popping." (Not suitable for freezing.)

Herbert H. Bateman

Herbert Bateman, *Representative (Virginia)*

Chinese Beef

SERVES 4

½ pound beef, thinly sliced
3 Tablespoons vegetable oil
1 teaspoon salt
3 ribs celery, sliced on bias
1 large onion, thinly sliced
4 ounces canned sliced mushrooms
4 ounces canned water chestnuts, chopped

¼ pound snow peas,
    fresh or frozen
1 Tablespoon cornstarch
5 Tablespoons soy sauce
½ Tablespoon sugar
½ cup water
1 cup rice, cooked

Brown beef in hot vegetable oil in skillet or wok. Add salt, celery, onions, mushrooms, water chestnuts and snow peas. Stir slowly a few minutes over high heat. Cover pan, turn down heat and simmer for 3 minutes. Just before serving, stir in combination of cornstarch, soy sauce, sugar and water. Serve over rice. Note: French style green beans may be substituted for snow peas. (Suitable for freezing.)

Laura G Bateman

Mrs. Herbert Bateman, *wife of Representative (Virginia)*

½ teaspoon coriander seed
¼ teaspoon anise seed
⅓ cup honey
¼ cup lemon juice
3 Tablespoons orange juice
3 Tablespoons lime juice
2 green onions, thinly sliced
1 teaspoon snipped fresh sage

1 teaspoon snipped fresh thyme
½ teaspoon snipped fresh rosemary
¼ teaspoon salt
⅛ teaspoon coarsely ground pepper
1½ pounds skinless, boneless chicken
  breast halves
lemon, lime and orange slices (optional)
fresh rosemary (optional)

In a small skillet cook and stir the coriander and anise seed over medium heat for 5 to 7 minutes or until seeds are fragrant and toasted, stirring constantly. Remove from heat. Let cool. Grind spices with a mortar and pestle. Set aside. For marinade; in a large non-metal bowl combine honey, lemon juice, orange juice, lime juice, onions, sage, thyme, rosemary, salt and pepper. Stir in spices. Rinse chicken; pat dry. Add chicken to marinade; turn to coat. Let stand at room temperature for 30 minutes, turning chicken occasionally. Remove chicken from the marinade, reserving marinade. Place chicken on the grill rack of an uncovered grill. Grill directly over medium coals for 12 to 15 minutes or until chicken is tender and no longer pink; turning once and brushing occasionally with remaining marinade during the first 10 minutes. If desired, garnish with citrus slices and rosemary. (20 minutes preparation time. Not suitable for freezing.)

Ron Kind

Ron Kind, *Representative (Wisconsin)*

Crock Pot German Style Pot Roast of Beef

3-4 pound brisket, rump roast,
 or pot roast
2-3 potatoes, pared and sliced
2-3 carrots, pared and sliced
1-2 onions, peeled and sliced

3-4 medium dill pickles, sliced
1 teaspoon dill weed
½ cup water or beef consommé
salt and pepper to taste

Put vegetables in bottom of crock pot. Salt and pepper meat, then put in pot. Add liquid. Add dill pickles and sprinkle with dill weed. Cover and cook on low for 10 to 12 hours (high 4 to 5 hours). Remove meat and vegetables with spatula. A wonderful dinner for a busy day and cold winter night.

Opal I. Karsten

Mrs. Frank Karsten, *wife of former Representative (Missouri)*

Beef 'N Berries
SERVES 8

1 4-pound boneless beef arm roast,
 blade roast or bottom round
 pot roast
½ cup flour
2 teaspoons salt
3 Tablespoons oil

5 ounces prepared horseradish
1 1-pound can whole cranberry sauce
3 Tablespoons ground cinnamon
1 can beef broth
4 whole cloves
2 Tablespoons onion flakes

Dredge meat thoroughly in flour mixed with salt. Heat oil in a Dutch oven and brown meat well on all sides. Mix remaining ingredients and pour over meat. Bring mixture to a boil, then reduce to a simmer for 2½ hours or until meat is tender. Serve meat with its tangy juice over mashed potatoes, noodles or rice. (30 minutes preparation time. Not suitable for freezing.)

Tom Tauke

Tom Tauke, *former Representative (Iowa)*

Orange-Mustard Glazed Chicken with Ginger
SERVES 6

6 boneless skinless chicken breasts (about 1½ pounds)
½ cup orange marmalade
1 Tablespoon Dijon mustard
2 teaspoons grated, peeled, fresh ginger root
season lightly with lemon pepper

If chicken breasts are large cut in half. Season with pepper and brown in heavy Teflon frying pan sprayed with Pam. Cook on medium high. When brown on both sides remove from pan and add marmalade, mustard and ginger, stirring into drippings. Simmer on low until combined. Put chicken into shallow baking pan and pour sauce over it. Put into a 350° oven and finish cooking until tender and well done. Serve with couscous. (45 minutes preparation time. Suitable for freezing.)

Mrs. David S. King, *wife of former Representative (Utah)*

Peppered Shrimp
SERVES 4

½ cup olive oil
½ head garlic, peeled and chopped
1 pound extra large shrimp
1 Tablespoon black pepper
½ teaspoon salt
1 Tablespoon oregano
2 lemons, juiced
½ cup white wine

Using a large frying pan, sauté garlic in olive oil. Add shrimp, pepper, oregano and salt. Add wine and lemon and stir. Shrimp will turn pink when cooked (5 to 8 minutes). Serve with French or Italian bread. Can be served as an appetizer or over pasta. Do not over-cook shrimp. (Not suitable for freezing.)

Michael Bilirakis, *Representative (Florida)*

Bloody Mary Pot Roast
SERVES 6

1 3-pound boneless chuck roast
1 6-ounce can Bloody Mary mix
½ cup red wine
2 Tablespoons all purpose flour

¼ teaspoon pepper
1 envelope dry onion soup mix
4 small onions
2 carrots, cut into 1″ slices

Place a 22″ × 18″ piece of aluminum foil in a 13″ × 9″ × 2″ pan. Place beef in pan, add Bloody Mary mix and wine. Sprinkle with flour, pepper and onion soup mix. Arrange vegetables around beef. Fold foil over and seal. Bake at 350° for 2 hours or until tender. (Suitable for freezing.)

Ginger Laughlin

Ginger Laughlin, *member of Congressional Club (Texas)*

Honey-Baked Chicken

2 2-pound chickens cut up, or 8 chicken breasts
½ cup butter
½ cup honey
¼ cup Dijon mustard
1 teaspoon salt
1 teaspoon curry powder

Preheat oven to 350°. Place chicken in shallow baking pan, skin side up. Melt butter and whisk in honey, mustard, salt and curry. Pour over chicken. Bake 1½ hours, basting every 15 minutes.

Marilyn Broyhill Beach

Mrs. Robert Beach, *daughter of former Senator James T. Broyhill (North Carolina)*

BITTERROOT
(LEWISIA REDIVIVA)

MONTANA

The state flower of Montana honors explorer Meriwether Lewis, who first collected bitterroot in western Montana's Bitterroot Valley. Although very bitter until cooked, Native Americans and early settlers considered the roots a treat and would often serve them garnished with venison gravy or huckleberry sauce.

Baked Salmon with Mustard and Tarragon
SERVES 4

1½ pounds center-cut salmon filet with skin
½ cup mayonnaise
2 Tablespoons Dijon mustard
lemon wedges

2 Tablespoons chopped fresh tarragon or 2 teaspoons dried
¼ teaspoon white wine vinegar

Preheat oven to 350°. Place salmon, skin side down, in ungreased roasting pan. Sprinkle with salt and pepper. Whisk mayonnaise, mustard, tarragon and vinegar in a small bowl to blend; season topping to taste with salt and pepper. Spread topping over top and sides of salmon, covering completely. Cover pan tightly with heavy-duty aluminum foil. Bake salmon covered until almost cooked through, about 35 minutes. Remove from oven; preheat broiler. Uncover pan and broil until topping is deep golden brown and salmon feels firm to touch, about 5 minutes. Cut salmon crosswise into 4 pieces. Slide spatula between salmon and skin and transfer salmon pieces to plates. Serve with lemon wedges. (45 minutes preparation time. Suitable for freezing.)

George (Buddy) Darden

Lillian B. Darden

George (Buddy) and Lillian Darden, *former Representative and Mrs. (Georgia)*

Veal "Mo"

1 cup sliced peeled onions
¼ cup oil
3 cups cubed veal (1-1½")
2½ cups fresh firm tomatoes,
  cut up
2 bay leaves
1 diced green pepper

1 cup sliced fresh mushrooms
2 teaspoons salt (or less)
dash of pepper
3 whole cloves
1 teaspoon sugar
¼ cup flour
6 Tablespoons water

In a large skillet lightly sauté onions, then remove from pan. To remaining oil in pan, add veal cubes. Cover and cook until tender. Add remaining ingredients, except flour and water. Cover and simmer for 30 minutes. Blend flour and water into smooth paste and add to meat mixture. Cook, stirring, for 5 minutes. Serve with rice. Note: Preparation time can be saved by cooking veal earlier. This dish can be made ahead and reheated. (1 hour or less preparation time. Suitable for freezing.)

"Mo" Udall, *former Representative (Arizona)*

Seafood Casserole

SERVES 12

1 pound crabmeat (fresh, frozen, or canned)
1 pound steamed small shrimp
1 cup mayonnaise
2 Tablespoons diced pimento
¼ cup chopped bell pepper
½ cup chopped onion
1 cup chopped celery

¾ teaspoon salt
2 teaspoons parsley, chopped
1 Tablespoon Worcestershire sauce
2 Tablespoons lemon juice
2 cups cracker crumbs (reserve ½ cup for topping)
2 Tablespoons butter
2 teaspoons paprika

Heat 1 tablespoon butter in skillet. Stir fry vegetables only until heated. Remove from heat. Mix all ingredients and pour into casserole dish. Sprinkle cracker crumbs and paprika on top. Bake at 350° for 25 minutes. (45 minutes preparation time.)

Mrs. Bob Riley, *wife of Representative (Alabama)*

18 Minute Chicken

SERVES 4

4 sheets (12″ × 28″ each) heavy aluminum foil
1 medium onion, sliced
4 skinless, boneless chicken breast halves
Dijon mustard (optional)
1 medium zucchini, sliced

1 medium yellow squash, sliced
2 medium carrots, cut into strips
½ pound fresh mushrooms, sliced
basil leaves
garlic powder
paprika
butter

Preheat grill to high. Center ¼ of onion and chicken on each foil sheet. Spread chicken with mustard. Top with squash, zucchini, carrots and mushrooms. Dot with butter, then sprinkle with seasonings. Wrap and seal to form 4 packets, leaving room for heat circulation inside packets. Grill 18 to 20 minutes on high in covered grill. (38 minutes preparation time. Suitable for freezing.)

David Hobson, *Representative (Ohio)*

Baked Salmon Filet

olive oil
salmon filet (at least ⅓ pound per serving)
oregano
garlic powder

pepper
tomato, sliced
onion, sliced
parsley
bread crumbs, Italian flavored

Lightly oil bottom of oven-proof pan. Place salmon in pan and sprinkle with seasonings to taste. Layer tomato slices, onion slices, and sprinkle parsley on salmon. Sprinkle with bread crumbs. Bake at 450°, 8 to 10 minutes depending on thickness of salmon, until firm and salmon flakes with a fork. Easy, quick and delicious. Serve with wild rice. (10 minutes preparation time. Not suitable for freezing.)

Gayle Kildee

Mrs. Dale Kildee, *wife of Representative (Michigan)*

Idaho Trout
SERVES 4

2-3 Tablespoons butter
4 trout, heads and tails intact

salt and pepper to taste
lemon wedges

Topping:
1 shallot
½ pound mushrooms
2 Tablespoons butter

3 parsley sprigs
salt and pepper to taste

Rinse and dry fish thoroughly. Cut 4 ovals of baking parchment or brown wrapping paper large enough to enclose fish. Generously spread butter in center of oval. Place fish in center and sprinkle with salt and pepper; include cavity. Spread topping over top of fish. Fold paper over fish folding edges over twice. (Moisten edges with beaten egg if brown paper is used.) Place on baking sheet and bake at 350° for 15 to 18 minutes. Garnish with lemon.

Topping: Chop shallots very fine. Add mushrooms chopped very fine. In heavy saucepan, melt butter and add mushroom and onion mixture. Cook for 3 to 5 minutes over medium high heat. Stir until all moisture has evaporated. Remove from heat. Add chopped parsley and season with salt and pepper. (Not suitable for freezing.)

Dirk Kempthorne, *Senator (Idaho)*

Whole Hog Bar-be-que
SERVES 30

1 whole hog - 80 to 100 pounds, dressed without head or feet, split to lay flat
but not separated
1 case of beer for cooks - 2 cooks are needed
2 40-pound bags of Kingsford charcoal
1 10-pound bag Match Light charcoal
lighter fluid
hickory wood or hickory nuts

Equipment:
drum cooker - 200 gallon size
2 pieces concrete wire 2' X 4'
roll of small wire, uncoated
2 pair leather gloves
pliers
shovel
wire cutters

Hog should be at room temperature. Put the 2 bags of Kingsford charcoal at the ends of the grill leaving charcoal in bag. Put Match Light charcoal in the middle. Tear open Kingsford and soak bag and charcoal with lighter fluid. Light Match Light and Kingsford. Close lid and let burn for 1 hour. This heats the grill while charcoal burns down.

While grill is heating, place hog, belly side down, on 1 piece of concrete wire. Place second piece of wire on top of hog. Wire corners and center together tightly with roll of wire to secure hog while cooking.

Check coals after 1 hour. You are ready to cook when coals are ashen, not flaming. Shovel the coals to the 4 corners of the grill; leaving a small amount of coals to cover the middle. This puts most of the heat under the thickest part of the meat. Vents of grill should be wide open during the burn down, then partially closed to cook.

Place hog on grill, belly side down. Add hickory chips, about 4 to 6 handfuls. It is very important not to open grill any more than necessary during cooking time, as heat is lost and will lengthen the cooking time. Add wood chips through side doors of cooker during cooking process.

After 4 hours check for doneness by wiggling the hind legs. If bone is loose and feels like it will pull out, the hog is done. If the bone is not loose, cook another hour. Skin should be nicely browned. When hog is done, lift up on side and hold for a couple of minutes to drain fat. Lay back on grill skin side down with lid closed for 30 minutes. Take hog off grill and place on table. Close lid of grill. Let meat cool for 1 hour (this is important).

Remove wire from hog. Pull skin off and put skin back on grill fat side down and close lid. Leave skin on grill until it pops or bubbles up. Remove as much fat as possible from meat. Now you are ready to chop the meat or have a Pig-Picking. By this time you should be out of beer!!! Cooks might need some help also.

Chopped pork bar-be-que is best when meat from the entire hog is combined. Chop to size you prefer. We like pieces about 2 inches or larger. The flavor of the meat is better. Serve your favorite bar-be-que sauce on the side. Pig-Pickings are much less work for the cooks. The meat freezes well in freezer bags. Special thanks to Charles Norwood III (my son) and Phillip McKagen for developing the details of the Southern tradition. (8 hours preparation time. Suitable for freezing.)

Charlie Norwood

Charlie Norwood, *Representative (Georgia)*

Deviled Crab Delight
SERVES 10 TO 15

1 pound white or claw crabmeat (1½ dozen fresh crabs)	1 Tablespoon lemon juice
50 Saltine crackers, crushed	2 Tablespoons dry white wine
1 medium onion, finely chopped	½ cup catsup
1 Tablespoon Worcestershire sauce	2 eggs, slightly beaten
1 Tablespoon prepared mustard	½ cup diced sharp cheese
2 Tablespoons Wesson oil	salt and pepper to taste
	20 foil tart cups or crab shells

Dampen cracker crumbs with water and mix well with all other ingredients. Stuff tart cups or crab shells with mixture. Bake in oven at 375° for 30 to 40 minutes until crab is light brown. Serve with lemon wedges. (40 to 50 minutes preparation time. Not suitable for freezing.)

Nancy Fleetwood Miller

Nancy Miller, *daughter-in-law of former Senator Jack Miller (Iowa)*

Pat's Tart and Tangy Salmon
SERVES 6 TO 8

1 3 to 4-pound salmon filet
1-2 teaspoons garlic powder

1 jar coarse ground mustard

Line a cookie sheet or shallow baking dish with foil. Place salmon filet on foil, skin side down. Sprinkle with garlic powder and spread whole jar of mustard on top of filet. Bake in 375° preheated oven about 45 minutes or until salmon is firm to the touch in the thickest part. The mustard will form a kind of crust. Slice and serve with garnishes of rosemary, thyme or other herb sprigs. Delicious served with wild rice, asparagus and fresh green salad. (45 to 60 minutes preparation time. Not suitable for freezing.)

Amy L. Bryant

Amy L. Bryant, *daughter of former Representative John Bryant (Texas)*

Grandma Butler's Yorkshire Pudding
SERVES 8

2 cups milk
2 cups flour
4 eggs
½ teaspoon salt
roast beef standing rib or good quality roast

Beat together eggs and salt. Add flour and milk. Batter should be thin. Remove cooked roast from pan. Pour batter into hot pan drippings. Bake starting at 450°, decrease heat to 350° after it puffs up and continue baking until golden brown, about 20-30 minutes. The secret for the best pudding is plenty of pan drippings. (Not suitable for freezing.)

Tony P. Hall

Tony Hall, *Representative (Ohio)*

Individual Beef Wellingtons
SERVES 4

4 1½-2" thick tenderloins of beef
3 Tablespoons liverwurst
1½ Tablespoons brandy, optional
1 egg yolk, beaten with little water

2 Tablespoons butter
salt and pepper
1 packet puff pastry, thawed

In a pan, sear steaks in butter 2 to 3 minutes each side. Sprinkle with salt and pepper; remove to cool. Mix liverwurst with brandy and spread over steaks. Roll out pastry and cut into 4 squares large enough to enclose each steak. Place steak in center of each pastry square and fold over to completely enclose. Seal seams with egg yolk-water mixture. Place on cookie sheet and bake in 400° preheated oven for 20 minutes or until golden brown. (Not suitable for freezing.)

Cecilia S. Marshall

Mrs. Thurgood Marshall, *wife of former U.S. Supreme Court Justice*

Mexican Beef
SERVES 4 TO 6

3 pounds boneless chuck roast cut in 2 inch chunks
7 ounces salsa
1 Tablespoon soy sauce
2 Tablespoons brown sugar
¼ teaspoon garlic powder
1 teaspoon salt
rice or noodles for 4 to 6 people

Brown meat in small amount of hot oil in Dutch oven. Mix all remaining ingredients and pour over meat. Cover and bake at 300° for 3 hours. Serve over rice or noodles. (3 hours preparation time. Suitable for freezing.)

Joanne Kemp

Mrs. Jack Kemp, *wife of former Representative and former Cabinet Secretary (New York)*

GOLDENROD
(SOLIDAGO CANADENSIS)

NEBRASKA

Goldenrod is a member of the sunflower family (Asteraceae or Compositae) which includes sunflowers, daisies, and asters. This large, global plant family is recognized by its flowers. What we typically call "flowers" are actually flowerheads composed of two different flowers. The central disk is composed of disk flowers while the petal-like outer flowers are called ray flowers.

1 dozen soft, flour taco shells
1 dozen corn taco shells
1½ pounds taco filling
  (see following recipe)
2 cups refried beans
  (see following recipe)
1 each tomato and onion, diced
½ head iceberg lettuce, chopped

1 can olives, sliced
1 pound sharp cheddar cheese, shredded
1 container fresh salsa (or see recipe
  in *The Congressional Club
  Cook Book*, twelfth edition,
  Page 435, Tomato Salsa)
1 can tomato sauce, heated (optional)

Taco Filling:

1½ pounds ground beef or
  ground turkey
¼ cup chopped onion
1 clove garlic, minced
1 teaspoon salt
¼ teaspoon pepper

1 teaspoon chili powder
½ teaspoon cumin
⅛ cup fresh cilantro, minced
1 cup canned tomato sauce
1 whole tomato diced
water

Refried Beans:

2-3 cups cooked beans
  (see recipe below)
¾-1½ cups oil
1 cup chopped onion

1 clove garlic, minced
½ cup cooked tomatoes
1 teaspoon chili powder
salt and pepper to taste

Basic Cooked Beans:

½ pound dried red kidney beans
½ cup chopped onion

water
salt to taste

Tacos:

Warm separated corn shells and stacked soft flour shells in oven at 250° for about 10 to 15 minutes. Remove a flour shell and spread with a heaping tablespoon of refried beans. Place a corn taco shell in the center and fold the flour shell up in a U-shape around the corn taco. Fill taco with 1 tablespoon of taco filling and serve. Each person may choose their own topping to complete their tacos. Heated tomato sauce may be poured over the top to help melt the cheese. Serve with left over refried beans. You may add guacamole and Spanish rice or Gazpacho (cold tomato soup) to make a nice meal.

Taco Filling:

Crumble beef into large flat skillet and brown meat completely; pour off all fat (beef) or water (turkey). Add onion and garlic and cook until onion is soft (about 5 minutes) while stirring frequently. Stir in dry seasonings, then tomato sauce. Continue cooking for about 15 more minutes. Add water if the mixture becomes too dry. Or for a "15 minutes to the table" version: 2 pounds ground beef or turkey, 1 package taco mix. Follow directions on the packet.

Refried Beans:

Mash beans with potato masher and add ½ cup of oil. Add ¼ cup of oil to skillet and cook onions and garlic until onion is soft. Add mashed beans and continue cooking until oil is absorbed by beans. Stir continually to prevent sticking. Stir in tomatoes, chili powder and salt and pepper to taste. You may add more oil to get the beans to the consistency you like. Makes 3 to 4 cups of refried beans.

Basic Cooked Beans:

Wash beans well and put into a large, heavy saucepan. Add onion and cover beans with water. Cover pan and bring to a boil, reduce heat and simmer until tender, about 3 hours. You may add more water if needed. When beans are tender, salt to taste. Or for a "15 minutes to the table" version; 1 can refried beans, heat on the stove and add a little water for smooth consistency. (2 hours 15 minutes preparation time. Taco filling suitable for freezing.)

Amy Swift Donovan, *daughter of former Representative Al Swift (Washington)*

Saxby's Quail
SERVES 4

10 quail
2 sticks butter
1 Tablespoon flour
2 Tablespoons Worcestershire sauce

2 Tablespoons lemon juice
2 cups water
1 cup fresh mushrooms, sliced

Salt and pepper the quail. Melt the butter and add the flour, Worcestershire sauce, lemon juice, and water. Let this come to a boil. Pour this mixture over the birds and add mushrooms. Bake in a covered baking dish for 2 hours at 350°. This is wonderful with grits. (2 hours preparation time. Not suitable for freezing.)

Saxby Chambliss, *Representative (Georgia)*

Chef Lagasse's Andouille-Crusted Fish with Lemon-Butter Sauce and Roasted Vegetable Relish

SERVES 4

Fish:

3 ounces Andouille or other smoked sausage, finely chopped
1 cup fresh white bread crumbs
1 teaspoon Creole or Cajun seasoning
1 Tablespoon olive oil
4 6-ounce filets tilapia, redfish, or red snapper

Lemon-Butter Sauce:

¼ cup Worcestershire sauce
1 whole lemon, peel and white
   pith removed
2 bay leaves
½ cup (1 stick) chilled unsalted
   butter, cut into pieces

Roasted Vegetable Relish:

2 yellow crookneck squash, halved
   lengthwise
2 Japanese eggplant, halved lengthwise
1 zucchini, halved lengthwise
3 Tablespoons olive oil
½ cup chopped, roasted pecans
¼ cup chopped, green onions
2 teaspoons chopped garlic
salt and pepper to taste

Fish: Preheat oven to 450°F. Cook sausage in heavy medium skillet over medium heat until fat is rendered, about 2 minutes. Cool. Mix in bread crumbs and ½ teaspoon Creole or Cajun seasoning. Heat olive oil in heavy large skillet over medium heat. Sprinkle fish with remaining ½ teaspoon Creole or Cajun seasoning. Add fish to skillet, flatter side up. Cook for 2 minutes. Turn fish onto baking sheet. Top each filet with ¼ of sausage mixture. Transfer to oven and bake until fish is cooked through, about 6 minutes. Meanwhile, prepare sauce.

Lemon-Butter Sauce: Bring Worcestershire sauce, whole peeled lemon and bay leaves to a boil in a heavy, medium-size saucepan. Boil until liquid is reduced to 2 tablespoons, about 6 minutes. Discard lemon and bay leaves. Reduce heat to low. Add butter and whisk just until smooth.

Roasted Vegetable Relish: Preheat oven to 450°F. Place squash, eggplant and zucchini on baking sheet. Drizzle with 2 tablespoons oil; toss to coat. Sprinkle with salt and pepper. Roast vegetables until golden brown in spots, turning once (about 20 minutes). Cool and dice. Heat remaining 1 tablespoon oil in heavy, large skillet over high heat. Add roasted vegetables and sauté 2 minutes. Mix in pecans, green onions and garlic. Season with salt and pepper.

Spoon hot relish onto plates. Top with fish. Spoon lemon-butter sauce around and serve. (40 minutes preparation time. Suitable for freezing.)

Alice M. Lancaster

Mrs. Martin Lancaster, *wife of former Representative (North Carolina)*

Blackened Yellow-Finned Tuna Steak
SERVES 6 TO 8

2-2½ pounds (2″ thick) very fresh yellow-finned tuna steak, skinned, filleted, and blood lines removed
clarified butter or olive oil to coat tuna
blackened seasoning to taste

Serve with either sauce below:

Wasabi Sauce:
1 cup soy sauce
2 Tablespoons wasabi mustard
1 Tablespoon finely chopped pickled ginger

Lemon Sauce:
1 cup mayonnaise
1 Tablespoon fresh chopped dill weed
juice of 1½ lemons
white pepper to taste

One hour ahead, generously baste tuna with butter or oil and pat on blackened seasoning. Refrigerate for 1 hour. Using a very, very hot grill or cast iron skillet, sear the tuna about 1 or 2 minutes on either side. It is best served rare. For sauces, simply blend listed ingredients together. Serve either or both sauces. (1 hour 10 minutes preparation time. Not suitable for freezing.)

Emilie Shaw

Mrs. Clay Shaw, *wife of Representative (Florida)*

Chicken with Lemon Cream Sauce

SERVES 4

1½ pounds boneless chicken breasts
¼ cup flour
½ teaspoon salt
¼ teaspoon pepper
5 Tablespoons butter, divided
½ medium onion, minced
½ teaspoon thyme

¼ cup chicken broth
2 Tablespoons lemon juice
1 teaspoon grated lemon rind
1 cup heavy cream
8 slices lemon
4 sprigs parsley, minced

Place each chicken breast between 2 pieces of waxed paper, spreading chicken out so that it lies flat. Using a mallet or a rolling pin, pound each chicken breast until about ¼" thick. On a plate, combine flour, salt and pepper. Dredge chicken, one at a time, in seasoned flour, turning until lightly coated. In a large skillet, melt 3 tablespoons butter over medium low heat. Add about half of the chicken. Cook for 3 to 4 minutes on each side until golden. Remove the chicken from skillet, and place on a plate, covering to keep warm. Add remaining 2 tablespoons butter to skillet, and cook the rest of the chicken as directed above. Sauté onion and thyme in the same skillet over medium-low heat until onion is soft. Add chicken broth and lemon juice. Deglaze the skillet by stirring mixture with a wooden spoon until all browned bits on bottom of skillet are dissolved. Stir in grated lemon rind and heavy cream. Cook over medium heat, stirring constantly, for about 3 minutes, until sauce thickens slightly. Place cutlets on a plate, and pour sauce over them. Garnish with lemon slices and parsley. (Not suitable for freezing.)

Sara R. Smith

Mrs. Adam Smith, *wife of Representative (Washington)*

Honey-Pecan Crusted Chicken

¼ teaspoon salt

¼ teaspoon pepper

4 6-ounce skinned chicken breast halves

8 4-ounce chicken drumsticks, skinned

½ cup honey

3 Tablespoons Dijon mustard

¾ teaspoon paprika

1 teaspoon garlic powder

1¼ cups finely crushed corn flakes (about 4 cups uncrushed cereal)

½ cup finely chopped pecans

cooking spray

Preheat oven to 400°. Sprinkle salt and pepper evenly over chicken; set aside. Combine honey, mustard, paprika and garlic powder in a small bowl; stir well. Combine corn flakes and pecans in a shallow dish; stir well. Brush both sides of chicken with honey mixture; dredge in corn flake mixture. Place chicken pieces on a large baking sheet coated with cooking spray. Lightly coat chicken with cooking spray, and bake at 400° for 40 minutes or until done. (1 hour preparation time. Not suitable for freezing.)

Loretta Symms

Mrs. Steve Symms, *wife of former Senator (Idaho)*

Chicken Divan

SERVES 6

2 10-ounce packages frozen broccoli

2 cans cream of chicken soup

1 teaspoon lemon juice

½ cup soft bread crumbs

½ cup shredded, sharp cheddar cheese

chicken breasts, cooked, boned and chopped into pieces (1 per person)

½ cup of mayonnaise

½ teaspoon curry powder

1 Tablespoon butter or margarine, melted

Cook broccoli in boiling, salted water until tender and drain. Arrange in greased 11½" × 7½" × 1½" baking dish. Place chicken on top of broccoli. Combine soup, mayonnaise, lemon juice and curry powder. Mix well in large bowl and pour over chicken. Sprinkle with cheese. Combine bread crumbs and butter. Sprinkle over top. Bake at 350° for 30 minutes. Serve with plain or curry rice.

Deane C. Walsh

Mrs. James Walsh, wife of Representative (New York)

Slow Oven Barbecued Brisket

SERVES 8

7-9 pound beef brisket
2 teaspoons chopped garlic
1 teaspoon celery seeds
freshly ground black pepper to taste
1 teaspoon ground ginger (optional)
4 large bay leaves, crumbled

1 6-ounce can tomato paste
1 cup soy sauce
1 cup Worcestershire sauce
½ cup tightly packed dark brown sugar
2 medium onions, thinly sliced

Preheat oven to 300°. Tear off 2 large pieces of foil, enough to completely enclose and seal in the brisket. Place the meat on the double sheets of foil and rub it on all sides with the garlic. Combine celery seeds, pepper, ginger, if using, and crushed bay leaves, then sprinkle on all sides. Mix tomato paste, soy sauce, Worcestershire sauce and brown sugar, and smear this on the meat. Score the fat side of the brisket and place the onions on top. Wrap in the foil and carefully seal by folding it down well. Place fat side up on a rack in a roasting pan. Cook in the foil for 5 to 6 hours. (20 minutes preparation time. Suitable for freezing.)

Steve Symms

Steve Symms, *former Senator (Idaho)*

Quick Italian Chicken
SERVES 6 TO 8

3 Tablespoons olive oil
1 large onion, cut into eighths
2 garlic cloves, minced
1 pound boneless chicken breast halves, skinned and cut into strips
2 6-ounce jars marinated artichoke hearts, undrained
1 7-ounce jar roasted red bell peppers, undrained
1 cup pitted black olives
salt and freshly ground pepper
¾ pound tricolor fusilli (or other pasta), freshly cooked
grated Parmesan cheese

Sauté onion and garlic in oil in heavy large skillet over medium heat until translucent, stirring occasionally, about 10 minutes. Add chicken and stir until cooked through, about 5 minutes. Mix in artichoke hearts and peppers along with their liquids. Add olives; season with salt and pepper. Pour over cooked pasta and toss well.

Melvin L. Watt, *Representative (North Carolina)*

SAGEBRUSH
(ARTEMISIA LUDOVISIANA)

NEVADA

Named for Artemis, the Greek goddess of the moon, members of the genus Artemisia were believed to contain the magical powers of the moon. It was considered helpful for travelers who thought it would protect them from fatigue, the sun, and animals they might encounter on their journey.

Makers Mark Flank Steak
SERVES 4 TO 6

1 large flank steak (about 2 pounds)
½ cup light soy sauce
3 Tablespoons vegetable oil
2 medium onions, chopped
3 large cloves garlic, chopped

1 Tablespoon minced, fresh ginger root
2 Tablespoons brown sugar
¼ teaspoon hot pepper sauce
½ cup Makers Mark bourbon

Trim all visible fat from steak. In a heavy-duty, gallon-sized plastic bag with zip top, mix together all the marinade ingredients. Add steak. Refrigerate at least 8 hours or as long as 24 hours. Cook on a hot grill for 8 minutes on the first side and 5 minutes on the second side for medium-rare steak. Increase the cooking time if a more well-done steak is desired. To serve, cut across the grain into 1" wide strips. (30 minutes preparation time.)

Deborah Boehner

Mrs. John Boehner, *wife of Representative (Ohio)*

Mediterranean Shrimp and Pasta
SERVES 4

1 pound medium size, fresh shrimp,
   unpeeled
8 ounces penne rigate, uncooked
5 green onions, chopped
3 cloves garlic, minced
2 Tablespoons olive oil
1 12-ounce jar artichoke hearts,
   drained

6 Roma tomatoes, chopped
1 cup sliced mushrooms
¼ cup dry white wine
2 teaspoons dried Italian seasoning
¼ teaspoon salt
¼ teaspoon pepper
¼ cup Kalamata olives, sliced
2 ounces crumbled feta cheese

Peel shrimp and devein, if desired. Set aside. Cook pasta according to package directions; drain and keep warm. Cook onions and garlic in olive oil in a large skillet over medium-high heat, stirring constantly until tender. Stir in artichoke hearts and next 6 ingredients. Bring to a boil; reduce heat and simmer 5 minutes. Add shrimp; cook for 3 minutes, stirring occasionally or until shrimp turn pink. Stir in olives; cook just until thoroughly heated. Serve over pasta and sprinkle with cheese. (30 minutes preparation time. Not suitable for freezing.)

Kyle Hard

Kyle Hard, *daughter of former Senator and former Cabinet Secretary Richard Schweiker (Pennsylvania)*

Corn Crab Cakes

SERVES 8

1 pound fresh lump crabmeat,
   cartilage removed
1 cup shoepeg corn
½ cup finely diced onion
½ cup finely diced green bell pepper
½ cup finely diced celery
1 cup mayonnaise

½ teaspoon dry mustard
pinch of cayenne pepper
salt and freshly ground pepper, to taste
1 egg, lightly beaten
1¼ cups Saltine cracker crumbs
2 Tablespoons olive oil
2 Tablespoons unsalted butter

Combine the crabmeat, corn, onion, bell pepper and celery in a mixing bowl, and toss well. In another bowl, combine the mayonnaise with the mustard and cayenne pepper. Stir into the crabmeat mixture, and add salt and pepper. Then using a rubber spatula, gently fold in the egg and ¼ cup of the cracker crumbs. Form the crab mixture into 8 patties. Carefully coat the patties with the remaining 1 cup cracker crumbs. Cover and chill crab cakes for at least 30 minutes, but no longer than a few hours. Heat 1 tablespoon of the oil and 1 tablespoon of the butter in a medium-size skillet. Cook the crab cakes over medium heat until golden on both sides, about 3 minutes per side, adding more oil and butter as necessary. Serve immediately. (2 hours preparation time. Not suitable for freezing.)

Caroline L. Skelton

Caroline Skelton, *daughter-in-law of Representative Ike Skelton (Missouri)*

Pasta & Vegetables

The Congressional Club
would like to thank
Diamond Chef Sponsor

PricewaterhouseCoopers LLP

Pasta & Vegetables

A Birthday and the Burning of the Mortgage

The celebration of 40 successful years as a club was a wonderful event, with a dramatic play and the spectacular burning of the mortgage.

The large cast for the play, "The Congressional Club," was made up of very enthusiastic members of the Club. The play itself had been written by a Club member from Pennsylvania, Nora Lynch Kearns. After the elaborate pageant, Mrs. Harry Truman brought the event to a dramatic close with the burning of the mortgage in a silver bowl.

The bowl was inscribed by the 76th Club and now is on display in the Archives Room.

Mexican Charro Beans
SERVES 10

3 cups dry pinto beans
1 cup salt pork, cubed (or bacon rind)
3 cloves garlic
3 Tablespoons cooking oil
½ onion, chopped

2 small tomatoes, chopped
2 fresh jalapeno peppers, chopped (optional)
1 teaspoon coriander

Pick and remove damaged pinto beans. Wash beans. Place beans in large bowl of water to soak for 4 to 6 hours. This may be done the night before. In a large cooking pot, heat 2 quarts water. Drain beans and add to cooking pot. Add salt pork and garlic. Cover and simmer for 2 hours or until beans are tender. In a separate skillet, sauté onions, tomatoes and coriander. Add sautéed mixture to beans. Additional water may be added if needed. Add jalapeno peppers. Cover and simmer for 15 minutes. Add salt to taste. (Suitable for freezing.)

Ruben Hinojosa

Ruben Hinojosa, *Representative (Texas)*

Teddy Smith's Creamed Potatoes
SERVES 6 TO 8

4 pounds Idaho baking potatoes
1 quart heavy cream
1 stick unsalted butter
salt and pepper to taste

Peel the potatoes and cut into 1" cubes. Place the potatoes into a double boiler or heavy-bottomed stock pot and cover with heavy cream. Place the stick of butter in the middle of the pot. Cook the potatoes at a simmer until done. Watch them carefully as they may foam up and boil over. When you add the salt and pepper to taste, the potatoes will thicken. They can be served in this state or put into a buttered casserole with bread crumbs and Parmesan cheese and reheated to serve later. If you plan to reheat this recipe, do it slowly at about 300°F. (1 hour preparation time. Not suitable for freezing.)

Freda Solomon

Mrs. Gerald Solomon, *wife of Representative (New York)*

Absolutely Scrumptious Scalloped Potatoes

Russet potatoes, sliced thin (food processor works great)
yellow onions, small dice
whole cream, half and half or milk (cream or half and half taste best)
salt and pepper to taste
grated cheddar cheese for topping (optional)

Use butter or Pam to grease an open, flat baking dish. Slice potatoes and dice onions. Layer into pan in 2 or 3 layers. Leave plenty of room for the cream so it does not boil over in the oven. Add salt and pepper with each layer. Pour in cream or milk. Put into a 425° oven for 20 minutes. Reduce heat to 350° for 45 minutes or until they feel tender when pierced by a fork. Timing depends on amount of potatoes. Grated cheese can be added 15 minutes before removal from oven if you wish. (20 minutes preparation time.)

Paula J Swift

Mrs. Al Swift, *wife of former Representative (Washington)*

Grandma Hospodor's Pirohi (Perogie)

Dough:
5 cups flour
3 whole eggs, beaten
1 teaspoon salt
1½ cups water (reserve ½ cup)

Filling:
½ pound extra sharp cheddar cheese
6 cooked and mashed potatoes

Topping:
½ pound butter
3 large yellow onions, chopped

Dough:

Mix beaten eggs and 1 cup of water. Add mixture to flour and mix well. Knead with hands for 5 minutes or mix in batches in a food processor. Dough should not be sticky. Add flour or water as needed until dough is smooth and soft to the touch, but not sticky. Shape into 4 balls. Cover and let stand for 30 minutes. Roll out dough to ¼″ thickness on a lightly floured board. Cut into squares of 2³/₈″.

Filling:

Grate cheese. While still hot, add cheese to potatoes that have been mashed. Mix thoroughly. If cheese does not melt, place in microwave in 30 second intervals on 75% power. Do not attempt to fill dough until filling is cold. (I recommend making filling the night before.) Fill dough by placing 1 teaspoon of mixture into center of square. Fold dough over to form a triangle. Moisten edges and press with a fork. Place on floured surface until ready to cook. May be frozen.

Cooking:

Bring 8 cups of water to a boil. Cook 2 dozen pirohi at a time. Cook for 8 minutes on rapid boil. Remove by slotted spoon and run under cold water. Drain. Sauté onions in butter until onions are clear. Add pirohi. You may continue to brown or serve as is.

This is a wonderful recipe for children. They love to press the pirohi closed with a fork. I have many fond memories of making pirohi with my grandmother and my brothers and cousins. (2-3 hours preparation time. Suitable for freezing.)

Mrs. Frank Pallone, Jr., *wife of Representative (New Jersey)*

NEW HAMPSHIRE

Lilacs are some of the most popular ornamental plants found in American gardens. Although they will grow in almost any soil, they do especially well in moist, fertile soils. Purple lilac can grow up to nine feet tall and produces a white flower with a very enjoyable scent.

Arroz Con Chili Y Queso
(Rice With Chili and Cheese)

4 cups cooked rice

1 pint sour cream or substitute

2 4-ounce cans sliced black olives

1 6-ounce can chopped green chilies
   (for spicier mixture add a second can)

1 pound shredded
   Monterey Jack cheese

paprika

salt

pepper

While rice is cooking, prepare mixture of sour cream, green chilies, black olives and paprika. Stir until blended. Add salt and pepper to satisfy taste.

Use 2 to 3 quart ovenproof casserole dish. Spray inside with Pam. Layer cooked rice to cover bottom of dish. Follow with layer of sour cream mixture. (Spread to cover entire rice layer.) Follow with layer of shredded cheese. Repeat layering to top of dish. Finish with shredded cheese. Bake in a 315° oven for 45 minutes to 1 hour, or until bubbling and cheese on top is completely melted. Recipe can be doubled or tripled as needed. Increase cooking time for larger casserole.

Mrs. Richard Bryan, *wife of Senator (Nevada)*

Curried Apricot Rice
SERVES 6

2 teaspoons butter

½ cup chopped onion

2½ cups low-sodium chicken broth

¼ cup dried apricots

1 teaspoon curry powder

1 cup brown rice

2 Tablespoons chopped parsley

Melt the butter in a medium saucepan. Add the onion and sauté until soft and translucent. Add broth, apricots and curry powder and bring to a boil. Add the rice. Cover, reduce heat and simmer for 30 minutes or until the liquid is absorbed. Stir in the chopped parsley. (15 minutes preparation time.)

Mrs. Robert Giaimo, *wife of former Representative (Connecticut)*

Tasty Tortellini
SERVES 4

3 packages cheese tortellini (prepackaged from the dairy section at store)
1 pint heavy cream
1 stick butter

½ teaspoon ground nutmeg
salt and pepper to taste
1 cup Parmesan cheese

Prepare tortellini per directions on package (do not overcook). Drain and put aside. In saucepan bring cream, butter, nutmeg, salt and pepper to a low simmer. Do not boil! Add pasta and ½ of cheese. Stir about 1 minute until creamy. Top with remaining cheese and serve. For a tasty variation, try topping with chicken or ham. (30 minutes preparation time.)

Shelly Hefner

Shelly Hefner, *daughter of Representative Bill Hefner (North Carolina)*

Sautéed Collard Greens with Garlic and Scallions
SERVES 4

2 teaspoons olive oil
3 cups shredded or
   chopped collard greens

1 clove garlic, minced
2 scallions, minced
1 Tablespoon crumbled feta cheese

In a large nonstick skillet or a wok heat oil over medium heat. Add collards and garlic and sauté, stirring constantly, until collards are just wilted or about 4 minutes. Add scallions just before collards are finished cooking. Serve hot, sprinkled with feta. Variation: Sauté a medium size, chopped ripe tomato with collards and garlic. (20 minutes preparation time. Suitable for freezing.)

Alma Rangel

Mrs. Charles Rangel, *wife of Representative (New York)*

Crawfish Fettuccine
SERVES 12

3 sticks butter
3 onions, chopped
2 green bell peppers, chopped
3 stalks celery, chopped
3 cloves garlic, minced
½ cup flour

1 pint half and half
1 pound Kraft jalapeno cheese, cubed
3 pounds crawfish tails
12 ounces fettuccine
Tabasco to taste
1 Tablespoon chopped parsley

In a saucepan, melt butter and sauté onions, bell pepper and celery until tender. Add garlic, flour and half and half. Mix well. Simmer on low heat for 20 minutes, stirring occasionally. Add cheese and stir until melted. Add crawfish and mix well. Meanwhile, cook noodles, drain and cool. Combine noodles and sauce. Add Tabasco to taste. Pour into 2 greased 3-quart casseroles or a greased 6-quart casserole dish. Bake uncovered in a 300° oven for 20 minutes until heated thoroughly. Garnish with parsley. (1 hour preparation time. Suitable for freezing.)

Catherine Cooksey

Catherine Cooksey, *daughter of Representative John Cooksey (Louisiana)*

Creamed Corn Baked

3 eggs
1 cup milk
3 Tablespoons self rising flour
⅛ teaspoon black pepper

2 cups creamed corn
3 Tablespoons sugar
½ teaspoon salt
2 Tablespoons butter, melted

Combine all ingredients. Pour into a greased 1½ quart casserole dish. Bake at 325° for 1 hour. (1 hour preparation time.)

Faye Flippo

Mrs. Ronnie Flippo, *wife of former Representative (Alabama)*

Pasta and Herbed Tomatoes and Cheese
SERVES 8

1 pound small pasta shells
8 medium tomatoes, peeled, seeded
  and coarsely chopped
4 cloves garlic, minced
1 cup chopped fresh basil
2 Tablespoons chopped fresh mint
2 teaspoons salt

1 teaspoon freshly ground pepper
¾ teaspoon red pepper flakes
½ cup olive oil
½ cup freshly grated Parmesan cheese
½ pound Fontina cheese, finely diced
fresh cracked pepper

In a medium bowl, toss together tomatoes, garlic, basil, mint, salt, black pepper, red pepper flakes and olive oil. Let stand at room temperature for 2 to 3 hours, tossing occasionally. Cook pasta until al dente. Drain and transfer to a large serving bowl. Spoon off ¼ cup of liquid from tomato mixture and toss with pasta to coat. While pasta is still warm, add Parmesan and Fontina and mix until cheeses begin to melt. Add tomatoes with liquid and blend until mixed. Serve warm or at room temperature. (1 hour preparation time.)

Bill Archer

Bill Archer, *Representative (Texas)*

Wild Rice Casserole
SERVES 8

1½ cups wild rice, washed thoroughly
3 cups hot chicken broth
1 cup dry white wine

1 cup pecan halves
1 can sliced water chestnuts
1 cup golden raisins

Put rice, broth and wine in a buttered 1½ quart casserole. Cover and bake in a 400° oven about 1 hour, until rice is tender but not too soft. Before serving, stir in pecans, water chestnuts and raisins. I have also used mushrooms, red grapes and almonds. (10 minutes preparation time. Not suitable for freezing.)

Dale E. Kildee

Dale E. Kildee, *Representative (Michigan)*

Red Beans and Rice
SERVES 12

2 pounds dried red beans
1 ham bone
1 pound smoked pork chop
1 ham slice, cut in small pieces
1 chopped green pepper
1 cup chopped onion
1 cup chopped celery

6 cloves garlic
2 bay leaves
½ cup chopped green onions
½ cup chopped parsley
½ teaspoon thyme
salt and pepper to taste
1½ pounds smoked sausage
Tabasco optional

Soak red beans overnight in cold water. Drain beans and place in large pot with other ingredients, except sausage. Add water to cover and get a slow boil going. Simmer for 1 hour. Blend ½ pound sausage with a little water and add to beans with the rest of the sausage sliced. Simmer another hour. Remove about 1 cup of beans and mash them to a paste, and return to beans to thicken beans. You can also mash beans in a pot with a heavy spoon. Add more water if needed to get thick consistency; add seasoning to taste. Ham and sausage may be salty, so taste. Add Tabasco to taste. Cook rice and serve beans over rice. (4 hours preparation time. Suitable for freezing.)

Dan Miller, *Representative (Florida)*

Our Favorite Baked Beans
SERVES 8 TO 10

1 pound ground beef
1 cup ketchup
1 2-pound can pork and beans
½ cup light molasses
½ cup chopped onion
½ cup brown sugar

1 medium chopped green pepper
½ cup Heinz BBQ sauce with
    mushrooms or ½ cup Heinz hickory
    flavored BBQ sauce
dash of garlic powder and salt

Brown and drain ground beef. Sauté green pepper and onion in grease from beef. Add remaining ingredients. Mix well. Tightly cover and bake in a 350° oven for 20 minutes. Uncover and cook for an additional 15 minutes. (Suitable for freezing.)

Trent Lott, *Senator (Mississippi)*

Favorite Lasagne
SERVES 8

1 pound hot Italian sausage
1 pound lean ground beef
2 cloves garlic, minced
1 28-ounce can crushed tomatoes
2 6-ounce cans tomato paste
1 Tablespoon dried basil
1 Tablespoon dried oregano

1 Tablespoon dried marjoram
1 16-ounce package lasagne
3 cups small curd cottage cheese
½ cup grated Parmesan
2 Tablespoons dried parsley
2 eggs, beaten
1 pound shredded mozzarella

Brown meat; spoon off fat. Add next 6 ingredients. Simmer for 30 minutes, stirring occasionally. Cook noodles in a large amount of boiling water until tender; drain and rinse in cold water. Combine next 4 ingredients. Ladle enough sauce into a 13″ × 9″ × 2″ baking dish to cover bottom of dish. Place noodles side by side over sauce. Top with sauce and dollop with cottage cheese mixture. Repeat layers with remaining ingredients. Top with shredded mozzarella. Bake in a preheated 375° oven for 30 minutes. Let stand 10 minutes before cutting in squares. May be made ahead and refrigerated. (30 minutes preparation time.)

Doc Hastings, *Representative (Washington)*

Butter Bean Casserole
SERVES 8

2 packages frozen lima beans
   (or fresh butter beans, cooked)
1 large can or approximately 3 cups
   diced or crushed tomatoes

1 small onion, chopped
1 green pepper, chopped
1 cup grated sharp cheddar cheese

Mix butter beans, tomatoes, onion, green pepper and one half of the cheese. Place mixture into a greased casserole dish and top with the remaining half of the grated cheese. Bake in 350° oven until warm and bubbly. This dish is best made with fresh butter beans and tomatoes. (20 minutes preparation time. Suitable for freezing.)

Mrs. Marshall (Mark) Sanford, wife of *Representative (South Carolina)*

Easy Spinach Casserole
SERVES 6 TO 8

2 packages frozen chopped spinach
1 can cream of celery soup
2 eggs
¾ cup mayonnaise
½ cup freshly shredded Parmesan
   or Romano cheese

¾ cup shredded sharp cheddar cheese
1 teaspoon fresh lemon juice
15 Ritz crackers, crumbled
¼ cup butter, melted

Cook the spinach according to directions until completely defrosted. The spinach can still be cool to the touch. Place the spinach in a colander and drain as thoroughly as possible. In a 1½ quart casserole dish, mix the soup, eggs and mayonnaise. Add the spinach, cheeses and lemon juice. Mix well and smooth the top. In a separate bowl, mix the cracker crumbs with the melted butter until the crumbs have absorbed all of the butter. Spread the crumb mixture on the top of casserole. Bake at 325° for about 45 minutes. (1 hour preparation time. Not suitable for freezing.)

James M Talent

James M. Talent, *Representative (Missouri)*

Red Cabbage
SERVES 6 TO 8

3 pounds red cabbage, cored and
   shredded
1½ cups beef broth
½ cup firmly packed brown sugar

½ cup cider vinegar
4 Tablespoons butter (½ stick)
¼ teaspoon freshly ground pepper
salt to taste if necessary

Combine all the ingredients in a 10 to 12 quart stainless steel pot. Bring to a boil, stir and cover. Simmer over low heat, stirring occasionally, for 1 hour and 15 minutes. Transfer to a casserole dish. If serving at a later time, reheat at 350° for 15 to 20 minutes. (Suitable for freezing a short time.)

Christiane English

Mrs. Philip English, *wife of Representative (Pennsylvania)*

Excelsior House Bacon-Wrapped Beans
SERVES 10 TO 12

2 cans whole green beans
½ pound bacon strips, cut in half
1 cup bean juice

¼ cup brown sugar
½ teaspoon allspice
salt and pepper

Wrap half slices of bacon around 10 to 12 beans; fasten with toothpicks and lay in a square glass baking dish. Mix bean juice and brown sugar together and pour over beans. Sprinkle bundles with allspice, salt and pepper. Bake at 400° for about 25 minutes or until bacon browns. Turn once during cooking and baste. (25 minutes preparation time. Suitable for freezing.)

Max Sandlin, *Representative (Texas)*

Company Sweet Potatoes
SERVES 12

6 large sweet potatoes
1 cup sugar
2 eggs
⅓ stick margarine

½ cup milk
1 teaspoon vanilla
1 teaspoon salt

Peel and slice sweet potatoes. Cook in boiling water to cover for 15 to 20 minutes or until tender. Drain thoroughly and mash. Whip sweet potatoes, sugar, eggs, margarine, milk, vanilla and salt until smooth. Spoon mixture into lightly buttered 13″ × 9″ × 2″ baking dish.

Topping:

1 cup brown sugar
⅓ cup flour

1 cup chopped pecans
⅓ stick margarine

Sift together brown sugar and flour. Sprinkle over top of potatoes. Sprinkle chopped pecans over topping and drizzle with melted margarine. Bake for 25 minutes at 325°. (25 minutes preparation time. Suitable for freezing.)

Mac Collins, *Representative (Georgia)*

Sweet Potato Casserole

3 cups cooked and mashed
    sweet potatoes
1 stick butter

1 cup sugar
½ cup Pet milk
1 egg

Topping:
1 cup brown sugar
⅓ cup butter (cut in)

⅓ cup flour
1 cup pecans, chopped

Mix the first 5 ingredients and pour into greased casserole. Top with the topping ingredients mixed together. Bake at 350° for 30 minutes.

Ruth Cross

Mrs. Ruth Cross, *daughter of former Representative Claude A. Fuller (Arkansas)*

Raclette Potatoes
SERVES 6

6 large baking potatoes
¼ cup butter, softened
1 clove garlic, crushed
1 teaspoon salt

¼ teaspoon pepper
1 8-ounce package sliced Swiss cheese
paprika

Bake potatoes. Blend the butter, salt, pepper and garlic. Slice 6 slits into each potato, not cutting all of the way through. Spread each slice with the butter mix. Fit the cheese pieces into the slits. Bake in a 350° oven for 10 to 20 minutes. Sprinkle with paprika.

Joe Knollenberg

Joe Knollenberg, *Representative (Michigan)*

Green Beans with Stewed Tomatoes and Mushrooms

SERVES 10

2 pounds fresh whole beans or 3 packages frozen beans
2 large shallots or 1 small onion, finely chopped
1 clove garlic
4 Tablespoons butter or margarine
1 pound mushrooms, sliced
4 cups stewed tomatoes without juice,
    coarsely chopped (2 28-ounce cans)
2 teaspoons salt
1 teaspoon pepper

Snap ends from beans and place in boiling, unsalted water. Bring water to boil again and cook for 2 minutes. If using frozen beans, cook according to package directions but be careful not to over-cook. (May microwave beans.) Peel and finely chop shallots and garlic. Sauté in butter over low heat until soft, about 4 minutes. Add sliced mushrooms and continue to cook at low heat for another 5 minutes. Add coarsely chopped tomatoes and raise heat to medium. Simmer for 10 minutes and add green beans. Cook for an additional 5 minutes until beans are warmed. Season with salt and pepper. (Suitable for freezing.)

Gina Sangmeister

Gina Sangmeister, *daughter-in-law of former Representative George Sangmeister (Illinois)*

PURPLE VIOLET
(VIOLA PEDATA)

NEW JERSEY

According to Greek myth, the God Zeus loved the nymph Io and turned her into a white heifer to hide her from his wife, Hera. Io, unhappy about having to eat the rough grass, began to cry. Her tears so moved Zeus that he changed her tears into sweet smelling violets.

Vidalia Onion Pie
SERVES 12

2 pounds of onions, thinly sliced
(preferably Vidalia)
1 stick of butter
3 eggs, well beaten
1 cup sour cream (or light
sour cream)

¼ teaspoon salt
½ teaspoon white pepper
¼ teaspoon Tabasco sauce
2 pie shells (unbaked)
grated Parmesan cheese

Sauté the onions in butter. Combine the eggs and sour cream mixture. Add to onions. Season the mixture with salt, pepper and Tabasco. Pour into the 2 pastry shells and top with Parmesan cheese. Bake at 400° for 20 minutes. Reduce the temperature to 325° and bake for an additional 20 minutes. This is a wonderful side dish with steak, lamb or chicken. (40 minutes preparation time. Suitable for freezing.)

Nancy Weldon

Mrs. Dave Weldon, *wife of Representative (Florida)*

Cousin Bonnie's Spicy Peanut Cous-Cous
SERVES 8

1 box cous-cous
2 cups chicken broth
2 navel oranges or 1 can Mandarin
oranges

Dressing:
¼ cup Chinese rice vinegar
3 Tablespoons olive oil
4 Tablespoons creamy peanut
butter

½ cup raisins
1 red pepper, chopped
½ cup roasted dry peanuts
¼ cup chopped chives

2 Tablespoons honey
Dash cayenne pepper or red pepper
flakes
2 Tablespoons orange juice

Cook cous-cous with chicken broth. While cooking, cut up oranges into ½" pieces. Add raisins, red pepper, nuts and chives. Mix dressing in jar and shake until mixed well. Add cous-cous to dry ingredients. Mix with dressing just prior to serving. (20 minutes preparation time. Not suitable for freezing.)

Fred Upton

Fred Upton, *Representative (Michigan)*

Creamy Whipped Potatoes
SERVES 12

5 pounds medium size potatoes

1 8-ounce container whipped cream cheese with chives

1 teaspoon garlic powder

¼ teaspoon ground black pepper

6 Tablespoons margarine or butter (¾ stick), optional

1 cup heavy or whipping cream

¼ cup sliced almonds

paprika

About 1½ hours before serving, peel potatoes; cut each into quarters. In a 5-quart sauce pot over high heat, boil potatoes, 1 teaspoon of salt and enough water to cover. Reduce heat to low; cover and simmer for 20 minutes or until potatoes are tender. Drain well. Preheat oven to 375°. In large bowl, combine potatoes, cream cheese, garlic powder, pepper, 4 tablespoons margarine or butter (½ stick) and 1 teaspoon salt. With potato masher, mash until smooth. Gradually add heavy cream, mixing well after each addition. Grease 13" × 9" glass baking dish or a shallow 3-quart casserole. Spoon potatoes into baking dish. To prepare this dish a day ahead, cover and refrigerate. Dot potatoes with 2 tablespoons margarine or butter (¼ stick). Sprinkle with sliced almonds and paprika. Bake for 30 minutes or until top is golden. An hour before serving, put the potatoes in the oven and heat for 30 minutes at 375°. (1½ hours preparation time. Not suitable for freezing.)

Mrs. William Clay, wife of Representative (Missouri)

Mexican Lasagna

2 pounds ground beef

1 medium onion, chopped

2 Tablespoons chili powder

3 cups tomato sauce

1 can sliced black olives

1 can green chiles, chopped

1 teaspoon sugar

1 carton cottage cheese

1 egg

8 ounces grated Monterey Jack cheese

4 ounces grated cheddar cheese

12 corn tortillas

Cook beef, onion and chili powder together and then add tomato sauce, olives, chiles and sugar. Beat egg and add to carton of cottage cheese. Starting with meat sauce, layer tortillas, cottage cheese and grated cheese in several layers. Bake at 350°. (30 minutes preparation time.)

Mrs. James Inhofe, wife of Senator (Oklahoma)

Spinach Timbales
SERVES 6 TO 9

1 package frozen chopped spinach
  or 1½ pounds fresh (9 cups cleaned
  and stems removed)
1 cup light cream
2 eggs

1 teaspoon salt
¼ teaspoon pepper
⅛ teaspoon nutmeg
¼ cup grated Jarlsburg or Gruyere cheese

Cook spinach, squeeze all the water out. Place cream, eggs and seasonings in a blender. Blend for a few seconds. Add spinach and cheese and blend for a few seconds longer. Butter 6 4-ounce timbale molds or 9 muffin cups and fill ¾ full with spinach mixture. Preheat oven to 350°. Set molds in a pan of boiling water. Water should come ½ to ⅔ of the way up sides of molds. Bake about 25 minutes. Let cool 5 minutes before removing molds. Timbales may be refrigerated at this point and reheated later. (50 minutes preparation time. Not suitable for freezing.)

Caryll Kyl

Mrs. Jon Kyl, *wife of Senator (Arizona)*

Risotto Milanese
SERVES 4

1 shallot, minced
2 Tablespoons butter, clarified
1 cup rice
1 cup shiitake mushrooms, sliced
pinch saffron

2 cups champagne
2-3 cups chicken broth
dash salt
dash white pepper
½ cup Parmesan cheese, grated

Sauté shallot in butter until golden. Add rice and sauté until butter is absorbed and rice is golden, not brown. Add mushrooms. Boil saffron, champagne and 2 cups of broth. Add 1 cup of this mixture to rice and simmer, gradually adding 2 more cups of mixture over 10 minutes and stirring constantly. Lower heat and cook for 10 minutes, always adding moisture and stirring. Use last cup of chicken broth if needed. After 20 minutes, add Parmesan cheese, salt and pepper to taste. Stir and serve immediately. (40 minutes preparation time. Not suitable for freezing.)

Ruthie McIntosh

Mrs. David McIntosh, *wife of Representative (Indiana)*

Cousin Tib's Peas and Water Chestnuts
SERVES 16 TO 20

½ cup butter or margarine
1 cup chopped onion
1 cup chopped celery
1 large sweet red pepper, chopped
4 cups frozen English (green) peas
1 18-ounce can sliced water chestnuts

1 10½-ounce can condensed
   cream of celery soup (undiluted)
¼ teaspoon salt
¼ teaspoon pepper
1 cup chow mein noodles

Melt butter in large skillet over medium heat. Add onion, celery and red pepper. Cook, stirring constantly until tender. Stir in peas and next 4 ingredients. Spoon into a lightly greased 2 quart baking dish. Sprinkle with chow mein noodles. Bake at 350° for 20 minutes or until hot. (20 minutes preparation time.)

Annie Laurie Rankin Sanders

Annie Laurie Rankin Sanders, *daughter of former Representative John E. Rankin (Mississippi)*

Sweet Potato Soufflé
SERVES 6

3 cups mashed sweet potatoes
  (peeled, cubed and boiled)
1 cup sugar
2 beaten eggs
¾ stick margarine
½ teaspoon nutmeg

½ cup drained pineapple
½ teaspoon salt
½ cup milk
1 teaspoon vanilla
½ teaspoon cinnamon

Topping:
⅓ cup flour
½ stick margarine

½ cup packed brown sugar
1 cup chopped pecans

After boiling sweet potatoes until tender, mash (use blender or processor.) Then mix in the remaining ingredients. Pour into baking dish. Mix topping ingredients thoroughly and sprinkle on top. Bake in 350° oven for 30 minutes. (30 minutes preparation time. Suitable for freezing.)

Carolina Reyes

Mrs. Silvestre Reyes, *wife of Representative (Texas)*

Mama's Cracked Wheat "Pilaf"
SERVES 4 TO 6

1 cube butter
handful of broken vermicelli
2 green onions, sliced, tops and all
1 cup cracked wheat

1 small can mushrooms with juice
1 10½-ounce can beef bouillon
  or consommé
1 10½-ounce can water

Cook butter, vermicelli and green onions slowly until vermicelli is brown. Add cracked wheat, mushrooms, bouillon and water. Bake uncovered 45 minutes at 300°. Will hold for serving indefinitely, and reheats well. (20 minutes preparation time. Suitable for freezing.)

Nancy Schulze

Mrs. Dick Schulze, *wife of former Representative (Pennsylvania)*

Pasta with Caramelized Scallops and Rosemary Beurre Blanc

SERVES 6

YUCCA
(YUCCA ELATA)
SPECIES SENT: YUCCA ARKANSANA

NEW MEXICO

Yucca elata is a widespread species that occurs in deserts and grasslands from southwestern Texas to New Mexico, Arizona, and south to Mexico. Also called soaptree yucca, the roots are used to make soap for washing clothes and shampooing hair.

¾ pound fresh or good quality fettuccine
1½ pounds sea scallops

Beurre Blanc:

½ cup dry white wine
3 Tablespoons white wine vinegar
¼ cup chopped shallot
1 Tablespoon chopped garlic
2 teaspoons chopped fresh
  rosemary leaves

½ cup heavy cream
1 stick (½ cup) cold butter
  cut into pieces
1 Tablespoon fresh lemon juice
2 Tablespoons olive oil

Garnish: chopped fresh rosemary and parsley leaves

In a large pot bring salted water to a boil for pasta. Remove tough muscle from side of scallop if necessary.

Beurre Blanc:
In a small, heavy saucepan simmer wine, vinegar, shallot, garlic and rosemary until reduced to about 3 tablespoons. Add cream and simmer until liquid is reduced by about half. Add butter all at once and cook over moderately low heat, swirling pan constantly, just until cream and butter are incorporated (consistency of Hollandaise.) Remove from heat and stir in lemon juice, salt and pepper to taste.

Pat scallops dry and season with salt and pepper. In large, heavy skillet heat oil over moderately high heat. Arrange scallops, without crowding in skillet, and cook until golden brown on all sides. You may need to remove excess liquid from pan to ensure browning. Cook pasta in boiling water until al dente and drain. Transfer pasta to a heated bowl and mix sauce into pasta. Arrange scallops on top of pasta and garnish with herbs. (40 minutes preparation time. Not suitable for freezing.)

Linda Dooley

Mrs. Calvin Dooley, *wife of Representative (California)*

Broccoli Soufflé
SERVES 6 TO 8

16-ounce bag frozen broccoli cuts
½ cup mayonnaise
1 can cream of chicken soup
1 cup shredded cheddar cheese
1 egg
1 medium onion
20-25 crushed Ritz crackers

Steam broccoli, drain any excess water. Mix broccoli, mayonnaise, soup, cheese, egg and chopped onion together. Pour into ungreased 9″ × 13″ Pyrex, top with crushed Ritz crackers. Bake at 350° for 30 minutes. Let stand for 10 to 15 minutes prior to serving. (40 minutes preparation time. Not suitable for freezing.)

Angelique M. Payton

Angelique Payton, *daughter-in-law of Representative Elton Gallegly (California)*

Broiled Tomatoes
SERVES 6

6 medium tomatoes
½ cup soft bread crumbs
¼ cup grated Parmesan cheese
2 Tablespoons snipped parsley
2 teaspoons snipped chives
¼ teaspoon pepper
⅛ teaspoon garlic powder

¼ teaspoon dried basil
¼ teaspoon dried dill
⅛ teaspoon dried thyme
⅛ teaspoon dried oregano
dash salt
3 Tablespoons butter, divided

Slice off tops of tomatoes. Place tomatoes in 8″ × 8″ × 2″ baking dish. Combine bread crumbs, Parmesan cheese, parsley, chives, pepper, garlic powder, basil, dill, thyme, oregano and salt. Spoon mixture over tomatoes. Top each with 1½ teaspoons butter. Bake at 350° about 25 minutes. (30 minutes preparation time. Not suitable for freezing.)

Mary Virginia Bliley

Mrs. Tom Bliley, *wife of Representative (Virginia)*

Macaroni with Spinach Sauce

3 pounds fresh spinach
salt and pepper
2-3 serrano chilies, chopped
3 Tablespoons butter
3 Tablespoons flour

2 cups hot milk
1 cup cream
2 pounds macaroni
1 cup grated Parmesan cheese

Wash the spinach and discard stems. Cook the spinach with water that clings to leaves. Add chilies and salt to taste. Remove from heat. Puree spinach mixture. Melt butter and stir in the flour. Add milk, cream, salt and pepper to taste. Stir with whisk. Sauce will thicken. Stir in spinach puree. Cook macaroni as directed. Drain thoroughly. In an oven-proof dish, add half of the spinach sauce. Add the macaroni and top with remaining sauce. Sprinkle with grated cheese. Bake in preheated oven at 350° for 20 minutes, until the cheese is golden brown. (Not suitable for freezing.)

Mrs. Ruben Hinojosa, *wife of Representative (Texas)*

Carrot-Yam Tzimmes
SERVES 8

2 pounds yams, pared and cut
   into ¾" slices
1 pound carrots, scraped and cut
   into ¾" slices
½ cup dried prunes

½ cup dried apricots
1 cup orange juice
1 Tablespoon grated lemon rind
¼ teaspoon ground nutmeg
¼ teaspoon ground ginger

Cook yams and carrots in 1" of simmering water in covered pan until barely tender (about 15 minutes). Drain. Preheat oven to moderate (350°.) Grease 2½ quart casserole. Place yams and carrots in casserole; stir in dried prunes and apricots. Pour orange juice over vegetables and fruits. Sprinkle with lemon rind, nutmeg and ginger. Can be prepared ahead to this point. Bake in a 350° oven for 30 minutes or until vegetables are tender to fork. Garnish with thin strips of orange rind. (50 minutes preparation time.)

Mrs. Jim Lloyd, *wife of former Representative (California)*

Light Lasagne
SERVES 12

lasagne noodles
1 cup chopped onion
1 Tablespoon olive oil
1 8-ounce light or nonfat cream
   cheese
1½ cup cream style nonfat cottage
   cheese
1 egg, beaten
2 Tablespoons basil, crushed
salt and pepper to taste

1 10-ounce can cream of mushroom
   soup, low fat, undiluted
½ cup skim milk
½ cup dry wine
1 pound frozen cocktail shrimp, thawed
1 6½-ounce can crab or artificial crabmeat
¼ cup grated Parmesan
½ cup grated sharp American or
   cheddar cheese

Cook lasagne according to directions. Sauté onions in olive oil. Blend in cream cheese. Stir in cottage cheese, egg, basil, salt and pepper. Combine soup, milk and wine. Stir in shrimp and crab. Layer cheese mixture over 4 lasagne noodles and top with soup and fish mixture. Repeat twice more. Sprinkle with Parmesan cheese. Bake uncovered at 350° for 45 minutes. Top with grated cheese. Bake 2 minutes, until bubbly. Let stand 10 minutes before cutting. (35 minutes preparation time.)

Mrs. Dirk Kempthorne, *wife of Senator (Idaho)*

Potatoes Supreme
SERVES 10

1 package unthawed frozen hash browns
1 can cream of chicken soup
1 cup Velveeta, grated
3 Tablespoons minced onion

8 ounces sour cream
½ cup margarine, melted
1 teaspoon salt
1½ cups corn flakes, crushed

Put potatoes, salt, onion and cheese in a 9" × 13" pan. Mix soup, sour cream and margarine. Add to potatoes. For topping, mix ½ cup melted margarine with 1½ cups crushed corn flakes. Spread on top of potatoes. Bake in a 325° oven for approximately 30 minutes. (15 minutes preparation time. Suitable for freezing.)

Stanley Greigg, *former Representative (Iowa)*

Roasted Potatoes
SERVES 8

2 pounds new potatoes, as small as possible
3 cloves garlic, peeled and chopped
¼ cup butter
1 teaspoon pepper
juice and grated peel of 1 lemon
1 Tablespoon dried parsley
mixed seasonings such as Mrs. Dash

Preheat oven to 400°. Wash and drip dry potatoes on paper towels. Combine with remaining ingredients, except for lemon, in roasting pan and cover with foil. Bake for 20 minutes, then uncover and bake for 15 minutes until golden brown. Sprinkle with lemon juice and lemon peel. (15 minutes preparation time.)

Carolyn Hobson

Mrs. David Hobson, *wife of Representative (Ohio)*

Vi's Hungarian Noodles
SERVES 8

2 cups flour
2 eggs
2 Tablespoons water

Put flour on pastry board. Make a "well" in center. Break eggs into well. Add water. Starting in the center, pull flour into well, mixing thoroughly to make a stiff dough. Knead until smooth. Place under glass bowl for about 10 minutes. Roll out on lightly floured board until very thin. Cut in 3" strips. Place strips on top of each other. Cut into fine strips crosswise (or lengthwise for longer noodles). Cook in salted boiling water for 5 minutes or until al dente. Rinse and drain. May be added to soups or casseroles. (5 minutes preparation time. Not suitable for freezing.)

Olga Esch

Mrs. Marvin Esch, *wife of former Representative (Michigan)*

Sweet Potato Casserole
SERVES 10 TO 12

3 cups canned sweet potatoes, mashed ½ teaspoon vanilla
½ cup sugar ½ stick butter, melted
2 eggs, beaten ½ cup milk
½ teaspoon salt

Topping:
½ cup brown sugar 1 cup nuts, chopped
½ cup flour ½ stick butter, melted

Combine in food processor sweet potatoes, sugar, eggs, salt, vanilla, butter and milk. Spoon into 9″ × 13″ baking dish. Mix together until crumbly, brown sugar, flour, nuts and butter. Spread over sweet potato mixture. Bake at 350° for 35 minutes. (45 minutes preparation time. Suitable for freezing.)

Julia H. Doolittle

Mrs. John Doolittle, *wife of Representative (California)*

Yam Cheeselets
SERVES 8

4 yams, cooked and sliced about ¾″ thick
1 Number 2 can crushed pineapple
1 Tablespoon lemon juice
¼ pound Swiss cheese, sliced

Preheat broiler compartment to 550°F. On a well oiled 8″ × 12″ shallow baking pan or ovenproof dish arrange yam slices. Spread each slice with crushed pineapple. Sprinkle with lemon juice. Top with cheese. Place 3″ from source of heat, and broil until cheese melts and bubbles. Serve with any hot meat. (Not suitable for freezing.)

Laura Y Bateman

Mrs. Herbert Bateman, *wife of Representative (Virginia)*

Marinated Carrots
SERVES 10

2 pounds sliced carrots
1 medium bell pepper, diced
1 medium onion, diced
¾ cup sugar
¾ cup white vinegar

¼ cup Wesson oil
1 can undiluted tomato soup
1 teaspoon salt
1 teaspoon pepper
1 teaspoon dry mustard

Boil carrots in unsalted water and drain. Add green pepper and onion. Mix remaining ingredients and add to carrots. Refrigerate overnight. Bake 325° about 30 minutes or until thoroughly heated. Delicious with ham or turkey. Adds great color. (40 minutes preparation time. Suitable for freezing.)

Tricia Lott

Mrs. Trent Lott, *wife of Senator (Mississippi)*

Vegetable Pie
SERVES 8

1 9" unbaked pastry pie shell
2 medium yellow squash, sliced
1 zucchini squash, sliced
1 onion, sliced
1 green or red pepper, sliced
1 pound fresh mushrooms, sliced

1 large tomato, sliced
1 block mozzarella cheese, grated
1 stick butter
2 Tablespoons mayonnaise
½ teaspoon salt
¼ teaspoon pepper

Preheat oven to 325°. Prebake pie shell only slightly in a removable bottom pie pan. (The deep dish kind with fluted sides.) Mix all vegetables, except tomatoes, salt and pepper. Lightly sauté these vegetables in butter to get water out. Line pie shell with sliced tomatoes. Add the sautéed vegetables. Mix grated cheese with 2 tablespoons of mayonnaise until it is pasty. Spread this on top of pie to seal. Bake for 30 minutes. To serve, use hot mitts to push bottom up which removes side of pan. Set pie pan bottom with pie on serving plate. This is great for brunch, luncheon or summer supper and men love it too! (45 minutes preparation time. Not suitable for freezing.)

Lana Bethune

Mrs. Ed Bethune, *wife of former Representative (Arkansas)*

NEW YORK

Pasture rose is a member of the Rosaceae (rose family), a large an easily recognizable plant family. The Rose family is comprised of more than 100 species found in temperate areas of the Northern Hemisphere. In addition to roses, many members of this family are species we frequently enjoy on our tables: strawberries, raspberries, cherries, peaches, apples, and pears.

Penne Pasta and Cheese
SERVES 12

2 Tablespoons (¼ stick) butter
3 large red bell peppers (about
   1½ pounds), cut into ½" pieces
5 stalks celery, diced
salt and pepper
1½ cups whipping cream
1½ cups half and half
1 pound blue cheese, crumbled

1 teaspoon celery seeds
cayenne pepper
3 large egg yolks
½ cup fresh celery leaves, chopped
1 pound penne
¾ cup freshly grated Parmesan
   cheese (about 2 ounces)

Melt butter in heavy large skillet over medium high heat. Add bell peppers and celery; sauté about 7 minutes. Remove from heat. Season with salt and pepper. In medium size saucepan, combine cream, half and half and blue cheese. Stir over low heat until cheese melts. Remove from heat. Add celery seed, cayenne, salt and pepper. Beat yolks in medium bowl; gradually whisk in half of cheese sauce. Return this mixture to saucepan; whisk to blend. Add celery leaves. Butter 13" × 10" × 2" (4 quart) baking dish. Cook pasta in salted boiling water (al dente), occasionally stirring. Drain. Return to same pot; add sauce and vegetables; gently stir to blend. Transfer to baking dish. (Can be made 1 day ahead to this point.) Cover; chill. Let stand at room temperature 1 hour before continuing. Preheat oven to 400°. Sprinkle Parmesan over top of pasta. Bake about 25 minutes until pasta is heated through, sauce is bubbling, and top is beginning to brown. (15 minutes preparation time. Not suitable for freezing.)

Mrs. Ike Skelton, *wife of Representative (Missouri)*

Superb Spinach
SERVES 6

1 package frozen chopped spinach
1 garlic clove, minced
2 slices bacon, chopped fine
½ cup onion, chopped fine

2 Tablespoons flour
1 teaspoon Lawry's seasoned salt
¼ teaspoon Lawry's seasoned pepper
1 cup milk

Cook spinach according to package directions. Drain well. Fry garlic, bacon and onion together until onions are tender and bacon is crisp. Remove from heat and add flour, salt and pepper, and blend thoroughly to a smooth paste. Slowly add milk, stirring constantly to keep smooth. Return to heat and add spinach, mix well, and heat thoroughly. (20 minutes preparation time. Not suitable for freezing.)

Mrs. Robert Badham, *wife of former Representative (California)*

Strawberry Pasta
SERVES 4

2 pints fresh strawberries
1 pound fettuccine
½ cup grated Parmesan cheese
4 Tablespoons butter
½ cup heavy cream

Pureé the strawberries in a food processor or blender. Then strain to remove seeds. Prepare pasta as directed on its package; drain and toss with cheese. Melt the butter with the cream in a small saucepan. Move the pasta to a serving bowl, cover with the strawberries. Add the butter cream sauce and mix well. If desired, garnish with strawberries and mint leaves. (30 minutes preparation time. Not suitable for freezing.)

Erin Bilbray-Kohn, *daughter of former Representative Jim Bilbray (Nevada)*

Pasta Salad

SERVES 12

2 cups uncooked pasta
  (we like penne regate)
2-3 tomatoes, cut up
2 cups broccoli, chopped
1 cup celery, chopped
1 green pepper, sliced
½ cup chopped green onions
  with tops

½ cup chopped parsley
½ cup grated carrot
1 can black olives, drained
4 ounces crumbled feta cheese
½ cup sliced pepperoni
  (usually cut into quarters)

Cook pasta, rinse and drain. Combine and toss all ingredients. Add favorite Italian or Ranch salad dressing. Refrigerate for 1 hour before serving.

Chris Cannon, *Representative (Utah)*

Fried Green Tomatoes

SERVES 4

4 medium green tomatoes
1 cup bread crumbs
2 eggs
½ cup Parmesan cheese
1 cup cooking oil

Cut unpeeled tomatoes into ½″ slices. Beat the eggs in a small bowl. Dip the tomato slices into the egg mixture first; then dip slices into the crushed bread crumbs. Heat the cooking oil in a frying pan. Cook the battered tomato slices in oil until both sides are brown. Drain off excess oil on paper towel, place slices on a dish, and sprinkle with Parmesan cheese. (10 minutes preparation time.)

Mrs. Jim Gibbons, *wife of Representative (Nevada)*

Holiday Mashed Potatoes
SERVES 12

5 pounds red potatoes
8 ounces cream cheese
8 ounces sour cream
2 teaspoons onion salt

1 teaspoon salt
¼ teaspoon pepper
1 stick margarine

Peel and cut up potatoes. Cook in salted boiling water until tender; drain. Mash slightly. Add remaining ingredients and beat until light and fluffy. May be served immediately or kept in the refrigerator for several days. If refrigerated, bake at 350° until heated. (30 minutes preparation time. Not suitable for freezing.)

Carolyn Snowbarger

Mrs. Vince Snowbarger, *wife of Representative (Kansas)*

Prosciutto and Pea Pod Pasta
SERVES 6

2 Tablespoons olive oil
sliced onion
1 clove garlic, minced
1 Tablespoon lemon juice
1 pound fettuccine

¼ cup white wine or chicken stock
¼ cup heavy cream
prosciutto ham
pea pods
basil shredded
pinch salt

Put olive oil in a nonstick pan. Add the sliced onion and sauté until translucent. Add garlic and sauté until it turns light brown. Add white wine (or stock) and reduce the liquid to half. Add heavy cream and again reduce the liquid a bit. It thickens as it cooks. Add the ham (as much as desired), pea pods, several leaves of freshly shredded basil, lemon juice and a pinch of salt. Meantime, the fettuccine should be cooked al dente (about 8 minutes.) Mix all the ingredients together and serve topped with Parmesan or some cheese which has been freshly shredded. (20 minutes preparation time. Not suitable for freezing.)

Dave McClory

Mrs. Robert McClory, *wife of former Representative (Illinois)*

Debe's Vegetable Casserole
SERVES 8 TO 10

2 sacks Birdseye frozen vegetables (water chestnuts, baby carrots, and broccoli)
1 cup celery, diced
1 cup onion, diced
1 cup mayonnaise
1½ cups grated sharp cheese
1 roll Ritz crackers, crushed
½ stick margarine, melted

Cook vegetables until barely tender and drain. Put vegetables in a greased casserole and add celery, onion, sharp cheese, and mayonnaise. Top casserole with Ritz crackers mixed with melted butter. Cook about 30 minutes at 350°. (30 minutes preparation time.)

Barbara Valentine

Mrs. Tim Valentine, *wife of former Representative (North Carolina)*

Okra and Tomato Casserole
SERVES 6 TO 8

3 Tablespoons oil or bacon grease
1 large white onion, chopped
4 cloves garlic, minced
1 20-ounce bag frozen cut okra
1 28-ounce can Italian style tomatoes, cut into large chunks
2 Tablespoons picanté sauce, medium hot
salt and pepper to taste
¼ cup bread crumbs

Over medium heat sauté the chopped onion in oil until soft. Add garlic and stir for 2 minutes. Add okra, stir until soft and ropey. Add tomatoes, cook 5 minutes. Add picanté sauce, salt and pepper. Pour into casserole. Top with bread crumbs. Bake at 350° for about 20 to 30 minutes. (It should be bubbling and bread crumbs brown.) (30 minutes preparation time. Not suitable for freezing.)

Mary Johnston

Mrs. J. Bennett Johnston, *wife of former Senator (Louisiana)*

Sweet Potato Soufflé
SERVES 6 TO 8

½ dozen sweet potatoes
1 stick melted butter
1 cup sugar
5 eggs
2 teaspoons vanilla flavoring
tiny marshmallows

Boil potatoes until soft, then peel. Beat in Mix Master, adding butter, sugar and eggs, 1 at a time. Add flavoring and mix well. Pour in buttered casserole and bake 1 hour at 350°. Before serving cover with marshmallows and brown top. (1 hour preparation time. Not suitable for freezing.)

Natalie C. Grant

Mrs. George Grant, *wife of former Representative (Alabama)*

Squash Casserole
SERVES 6 TO 8

6 medium "yellow neck" squash
½ stick butter or margarine
1 Tablespoon sugar
1½ teaspoons salt
¼ plus teaspoon pepper
1 cup grated sharp cheese
2 hard cooked eggs
paprika

Scrub squash; slice and boil until tender, 10 to 20 minutes. Boil eggs and grate cheese. When squash is tender, drain and mash or mix with electric mixer. Add remaining ingredients, dice egg and mix thoroughly. Pour into well greased round or square 1½ quart casserole. Sprinkle with paprika and bake at 400° for 20 minutes, uncovered. Can be frozen or fixed a day ahead and kept in the refrigerator. Remove from refrigerator 1 hour before baking. (Suitable for freezing.)

Mary Virginia Bliley

Mrs. Tom Bliley, *wife of Representative (Virginia)*

Linguine with Shrimp Scampi and Broccoli
SERVES 4

1¼ pounds medium to large shrimp, shelled and deveined
3 large garlic cloves
salt and pepper to taste

6 Tablespoons olive oil
4 Tablespoons butter
1½ pounds broccoli, medium flowerets
9-10 ounces fresh linguine

Combine garlic, shrimp, pinch of salt and pepper, and 4 tablespoons olive oil in a medium bowl. Cover and marinate in refrigerator at least 1 hour. Remove shrimp from marinade and reserve marinade. Put 2 to 4 tablespoons of butter in a large warm bowl for tossing pasta. Cook broccoli until just tender. Heat remaining 2 tablespoons of olive oil and 2 tablespoons of butter over medium to high heat in a large, heavy skillet. Add shrimp and sauté. Cook pasta uncovered over high heat in boiling water, about 2 minutes for fresh linguine. Drain well. Add linguine to bowl and toss. Add shrimp and broccoli. Add remaining marinade to skillet used to cook shrimp, cook about 1 minute. Pour over pasta and toss until blended. (Not suitable for freezing.)

Laura Margaret Bateman

Laura Margaret Bateman, *daughter of Representative Herb Bateman (Virginia)*

Sweet and Sour Carrots
SERVES 8 TO 10

3 pounds carrots, sliced and cooked tender and crisp

1 onion, sliced
1 green pepper, sliced

Marinade:
1 cup sugar
1 cup oil
1 cup vinegar

1 teaspoon dry mustard
1 can (10-ounce) tomato soup

Cook 3 pounds carrots, sliced thin, until tender and crisp. Make marinade and add to drained carrots. Slice onion and pepper thinly and add to carrot mix. Chill overnight (or at least 6 hours). Drain, add salt and pepper to taste, and serve. (20 minutes preparation time. Not suitable for freezing.)

Mary Jo Smith

Mrs. Robert Smith, *wife of Senator (New Hampshire)*

Caramelized Onion Pudding
SERVES 8 TO 10

8 Tablespoons unsalted butter
6 cups thinly sliced (in rounds) onions
6 large eggs
2 cups heavy cream

4 Tablespoons sugar
2 teaspoons salt
2 teaspoons baking powder
3 Tablespoons all-purpose flour

In skillet over moderate heat, heat butter until hot, but not smoking. Add onions and cook, covered, until softened, about 20 minutes. Remove cover and continue cooking, stirring occasionally, until golden. Remove from heat and reserve. In bowl, beat eggs and slowly whisk in cream. Combine dry ingredients, and slowly whisk into egg mixture. Stir in onion mixture. Pour into a well-buttered 9″ × 13″ casserole and bake in a preheated 350° oven until set, about 45 minutes. Cut into 2″ squares. Serve immediately. (50 minutes preparation time. Not suitable for freezing.)

Bobbi Powell

Mrs. Walter Powell, *wife of former Representative (Ohio)*

White Potato Casserole
SERVES 12

5 pounds large russet potatoes
8 ounces cream cheese
8 ounces sour cream

¼ cup butter or margarine
½ cup grated sharp cheese
2 teaspoons garlic salt or to taste

Peel and cook potatoes. Drain, mash, and add margarine. Add all other ingredients except sour cream and stir well. Fold in sour cream. Put into a 9″ × 2″ × 13″ greased casserole. Bake at 350° to 400° until it gets bubbly (30 minutes). This recipe can be made in advance and refrigerated uncooked. Instant potatoes can be substituted for fresh. This is an Etheridge family favorite. (30 minutes preparation time. Suitable for freezing.)

Faye Etheridge

Mrs. Bob Etheridge, *wife of Representative (North Carolina)*

FLOWERING DOGWOOD
(CORNUS FLORIDA)

NORTH CAROLINA

Found in woodlands from East Texas to Florida, and north to Canada, Cornus florida, make an ideal accent for small yards and patio areas. In the fall their leaves turn a lovely shade of scarlet and the clusters of red berries provide great color and are a wonderful food source for hungry birds.

Texas Drunken Beans

SERVES 5

2 cups pinto beans
1 teaspoon salt
1 clove garlic
small piece pork fat
1 Tablespoon bacon fat

1 medium tomato, chopped
½ green pepper, chopped
2 Tablespoons chopped onion
1 can beer

Cook beans, salt, garlic and pork fat with water to cover, until they are tender. Drain, reserving the liquid. In an earthenware casserole, sauté the tomato, pepper and onion in the bacon fat until soft. Stir in the beans and simmer 5 minutes. Add the reserved liquid and simmer another 10 minutes. Stir in the beer and serve the beans at once, hot. (1 hour 45 minutes preparation time. Suitable for freezing.)

Kika de la Garza

Kika de la Garza, *former Representative (Texas)*

Copper Pennies

SERVES 8

2 pounds carrots, sliced in rounds
   (like pennies)
1 medium onion
3 celery sticks
1 medium green pepper
¾ cup apple cider vinegar

1 can condensed tomato soup
1 cup sugar
1 Tablespoon Worcestershire sauce
1 Tablespoon dry mustard
¼ cup oil

Slice carrots and cook in salted water until tender. Chop onion, celery and green pepper until fine and mix together with carrots in bowl. Mix all other ingredients together in saucepan and bring to a boil. Stir until well blended. Pour hot liquid over vegetable mixture and blend well. Let cool. Refrigerate several hours or overnight. May be served cold or warm. I prefer it cold. (30 minutes preparation time.)

Sally J. Roemer

Mrs. Tim Roemer, *wife of Representative (Indiana)*

String Beans in Tomato Sauce

SERVES 4 TO 6

1 pound fresh green or yellow string beans or 2 10-ounce packages frozen
2 Tablespoons virgin olive oil
2 large onions, peeled and chopped
1 small clove garlic, minced (optional)
2 teaspoons tomato paste
1 8-ounce can tomato sauce or 2-4 fresh tomatoes, peeled and chopped
3 Tablespoons fresh parsley, chopped
1-2 teaspoons dried oregano, or ½ cup fresh oregano leaves torn in small pieces
½ cup fresh dill torn in small pieces
salt and pepper to taste
hot water to cover

Remove tips and strings from green/yellow beans; wash and drain. In a 4-quart saucepan heat the oil and sauté the onions and garlic. Add tomato paste, tomato sauce or fresh tomatoes until sauce is slightly thickened. Add string beans, parsley, oregano, dill, salt and pepper and stir. Add just enough water to cover and cook until tender. This may take 30 to 45 minutes. (45 to 50 minutes preparation time. Not suitable for freezing.)

Evangeline Charas-Gekas

Mrs. George Gekas, *wife of Representative (Pennsylvania)*

Don's Cheese Grits

SERVES 6

4½ cups water
⅓ cup soy sauce
2 cloves garlic, crushed
1 teaspoon Tabasco

1 teaspoon coarsely ground pepper
1 cup coarse grits
½ stick butter
2 cups grated extra sharp cheddar cheese

Bring water, soy sauce, garlic, Tabasco and pepper to a boil. Add grits. Simmer approximately 30 to 45 minutes, stirring occasionally, until mixture begins to thicken. Just prior to serving, add butter and cheese. Allow butter and cheese to melt and blend well. Delicious with steak or fish. (45 minutes preparation time. Not suitable for freezing.)

Don Fuqua

Don Fuqua, *former Representative (Florida)*

Sam's Copper Pennies

2 pounds carrots

1 medium green pepper, diced

3 medium onions, (Vidalia) thinly sliced

Dressing:

1 can tomato soup, undiluted

1 teaspoon Worcestershire sauce

¾ cup sugar

½ cup salad oil

¾ cup vinegar

1 teaspoon prepared mustard

Slice carrots about ¼" thick and cook in salted water until tender. Drain and add carrots, peppers and onions to dressing. Chill at least 8 hours. Will keep several months in the refrigerator. (20 minutes preparation time. Not suitable for freezing.)

Sam Nunn, *former Senator (Georgia)*

Stuffed Onions

SERVES 6

6 large onions (white or Vidalia)
   3" in diameter

½ cup butter

⅓ cup shallots

2 teaspoons garlic

1¼ cups toasted and finely chopped
   pecans

1¾ cups fresh bread crumbs

1¾ cups Gruyere cheese

salt and pepper

1 teaspoon dried rosemary, crushed

¾ cup canned chicken broth

½ cup white wine

3 Tablespoons butter

Cut off ends of onions. Peel skin. Cook in boiling water for 10 minutes and drain. Cut a cone-shaped core from onion top. Scoop out inside, leaving shell about ¼" thick. Melt ½ cup butter in skillet or wok. Chop shallots and sauté 2 to 3 minutes. Add garlic and pecans. Cook 2 minutes more. Toss in bread crumbs and cheese. Stir until cheese is almost melted; 2 more minutes. Remove from heat. Add salt, pepper and rosemary. Mix. Fill onions, mounding slightly. Can be prepared ahead. Preheat oven to 350°. Combine broth and wine. Bake onions (can brush with butter or omit) in a single layer, uncovered for 1 to 1¼ hours, basting often, every 15 minutes. (30 minutes preparation time. Not suitable for freezing.)

Andrew Jacobs, Jr., *former Representative (Indiana)*

New Orleans Mirlitons (Chayote)

SERVES 6 TO 8

6 medium mirlitons (chayote)
liquid crab boil
½ pound boiled shrimp, chopped
   (or 1-2 cans of crabmeat
   or use 1 can of each)
½ pound seasoned sausage, chopped

3-4 pats of butter
1 medium onion, finely chopped
⅛ cup chopped fresh parsley
seasoned bread crumbs
Parmesan cheese
salt and pepper

Boil mirlitons (chayote) in water seasoned with 1 to 2 tablespoons of crab boil and salt until tender when pierced with a fork. Allow to stand in the water for about 15 minutes after removing from fire. Cut the vegetables in half and scrape flesh into casserole dish discarding the skin and the seed. Cut into small pieces. Sauté onion, parsley and sausage in the butter until onions are tender; add to the mirlitons. Add seafood and mix thoroughly. Mix in some seasoned bread crumbs, and season to taste. Sprinkle a layer of Parmesan cheese and then a layer of bread crumbs. Bake until golden brown at 350°. (60 minutes preparation time. Suitable for freezing.)

Brian and Karen Bilbray, *Representative and Mrs. (California)*

Sunday Artichokes

SERVES 8

½ cup butter or margarine
2 cups fresh mushrooms, sliced
1 teaspoon salt
1 teaspoon crushed sweet basil
½ teaspoon crushed oregano
¼ teaspoon garlic powder

1 Tablespoon fine dry bread crumbs
2 Tablespoons lemon juice
2 8-ounce packages frozen artichoke
   hearts, thawed (or 2 cans
   artichoke hearts)
½ cup Parmesan cheese

Melt butter in a large, heavy skillet. Sauté mushrooms until golden. Sprinkle with salt, basil, oregano and garlic powder during cooking. Stir in bread crumbs and lemon juice, mixing well. Arrange artichoke hearts in a lightly buttered, shallow, glass baking dish. Spoon mushroom mixture over artichokes. Sprinkle cheese over all. Bake at 350° for 25 to 30 minutes until juices bubble and cheese is browned. (45 minutes preparation time. Not suitable for freezing.)

Ralph Regula, *Representative (Ohio)*

TexGrec Green Beans
S E R V E S   4

3 quarts boiling, salted water
2 Tablespoons olive oil
1 pound green beans

⅔ cup fresh salsa
4 ounces feta cheese

Blanch the green beans. Drop into boiling, salted water. Bring back to a boil rapidly and cook until tender, but still a bit crisp. Remove from the hot water and chill with cold water or ice water to stop the cooking so they will remain al dente. Drain and set aside. Meanwhile, measure out the fresh salsa. Most grocery stores now carry delicious salsa, hot and mild. Take your pick. Crumble (I just chop it up) the feta cheese. About 3 minutes before dinner is served, heat the oil in a frying pan large enough to toss the beans quickly and conveniently. Add the beans and toss over a high heat until warm. Add salsa and continue to toss, heating and mixing the ingredients until hot enough to serve. Do this quickly so you do not overcook the beans. Remove from the heat and add the crumbled feta. Toss just enough for the cheese to mix and melt a bit. Serve immediately. Description: Unusual, but not strange, these beans are a great accompaniment to a meal that needs a little kick in the pants or it can hold it's own with a spicy South-of-the-Border table. (10 minutes preparation time.)

Al Swift, *former Representative (Washington)*

Bestamor Sabo's Potato Comle
S E R V E S   8

1 cup mashed potatoes
3½ cups grated potatoes
1 Tablespoon salt

½ cup graham flour
3 cups white flour
1 stick of butter, melted

Mix together all ingredients. Form into large balls and drop into boiling salted water. Boil for 50 minutes. Serve with melted butter. (1½ hours preparation time.)

Martin Sabo, *Representative (Minnesota)*

Jackie's Corn Casserole
SERVES 8

1 16-ounce can of cream-style corn
1 16-ounce can of whole kernel corn
1 medium bell pepper, chopped
1 small red pepper, chopped or pimento
⅔ cup milk
1 egg, beaten

1 cup cracker crumbs
1 cup cheddar cheese, grated
salt and pepper to taste
¼ cup margarine, melted
¼ cup sugar

Mix all ingredients together and bake in a greased dish for 1 hour in a 350°oven. (20 minutes preparation time. Not suitable for freezing.)

Danny K. Davis, *Representative (Illinois)*

Southern Spaghetti Squash
SERVES 6 TO 8

1 medium or large spaghetti squash
4-6 Tablespoons butter

salt and pepper to taste
grated Romano or Parmesan cheese

Take a medium or large spaghetti squash, rinse it, and slice it length-wise right down the middle. Scoop out all seeds. Place the 2 halves open side down on a vegetable steamer in a covered pot, with a small amount of water below the steamer grate. Cook until the squash is soft to a fork poked into it. Note: if you do not have a steamer, boil the 2 halves, but be careful not to over boil. Remove both halves of the squash from the pot and place open side up on a baking sheet. Take a large fork and gently scrape the squash away from the rind. It should come away from the rind in spaghetti-like strands. Leaving the squash strands in the rinds, gently stir in butter or margarine to taste, usually about 2 or 3 tablespoons per half. Also, gently stir in salt and pepper, to taste. Sprinkle each half with grated Romano or Parmesan cheese. Top off with a small amount of pepper and seasoning salt for taste and appearance. Place both halves of squash on the baking pan in the oven broiler rack, and broil for a few minutes until the top is browned. Serve immediately, while steaming hot.

Bob Barr, *Representative (Georgia)*

Northwest Twice Baked Potatoes
SERVES 8

8 large Washington russet potatoes
¾-1 cup milk
3 Tablespoons butter
1 cup shredded Tillamook sharp cheddar cheese
½ cup chopped chives, dried or fresh
1 extra large or 2 small beaten eggs
salt and pepper to taste

Wash and scrub potatoes. Bake at 400° for 45 to 60 minutes, or microwave on high turning once until knife inserts easily through the center of potatoes. Set aside until cool. Take a slice from top of each potato. Carefully scoop out inside into large mixing bowl. Mash. Add milk, butter and beaten egg. Salt and pepper to taste. Whip until fluffy. Fold in chives and cheddar cheese. Fill potato shells; mound generously. Place in oven-proof dish and bake in preheated 350° oven for 15 to 20 minutes until lightly browned. May be made ahead and refrigerated.

Claire Hastings

Mrs. Doc Hastings, *wife of Representative (Washington)*

Collin County Apples (County in District IV)

large white onions
bouillon cubes
butter or margarine

Remove outer peel and inner core of onion. Place bouillon cube in decored onion. Wrap securely in foil. Place in oven on baking sheet. Bake at 400° for 1½ hours, unwrap, butter and enjoy! (15 minutes preparation time. Not suitable for freezing.)

Mary Ellen Hall   Ralph M. Hall

Ralph and Mary Ellen Hall, *Representative and Mrs. (Texas)*

Lasagna
SERVES 8

1 small onion
2 Tablespoons salad oil
1½ pounds ground beef
½ pound mild Italian sausage
1 package sliced pepperoni

1 12-ounce can tomato paste
2 28-ounce cans tomato purée
1 1-pound box lasagna noodles
1 pound ricotta cheese
1 pound shredded mozzarella cheese

Sauté onion in oil. Brown meat. Add purée and paste and 52 ounces of water. Stir while cooking on medium heat until it reaches a slow boil. Simmer for 1 hour and 20 minutes. Cook noodles according to package directions. To assemble casserole, spoon some sauce in the bottom of a 9″ × 13″ baking dish. Place ½ of the noodles in dish. Crumble ½ of the ricotta cheese on noodles. Spread ½ of the mozzarella cheese on this. Cover with sauce. Place the other ½ of noodles. Place the other ½ of ricotta cheese crumbled. Place the other ½ of the mozzarella cheese. Cover with sauce. Spread pepperoni on top of sauce. Cover with foil. Bake for 45 minutes at 350°. Remove foil. Bake 10 more minutes. Serve with remaining sauce. (3 hours preparation time. Not suitable for freezing.)

Jackie Poston

Jackie Poston, *daughter of former Representative Wylie Chalmers (Ohio)*

Apples and Onions
SERVES 8

8-10 Granny Smith apples, sliced
2-4 onions, sliced
¼-½ cup butter

salt and pepper
¼-½ cup brown sugar

Alternate ingredients in casserole dish and bake at 350°. Vary number of apples and onions according to size. Results should be mushy. (30 minutes preparation time. Not suitable for freezing.)

Deba Leach

Mrs. Jim Leach, *wife of Representative (Iowa)*

Cheese Stuffed Manicotti
SERVES 6

Sauce:

⅓ cup oil

1½ cups chopped onion

3 cloves garlic, chopped

2 16-ounce cans tomatoes in liquid

1 16-ounce can tomato paste

2 Tablespoons chopped parsley

2 teaspoons salt

2 teaspoons sugar

1½ teaspoons dry oregano

1½ teaspoons dry basil

¼ teaspoon pepper

Filling:

15 ounces ricotta cheese

8 ounces mozzarella cheese

½ cup Parmesan cheese

2 eggs, beaten

1 teaspoon salt

¼ teaspoon pepper

1 Tablespoon parsley or more

1 package manicotti noodles

Make sauce by sautéing onion and garlic in hot oil until translucent (about 5 minutes). Add rest of ingredients, mashing tomatoes. Simmer, covered for 1 hour. Mix all ingredients for the filling. Cook 1 package manicotti as directed on box. Cool under cold water and drain well. With teaspoon, stuff filling into cooked noodles. Cover bottom of baking dish with small amount of sauce. Place cheese-stuffed noodles in dish and pour remaining sauce on top. Sprinkle extra Parmesan on top. Bake at 350° for 30 minutes. (1 hour preparation time. Suitable for freezing.)

Anita Skelton

Anita Skelton, *daughter-in-law of Representative Ike Skelton (Missouri)*

Desserts & Sweets

Desserts & Sweets

ONE HUNDRED YEARS OF GREAT FIRST LADY FASHIONS

One room you don't want to miss is the Congressional Club Museum Room,
which displays exact replicas of gowns worn by every First Lady since Mary Todd Lincoln. Miss Evyan
of Evyan Perfumes was inspired to create this collection of First Lady Dolls in 1962. She personally
designed the forty-eight inch, lady-like mannequins, and dressed them in miniature reproductions of the
inaugural ball or other special gowns of 18 of our First Ladies, just as they are displayed in the
Smithsonian's Museum of American History. Each begowned mannequin is showcased
in a cabinet of antique white and gold, custom-made in Florence, Italy.
The Evyan Collection of One hundred Years of Great First Lady Fashions, as it is officially
known, now covers 138 years from Mrs. Lincoln through Mrs. Hillary Rodham Clinton.

Florida Key Lime Pie
SERVES 6 TO 8

1 14-ounce can sweetened condensed milk
½ cup Key lime juice (available bottled in some food stores, but fresh juice is best!)
3 large eggs, separated
3 Tablespoons sugar
1 9" baked pie shell

Mix together condensed milk, Key lime juice and 3 egg yolks. Pour into pie shell and
bake at 350° for 10 to 15 minutes. Beat 3 egg whites until it begins to form peaks for
meringue. Gradually add 3 Tablespoons of sugar and beat at high speed until stiff peaks
form. Put meringue on top of pie and bake for another 10 minutes at 350° or until
meringue is golden brown. Chill pie until ready to serve. (30 minutes preparation time.
Suitable for freezing.)

Dan Mica, *former Representative (Florida)*

Holiday Almond Roca
SERVES 4 TO 6

1 pound real butter (no substitutes)
3 cups granulated white sugar
1 pound whole shelled almonds (unsalted)
1 giant Hershey milk chocolate bar

Place butter and sugar in large heavy saucepan or Dutch oven. Blend sugar and butter over medium heat, stirring continually. When mixture begins to bubble increase heat, time for 5 minutes, stir constantly. Mixture will begin to brown. Add whole almonds and continue cooking on high heat; stirring constantly for 7 to 10 minutes. Mixture should be smooth and resemble a brown thick syrup. Quickly pour onto a large, sided cookie sheet. (Caution, this liquid is extremely hot!) Set aside to cool, refrigerate if necessary. Melt Hershey bar in a saucepan or medium mixing bowl in microwave. Spread on one side of candy block. Allow to harden. Turn and frost other side of block. Break into small pieces. Place in suitable gift giving containers. This is a yummy treat for friends and neighbors.

Claire Hastings

Mrs. Doc Hastings, *wife of Representative (Washington)*

Empanadas de Jalea
Apricot Jelly Turnovers

Dough:	Filling:
5 cups flour	Apricot fruit jam
2 cups shortening	
1 12-ounce can coca cola	

Cut in flour and shortening with pastry blender. Make well in center and add ½ coca cola. Stir with fork until mixture becomes dough. Add additional coca cola as needed, about ¾ can. Press together to form dough. Pinch off small amounts of dough and shape into small round patties. Roll out patties on a lightly floured board. Spoon apricot filling into center of round patties. Fold over and seal edges with fork. Place turnovers on cookie sheet and bake at 350° for 15 to 20 minutes. (Not suitable for freezing.)

Marty L. Hinojosa

Mrs. Ruben Hinojosa, *wife of Representative (Texas)*

Bartlett Brownies
SERVES 10 TO 12

1 cup flour
1 teaspoon baking powder
1 cup sugar
5 Tablespoons margarine
2 eggs

2 squares Hershey's baking chocolate, melted
¼ teaspoon salt
1 teaspoon vanilla
1 cup chopped walnuts

Mix thoroughly and place in a buttered 13″ × 9″ pan and bake at 350° for 30 minutes. (3 minutes preparation time. Suitable for freezing.)

[signature]

Roscoe Bartlett, *Representative (Maryland)*

Sour Cream Coffee Cake
SERVES 16

1 cup butter
2 cups sugar
2 eggs
1 teaspoon vanilla
1 cup sour cream
2 cups flour

1 teaspoon baking powder
½ teaspoon salt
½ cup pecans
½ teaspoon cinnamon
4 Tablespoons brown sugar

Beat the sugar, butter and eggs to a creamy mixture. Fold in the sour cream and vanilla. Mix together the flour, baking powder and salt, and stir into the mixture until the batter is smooth. Pour ½ of the batter into a spring form or bundt pan. Mix together the pecans, cinnamon and brown sugar to make a topping. Sprinkle ⅔ of the pecan mixture over the batter. Add the rest of the batter and then sprinkle the remainder of the pecan mixture on top of the batter. Bake at 350° for 55 to 60 minutes. (15 minutes preparation time. Suitable for freezing.)

[signature]

Mrs. Ted Strickland, *wife of Representative (Ohio)*

SCARLET CARNATION
(DIANTHUS ARMERIA)

O H I O

Scarlet carnation is a member of the Caryophyllaceae, a family of 89 genera and more than 2,000 species that grow in temperate and warm temperate regions. The family name is derived from the Latin word, caryophylum, which means "clove" and refers to the clove-like smell of some carnations.

Oatmeal Cake

1 cup oatmeal
1 stick butter
1½ cups boiling water
1 cup brown sugar
1 cup white sugar
2 eggs

1 teaspoon baking soda
1 teaspoon salt
1 teaspoon vanilla
1 teaspoon cinnamon
1⅓ cups flour

Topping:
6 Tablespoons butter
½ cup white sugar

¼ cup evaporated milk
1 teaspoon vanilla

Mix first 3 ingredients together and let stand for 20 minutes. Mix together next 8 ingredients, combine with oatmeal mixture. Pour into mini bundt pan. Bake at 350° for 40 minutes. Mix together topping ingredients and boil for 2 minutes. Let cool and beat until thick and pour over cooled cake. When I had trouble getting our four children to eat oatmeal in the mornings, this worked like magic.

Kay Inhofe

Mrs. James Inhofe, *wife of Senator (Oklahoma)*

German Chocolate Upside Down Cake
SERVES 24

1 cup coconut
1 cup chopped pecans
1 box German chocolate cake mix
1 box confectioners' sugar

1 8-ounce package cream cheese, softened
1 stick margarine, melted
5 Tablespoons milk

In a 9″ × 13″ pan, spread the coconut and chopped pecans. Mix the cake mix as directed on the box and pour over the coconut and pecans. Mix together the confectioners' sugar, softened cream cheese, melted margarine and milk until the mixture is smooth and creamy. Spread over the cake batter. Bake at 350° for 40 to 50 minutes or until done. (15 minutes preparation time. Suitable for freezing.)

Frances Strickland

Mrs. Ted Strickland, *wife of Representative (Ohio)*

Chocolate Buttermilk Cake
with Sour Cream Frosting
SERVES 10 TO 12

2 sticks unsalted butter, softened
1½ cups granulated sugar
2 eggs
½ cup cocoa powder
1 teaspoon baking soda
1 teaspoon baking powder
1 teaspoon ground cinnamon
2 cups sifted all-purpose flour
1½ cups buttermilk
1 Tablespoon instant coffee, dissolved in 1 Tablespoon hot water

Sour Cream Frosting:
1 cup sour cream
1 cup confectioners' sugar, sifted after measuring
1 cup heavy whipping cream

Preheat oven to 350°. Butter a 10" springform pan. Line the bottom with a round of wax or parchment paper and lightly butter the paper. With an electric mixer, cream together the butter and sugar until light and fluffy. Add the eggs, 1 at a time, and continue beating until thick and light. Sift together the cocoa, baking soda, baking powder, cinnamon and flour. With the mixer on low speed, add the dry ingredients in 4 portions, alternating with the buttermilk and coffee. Beat until perfectly blended. Pour batter into the prepared pan and bake for 60 minutes, or until cake tester comes out clean. Run a knife or spatula around the edges of the cake. Let the cake cool completely in the pan. Make the frosting shortly before needed. Mix together the sour cream and the sugar. Whip the heavy cream until it is firm, then mix the 2 creams together. Release the cake and turn it out upside down on a platter. Use a long serrated knife to cut the cake into layers. Spread the frosting generously over 1 layer and top with the other layer. Swirl the frosting over the entire top and sides of cake. Refrigerate until ready to serve. (45 minutes preparation time. Not suitable for freezing.)

Carol Laxalt

Mrs. Paul Laxalt, *wife of former Senator (Nevada)*

Death by Chocolate
SERVES 24

1 package Betty Crocker walnut brownie mix
½ cup Kahlua (optional)
3 boxes Jello chocolate mousse (4 serving size)
1 bag Heath Bits-O-Brickle (or chop Heath bars to equal 7½ ounces)
1 large container Cool Whip

Prepare and bake brownie mix according to package directions. Take Cool Whip out of the freezer and set aside when you remove the brownies from the oven. (Optional: After removing brownies from the oven, stab holes in brownies with a fork and pour Kahlua over them.) Allow to cool for at least 30 minutes while preparing the mousse mix according to package directions. Using a straight sided trifle bowl, layer the following: ½ of the brownie mix, broken up into bite size pieces, ½ of the mousse mix, ½ of the Cool Whip and ½ of the brickle mix. Repeat layers as above with remaining ingredients. Cover with plastic wrap and refrigerate for at least 3 hours. Best if prepared a day ahead and refrigerated overnight. (1½ hours preparation time. Not suitable for freezing.) Should serve 24, or one chocolate-a-holic!

Peatsy Hollings

Mrs. Ernest F. Hollings, *wife of Senator (South Carolina)*

Lemon Chocolate Dessert
SERVES 15 TO 18

1 14½-ounce can evaporated milk
1 3-ounce package lemon Jello
¾ cup sugar
1½ cups boiling water
3 Tablespoons lemon juice
1 Tablespoon grated lemon rind
25 chocolate wafers, crushed fine
¼ cup butter, melted

Chill can of evaporated milk overnight in refrigerator. Mix Jello and sugar. Dissolve in boiling water. Chill until almost completely set. Stir in lemon juice and rind. In large mixing bowl, whip milk until it resembles soft whipped cream. Add Jello mixture and continue whipping for about 2 minutes. In 13″ × 9″ × 2⅝″ pan, place chocolate wafer crumbs, reserving 1 tablespoon of crumbs. Add melted butter to crumbs in pan, mix, press firmly into bottom of pan. Cover with whipped lemon mixture. Sprinkle on remaining chocolate crumbs. Refrigerate until ready to serve. (30 minutes preparation time. Not suitable for freezing.)

Claire Schweiker

Mrs. Richard S. Schweiker, *wife of former Senator
and former Cabinet Secretary (Pennsylvania)*

Lloyd's Favorite Gingerbread
SERVES 8 TO 12

3 eggs, well beaten
1 cup sugar
2 cups flour
1 teaspoon cinnamon
1 teaspoon ground ginger

1 teaspoon ground cloves
1 cup oil
1 cup dark molasses
2 teaspoons baking soda dissolved in ⅛ cup hot water
1 cup boiling water

Mix eggs and sugar. Add flour and spices. Then add the oil and molasses and mix thoroughly. Dissolve 2 teaspoons baking soda in hot water and add to batter. Mix well. Lastly add 1 cup hot water, batter will be soupy. Pour in a greased 9″ × 13″ baking pan and bake at 375° for 30 minutes. Cool. We serve it with apple sauce or frozen vanilla yogurt. Sometimes, we splurge and add whipped cream. (20 minutes preparation time. Suitable for freezing.)

Lloyd Doggett

Lloyd Doggett, *Representative (Texas)*

Never Fail Peanut Blossoms

1 cup granulated sugar
1 cup packed brown sugar
1 cup butter or margarine
1 cup creamy peanut butter
2 eggs
¼ cup milk

2 teaspoons vanilla
3½ cups sifted all-purpose flour
2 teaspoons baking soda
1 teaspoon salt
2 10-ounce packages Hershey Kisses

Cream sugars, butter and peanut butter. Beat in eggs, milk and vanilla. Sift together flour, soda and salt. Stir into egg mixture. Shape into balls and roll in additional granulated sugar. Place on ungreased cookie sheet. Bake in 375° oven for 10 to 12 minutes. Immediately press a Hershey Kiss into each cookie. Makes 6 to 7 dozen. (20 minutes preparation time. Not suitable for freezing.)

Dolores Mascara

Mrs. Frank Mascara, *wife of Representative (Pennsylvania)*

Ice Cream Pie

SERVES 8

½ cup peanut butter
½ cup light corn syrup
2½ cups Rice Krispies
2 pints vanilla ice cream
¾ cup sugar

½ cup cocoa
½ cup cream
4 Tablespoons of butter
1 teaspoon vanilla

Stir together peanut butter and corn syrup. Add Rice Krispies until coated. Press into a 9″ pan. Spread ⅓ of ice cream into crust and freeze. To make fudge sauce, cook sugar, cocoa, cream and butter until smooth and boils. Remove from heat and add vanilla. Cool slightly. Pour 1¼ cup fudge sauce over the ice cream and freeze. (45 minutes preparation time. Suitable for freezing.)

John Shadegg

John Shadegg, *Representative (Arizona)*

Christmas Cranberry-Apple Casserole

SERVES 8

3 cups sliced apples
2 cups fresh cranberries
1¼ cups sugar

Topping:
1½ cups quick cooking oatmeal
1 cup chopped nuts
1 cup brown sugar
¾ cup melted margarine

Mix apples, cranberries and sugar together and put into a 2-quart baking dish. Combine topping ingredients and spread on top of fruit. Bake in a 325° oven for one hour. (1¼ hour preparation time. Not suitable for freezing.)

Ethel Schwengel

Mrs. Fred Schwengel, *wife of former Representative (Iowa)*

Flan de Naranja Orange Soufflé

Soufflé:

½ cup sugar
2½ cups half and half
1" piece vanilla bean
3 whole eggs
3 egg yolks

⅔ cup sugar
3 Tablespoons Grand Marnier liqueur
orange sections for garnish
orange sauce

Orange Sauce:

¼ cup sugar
½ cup hot tap water

3 Tablespoons Grand Marnier liqueur
1 orange, peeled and sectioned

Soufflé: Heat oven to 350°. Set a 1-quart soufflé dish in the oven to warm. Melt the ½ cup sugar in a heavy skillet over high heat, stirring constantly until sugar is a deep golden color. Pour the caramelized sugar into the warmed soufflé dish, turning to coat the bottom and sides. Heat the half and half with the vanilla bean. Do not boil. Beat the eggs with the ⅔ cup sugar until light and lemon-colored. Stir in the Grand Marnier. Remove the vanilla bean from the half and half. Split the pod and scrape the seeds into the egg mixture. Discard the pod. Gradually pour the half and half into the egg mixture, stirring constantly with a wooden spoon. Strain the custard into the prepared soufflé dish. Set the soufflé dish in a deep roasting pan. Add very hot, but not boiling, water to the roasting pan to a depth halfway up the sides of the soufflé dish. Bake 1 hour or until a knife inserted in the center of the custard comes out clean. Do not allow water bath to boil during baking. Cool on a wire rack; refrigerate overnight. When ready to serve, loosen edges of custard, invert into a serving platter. Garnish with orange sections and serve with orange sauce.

Orange Sauce: Melt the ¼ cup sugar in a heavy skillet over high heat, stirring constantly until sugar is a deep golden color. Remove from heat; cool slightly. Add water to the caramelized sugar, stirring constantly. Return to heat and bring to a boil. Boil and stir until the mixture forms a thick syrup. Remove from heat. Stir in the Grand Marnier and orange sections. Cool. (90 minutes preparation time. Not suitable for freezing.)

Caryll Kyl

Mrs. Jon Kyl, *wife of Senator (Arizona)*

OKLAHOMA

A symbol of hospitality and good fellowship, mistletoe is most famous for the custom of kissing under it during the Christmas season. In English homes and bars, a kissing bough, made with evergreen branches and studded with candles and apples, was hung from the rafters for the holidays. A sprig of mistletoe hung from the center and, everytime someone was kissed beneath it, a berry was picked. When all the berries were gone, kissing privileges stopped.

Flan de la Familia Castillo
Caramelized Custard "Flan"
SERVES 10 TO 12

2 cans evaporated milk	3 Tablespoons vanilla extract
2½ cups granulated sugar	¼ cup white rum (optional)
6 large eggs	3 Tablespoons cornstarch

Pour ½ cup of sugar in a round baking dish. Place dish on top of the stove. Move the dish around until the sugar is caramelized. With the help of a spoon, coat the inside of the dish. Set aside to cool. Pour ½ cup of the evaporated milk into a cup and set aside. In a large bowl, pour the rest of the evaporated milk. Slowly add the remaining 2 cups of the sugar, mixing with a wooden spoon until well dissolved. Or you can use an electric mixer at low speed. Add eggs one by one, mixing all the time. Add the vanilla and rum. Add the cornstarch to the milk that was set aside in the cup and dissolve thoroughly. Add to the ingredients in the large bowl and continue mixing. After all is well mixed, pour the batter through a large sieve into the cool caramelized baking dish. In the oven, put a shallow large pan with 1″ of water. Into it place the flan's round baking dish. Cook at 350° for 1 hour. Remove from the oven when a knife inserted in the middle comes out clean. When it gets cooler, place flan in the refrigerator for at least 2 hours (tastes better if it is cool). To unmold so that it does not break, gently shake the dish with a rotating motion to carefully free the flan in case it is sticking to the bottom. When the flan moves inside the dish, hold a large plate over the opening of the pan. Turn it over quickly onto the plate. (1 hour preparation time. Not suitable for freezing.)

Lelia Castillo de Colorado

Mrs. Antonio Colorado, *wife of former Delegate (Puerto Rico)*

Marshmallow-Nut Fudge

1 1-pound bag miniature marshmallows
1 12-ounce bag chocolate chips
1 cup nuts
1 can sweetened condensed milk

Place marshmallows in a buttered pan. Melt chocolate chips on very low heat; remove from heat. Add condensed milk and nuts. Pour over marshmallows. Allow to cool several hours, or overnight, before cutting into squares. Makes 24 squares. (30 minutes preparation time. Suitable for freezing.)

Connie S. Hansen

Mrs. George Hansen, *wife of former Representative (Idaho)*

Blackberry Cobbler
SERVES 6

2 pints fresh blackberries
1 cup sugar (or to taste)
enough water to cover berries in pot
1½ cups Crisco
3 cups flour

Bring blackberries, sugar and water to boil (sweetened to taste). Lower heat and simmer for 15 minutes. Mix Crisco and flour until mixture crumbles. Add 1 tablespoon of cold water to mixture. Roll dough until thickness is ⅛" thick. Pour blackberry mixture into an 8" × 11" casserole dish. Cut dough into strips. Lay across top of mixture. Bake until slightly brown; remove. Add second layer of strips criss-crossing first layer. Bake until brown. (30 minutes preparation time. Not suitable for freezing.)

Stacy H Hefner

Mrs. Charlie Rose, *wife of former Representative (North Carolina)*

Snickerdoodles

2½ cups flour
2 teaspoons cream of tartar
1 teaspoon baking soda
½ teaspoon salt
1½ cups sugar
1 cup shortening
2 eggs
cinnamon and sugar mixed as for cinnamon toast

Sift together flour, cream of tartar, baking soda and salt. Set aside. Mix sugar, shortening and eggs together; beating at medium speed until light and fluffy. Stir in dry ingredients to form dough. Form walnut-sized balls and roll in cinnamon/sugar mixture. Place on ungreased cookie sheet. Bake 10 minutes at 400°. (1½ hours preparation time. Suitable for freezing.) Makes 5 dozen.

Harris Fawell, *Representative (Illinois)*

Ornamental Candied Pansies

2 dozen live pansies
2 envelopes unflavored gelatin
2 cups warm water
2 cups super-fine sugar

Sprinkle 2 envelopes unflavored gelatin over 2 cups of warm water. Stir with a wire whisk until the gelatin dissolves. Dip pansies, one at a time, into the gelatin mixture, shaking to remove excess liquid. Sprinkle all sides of pansies with super-fine sugar, covering them completely. Place pansies on baking sheets and let stand 30 minutes or until dry and firm. (30 minutes preparation time. Not suitable for freezing.) Makes 24.

Mrs. Richard Ichord, *wife of former Representative (Missouri)*

Yummy Butter Cake
SERVES 12

1 (2-layer size) package yellow cake mix, pudding included type
4 eggs
1 stick (½ cup) butter, melted
8 ounces cream cheese, softened
1 teaspoon vanilla
1 pound powdered sugar

Preheat oven to 350°. Mix 1 slightly beaten egg with dry cake mix and butter to a moist dough consistency. Grease a 13″ × 9″ × 2″ pan. Press mixture evenly in pan. Soften cream cheese and beat in electric mixer with remaining eggs and vanilla until creamy. Beat in powdered sugar gradually until smooth; this takes several minutes. Pour over crust. Bake at 350° (325° if using a glass pan) 35 to 40 minutes. Watch carefully so base does not get too brown. The cheese mixture sinks into the center somewhat leaving a firmer crust around the edges. Powdered sugar, pecans, fresh fruit or fruit sauce can be served over the top of the baked cake. (1 hour preparation time. Not suitable for freezing.)

Helen Green

Mrs. Gene Green, *wife of Representative (Texas)*

Spice Cake
SERVES 12

2 cups sugar
1 cup oil
3 eggs (1 at a time)
2 small jars apricot baby food
2 cups flour

1 teaspoon baking soda
1 teaspoon cinnamon
1 teaspoon nutmeg
½ teaspoon salt

Mix all ingredients. Bake for 1 hour at 350° in a greased bundt pan. Dust with powdered sugar once cake is cool. (30 minutes preparation time. Not suitable for freezing.)

Karyn Frist

Mrs. Bill Frist, *wife of Senator (Tennessee)*

Francie's One-Step Pound Cake

2¼ cups Pillsbury's Best unbleached or all-purpose flour
2 cups sugar
½ teaspoon salt
½ teaspoon baking soda
1-2 teaspoons grated lemon or orange peel, if desired
1 teaspoon vanilla
1 cup butter or margarine, softened
1 carton (8 ounces) pineapple or Mandarin orange yogurt or 1 cup dairy sour cream
3 eggs, (¾ cup)

Glaze Topping: (Optional)
1 cup powdered sugar
1-2 Tablespoons fresh or concentrated lemon juice

Combine all ingredients in a large mixing bowl. Blend at low speed, then beat 3 minutes at medium speed. Pour into a greased and floured 10" bundt or tube pan. Bake at 325° for 60 to 70 minutes, or until top of cake springs back when touched lightly in center. Cool cake upright in pan 15 minutes. Remove from pan and cool completely before cutting and serving. If glazing cake, combine powdered sugar and enough lemon juice to make a drizzling consistency. Glaze cooled cake. (60 to 70 minutes preparation time. Not suitable for freezing.)

Evangeline Choras-Gekas

Mrs. George Gekas, *wife of Representative (Pennsylvania)*

Pistachio Cake
SERVES 12

1 box white cake mix
1 package instant pistachio
  pudding
¾ cup oil
4 eggs
¾ cup plus 1 Tablespoon water

Topping:
2 Tablespoons margarine
⅓ cup water
1 teaspoon vanilla
2 cups confectioners' sugar
nuts to sprinkle on top

Mix first 5 ingredients in large mixing bowl until smooth. Pour into greased pan. Sprinkle chopped nuts on top. Bake in 350° oven for 40 minutes or until done. While cake is baking, mix topping ingredients. In saucepan, bring to boil and boil for 1 minute. When cake is done, poke holes with meat fork and spoon topping into holes and on top. Put back into oven for 5 minutes. Cool. Serve with dollop of Cool Whip. (15 minutes preparation time. Not suitable for freezing.)

Dolores Mascara

Mrs. Frank Mascara, *wife of Representative (Pennsylvania)*

Chocolate Chip Cookies

1 cup butter
⅔ cup light brown sugar
1⅓ cups granulated sugar
½ teaspoon vanilla
2 extra large eggs

3 cups flour
1 teaspoon baking soda
1 teaspoon salt
1 24-ounce bag semi-sweet chocolate chips
2 cups walnut pieces

Cream together butter and sugars; blend in vanilla. Beat in eggs. Add flour, baking soda and salt. Stir in chips and walnuts. Scoop, tightly packed in a small ice cream scoop. Cookie should resemble a golf ball. Bake at 325° for 12 to 15 minutes. Remove when browned, but somewhat underdone. Let cookies finish cooking for several minutes outside the oven. Makes 5 dozen. (15 minutes preparation time. Suitable for freezing.)

Nancy Weldon

Mrs. Dave Weldon, *wife of Representative (Florida)*

Jurich Family Nut Roll

SERVES 48

Dough:
5½ cups flour
⅓ cup sugar
1 teaspoon salt
½ pound butter, softened
1 Tablespoon vanilla
2 Tablespoons grated lemon peel
¾ cup sour cream
1 package cake yeast, or 2 packages instant yeast, dissolved according to package directions
4 eggs, beaten

Nut Filling Mixture:
½ cup honey or sugar
2 cups ground walnuts
½ cup golden raisins
2 Tablespoons butter
¼-½ cup milk
cooking spray
1 egg, beaten
1 Tablespoon water
½ cup powdered sugar

Dough: Mix flour, sugar, salt, butter, vanilla and lemon peel. Work until it resembles pie dough. Heat sour cream until just lukewarm and add yeast mixture. Combine. Add beaten eggs, mixing several minutes. Combine thoroughly with dough mixture. Put in buttered glass bowl, covered with damp towel. Let rise 1½ hours (or until doubled in size).

Nut Filling Mixture: In saucepan, combine all ingredients and stirring constantly, cook over low heat for 3 minutes. Cool completely.

Divide risen dough into 4 equal portions. Roll 1 portion onto pastry board, forming a rectangle. Spread ¼ of the nut filling onto rolled dough, leaving ½" at borders. Roll up jelly-roll fashion, making sure to seal ends, and place seam-side down onto baking sheet coated with cooking spray. Repeat with other 3 portions. Let nut rolls rise again for 1 hour. Preheat oven to 350°. Beat egg and water together in small bowl. Using pastry brush, baste the 4 nut rolls with beaten egg and water mixture. Bake for 25 to 30 minutes, or until nicely browned. Cool on rack. When cool, sift powdered sugar over each nut roll. Slice into 1½" slices, cut crosswise. Each nut roll serves 12. I like to warm the slices in microwave for 12 seconds and serve with whipped butter! (4 hours preparation time. Suitable for freezing.)

Emily Esch

Emily Esch, *daughter of former Representative Marvin Esch (Michigan)*

Mother's Vanilla Ice Cream
SERVES 10 TO 12

5 large eggs
2 cups sugar
dash salt
2 Tablespoons Karo syrup (light)
1 teaspoon lemon extract

1 large can milnot or evaporated milk
1 pint of half and half
1 small carton whipping cream (8 ounces)
whole milk

Beat eggs until pale yellow. Gradually add sugar and dash of salt. Continue beating. Add Karo syrup, vanilla and lemon extract while beating. Turn mixer to slow speed. Add the milnot or evaporated milk, half and half and whipping cream. Put in 1 gallon size ice cream freezer. Add enough milk to fill to ¾ full. Stir this mixture and freeze with crushed ice and rock salt. Makes 1 gallon. (Suitable for freezing.)

Glenn English, *former Representative (Oklahoma)*

Aunt Mary's Carrot Cake
SERVES 12

4 eggs
1½ cups sugar
1½ cups vegetable oil
½ teaspoon salt
1 teaspoon ground cinnamon
2 teaspoons baking soda

2 teaspoons baking powder
3¼ cups flour
2 cups finely grated carrots
1 8-ounce can crushed pineapple, drained
1 cup chopped dates
1 cup chopped pecans

Beat the eggs. Gradually beat in the sugar. Stir in the oil. Combine salt, cinnamon, baking soda, baking powder and flour. Stir into the egg mixture. Add the carrots and pineapple. Mix well. Stir in the dates and nuts. Grease a 10" angel cake pan, then line the bottom with wax paper. Turn mixture into the pan and bake in a 350° oven for 1 hour and 15 minutes or until top springs back when touched. Cool for 15 minutes on rack, then remove from pan. (20 minutes preparation time. Suitable for freezing.)

Mrs. Ron Klink, *wife of Representative (Pennsylvania)*

Sleep-Over Coffee Cake

SERVES 8 TO 10

OREGON GRAPE
(BERBERIS AQUIFOLIUM)

OREGON

Oregon grape berries are eaten by a variety of wildlife and make a tasty jelly. Native Americans extracted a yellow dye from the bark and wood. Symbolizing sourness and ill temper, Berberis is believed to have been one of the four thorny plants used to make the crown of thorns worn by Christ.

Cake:

2 cups flour
1 cup sugar
1 cup buttermilk
⅔ cup butter or margarine, softened
½ cup brown sugar
2 large eggs

1 teaspoon dry milk powder
1 Tablespoon cinnamon
1 teaspoon baking soda
1 teaspoon baking powder
½ teaspoon salt

Topping:

½ cup brown sugar
½ cup walnuts or pecans, chopped
½ teaspoon ground nutmeg
¼ cup butter or margarine, melted

Grease and flour a 9″ × 13″ baking pan. In large bowl of electric mixer, combine cake ingredients. Mix at low speed until well-blended, about 4 minutes. Place in prepared pan. Mix dry topping ingredients only and sprinkle over batter evenly. Refrigerate overnight. The next morning, drizzle with melted butter. Place in pre-heated 350° oven and bake for 30 minutes, until top is a rich golden brown. Cool for 15 minutes and serve warm. Fabulous when entertaining house guests. (20 minutes preparation time.)

Suzie Dicks

Mrs. Norm Dicks, *wife of Representative (Washington)*

Caramel Rum Flan

S E R V E S   8

1½ cups sugar, divided
1 quart milk
6 eggs, extra large
2 yolks

½ cup table cream
⅓ cup dark rum
whipped cream and berries if desired

Preheat oven to 350°. Combine ½ cup sugar and 3 tablespoons water in a saucepan. Heat over high heat until syrup turns amber color. Do not stir. Pour syrup into a 2-quart soufflé dish and tip dish back and forth until syrup covers the bottom. Refrigerate. In saucepan, bring milk and remaining cup of sugar just to a boil. Stir to mix sugar. Place whole eggs and extra yolks in a large mixing bowl and beat. Slowly add hot milk while beating. Stir in cream and rum. Pour egg mixture into the soufflé dish and set into a pan with enough hot water to come up half way on the soufflé dish. Place in oven and bake 1 hour or until a knife inserted in middle comes out clean. Lift from water bath and chill. To serve, run knife around edge of dish and turn out onto dish with lip to catch sauce. Serve with whipped cream and berries. (30 minutes preparation time. Not suitable for freezing.)

Mrs. Mark Andrews, *wife of former Senator (North Dakota)*

Bartlett Pear Pudding

S E R V E S   8   T O   1 0

½ cup sugar
1 Tablespoon cornstarch
3 cups canned pears and juice
½ teaspoon cinnamon
2 cups flour

2 Tablespoons sugar
2 teaspoons baking powder
1 teaspoon salt
⅓ cup shortening
¾ cup milk

Mix 1 cup sugar and the cornstarch in saucepan. Gradually stir in 1 cup water. Boil 1 minute, stirring constantly. Add the Bartlett pears and juice. Pour into a 10″ × 6″ × 2″ buttered baking pan. Dot with butter and sprinkle with cinnamon. Mix together flour, sugar, baking powder, salt, shortening and milk. Spoon this on top of pears and bake at 400° for 30 minutes. Serve warm, decorated with pear halves and cherries. (5 minutes preparation time. Not suitable for freezing.)

Mrs. Roscoe Bartlett, *wife of Representative (Maryland)*

"Crooked Lake Taffy Pull"

2 cups white sugar
2 cups corn syrup
¼ cup vinegar
1 Tablespoon butter

1 Tablespoon vanilla (my mother
and brother liked 2 drops of
peppermint flavoring in theirs)

Combine sugar, corn syrup and vinegar in large saucepan. Cook until a small amount dropped into cup of cold water becomes brittle. Remove from fire and add butter and vanilla. Pour in equal portions onto 3 to 8 buttered ceramic plates. As soon as it is cool enough to handle, butter both hands, pick up warm taffy and pull with both hands into skeins. Double back and pull again until too stiff to pull anymore or until ends clicked together make clicking sound. Twist into a rope and cut into pieces by hitting along rope with knife handle. This was a "once a summer" treat at our lake in Northern Michigan where we had no electricity or running water. Enough for 3 to 8 children to pull.

Mrs. Nick Smith, *wife of Representative (Michigan)*

Double Chocolate Biscotti
SERVES 15

⅓ cup butter, room temperature
⅔ cup sugar
¼ cup unsweetened cocoa
2 teaspoons baking powder

2 eggs
1¾ cups flour
4 ounces white chocolate, coarsely chopped
6 ounces semi-sweet chocolate chips

In a large bowl, beat butter until light. Add sugar, cocoa powder and baking powder. Beat until fluffy. Mix in eggs. Mix in as much of the flour as you can. Stir in the remaining flour by hand. Add the white chocolate and semi-sweet chocolate chips. Divide dough in half. Shape each portion into a 9" roll. Place both on a greased cookie sheet 4" apart. Flatten each roll until 2" wide. Bake at 375° for 20 to 25 minutes or until fairly firm to the touch. Cool slightly. Cut with serrated knife. Cut each roll into ½" diagonal slices. Lay slices, cut side down, on baking sheet. Bake at 325° for 8 minutes. Turn slices over and bake for 8 minutes more until biscotti are dry and crisp. (50 minutes preparation time. Suitable for freezing.)

Mrs. John E. Sununu, *wife of Representative (New Hampshire)*

Kentucky Jam Cake

Cake:

1¾ cups flour
1½ cups sugar
1 cup salad oil
1 cup buttermilk
1 cup blackberry jam
1 teaspoon baking soda
1 teaspoon baking powder
1 cup chopped nuts

1 teaspoon cinnamon
1 teaspoon nutmeg
1 teaspoon allspice
1 teaspoon vanilla
½ teaspoon cloves
½ teaspoon salt
3 eggs

Caramel Frosting:

1 stick butter
1½ cups brown sugar

⅓ cup cream
1½ cups confectioners' sugar

Cake: Mix all ingredients together and beat. Grease and flour two 9″ pans. Fill pans with cake batter and bake 30 to 35 minutes at 350°. Ice with caramel frosting.

Frosting: Combine first 3 ingredients. Bring to a boil for 2 minutes. Sift sugar and beat into mixture.

Hint: For best results, an apple cut in half and placed in the cake box will keep the cake fresh several days longer. (Suitable for freezing.)

Ron Lewis

Ron Lewis, *Representative (Kentucky)*

Carol's Buttermilk Cake
SERVES 12

Cake:
2 cups flour
2 cups sugar
½ cup buttermilk
1 teaspoon baking soda
1 teaspoon vanilla

1 cup water
2 sticks margarine
2 eggs
2 squares unsweetened chocolate

Frosting:
½ cup margarine or butter
1 square unsweetened chocolate
¼ cup milk

1 teaspoon vanilla
2½ cups powdered sugar

Cake: Bring water and chocolate to a boil. Mix dry ingredients together; add buttermilk, vanilla and eggs. Pour water and chocolate mixture over dry ingredients. Mix together. Pour into 11″ × 16″ ungreased pan and bake for 30 minutes at 375°.

Frosting: Melt butter and chocolate. Mix with milk, vanilla and powdered sugar until smooth. Frost cake when cool. (20 minutes preparation time. Not suitable for freezing.)

Pat Williams

Pat Williams, *former Representative (Montana)*

Zach's Favorite Coconut Cake
SERVES 10

1 box of yellow cake mix
1 can of Eagle Brand milk
1 can cream of coconut

1 10-ounce Cool Whip
1 cup flaked coconut

Mix and bake cake as directed on back of box. As soon as cake comes out of the oven, prick holes in cake all over with fork. Immediately pour Eagle Brand milk over cake. Wait 5 minutes and pour cream of coconut on cake. Let cool and top with Cool Whip and sprinkle with coconut. (45 minutes preparation time. Not suitable for freezing.)

Kimberly W. Wamp

Mrs. Zach Wamp, *wife of Representative (Tennessee)*

Chocolate Bread Pudding
SERVES 6

3 cups milk
2 squares Baker's chocolate
1½ cups soft bread crumbs
3 eggs

½ teaspoon salt
1 cup sugar
1 teaspoon vanilla

Heat milk and chocolate in double boiler. Beat until smooth and add crumbs. Let soak for 10 minutes. Beat eggs slightly. Add salt, sugar and vanilla. Turn into milk mixture. Place in buttered dish, set in a pan of hot water and bake in a 375° oven until firm. Serve cold topped with whipped cream if desired. This is Sam's mother's recipe and one of his favorites. (30 minutes preparation time. Not suitable for freezing.)

Sam Johnson

Sam Johnson, *Representative (Texas)*

Lemon Chess Pie

1 Tablespoon flour
1½ cups sugar
3 eggs
½ cup (1 stick) unsalted butter, melted
juice and rind of 1 medium to large lemon
½ cup buttermilk
1 teaspoon vanilla
1 9″ unbaked pastry shell (preferably butter)

Preheat oven to slow, 325°. Combine flour and sugar in a large bowl. Add eggs and melted butter and whisk with wire whisk or mix in an electric mixer at low speed, just until blended. Stir in lemon rind and juice, buttermilk and vanilla. Pour into pastry shell. Bake at 325° for 45 minutes or until top is lightly golden. Cool completely on wire rack. Can also be chilled or served at room temperature. Garnish with whipped cream and lemon slices, if desired.

Eulada P. Watt

Mrs. Melvin Watt, *wife of Representative (North Carolina)*

Grandma Smith's Famous Christmas Cake
SERVES 8 TO 12

2¼ cups flour
1 cup sugar
¼ teaspoon salt
1 teaspoon baking powder
1 teaspoon baking soda
1 cup chopped nuts
1 cup chopped dates

1 cup chopped raw cranberries
grated peel of 2 oranges
2 eggs, well-beaten
1 cup buttermilk
¾ cup oil
1 cup sugar
1 cup orange juice

(Prepared somewhat like Baba au Rhum...) Sift flour, measure and sift into a bowl with sugar, salt, baking powder and baking soda. Stir in nuts, dates, cranberries and peel. Combine eggs, buttermilk and oil; stir into flour and mix until well-blended. Pour into well-greased 10″ tube (bundt) pan. Bake at 350° for 1 hour. Let stand about 15 minutes. Remove cake from pan and place on a rack over a pan. Heat the sugar with orange juice until dissolved; pour over cake, catching drippings and pouring back over cake several times. Set cake in deep dish and pour over remaining drippings. Cover and refrigerate for at least 24 hours. Top with whipped cream. Caution: In order not to break cake apart; invert over plate to take from pan. Use plate to reverse it, etc., as you put it onto a rack, then back onto a serving plate. (20 minutes preparation time. Not suitable for freezing.)

Bob Smith

Robert C. Smith, *Senator (New Hampshire)*

Never Fail Chocolate Cake
SERVES 12

4 Tablespoons cocoa
2 cups sugar
¾ cup shortening
pinch salt
2 eggs, unbeaten

2 teaspoons baking soda
1 cup sour milk
3 cups flour
2 teaspoons vanilla
1 cup boiling water

Mix cocoa, sugar, shortening and salt. Add unbeaten eggs and beat well. Add sour milk, flour and vanilla. Beat well. Add boiling water in which baking soda has been dissolved. Pour into greased and floured 13″ × 9″ cake pan. Bake at 350°. Begin checking after 30 minutes. (Not suitable for freezing.)

Vicki Tiahrt

Mrs. Todd Tiahrt, *wife of Representative (Kansas)*

Dutch Pastries

SERVES 20

2 17¼-ounce packages (4 sheets) frozen puff pastry
1 8-ounce can almond paste (not filling)
1 egg white, slightly beaten
⅓ cup granulated sugar
⅓ cup brown sugar
granulated sugar for sprinkling on tops
water to brush over tops and to seal
flour to keep pastry from sticking when rolling out

Thaw puff pastry according to directions. In bowl, mix together egg white, sugars and almond paste. Set aside. On lightly floured surface roll each sheet of thawed puff pastry into a rectangle about 12" × 10". Cut each rectangle into strips 10" × 2½". Shape a rounded tablespoon of the almond filling into a 9" long rope. Place this down the center of 1 strip. Roll up strip lengthwise. Brush edge and ends with water; pinch to seal. Repeat with strips and filling. Place filled strips, sealed side down, on ungreased baking sheet. Brush with water, sprinkle with sugar. Bake in 375° oven for 20 to 30 minutes or until pastry is golden.

To freeze, place cooled, baked pastries between layers of waxed paper in an airtight freezer container. Seal, label, and freeze for up to 3 months. To thaw, let pastries stand at room temperature for 30 minutes. May be refreshed in a 300° oven for 2 or 3 minutes. (40 minutes preparation time. Suitable for freezing.)

Arlene Kyl

Mrs. John Kyl, *wife of former Representative (Iowa)*

MOUNTAIN LAUREL
(KALMIA LATIFOLIA)

PENNSYLVANIA

The mountain laurel's genus name, Kalmia, honors Peter Kalm, a professor of natural history who spent four years exploring and collecting plant material in Pennsylvania, New York, and New Jersey. Mountain laurel was also known as the "spoon tree" because Native Americans used its wood to make spoons, small dishes, and other utensils.

Sherry's Sugar Cookies

1 cup sugar
1 cup powdered sugar
1 cup margarine
1 cup oil
2 eggs
1 scant teaspoon almond flavoring

1 scant teaspoon vanilla flavoring
4 cups flour
1 teaspoon salt
1 teaspoon cream of tartar
1 teaspoon baking soda

Combine sugars, margarine, oil, eggs, vanilla and almond extracts and mix until creamy. Add flour and other dry ingredients. Place dough in refrigerator to chill (about 1 hour). Roll into small balls about 1" in diameter. Roll each in additional sugar and place on cookie sheet. Press with fork to flatten. Bake at 350° until lightly browned at edges (about 15 minutes). Makes 5 dozen. (15 minutes preparation time. Suitable for freezing.)

Mrs. Wes Watkins, *wife of Representative (Oklahoma)*

Shirley Nygren's Brown Sugar Cookies

1 cup butter
2 cups brown sugar
2 eggs
¼ cup sweet or sour cream
3½ cups flour

2 teaspoons baking powder
¼ teaspoon soda
½ teaspoon salt
1 teaspoon vanilla

Cream butter and sugar. Add eggs and cream. Mix together the other ingredients and add to butter, sugar and egg mixture. Add vanilla last. Chill dough. Roll out and cut in shapes. Bake at 400° for 6 minutes. (Suitable for freezing.)

Mrs. Martin Sabo, *wife of Representative (Minnesota)*

Marge Coyne's Crumb Cake
SERVES 18

2 cups all-purpose flour
1 cup sugar
¼ teaspoon salt
1 teaspoon soda
1 teaspoon ground cloves
3 Tablespoons butter, melted

1½ teaspoons cinnamon
½ teaspoon allspice
½ teaspoon nutmeg
½ cup shortening
2 Tablespoons molasses
1 egg, well-beaten

1 cup buttermilk (If you do not have buttermilk, put 1 tablespoon vinegar into a 1 cup measure and then fill with milk. Let stand 5 minutes before using.)

Topping:
1 Tablespoon flour
4 Tablespoons sugar

½ teaspoon cinnamon

Mix well the first 8 dry ingredients, then blend shortening into dry mixture with pastry blender. Add molasses, egg and milk and beat well. Pour into greased and floured 8″ × 10″ cake pan. Spread butter across top of cake with back of spoon. Mix together flour, sugar and cinnamon topping and sprinkle over top of cake. Bake in moderate oven (350°) for 25 minutes. Cut in squares and serve hot or cold. (1 hour preparation time. Suitable for freezing.) Offered with the permission of Marge Coyne, from Cushing, Oklahoma.

Wes Watkins

Wes Watkins, *Representative (Oklahoma)*

Impossible Pumpkin Pie
SERVES 6 TO 8

¾ cup sugar
½ cup Bisquick
2 Tablespoons butter or margarine
1 can (16 ounces) pumpkin

2 eggs
2½ teaspoons pumpkin pie spice
2 teaspoons vanilla
1 can evaporated milk

Heat oven to 350°. Grease pie plate. Beat all ingredients until smooth. Pour into pie plate. Bake until knife comes out clean, about 50 to 55 minutes. (10 minutes preparation time. Suitable for freezing.)

Edward R Royce

Edward R. Royce, *Representative (California)*

Angel Chocolate Pie
SERVES 6

½ pint whipping cream
5 Tablespoons sugar
2 Tablespoons cocoa
3 egg whites
½ teaspoon cream of tartar

1 cup sugar
1 teaspoon vanilla
1 cup chopped pecans
18 soda crackers, crushed finely
½ cup coconut

Crust: Beat egg whites until stiff. Add cream of tartar. Gradually add sugar. Continue beating, adding vanilla. Fold in by hand chopped pecans and finely crushed soda crackers. Pour and shape into 9" pie pans which have been buttered lightly. Bake slowly at 325° until golden brown. Cool.

Beat whipping cream, sugar and cocoa. Pour into cooled pie shell. Garnish with coconut. Store in ice box. These pies keep well for several days. (45 minutes preparation time.)

Patsy Riley

Mrs. Bob Riley, *wife of Representative (Alabama)*

Snickerdoodle Cookies

¼ cup solid vegetable shortening
½ cup butter
2 teaspoons vanilla
1½ cups sugar
2 eggs
2¾ cups flour

2 teaspoons cream of tartar
1 teaspoon baking soda
¼ teaspoon salt
3 Tablespoons sugar mixed with
　½ teaspoon ground cinnamon
　to coat cookies

In a large bowl, mix shortening, butter, vanilla, sugar and eggs thoroughly. In a medium bowl, combine all dry ingredients, except sugar-cinnamon mixture, and stir into shortening mixture. Roll dough into balls the size of small walnuts. Roll the balls of dough in sugar-cinnamon mixture. Place about 2" apart on ungreased cookie sheets. Bake at 375° for 10 minutes. Makes about 3 to 4 dozen cookies. (1 hour preparation time. Suitable for freezing.)

Jennifer H. Canady

Mrs. Charles T. Canady, *wife of Representative (Florida)*

Chocolate Brioche Bread Pudding

SERVES 6 TO 8

12 ounces brioche loaf

4 ounces unsalted butter
  (room temperature)

1 quart whole milk

12 ounces semi-sweet chocolate

1 ounce pure vanilla extract

6 large eggs

10 ounces granulated sugar

4 medium sized ripe bananas

2 teaspoons cinnamon

¼ teaspoon unsalted butter, sliced thin

Preheat oven to 350°. Cut the brioche into large ½" slices. Coat the inside of a casserole dish with butter. In a medium saucepan, heat the milk until scalding. Slowly whisk in the chocolate until melted. Add the vanilla. In a large bowl, whip the eggs with the sugar until pale in color. Slowly temper the scalding milk to the egg mixture. Whisk until smooth. Let cool. Dip ½ of the brioche into the egg mixture and layer in the bottom of the casserole dish. Slice the bananas thin and toss with the cinnamon. Arrange the bananas on top of the brioche and repeat the layer using the remaining brioche. Pour the remaining liquid on top of the brioche and place the butter slices on top of the pudding. Cover with foil and bake for 25 to 30 minutes. Remove the foil and continue baking another 10 minutes until crisp and golden brown. Cool and serve with a warm bourbon or Kahlua cream sauce. (50 to 60 minutes preparation time. Not suitable for freezing.)

Krista Hubbard

Krista Hubbard, *daughter of former Representative Carroll Hubbard (Kentucky)*

Mom's Ginger Cookies

Cookies:

1 cup sugar	3¼ cups flour
1 cup shortening	1 teaspoon baking soda
2 eggs, beaten	½ teaspoon cinnamon
½ cup molasses	½ teaspoon cloves
1 cup raisins	½ teaspoon ginger
1 cup boiling water	½ teaspoon salt

Frosting:

4 cups powdered sugar	1 Tablespoon vanilla
2 Tablespoons butter	½ cup evaporated milk

Cookies: Cream sugar and shortening together. Add beaten eggs, molasses, soda, salt, spices and flour. Put raisins in boiling water to soak for 10 minutes, then add to mixture and stir. Drop batter on greased cookie sheet. Bake at 350° for 10 minutes. (Suitable for freezing.)

Frosting: Melt butter, add milk, vanilla, and powered sugar. Stir until smooth. When cool, frost cookies with butter cream frosting. (Suitable for freezing.)

Carol Williams

Mrs. Pat Williams, *wife of former Representative (Montana)*

Homemade Vanilla Ice Cream

3 eggs	¼ teaspoon salt
2 cups whole milk	4 cups evaporated milk
1 cup sugar	4 Tablespoons vanilla

Scald whole milk and eggs together. Add sugar and salt. Stir until dissolved. Add evaporated milk. Stir in vanilla. Cool mixture, pour into ice cream freezer container. Follow directions for individual freezers. (1 hour preparation time. Suitable for freezing. Makes ½ gallon.)

Tom DeLay

Tom DeLay, *Representative (Texas)*

Regula Angel Pie
SERVES 6

1⅓ cup graham cracker crumbs
¼ pound melted butter or margarine
4 egg whites
¼ teaspoon salt
1 teaspoon vinegar

1 cup sugar
1½ cups heavy cream, whipped
1 cup shredded coconut
2 Tablespoons sugar
1 teaspoon vanilla

Combine graham cracker crumbs and butter; pat firmly into a 9″ pie pan. Beat egg whites until frothy. Add salt and vinegar and beat until stiff. Gradually add the 1 cup sugar, 2 tablespoons at a time, beating thoroughly after each addition. Spread in prepared crust and bake in a 275° oven for 1¼ hours. Cool. Into whipped cream, fold ½ cup coconut, remaining sugar and vanilla. Spread whipped cream over top of pie. Toast remaining coconut and sprinkle over whipped cream. (1 hour 30 minutes preparation time. Not suitable for freezing.)

Mary A. Regula

Mrs. Ralph Regula, *wife of Representative (Ohio)*

Fresh Strawberry Pie
SERVES 6

1 pie crust, baked
1 cup sugar
2 Tablespoons cornstarch
1 cup water

4 Tablespoons strawberry Jello
(½ package)
1 quart fresh strawberries,
rinsed and stemmed

In a medium saucepan, mix together the sugar and cornstarch. Add the water and stir constantly until the mixture comes to a boil. Cook 1 more minute to allow the mixture to thicken. Sprinkle in the Jello. Stir to dissolve. Set aside to cool. Place prepared strawberries in the pie crust. Pour the Jello mixture over the top of the berries, taking care to coat each of the berries. Refrigerate 4 to 5 hours before serving. (30 minutes preparation time. Not suitable for freezing.)

Jennifer H. Canady

Mrs. Charles T. Canady, *wife of Representative (Florida)*

Lemon Cheese Cake
SERVES 12

graham cracker crust (in a 9" × 12" rectangular pan)
1 large can Pet milk, chilled overnight
1 small package lemon Jello
½ cup boiling water
1 8-ounce package cream cheese
1 cup sugar
1½ lemons, juiced
1 teaspoon vanilla
¼ cup graham cracker mixture to sprinkle on top

Put Pet milk in refrigerator overnight. Mix Jello and water. Cool. Blend cream cheese, sugar, juices of 1½ lemons and vanilla with Jello mixture. Whip chilled Pet Milk until thick and frothy. Fold Jello mixture into whipped milk. Pour into graham cracker crust in 9" × 12" pan. Sprinkle small amount of graham cracker mixture over top for color. Chill. Cut in squares to serve. This is a very light, great summertime dessert.

Betty Chapman

Mrs. Jim Chapman, *wife of former Representative (Texas)*

Cranberry Cream Freeze
SERVES 10

3 ounces cream cheese
2 Tablespoons sugar
2 Tablespoons mayonnaise
1 1-pound can whole cranberry sauce
1 8¼-ounce can crushed pineapple
½ cup pecan pieces
1 cup whipped cream

Whip cream cheese. Stir in sugar and mayonnaise. Mix in cranberry sauce and fold in crushed pineapple, pecans and whipped cream. Freeze mixture in loaf pan until solid. Cut in ½" slices. (20 minutes preparation time. Suitable for freezing.)

Beverly Tauke

Mrs. Tom Tauke, *wife of former Representative (Iowa)*

Kahlua Betty

SERVES 8

8 betties (ice cream sandwiches)
8 ounces Cool Whip

½-¾ cup Kahlua
1 loaf pan

Line loaf pan with betties. Prick with fork and pour ½ Kahlua over betties. Spread ½ Cool Whip over Kahlua. Repeat layers. Put in freezer. When ready to serve, slice and place on dessert plates. For a different flavor, sprinkle toasted sliced almonds over each slice. In Georgia, Betty was the name given to an ice cream sandwich when I was growing up. (20 minutes preparation time. Suitable for freezing.)

Luella Rowland

Mrs. J. Roy Rowland, *wife of former Representative (Georgia)*

RHODE ISLAND

During his exile, Napoleon Bonapart promised his followers that he would "return with the violets in the spring." He did so, returning to Paris on March 20, 1815. Thus, the violet became the symbol of his followers.

Watergate Cake

SERVES 8

1 package yellow cake mix
1 package of vanilla pudding
½ cup of vegetable oil
½ cup 7-Up or Sprite
1 cup of walnuts or pecans, chopped very fine
1 egg, beaten
1 cup shredded coconut

Glaze:
¼ cup lemon juice
1 cup powdered sugar

Mix all ingredients together. Beat for 3 minutes at medium speed. Pour batter into greased and floured 10" tube pan. Bake in preheated oven at 350° for 45 minutes or until cake springs back when patted with fingertips. Allow the cake to cool to the touch and then drizzle a glaze of ¼ cup lemon juice and 1 cup of powdered sugar. (45 minutes to 1 hour preparation time. Suitable for freezing.)

Vera D. Davis

Mrs. Danny Davis, *wife of Representative (Illinois)*

Chocolate Delight

SERVES 15

1 cup flour
1 stick margarine
1 cup chopped nuts
1 8-ounce cream cheese

1 cup powdered sugar
1 cup Cool Whip
3 small boxes instant chocolate pudding

Crust: Cream flour and margarine, add chopped nuts. Mix well. Press in a 9″ × 13″ baking pan. Bake at 300° until brown. Cool.

Filling: In a mixing bowl, mix the cream cheese and powdered sugar. Fold in Cool Whip. Pour into cooled crust. In separate bowl, prepare the chocolate pudding per directions on box. Pour chocolate pudding on top of cream cheese mixture. Top with more Cool Whip and sprinkle with nuts. Refrigerate until ready to serve. (12 minutes preparation time. Not suitable for freezing.)

Carolina Reyes

Mrs. Silvestre Reyes, *wife of Representative (Texas)*

Chocolate Raspberry Squares

1¼ cups all-purpose flour
1¼ cups Quaker oats (quick or old fashioned, uncooked)
⅓ cup granulated sugar
⅓ cup firmly packed brown sugar
½ teaspoon baking powder

¼ teaspoon salt
¾ cup (1½ sticks) margarine or butter, chilled and cut into pieces
¼ cup chopped almonds
¾ cup raspberry preserves
1 cup (6 ounces) semi-sweet chocolate pieces

Heat oven to 375°F. In a large bowl, combine flour, oats, sugars, baking powder and salt. Cut in margarine with a pastry blender or 2 knives until mixture is crumbly. Reserve 1 cup oat mixture for topping. Stir in almonds. Set aside. Press remaining oat mixture onto bottom of ungreased 8″ square baking pan. Bake 10 minutes. Spread preserves evenly over partially baked crust to within ¼″ of edges. Sprinkle remaining oat mixture over chocolate pieces, patting gently. Bake 30 to 35 minutes or until golden brown. Cool completely.

Christine Rogan

Mrs. James Rogan, *wife of Representative (California)*

Idell's Raspberry Delight
SERVES 6

1 can Eagle Brand milk (chilled)
½ cup lemon juice
1 Tablespoon raspberry jam
  (black seedless)

½ cup finely chopped pecans
½ pint whipping cream, whipped stiff
1 graham cracker crust

Mix ingredients together, folding whipped cream in last. Put in graham cracker crust and refrigerate overnight. (Suitable for freezing.)

Jim Chapman, former Representative (Texas)

Father's Day Dessert
SERVES 8 TO 10

⅓ cup sugar
2 envelopes unflavored gelatin
2 Tablespoons finely shredded lemon
  peel (set aside)
¾ cup lemon juice
½ cup water

3 egg yolks
3 cups whipping cream
½ cup sugar
1 teaspoon vanilla
2-3 cups fresh raspberries

In heavy medium-size saucepan, combine ⅓ cup of sugar and gelatin. Stir in lemon juice, water and egg yolks. Cook, whisking constantly, over medium heat until mixture just comes to a boil. Pour into bowl. Stir in lemon peel. Cover with plastic wrap. Chill 30 minutes. In large bowl, beat whipping cream, ½ cup sugar and vanilla until soft peaks form. Fold in lemon mixture. Chill until mixture mounds, stirring occasionally. Spoon ⅓ of mixture into glass bowl. Top with ½ of raspberries. Repeat layers. Top with remaining ⅓ mixture. Garnish with raspberries, lemon peel and mint. Cover and chill for 3 or more hours. (30 to 45 minutes preparation time. Not suitable for freezing.)

Kathleen Waters, daughter of former Representative John Foley (Maryland)

Scripture Cake

Judges 5:25 — 1 cup butter
Jeremiah 6:20 — 2 cups sugar
I Samuel 14:25 — 2 Tablespoon honey
Jeremiah 17:11 — 6 eggs
I Kings 4:22 — 4½ cups flour
Amos 4:5 — 2 teaspoons baking powder
Leviticus 2:13 — 1 teaspoon salt
2 Chronicles 9:9 — ½ teaspoon nutmeg
½ teaspoon allspice
½ teaspoon cinnamon

Judges — ½ cup milk
1 Samuel 30:12 — 2 cups raisins
Nahum 3:12 — 2 cups dried figs, chopped
Numbers 17:8 — 2 cups chopped almonds

Cream butter, sugar and honey. Add eggs, 1 at a time, beating well after each addition. Combine dry ingredients and blend into butter mixture alternating with milk. Stir in raisins, figs and almonds. Bake in a greased and floured tube pan for 40 to 50 minutes at 350°. Cool 10 minutes; invert onto serving plate. (Suitable for freezing.)

Mrs. Ron Lewis, *wife of Representative (Kentucky)*

Mystery Bars
SERVES 32

1 cup flour
½ cup butter
1½ cups brown sugar
2 eggs
1 teaspoon vanilla

2 Tablespoons flour
½ teaspoon baking powder
¼ teaspoon salt
½ cup shredded coconut
1 cup chopped pecans

Cream butter and ½ cup brown sugar until smooth. Add 1 cup flour and mix. Pat into greased 8″ × 10″ pan and bake at 300° for 20 minutes. Remove from oven and cool. Beat eggs and add 1 cup brown sugar and vanilla. Mix well. Add 2 tablespoons flour, baking powder and salt. Add coconut and nuts. Spread over baked pastry. Bake at 350° for 25 minutes. When cool cut into squares. (45 minutes preparation time. Not suitable for freezing.)

Kathleen F. Mackie

Mrs. John Mackie, *wife of former Representative (Michigan)*

Italian Chews

¼ cup butter
1 cup sugar
2 eggs
2 Tablespoons milk
1 teaspoon vanilla

1 cup flour
1 teaspoon baking powder
1 cup chopped dates
1 cup chopped walnuts
powdered sugar

Cream together first 5 ingredients. Sift together flour and baking powder and add to creamed mixture. Add dates and nuts. Place in square, greased baking pan and bake for 30 minutes at 375°. When cool, cut in bite size squares and sprinkle with powdered sugar. (30 minutes preparation time. Suitable for freezing.) Makes 36 pieces.

Patricia S. Mica

Mrs. John Mica, *wife of Representative (Florida)*

Mamie's Rum Raisin Ice Cream

1 cup dark seedless raisins
½ cup dark Jamaican rum
2 cups half and half

1 cup whipping cream
¾ cup sugar
1 teaspoon vanilla

Plump the raisins in rum, preferably soaking them overnight. Heat the half and half and cream with the sugar, stirring frequently to dissolve the sugar. Do not boil. Cool. Add vanilla. Cover and refrigerate at least 1 hour or preferably overnight. Combine rum-soaked raisins and sweetened cream mixture. Pour into the chilled canister of your ice cream machine and freeze according to the manufacturer's directions.

Mrs. Frank Miller, *daughter of former Representative Edward V. Long (Missouri)*

Star Cookies

6 egg whites, beaten until stiff
1 pound powdered sugar
1 ounce cinnamon
1 pound unbleached almonds, ground fine
2 cups flour, more or less, to roll out for cutting

To the stiffly beaten egg whites, add powdered sugar and cinnamon. Take out 1 cup of mixture for icing. Add almonds to egg white mixture. Put flour on cutting board and work into mixture. Roll out to ½" thick to be cut with star shaped cookie cutters. Place star cut cookies on greased cookie sheet. Carefully ice each cookie, being sure to ice to each point. Ice cookies before baking at 350° for 12 minutes. To store, cut an apple in fourths and place between cookies in a tin cookie container. Makes 70 cookies. (1 hour preparation time. Suitable for freezing.)

Mrs. Walter Moeller, *wife of former Representative (Ohio)*

Carolyn's Carrot Cake
SERVES 10

2 cups sugar
2 cups plain flour
2 teaspoons baking soda
2 teaspoons cinnamon

1 teaspoon salt
1½ cups vegetable oil
4 eggs
3 cups carrots, grated

Icing And Filling:
1 stick butter, softened
1 8-ounce package cream
   cheese, softened

1 box powdered sugar
2 teaspoons vanilla
1 cup pecans, chopped

Sift together sugar, flour, soda, cinnamon and salt. Add oil, eggs and grated carrots. Pour into 3 greased and floured 9″ cake pans. Bake in 350° oven for 30 to 35 minutes. Let cool and frost with icing. For icing, cream butter with cream cheese and add powdered sugar. Stir until smooth. Blend in vanilla and pecans. Spread between layers and frost cake with remainder. (30 minutes preparation time. Suitable for freezing.)

Mrs. Henson Moore, *wife of former Representative (Louisiana)*

Swedish Apple Pie
SERVES 6 TO 8

3-4 Granny Smith green apples,
   peeled, cored and sliced
1 Tablespoon plus 1 cup sugar
1 Tablespoon cinnamon

1 cup flour
¾ cup butter, softened
1 egg, beaten
½ cup chopped walnuts

Preheat oven to 350°. Fill pie pan ¾ full with apple slices. Sprinkle apples with 1 tablespoon sugar and 1 tablespoon cinnamon. Combine 1 cup sugar, flour, butter, egg and walnuts together and spread over apples. Bake for 45 minutes or until golden brown. Cool. Serve with vanilla ice cream. Can be made the day before. (20 minutes preparation time. Not suitable for freezing.)

Mrs. Carlos Moorhead, *wife of former Representative (California)*

SOUTH CAROLINA

Yellow jessamine is a high-climbing evergreen vine common in many parts of the South. Although it blooms primarily from January to April, some plants may bloom throughout the year. The common name, jessamine, is a variation on the Persian name Jasmin.

Old-Fashioned Tennessee Jam Cake

SERVES 10 TO 12

Cake:

1 cup shortening	1 teaspoon ground cloves
1 cup sugar	1 teaspoon allspice
4 eggs	1 teaspoon cinnamon
1 cup buttermilk	1 scant teaspoon baking soda
1 cup blackberry or raspberry jam	1 cup black walnuts
3 cups sifted flour	

Caramel Icing:

2 cups brown sugar (pressed down)	½ cup (small can) evaporated milk
1 stick butter or margarine	1½ cups powered sugar

Cake: Cream shortening and sugar. Add eggs and beat until they change color. Add buttermilk and jam. Mix well. Add dry ingredients. Bake in two 9″ cake pans, greased and lined with wax paper at 350° until sides leave pans. Ice with caramel icing.

Caramel Icing: Bring first 3 ingredients to a boil, stirring constantly. Cook for 3 minutes. Remove from heat and add 1½ cups powdered sugar, beating until smooth enough to spread. Good on chocolate, yellow, or white cakes as well.

This cake has been a favorite of Bill's family since before he was born. We always have it at Christmas. (Suitable for freezing.)

Kathryn M. Jenkins

Mrs. William L. "Bill" Jenkins, *wife of Representative (Tennessee)*

Mama Owen's Brown Sugar Cookies

¼ pound butter

2 eggs

2 cups brown sugar

1 cup self-rising flour

1 teaspoon vanilla

1½ cups pecans, chopped coarsely

¼ teaspoon salt

1 teaspoon baking powder (only use
   if not using flour that is self-rising)

Mix together ingredients and pour in a 9″ × 12″ slightly greased pan. Bake for 35 minutes at 350°. Let stand in pan before cutting. Makes 24 cookies. (30 minutes preparation time.)

Katie Owen Morgan

Mrs. Robert Morgan, *wife of former Senator (North Carolina)*

Potato Chip Cookies

1 pound butter

1 cup sugar

2 cups coarsely crushed potato chips

2 teaspoons vanilla

3½ cups flour

powdered sugar

Cream butter and sugar together with vanilla. Add flour and potato chips. Mix well. Form into balls approximately the size of walnuts. Place on a cookie sheet and make an indentation on top. Bake in 350° oven for 18 minutes. Cool slightly then top with sifted confectioners' sugar. Enjoy! Yields 6 dozen cookies.

James Rogan

James Rogan, *Representative (California)*

Wilson Chocolate Chip Cookies

1 cup shortening
2 cups sugar
3 eggs
2½-3 cups sifted flour
1 teaspoon soda
½ teaspoon salt

2 teaspoons vanilla
1 package chocolate chips
  (small or large packages)
1 cup chopped nuts (black
  walnuts or pecans)

Cream shortening and sugar. Add eggs. Add dry ingredients and mix thoroughly. Stir in chocolate chips and nuts. Bake at 375° until light brown (about 10 minutes). Dough can be refrigerated for a few days. This recipe has been made by my mother, Maude Wilson Jenkins Hurd, and her sister Mae Wilson Price all of my life. My Aunt Mae always used black walnuts, shaped the dough into rolls, and refrigerated them. She would then slice the dough and place the chocolate chips on top of each cookie. No family gathering was complete without her cookies. Makes 4 to 6 dozen.
(10 minutes preparation time. Suitable for freezing.)

Bill Jenkins, *Representative (Tennessee)*

Oatmeal Chocolate Chip Cookies

2 cups butter or margarine
2 cups brown sugar
2 cups white sugar
4 eggs
2 teaspoons vanilla
5 cups oatmeal, measured, then
  pulverized in blender or food processor

4 cups flour
2 teaspoons baking soda
2 teaspoons baking powder
1 teaspoon salt
1 to 2 12-ounce packages chocolate chips
3 cups nuts, chopped (optional)

Cream together butter, brown sugar and white sugar. Mix in eggs and vanilla. In separate bowl, mix together oatmeal, flour, baking soda, baking powder and salt. Mix all ingredients together. Add chocolate chips and chopped nuts. Bake golf ball-size cookies 2″ apart on an ungreased cookie sheet for 6 to 8 minutes at 375°. Makes 10 dozen. (15 to 20 minutes preparation time. Suitable for freezing.)

Jill Darling, *daughter of Senator Mike DeWine (Ohio)*

Michigan Caramel Apple Pie
SERVES 6 TO 8

5½ cups peeled, sliced tart apples (about 2 pounds)
¼ cup water
¾ cup each sugar and graham cracker crumbs
1 Tablespoon all-purpose flour
½ teaspoon each ground cinnamon and nutmeg
½ cup chopped pecans
⅓ cup butter or margarine, melted
½ pound caramels (you can use the popular Kraft cellophane-wrapped caramels or try "gourmet" caramels if you are feeling fancy!)
½ cup milk

Mixer Pie Dough Shell:
1 cup all-purpose flour
½ teaspoon salt
⅓ cup chilled shortening
1 Tablespoon chilled butter
2 Tablespoons water

In a 3 to 4 quart pan, combine apples and water. Bring to a steady boil; boil for 1 minute. Pour into a 10″ × 15″ rimmed baking pan to cool quickly. Spoon apples into pastry shell. Combine sugar, cracker crumbs, flour, cinnamon, nutmeg, pecans and butter; sprinkle over apples. Bake in a 425° oven for 10 minutes. Reduce oven temperature to 350°; continue to bake until apples are tender when pierced, about 20 minutes. Meanwhile, combine caramels and milk in the top of a double boiler. Stir over simmering water until melted and smooth. Pour caramel sauce over pie. Continue to bake until caramel just begins to bubble at pie edges, about 10 minutes. Let cool.

Mixer Pie Dough Shell: Sift together first 2 ingredients. Measure and combine the remaining 3 ingredients. Place flour, salt, shortening and butter in a large mixer bowl. Scraping the bowl constantly, blend at low speed for 1 minute. Add the water. Mix about 10 seconds longer, or until the dough begins to cling to the beaters. Should the dough be too crumbly, incorporate 1 teaspoon to 1 tablespoon of water with your hands so that the dough forms into a ball. Roll on floured surface and fit into pie pan, crimping edges.

John Dingell, *Representative (Michigan)*

Dirt Dessert

1 20-ounce package Oreo cookies
8 ounces cream cheese
1½ sticks butter
1 cup powdered sugar

2 small packages instant chocolate pudding
9 ounces Cool Whip or whipped cream
gummi worms, if desired

This dessert is to be served in an 8″ flower pot. Crush the Oreo cookies and set aside. Cream together cream cheese, butter and powdered sugar. Add the chocolate pudding to the creamed mixture. Fold in Cool Whip/whipped cream. Begin with a layer of Oreos on the bottom of flower pot. Top it with a layer of the pudding mixture. Continue layering as described. Finish it with a thick layer of Oreos to resemble "dirt". Add gummi worms if desired (within whole pot or on top only). Serve it up with a garden trowel. It is great for kid's or school parties and is something a young child can make with their dad! (Not suitable for freezing.) I make this with my 10 yr. old son, Jimmy.

Jim Gibbons and Jimmy Gibbons, *Representative (Nevada)*

Chocolate Sheet Cake with Icing
SERVES 24

Cake:

2 sticks margarine

4 Tablespoons cocoa

1 cup water

2 cups flour

2 cups sugar

1 teaspoon baking soda

2 eggs, beaten

½ cup buttermilk

1 teaspoon vanilla

Icing:

1 stick margarine

4 Tablespoons cocoa

6 Tablespoons buttermilk

1 box powdered sugar

1 teaspoon vanilla

½-¾ cup chopped nuts (pecans)

Cake: Bring to a boil 2 sticks margarine, 4 tablespoons cocoa and 1 cup water. Sift together flour, sugar, baking soda and add to boiled mixture. Then add eggs, buttermilk and vanilla. Pour into greased and floured 11″ × 17″ cookie sheet. Bake for 30 minutes at 350°.

Icing: Melt margarine, cocoa, buttermilk. Bring to boil and remove from heat. Add powdered sugar, vanilla and nuts. (Suitable for freezing.)

Phyllis Burns

Mrs. Conrad Burns, *wife of Senator (Montana)*

Butter Thins

1 cup butter, softened

¾ cup sugar

1 teaspoon vanilla

1¾ cups flour

1 cup coconut (1 can of Bakers)

powdered sugar

Beat butter until creamy; add sugar, vanilla and coconut. Gradually add flour. Shape into a brick 12″ × 3″ × 1″ and freeze. Slice ¼″ thick or thinner. Bake at 300° for 15 minutes or until light brown. Sprinkle with powdered sugar while hot. (20 minutes preparation time. Suitable for freezing.) Makes 2½ dozen.

Chet Edwards

Chet Edwards, *Representative (Texas)*

Coconut Cake

1 package yellow or white cake mix, with pudding in the mix
¼ cup oil
1½ cups water
2 cups coconut
2 eggs
1 can cream of coconut
1 medium size carton of whipped topping

Combine the cake mix, oil, eggs, water, 1 cup cream of coconut and 1 cup coconut. Blend well. Bake at 350° for 35 minutes in a 9″ × 13″ pan. When cake is done punch holes (with fork) in cake and pour the rest of the cream of coconut over the cake. Let cool and frost with 1 cup coconut and whipped topping. Refrigerate. (35 minutes preparation time. Not suitable for freezing.)

Carol Myers

Mrs. John Myers, *wife of former Representative (Indiana)*

Raisin Cake (Depression Cake)
SERVES 10 TO 12

2 cups strong coffee
2 cups sugar
2 sticks margarine or butter
½ teaspoon salt
2 teaspoons cinnamon
1 teaspoon cloves

¼ teaspoon nutmeg
1 box raisins
2 teaspoons baking soda dissolved
  in ¼ cup of hot water
4 cups flour

In a large pot, mix sugar, margarine, salt, spices and raisins. Pour in strong coffee (you may use instant). Bring mixture to a boil. Continue to boil for 5 minutes. Cool completely and add baking soda and water mixture. Add flour, 1 cup at a time. Mix well. Pour into large pan 13″ × 9″ × 2″ and bake at 350° for 45 minutes. (30 minutes preparation time. Not suitable for freezing.)

Frank Pallone Jr.

Frank Pallone, Jr., *Representative (New Jersey)*

Fruit Cookie Delights

½ cup chopped dates
½ cup chopped candied cherries
½ cup chopped candied pineapple
½ cup raisins
¼ cup chopped pecans
¼ cup chopped walnuts
1 11-ounce box pie crust mix

½ teaspoon baking soda
1 cup sugar
¼ teaspoon ground cinnamon
⅛ teaspoon grated nutmeg
⅛ teaspoon ground cloves
2 eggs

In medium bowl, combine dates, cherries, pineapple, raisins and nuts. Mix well. In large bowl, combine pie crust mix, baking soda, sugar and spices. Stir to mix. Add the eggs and beat well. Stir in fruit mixture. Mix well. Drop from a teaspoon onto foil-lined cookie sheets, spacing the cookies about 2" apart. Bake for about 10 minutes, until light brown. Remove from cookie sheets and place on racks to cool completely before serving. Makes 3½ dozen. (45 minutes preparation time. Suitable for freezing.) 375° oven.

Mrs. W. G. (Bill) Hefner, *wife of Representative (North Carolina)*

Texas Sweeties

Cookie:
1 cup softened butter/margarine
2 cups sugar
3 eggs, beaten
1 Tablespoon almond extract

3½ cups flour
1 Tablespoon baking powder
½ teaspoon salt

Glaze:
confectioners sugar
milk

almond extract

Cream butter and sugar. Add eggs and extract. Mix and add remaining ingredients. Roll in 1½" balls and place on greased cookie sheet. Bake at 375° for 10 to 12 minutes. When cool, glaze. (20 minutes preparation time. Suitable for freezing.) Makes 3 dozen.

Mrs. Ron Paul, *wife of Representative (Texas)*

Carrot Cake

PASQUEFLOWER
(ANEMONE PATENS)

SOUTH DAKOTA

Anemones are members of the buttercup family and their flowers have no petals. Rather, the flowers are comprised of showy sepals we call petals. The appearance of the pale blue to lavender flowers heralds the arrival of spring in the western grasslands.

Cake:

2 cups sugar
4 eggs
1½ cups vegetable oil
1 teaspoon cinnamon
½ teaspoon allspice
3 cups grated raw carrots

1 teaspoon vanilla
2 cups flour, sifted
2 teaspoons baking soda
¾ teaspoon salt
1 cup chopped walnuts

Frosting:

1 package cream cheese, softened
1 box confectioners' sugar

½ cup butter, softened
2 teaspoons vanilla

Cake: Beat sugar, eggs and oil together until fluffy. Add cinnamon, allspice, carrots, vanilla, flour, baking soda, salt and nuts. Pour batter into greased and floured 9″ × 13″ cake pan or into two 9″ cake pans. Bake at 375° for 50 minutes for 9″ × 13″ pan or 35 minutes for 9″ pans. Cool before frosting.

Frosting: Mix together cream cheese, confectioners' sugar, butter and vanilla. Spread onto cooled cake. (Not suitable for freezing.)

Jane Portman

Mrs. Rob Portman, *wife of Representative (Ohio)*

Strawberry Pie
SERVES 6

2 cups fresh strawberries, crushed
¾ cup sugar
2 Tablespoons cornstarch
1½ Tablespoons butter
few drops red food coloring
baked pie shell
1 3-ounce package Philadelphia cream cheese
whole strawberries to cover bottom of pie shell
1 cup whipping cream, whipped

Combine crushed strawberries with sugar and cornstarch (mixed together). Cook until thick. Add butter. Let cool. Add red food coloring for extra color. Bring cream cheese to room temperature and spread on baked pie shell. Cover bottom of pie shell with fresh whole strawberries. Pour on the crushed strawberry mixture. Cover with whipped cream and refrigerate. (30 minutes preparation time. Not suitable for freezing.)

Florence Long

Mrs. Edward V. Long, *wife of former Representative (Missouri)*

Caramels
SERVES 15

2 cups sugar
1 cup butter
1 pint whipping cream

1½ cups white corn syrup
2 teaspoons vanilla

Boil sugar, butter, cream and white syrup. When it is boiling, stir in 1 cup cream. Continue boiling slowly, stirring occasionally for 1 hour or more until firm ball stage (test in cool water). Remove from heat and add 2 teaspoons vanilla. Pour into a greased 9″ × 13″ pan. Cool in refrigerator. Cut and wrap. (1½ hours preparation time. Suitable for freezing.)

Karen Andrews

Karen Andrews, *daughter of former Representative Mark Andrews (North Dakota)*

Key Lime Cheesecake

1¼ cups graham cracker crumbs
2 Tablespoons sugar
¼ cup butter, melted
1 teaspoon lime rind, grated
3 8-ounce packages cream cheese, softened

¾ cup sugar
3 eggs
¼ cup Key lime juice
1 teaspoon vanilla
2 cups sour cream
3 Tablespoons sugar

Combine first 4 ingredients; stir well. Press crumb mixture evenly over bottom and up sides of a 9″ spring form pan. Bake at 350° for 5 to 6 minutes. Let cool. Beat cream cheese until light and fluffy. Gradually add ¾ cup sugar, beating well. Add eggs, 1 at a time, beating well after each addition. Stir in lime juice and vanilla. Pour mixture into prepared pan. Bake at 375° for 45 minutes or until set. Combine sour cream and 3 table-spoons sugar; stir well, and spread evenly over cheesecake. Bake at 500° for 5 minutes. Let cool to room temperature on a wire rack. Chill at least 8 hours. To serve, carefully remove sides of spring form pan. (45 minutes preparation time. Not suitable for freezing.)

Mrs. Saxby Chambliss, *wife of Representative (Georgia)*

Mexican Fruit Cake

Cake:
2 cups plain flour
2 eggs, beaten
20 ounces canned crushed pineapple (undrained)

1 cup chopped nuts
2 cups sugar
2 teaspoons baking soda
1 teaspoon vanilla

Icing:
2 cups powdered sugar
8 ounces cream cheese

1 stick margarine
1 teaspoon vanilla

Cake: Mix all ingredients in a bowl with mixer. Pour into greased and floured 9″ × 12″ metal or glass pan. Bake at 350° for 35 minutes. Check center of cake for doneness.

Icing: Combine ingredients. Frost while cake is warm. (30 minutes preparation time. Not suitable for freezing.)

Glenn Poshard, *Representative (Illinois)*

Gerry's Favorite Chocolate Lush
SERVES 9

1 cup flour
½ teaspoon salt
2 teaspoons baking powder
¾ cup sugar
2 Tablespoons cocoa
2 Tablespoons oil

½ cup milk
1 teaspoon vanilla
½ cup chopped nuts
¾ cup brown sugar
2 Tablespoons cocoa
2 cups hot water

Combine flour, salt, baking powder, sugar and cocoa. Add oil, milk, vanilla and chopped nuts. Mix until well-blended. Spread into ungreased 8" × 8" × 2" pan. Combine brown sugar, cocoa and hot water; pour over top of batter. Bake at 350° for 45 minutes. Cut into squares. Invert the squares onto serving plate and top with chocolate "lush" from bottom of pan. Serve warm or cold with cream or ice cream. (55 minutes preparation time. Suitable for freezing.)

Gerry Sikorski, *former Representative (Minnesota)*

Kentucky Bourbon Balls

10 Tablespoons of good Kentucky bourbon
6-8 ounces pecan halves or 1 for each ball (Some can be made without
  pecans or a pecan can be added to top after dipping.)
2 pounds powdered sugar
½ cup melted butter
16 ounces unsweetened chocolate
paraffin, cut ¼" across the cake of paraffin

Soak pecans in 4 tablespoons of bourbon for 4 hours. Cream sugar and butter. Add whiskey (bourbon) by the tablespoon until you have a smooth fondant. Wrap a pecan in a ball of fondant and chill and dry for 4 hours or overnight for easy dipping. Dip pieces into chocolate which has been melted with paraffin in a double boiler. Use fork to lift pieces from chocolate mixture and place on wax paper to dry. Put in tins or boxes. Refrigerate. Makes 60 to 80 pieces. (1 to 2 hours preparation time.)

Mary Hamilton O'Neal, *daughter of former Representative Emmet O'Neal (Kentucky)*

Penuche Applesauce Cake
SERVES 12

Cake:

2½ cups flour
1½ cups sugar
¼ teaspoon baking powder
1½ teaspoons baking soda
1½ teaspoons salt
¾ teaspoon cinnamon
½ teaspoon ground cloves

½ teaspoon ground allspice
½ cup butter or margarine
½ cup water
2 cups applesauce
2 eggs
1 cup raisins, chopped
¾ cup walnuts, chopped

Penuche Icing:

⅓ cup melted butter
1 cup brown sugar

½ cup milk or cream
confectioners' sugar

Cake: Sift dry ingredients together. Add softened butter, water and applesauce. Beat 2 minutes at medium speed. Add eggs, beat another 2 minutes. Add raisins and nuts, blending well. Bake in greased 13″ × 9″ pan for 45 to 50 minutes. Ice when cool.

Icing: Combine butter and brown sugar in a pan and bring to a boil; add milk. Remove from heat and cool. Add enough confectioners' sugar until mixture is of good spreading consistency. (Suitable for freezing.)

Frank R. Wolf, Representative (Virginia)

Holiday Sugar Cookies

Sugar Cookie Dough:

2 cups all-purpose flour

¼ teaspoon salt

¾ cup butter, at room temperature

1 cup granulated sugar

1 large egg

1 teaspoon vanilla

Icing:

2 cups plus 1 Tablespoon confectioners' sugar

2 Tablespoons milk

assorted colors of liquid food coloring

Dough: Mix flour and salt. Beat butter and sugar in large bowl with electric mixer until fluffy. Beat in egg and vanilla until blended. Gradually stir in flour mixture until well blended. Flatten dough; wrap and refrigerate at least 2 hours or until firm enough to roll. Heat oven to 350°. Lightly grease cookie sheets. On lightly floured surface, roll dough to ¼" thickness. Cut out shapes with tin cookie cutters. Place 1" apart on cookie sheets. Chill and reroll scraps. Bake cookies for 8 to 10 minutes until lightly browned around the edges. Cool on sheet for 2 minutes before removing to racks.

Icing: Beat the sugar and milk in a medium size bowl with an electric mixer until smooth and glossy, about 2 minutes. Divide into small bowls or custard cups. Add 1 small drop of food coloring at a time. (If icing is too runny, add more confectioners' sugar; if too stiff, add more milk.) These cookies are so much fun to make and decorate. They make wonderful Valentine's day cookies, as well as Christmas and Easter cookies. Makes about 36 cookies approximately 3" in size. (Not suitable for freezing.)

Gayle Wicker

Mrs. Roger Wicker, *wife of Representative (Mississippi)*

Chocolate Chip Caramel Bars
SERVES 16

1 18½-ounce package German chocolate cake mix
¾ cup butter, melted
⅓ cup evaporated milk
1 pound caramels (about 50 individually wrapped)
⅓ cup evaporated milk
8 ounces semi-sweet chocolate chips

Heat oven to 350°F. Lightly grease and flour a 9″ × 13″ × 2″ pan. In larger mixing bowl, combine cake mix, butter and ⅓ cup milk; mix well. Pat half of mixture in prepared pan. Bake about 10 minutes. Cool. In double boiler or microwave-safe bowl in microwave, melt caramels with ⅓ cup milk. Spread over cooled layer in pan. Sprinkle with chocolate chips, then remaining cake mix mixture. Bake about 15 minutes. Cool. (20 minutes preparation time. Not suitable for freezing.)

Jawni Kind

Mrs. Ron Kind, *wife of Representative (Wisconsin)*

Michigan Apple Cake
SERVES 12

Cake:

1 cup cooking oil	1 teaspoon baking soda
1½ cups sugar	2 teaspoons cinnamon
2 eggs plus 1 egg white	½ teaspoon salt
1 teaspoon vanilla	3 apples, peeled, cored and diced
2 cups flour	1 cup chopped nuts

Frosting:

½ cup margarine	1 egg yolk
1½ cups confectioners' sugar	½ teaspoon vanilla

Preheat oven to 350°. In large bowl, beat oil and sugar until smooth. Beat in eggs, egg white and vanilla. Stir in flour, baking soda, cinnamon and salt. Beat well. Stir in apples and nuts. Pour into greased 13″ × 9″ pan. Bake for 45 minutes or until center springs back when pressed lightly. Cool.

Frosting: Beat margarine in bowl until fluffy. Add sugar, egg yolk and vanilla. Beat until smooth. Spread over cooled cake. (15 minutes preparation time. Not suitable for freezing.)

Gayle Kildee

Mrs. Dale E. Kildee, *wife of Representative (Michigan)*

Italian Coconut Cream Cake

SERVES 12

Cake:

2 cups sugar

6 egg yolks (save the whites)

1 stick margarine

½ cup Crisco

2 cups sifted flour

1 teaspoon baking soda

1 cup buttermilk

2 cups Angel flake coconut

½ cup chopped pecans

1 teaspoon vanilla

5 egg whites

Icing:

8 ounces cream cheese

1 stick margarine

1 box powdered sugar

1 teaspoon vanilla

1 cup coconut

Cake: Cream sugar, egg yolks, margarine and Crisco together. Add flour, baking soda, buttermilk, coconut, pecans and vanilla. Beat egg whites and fold into above mixture. Bake in three generously greased and floured, 9″ round cake pans at 350° for metal pans and 325° for glass pans, 30 to 35 minutes.

Icing: Cream together cream cheese and margarine. Add powdered sugar and vanilla. Frost cake and sprinkle with coconut on top, sides and between layers. (30 minutes preparation time. Suitable for freezing.)

Jo Poshard

Mrs. Glenn Poshard, *wife of Representative (Illinois)*

IRIS
(IRIS VERSICOLOR)

TENNESSEE

Because of its multi-hued flowers, ancient Greeks named this genus Iris, after the goddess of the rainbow. Early physicians used irises to treat a variety of diseases. Irises are still used medicinally today by herbalists throughout the world.

Jane's Fresh Strawberry Pie
SERVES 8

Crust:

¼ pound butter (1 stick)

1 cup flour

2 Tablespoons sugar

Filling:

5-6 cups hulled strawberries

1 cup sugar

2 Tablespoons cornstarch

⅔ cup orange juice

Crust: Melt butter (in pie plate, if desired). Add flour and sugar. Mix and pat down to form the crust. Bake at 400° for 8 to 10 minutes until lightly browned.

Filling: Mash 1 cup of fresh strawberries. Mix sugar and cornstarch in a saucepan. Mix in mashed fruit and orange juice. Stir over medium heat and allow to boil for 1 minute. Cool. Pour half of glaze into baked pie shell. Fill pie shell with 4 to 5 cups of fresh, clean strawberries. Pour remaining glaze over fruit. Refrigerate for 3 hours before serving. (45 minutes preparation time. Not suitable for freezing.)

Anne Wagner

Anne Wagner, *daughter of former Representative Laurie C. Battle (Alabama)*

Lemon Angel Dessert
SERVES 24

6 eggs, separated

1 cup sugar

½ cup lemon juice

1 teaspoon grated lemon rind

1 envelope gelatin

½ cup cold water

2 angel food cakes

1 cup whipping cream

In top of double boiler, combine slightly beaten egg yolks, ½ cup sugar, lemon juice and lemon peel. Cook mixture over simmering water (stirring constantly) until mixture thickens. Remove from heat and stir in gelatin that has been softened in ½ cup cold water. Cool mixture until partially set. Tear angel food cake into bite size pieces and place in a 9″ × 13″ glass dish. Beat egg whites until foamy and add ½ cup sugar gradually. Continue beating until egg whites hold peaks. Then, fold into lemon mixture. Whip ½ cup cream and fold into lemon mixture. Spoon lemon mixture over the cake pieces and refrigerate at least 6 hours. Cut into squares and top with a dab of whipped cream. (Whip the other ½ cup cream.) This is a great do-ahead dessert. (1 hour 30 minutes preparation time. Not suitable for freezing.)

Alice Baesler

Mrs. Scott Baesler, *wife of Representative (Kentucky)*

Pecan Tarts
SERVES 24

Cheese Pastry:

1 3-ounce package cream cheese
½ cup margarine or butter

1 cup sifted flour

Filling:

1 egg
¼ cup brown sugar
1 Tablespoon margarine

1 teaspoon vanilla
dash salt
⅔ cup broken pecan pieces

Cheese Pastry: Let cream cheese and butter or margarine soften and blend. Stir in flour and chill for 1 hour. Shape into 24 individual 1″ balls and place 1 ball in each tiny ungreased muffin tin cup. Press dough on bottom and sides of each cup.

Pecan Filling: Preheat oven to 325°. Beat together egg, sugar, margarine, vanilla and salt until smooth. Place a few pecan pieces in each cup. Pour 1 teaspoon filling mixture over top. Add a few more pecan pieces. Bake at 325° for 25 minutes. Cool. Remove from pans. (45 minutes preparation time. Suitable for freezing.)

Nancy Hamilton

Mrs. Lee H. Hamilton, *wife of Representative (Indiana)*

Ginger Snaps

¾ cup butter-flavored Crisco
1 cup sugar
¼ cup light molasses
1 egg
2 cups flour

¼ teaspoon salt
2 teaspoons baking soda
1 teaspoon cinnamon
1 teaspoon cloves
1 teaspoon ginger

Mix ingredients as listed. Roll into small balls. Roll balls in sugar. Place 2″ apart on lightly greased cookie sheet. Bake in 375° oven for 12 minutes. Makes 4 dozen cookies. (Suitable for freezing.)

Patricia Kempthorne

Mrs. Dirk Kempthorne, *wife of Senator (Idaho)*

Balish Cookies

4½ cups sifted flour
2 teaspoons baking powder
½ teaspoon salt
½ pound butter
½ cup sugar

½ teaspoon baking soda
1 cup sour cream
3 egg yolks (beaten)
fruit or nut filling (jam or preserves)
powdered sugar

Sift the flour with the baking powder and the salt. Work the butter into the flour mixture, as if making pie dough. Add the sugar. In a separate bowl, mix the sour cream and the baking soda, then add the egg yolks and blend. Pour the sour cream mixture into the flour mixture and knead until smooth. Roll out the dough thinly and cut into 2" squares. Place a heaping teaspoon of the filling in the center of each square. Fold over 2 opposite corners of each square until they meet in the middle of the square, then overlap ⅛". Place the cookies on a cookie sheet and bake 10 minutes or until done (just <u>before</u> cookie turns light brown). Sprinkle powdered sugar over the cookies while warm. Makes 5 dozen. (1 hour preparation time. Suitable for freezing.)

Karen M. DeWine

Karen DeWine, *daughter-in-law of Senator Mike DeWine (Ohio)*

Chocolate Pound Cake
SERVES 8 TO 12

3 cups sugar
¾ pound butter or margarine
5 eggs
3 cups all-purpose flour

4 Tablespoons cocoa
1 teaspoon baking powder
1 cup milk
1 teaspoon vanilla

Preheat oven to 325°. Grease and flour 10" tube pan. In large mixing bowl, cream sugar and butter. Beat in eggs. Sift flour, cocoa and baking powder together 3 times. Then add flour mixture, milk and vanilla to sugar, butter and egg mixture. Mix well. Bake for 1 hour and 20 minutes. (1 hour 35 minutes preparation time. Suitable for freezing.)

Jerry Moran

Jerry Moran, *Representative (Kansas)*

Chocolate Cheesecake
SERVES 12

Crust:
1¾ cups chocolate wafer crumbs
½ cup finely ground pecans, walnuts or macadamia nuts
¾ stick of unsalted butter, melted

Filling:
3 8-ounce packages of cream cheese
1 teaspoon vanilla
1 cup sugar
dash of salt
3 eggs, separated
1 cup sour cream
12 ounces semisweet or milk chocolate, melted and cooled

Crust: Butter the sides of a 9″ spring form pan. Mix the chocolate wafer crumbs and ground nuts. Gradually add the melted butter and mix well. Press the crust mixture into the bottom of the pan.

Filling: Beat the cream cheese until smooth. Add vanilla, sugar and salt. Mix well. Add the egg yolks, 1 at a time, and blend until smooth. Add chocolate and sour cream, blending thoroughly. Beat the egg whites in a separate bowl until they form peaks. Fold the egg whites gently into the cream cheese mixture. Pour the mixture into the crust and bake for about 1 hour at 375°. The center of the cheesecake may still be soft. Cool completely before refrigerating. (1 hour 30 minutes preparation time. Not suitable for freezing.)

Brenda Lyons Talent

Mrs. James M. Talent, *wife of Representative (Missouri)*

Honey Walnut Cake "Karethopita"

SERVES 24

1 pound butter
2 cups sugar
12 eggs
2 cups flour

4 teaspoons baking powder
dash of salt
2 cups finely chopped walnuts

Syrup For Topping:
3 cups water
3 cups sugar

1 teaspoon lemon
1 teaspoon whiskey

Beat butter and sugar together. Gradually add 1 egg at a time. Blend in other ingredients. Pour into greased 9″ × 13″ pan and bake in a 375° oven. Cook syrup for 10 minutes. Let syrup and cake cool before spooning syrup over cake. (1 hour preparation time. Suitable for freezing.)

Ben Gilman

Ben Gilman, *Representative (New York)*

Baked Milk Custard "Yalatopouriko"

SERVES 24

2 quarts milk
⅔ cup farina
2 teaspoons butter
1½ cups sugar

12 eggs
1 teaspoon vanilla
8 sheets filo dough (strudel leaves)

Syrup:
1 cup sugar
1 cup water

1 teaspoon lemon juice

Boil milk in double boiler; add farina and butter and cook until thick. Set aside to cool. Mix sugar, eggs and vanilla together. Add cooled milk mixture, stirring all together. Place 4 layers of filo dough on bottom of a greased 9″ × 14″ pan. Each layer should be brushed with melted butter. Add mixture and put additional 4 layers of filo on top. Sprinkle with cinnamon and with the point of a knife make air holes on top. Bake at 375°, removing from oven when knife comes out clean. Pour cool syrup over cool pudding after cutting lines down pan. (45 minutes preparation time. Not suitable for freezing.)

Georgia Gilman

Mrs. Ben Gilman, *wife of Representative (New York)*

Mom Burn's Burnt Sugar Ice Cream

¾ cup sugar
3 cups milk
5 eggs
2½ cups sugar
1 Tablespoon flour

dash of salt
1-2 cans Carnation milk
1 teaspoon vanilla
milk to fill ice cream freezer

In heavy saucepan, place ¾ cup sugar on heat and let it melt until bubbly and dark. Reduce heat and add 3 cups milk. Stir and cook until the burnt sugar is dissolved before adding the egg, sugar and flour mixture. Beat together 5 eggs, 2½ cups sugar and 1 tablespoon flour. Add this mixture to milk and burnt sugar. Cook this mixture until it thickens. Add a dash of salt, 1 or 2 cans of Carnation milk, vanilla and enough milk to fill the ice cream freezer. Freeze according to ice cream freezer directions. (45 minutes preparation time. Suitable for freezing.)

Phyllis Burns

Mrs. Conrad Burns, *wife of Senator (Montana)*

Buttermilk Pie
SERVES 6

1 cup sugar
2 Tablespoons flour with a pinch of salt
2 eggs, beaten
⅔ stick of margarine or butter
⅔ cup buttermilk
1½ teaspoons vanilla
9" unbaked pie shell

Mix sugar and flour together until well blended. Beat eggs and add dry ingredients. Add butter or margarine. Mix and add buttermilk and vanilla. Pour into pie shell. Bake at 375° until it begins to brown. Reduce heat to 300° and bake until done, 45 minutes to 1 hour. (1 hour 30 minutes preparation time. Not suitable for freezing.)

Louise Broyhill

Mrs. James T. Broyhill, *wife of former Senator (North Carolina)*

Do's Delicious Cheesecake
SERVES 25

1 small box sugar-free lemon flavored
    gelatin dessert
1 cup hot water
1 cup lemon wafer cookies, crushed
3 Tablespoons plus 2 teaspoons
    margarine, melted

1½ Tablespoons water
8 ounces light cream cheese
¾ cup sugar
½ cup non-fat vanilla yogurt
1 8-ounce package light whipped topping
1 teaspoon vanilla extract

Our Grandmother, Dorothy Billet, has always made this delicious and beautiful no-bake cheesecake. Mix gelatin in hot water and set aside to cool. Combine crumbs and margarine, mixing well. Lightly mix in 1½ tablespoons of water and press firmly in bottom of 9″ × 13″ glass dish. Cream the cheese and sugar; add the gelatin mixture to this. Add yogurt, then whipped topping and vanilla. Spoon mixture into the crumb crust. Chill pie in refrigerator. Decorate with fresh strawberries surrounded with sliced kiwi (optional). (15 minutes preparation time. Suitable for freezing.)

Susan Livingston

Susan Livingston, *daughter of Representative Bob Livingston (Louisiana)*

Deep Dark Chocolate Cake
SERVES 15

1¾ cups flour
2 cups sugar
¾ cup Hershey's cocoa
1½ teaspoons baking soda
1½ teaspoons baking powder
1 teaspoon salt

2 eggs
1 cup milk
½ cup oil
2 teaspoons vanilla
1 cup boiling water

Combine dry ingredients in large bowl. Add remaining ingredients <u>except</u> boiling water. Beat at medium speed for 2 minutes. Stir in boiling water with a spoon. Batter will be thin. Pour into greased and floured pans (either two 9″ or three 8″ layer pans or one 13″ × 9″ pan). Bake at 350° for 30 to 35 minutes for layer pans or 35 to 40 minutes for a 13″ × 9″ pan. Cool. Frost. (15 minutes preparation time. Suitable for freezing.)

Mary Brownback

Mrs. Sam Brownback, *wife of Senator (Kansas)*

Macadamia Delights

2 cups flour
½ teaspoon baking soda
¼ teaspoon salt
¾ cup unsalted butter, slightly
  softened
¾ cup packed dark brown sugar
½ cup white sugar

2 eggs
2 teaspoons vanilla extract
1 cup shredded sweetened coconut
1 cup coarsely chopped macadamia
  nuts
12 ounces white chocolate, broken
  into chunks

Preheat the oven to 300°. Combine flour, baking soda and salt in a small bowl. Mix well. In a large bowl mix the butter and sugars until coarsely blended. Add the eggs and vanilla, blend until smooth. Gradually add the flour mixture and blend until smooth. Add the coconut and mix thoroughly. Then add the macadamia nuts and white chocolate to the blended dough. Use a large spoon to fold these ingredients into the dough. To form the cookies, take about a table-spoon of dough and roll it into a ball. Place the balls on an ungreased cookie sheet, about 2" apart. When you have prepared a full cookie sheet, place the cookie sheet into the freezer for about 5 to 10 minutes to harden the cookie dough. Then place the cookie sheet in the oven and bake for 18 to 23 minutes. The cookies should be a light brown when done. Makes 4 to 5 dozen cookies. (1 hour preparation time. Suitable for freezing.)

Brenda Lyons Talent

Mrs. James M. Talent, *wife of Representative (Missouri)*

BLUEBONNET
(LUPINUS TEXENSIS)

TEXAS

Fields of these striking blue flowers announce the arrival of spring in the Lone Star State. The legend of the bluebonnet tells the story of a tribe of Comanche who were experiencing a time of severe drought and star-vation. A young girl burned a doll, her most prized possession, and scattered the ashes as an offering to the Great Spirit. The next morn-ing, everywhere the ashes had fallen, a blue flower had sprung up. And, in the distance, the rain began to fall.

Every spring, the Great Spirit sends bluebonnets to remind the people of Texas of the little girl who was willing to sacrifice her beloved doll to save her people.

Dorothea's Italian Biscotti (Dipping Cookies)

9 large eggs
8 cups flour
2½ cups sugar
3 sticks margarine, melted

6 teaspoons baking powder
2 teaspoons anise seeds or 1 ounce
anise flavoring
⅛ cup cooking oil (for hands)

Beat eggs and sugar. Add margarine and flour. Mix into a soft dough. Oil hands and pat dough into 8 sections. Roll into 2" wide and 8" long logs. Place onto greased cookie sheets. Use remainder of oil if you wish. Place on oven rack (second from bottom). Bake at 375° for 20 minutes until firm. The tops should not be hard, but crusty and light in color. Remove, slice diagonally ½" thick and place back in oven for 5 minutes. Carefully turn and bake additional 5 minutes. (½ hour preparation time. Not suitable for freezing.)

Mrs. Frank Pallone, Jr., *wife of Representative (New Jersey)*

Key Lime Pie
SERVES 6

Crust:
4 ounces graham cracker crumbs
5 ounces granulated sugar
1 Tablespoon butter

Filling:
5 egg yolks
12 ounces sweetened condensed milk
5 ounces Key lime juice

Crust: Melt butter. Mix with crumbs and sugar. Pat into 10" pie pan. Bake at 350°F for 5 minutes.

Filling: Mix egg yolks, condensed milk and lime juice well. Pour into crust. Bake at 300°F for 25 minutes.

Tolise Norwood, *daughter of former Representative E. C. "Took" Gathings (Arkansas)*

Cherry Cheesecake
SERVES 20

20 single graham crackers, crushed
¼ cup melted butter
¼ cup sugar
2 8-ounce packages cream cheese
1½ cups sour cream
½ cup sugar

2 eggs
2 Tablespoons melted butter
2 teaspoons vanilla
1 cup sour cream
½ cup sugar
1 can cherry pie filling

Mix crushed graham crackers, ¼ cup melted butter and ¼ cup sugar together and press into bottom of a 9″ × 13″ pan. Beat cream cheese with 1½ cups sour cream and ½ cup sugar. When creamy, add 2 eggs, 2 tablespoons melted butter and 2 teaspoons vanilla. Pour over crust and bake at 325° for 30 to 40 minutes. Mix 1 cup sour cream and ½ cup sugar. Put on top and return to oven for 5 minutes at 350°. Cool and top with cherry pie filling. (15 minutes preparation time. Not suitable for freezing.)

Sue Neumann

Mrs. Mark W. Neumann, *wife of Representative (Wisconsin)*

Chocolate Chip Bars
SERVES 20

½ cup butter or margarine
2 cups light brown sugar
2 eggs
2 teaspoons baking powder
1 teaspoon salt

1 teaspoon vanilla
1½ cups flour
1 cup chocolate chips
½ cup chopped nuts (if desired)

Melt butter or margarine. Mix in brown sugar. Stir in eggs. Add baking powder, salt and vanilla. Stir in flour until blended. Mix in chocolate chips and nuts (if desired). Bake in greased 9″ × 13″ pan for 22 minutes at 350°. When cool, dust with powdered sugar if desired. Especially good served warm with ice cream. (10 minutes preparation time. Suitable for freezing.)

Mark W. Neumann

Mark W. Neumann, *Representative (Wisconsin)*

Pineapple Chiffon Pie
SERVES 8

Keebler ready baked shortbread crust
2 cups sour cream
1 8-ounce can crushed pineapple, juice and all
1 large instant vanilla pudding mix

Mix all ingredients together and pour into crust. Refrigerate (about 4 hours). Top with Cool Whip. (15 minutes preparation time. Not suitable for freezing.)

Mary C. Bunning

Mrs. Jim Bunning, *wife of Representative (Kentucky)*

Southern Pralines

1½ cups sugar
¾ cup firmly packed brown sugar
½ cup half and half
6 Tablespoons butter or margarine
2 cups pecans

Combine all ingredients in large saucepan. Cook and stir gently and slowly until sugar dissolves. Cover and continue to cook over medium heat until sugar crystals are washed down from sides of pan. Uncover, and cook to soft boil stage (240°) stirring constantly. Remove from heat and stir mixture with a wooden spoon until it thickens. Work quickly, drop tablespoons of candy onto greased wax paper. Makes 1½ to 2 dozen. (This is a tradition at our home during Christmas. It is my favorite holiday sweet. Also, good for hostess gifts, my wife gives them when we go to friends' homes during the holidays.) (20 minutes preparation time.)

Bob Clement

Bob Clement, *Representative (Tennessee)*

Grandma Alden's _Real_ Mississippi Mud Pie

Pie:

2 eggs

1 cup sugar

½ cup melted butter or margarine

½ cup unsifted all-purpose flour

⅓ cup Hershey's cocoa

¼ teaspoon salt

1 teaspoon vanilla

½ cup chopped nuts (optional)

ice cream (optional)

Hot Fudge Sauce:

¾ cup sugar

½ cup cocoa

⅓ cup butter or margarine

1 5-ounce can evaporated milk

⅓ cup light corn syrup

1 teaspoon vanilla

Pie: Beat eggs in small mixer bowl. Blend in sugar and melted butter. Combine flour, cocoa, and salt; add to butter mixture. Stir in vanilla and nuts. Pour into lightly greased 8" pie pan. Bake at 350° for 25 to 30 minutes (pie will not test done). Cool; cut into wedges. Serve topped with ice cream and hot fudge sauce.

Sauce: Combine sugar and cocoa in a small saucepan. Blend in evaporated milk and corn syrup. Cook over medium heat; stirring constantly until it boils. Boil for 1 minute. Remove from heat. Stir in butter and vanilla. Serve warm. This pie <u>literally</u> melts in your mouth! (20 minutes preparation time. Suitable for freezing.)

Jacquelyn Orton

Mrs. William Orton, _wife of former Representative (Utah)_

Chocolate Pecan Tart
SERVES 6

Crust:

1 cup flour

1 stick butter

1 Tablespoon sugar

3 Tablespoon cold water

Filling:

1 stick butter

¼ cup honey

¾ cup dark brown sugar

½ cup heavy cream

3 Tablespoons sugar

2 cups chopped pecans

Topping:

¾ cup heavy cream

4 ounces bittersweet chocolate

Crust: Mix ingredients together and bake shell 15 minutes with pastry weights. Remove weights and bake for an additional 3 minutes without weights. Use a 9″ pie pan.

Filling: Melt butter and honey on high heat. Add sugar and dissolve. Boil for 1 minute without stirring. Add ½ cup heavy cream and stir until smooth. Add nuts, stir, and remove from heat. Pour filling in crust shell and bake for 18 to 20 minutes at 350°. Do not burn!

Topping: Bring ¾ cup cream to boil. Add chocolate and remove from heat. Stir until dissolved. Pour over pecan filling. Keep at room temperature until served. Refrigeration will cause tart to become quite hard and chewy.

The resulting tart will be approximately 1½″ deep caramel pecan filling in a toasty brown sweet tart crust topped with approximately ¼″ deep chocolate cream. (1 hour preparation time. Not suitable for freezing.)

William Orton, *former Representative (Utah)*

Bonnie Braun's Ice Cream Bars

SERVES 8 TO 12

3 cups Rice Krispies
1 cup coconut
1 cup brown sugar

1 stick real butter, melted
½ cup nuts
½ gallon vanilla ice cream

Take ice cream out of freezer to soften. Mix other 5 ingredients and bake in oven at 300° for 20 minutes; stirring occasionally. Cool. Pat half of browned Rice Krispies into a buttered 9″ × 13″ pan. Spoon ½ gallon ice cream over this. Smooth ice cream out and pour second half of Rice Krispies over ice cream and pat lightly. Return to freezer until firm. (2 to 3 hours preparation time. Suitable for freezing.)

Georgia J. Costello

Mrs. Jerry F. Costello, *wife of Representative (Illinois)*

Louise's Southern Black Walnut Cake

SERVES 12

Cake:
½ cup shortening
1 stick margarine
2 cups sugar
4 eggs
½ teaspoon black walnut flavoring

2½ cups flour
½ teaspoon salt
1 teaspoon baking soda
1 cup buttermilk

Icing:
1 stick margarine
2 cups sugar
½ cup sweet milk

1 Tablespoon white Karo syrup
1½ cups black walnuts

Cake: Cream shortening, margarine, and sugar until fluffy. Add eggs, 1 at a time. Add flavoring and beat well. Add sifted dry ingredients alternately with buttermilk. Mix 3 minutes. Bake in 8″ pans at 350° for 20 minutes. This recipe will make 6 thin layers.

Icing: Melt margarine in heavy pan. Add sugar, milk and syrup. Bring to boil, boiling for 1 minute. Remove from heat, add 1½ cups of black walnuts. Beat for 2 minutes. Spread between layers and on top of cake. (1 hour preparation time. Suitable for freezing.)

W. B. Bill Hefner

W.G. (Bill) Hefner, *Representative (North Carolina)*

UTAH

Often found in association with sagebrush, sego lily occurs on hillsides and dry open plains from the Dakotas, south to New Mexico, and west to California. The tulip-like flowers, which vary in color from yellow to peach to white, bloom in June and July. The species name, nutallii, honors Thomas Nutall, a botanist who explored the West in the early 1800s.

Bonnie's Red Velvet Cake
SERVES 10

Cake:

1 yellow butter cake mix
2 ounces red food coloring

3 Tablespoons Nestle Quick

Frosting:

1 stick butter or margarine
½ cup Crisco
1 cup sugar

3 Tablespoons flour
⅔ cup milk
1 teaspoon vanilla

Cake: Follow directions on cake mix box. Mix together food coloring and Nestle Quick, and add to cake batter. Bake in two 9" round cake pans in a 350° oven for 23 to 28 minutes. Cool and frost.

Frosting: Cream ¼ pound butter or margarine, ½ cup Crisco and 1 cup sugar. Add 3 tablespoons flour; 1 tablespoon at a time. Then add ⅔ cup milk and 1 teaspoon vanilla. Beat with electric mixer for 12 minutes. (30 minutes preparation time. Not suitable for freezing.)

Barbara Battle

Barbara Battle, *daughter-in-law of former Representative Laurie Battle (Alabama)*

Pineapple Cheese Pie
SERVES 16

1 8-ounce package of cream cheese, softened
1 14-ounce can Eagle Brand sweetened condensed milk
¼ cup lemon juice
1 15¼-ounce can crushed pineapple, well drained
2 8-ounce cartons of Cool Whip
¼ cup chopped pecans
2 9" graham cracker pie crusts

Combine cream cheese, condensed milk, lemon juice and pineapple; mixing until well blended. Fold in Cool Whip. Pour into crusts and sprinkle with pecans. Chill several hours or overnight. (15 minutes preparation time.)

Barbara C. Harris

Mrs. Claude Harris, Jr., *wife of former Representative (Alabama)*

Texas Rangers Blueberry Cobbler
SERVES 20

1 stick butter or margarine
2 cups sugar
¾ cup milk
1 cup flour

2 teaspoons baking powder
⅛ teaspoon salt
2-4 cups blueberries
cinnamon

Heat oven to 350°. Melt margarine in a 9″ × 13″ dish. In separate bowl mix 1 cup sugar, milk, flour, baking powder and salt. Pour over melted margarine. If using canned fruit, drain. Top flour mixture with fruit and sprinkle with remaining cup of sugar. Then sprinkle a little cinnamon on top. Bake for 30 to 45 minutes until crust is golden. (1 hour preparation time. Suitable for freezing.)

Cathy Brady

Mrs. Kevin Brady, wife of *Representative (Texas)*

Dump Cake
SERVES 12

1 box German chocolate cake mix with pudding
1 small package Jello chocolate instant pudding
4 eggs
½ pint sour cream
1 12-ounce package chocolate chips
½ cup cooking oil
½ cup warm water
¼ cup powdered sugar

Dump all ingredients except powdered sugar together and mix well. Grease bundt pan well and pour mixture into pan. Bake for 50 minutes at 350°. Do not over-bake. Cool for 10 minutes <u>only</u> (it will stick if cooled longer) and remove from pan. Sift powdered sugar over cake when cool. (15 minutes preparation time. Suitable for freezing.)

Lee Hamilton, *Representative (Indiana)*

Pecan Pie

SERVES 16

4 beaten eggs
1¼ cups sugar
¾ cup dark (or white) Karo syrup
5 Tablespoons melted butter

1¼ teaspoons vanilla flavoring
2 cups (or more) chopped pecans
2 unbaked regular 9" pie crusts

To the beaten eggs, add sugar, Karo syrup, melted butter and vanilla flavoring. Mix well after each addition. Add pecans, dividing evenly in the 2 crusts. Bake slowly in 275° preheated oven for 30 to 40 minutes until custard is "set" or pie rises slightly. Since ovens vary, check pies. (1 hour preparation time. Suitable for freezing.)

Frances Hagan

Mrs. G. Elliott Hagan, *wife of former Representative (Georgia)*

Coca Cola Cake

SERVES 24

Cake:
2 cups sugar
2 cups plain flour
2 sticks margarine
1 cup Coca Cola
2 teaspoons cocoa
½ teaspoon salt

1 teaspoon vanilla
2 eggs
1½ cups mini marshmallows
½ cup buttermilk
½ teaspoon soda

Topping:
1 stick margarine
6 Tablespoons Coca Cola
2 Tablespoons cocoa

1 teaspoon vanilla
1 box confectioners' sugar
1 cup chopped pecans

Cake: Sift flour and sugar together, set aside. Mix margarine, cocoa and Coca Cola. Heat on low temperature to melt margarine. Pour over flour and sugar. Mix well. Add the remaining ingredients and bake at 350° for 30 minutes in a 9" × 13" casserole dish.

Topping: Mix margarine, cocoa and Coca Cola in saucepan. Heat to a boil, pour over sugar and flavoring. Add pecans and spread over hot cake. (30 minutes preparation time. Suitable for freezing.)

Julie W. Collins

Mrs. Mac Collins, *wife of Representative (Georgia)*

Strawberry Cheesecake Trifle

SERVES 12 TO 16

2 8-ounce packages cream cheese, softened
2 cups powdered sugar, sifted
1 8-ounce carton sour cream
2 teaspoons vanilla
½ teaspoon almond extract
1 cup whipping cream
1 teaspoon vanilla

1 Tablespoon sugar
1 angel food cake, cut into 1" cubes
2 quarts fresh strawberries, hulled and sliced
3 Tablespoons sugar
3 Tablespoons Amaretto
fresh whole strawberries

Combine cream cheese and powdered sugar in a large mixing bowl. Beat at high speed with an electric mixer until well blended. Stir in sour cream, 2 teaspoons vanilla and ½ teaspoon almond extract. Beat whipping cream until foamy. Add 1 teaspoon vanilla and 1 tablespoon sugar; beat until peaks form. Fold whipping cream into cream cheese mixture. Add cake and stir gently to coat well. Combine sliced strawberries, 3 tablespoons sugar and Amaretto. Layer strawberries and cream cheese mixture into trifle bowl or large crystal/china bowl. Begin and end with strawberries. Chill. Garnish with whole strawberries. (30 minutes preparation time. Not suitable for freezing.)

Lucy Goode

Mrs. Virgil Goode, *wife of Representative (Virginia)*

Cooked Fudge Frosting

2 cups sugar
½ cup cocoa
½ cup shortening

dash of salt
1 teaspoon vanilla
⅔ cup canned milk (1 small can)

Stir all ingredients together in large saucepan. Bring to a good boil over medium heat. Boil for 2 minutes. You may need extra minutes if the weather is rainy or high humidity. Cool by placing pan in a sink of cold water, add ice to cool water. Beat frosting, while the pan is in the water, until it is thick enough to spread. If frosting gets too thick, add more canned milk. (30 minutes preparation time. Not suitable for freezing.)

Cynthia L Staton

Cynthia Staton, *daughter of former Representative Mick Staton (West Virginia)*

"Chocolate Tart"
SERVES 10

¼ pound butter
4 ounces unsweetened or semi-sweet chocolate
1½ cups sugar
3 large eggs (crack into a bowl and mix just to break yolks)
½ teaspoon vanilla
¼ cup chopped walnuts
pie crust

Preheat oven to 350°. Line a 9″ tart pan with pie crust. Melt butter and chocolate together in a large saucepan (over medium heat). Add sugar and mix well. Take off heat. Add 1 to 2 tablespoons chocolate to eggs and mix. Pour back into the chocolate mixture and blend well. Add vanilla, then add walnuts. Pour into pie shell. Bake for 30 minutes or until toothpick comes out clean. Whipped cream is great served on top! (25 minutes preparation time. Suitable for freezing.)

Gary A. Condit, *Representative (California)*

Sanibel Blizzard

For each serving:
1 scoop good quality vanilla ice cream or frozen yogurt
sliced Florida fresh strawberries
crumbled almond macaroon
1 Tablespoon Cointreau or Grand Marnier

Place scoop of ice cream in individual dish. Cover with sliced fresh strawberries. Sprinkle with macaroon crumbs. Drizzle with 1 tablespoon of orange flavored liquor over all.

Porter Goss, *Representative (Florida)*

Banana Cake
SERVES 12

Cake:
3 bananas
2 cups flour (sifted)
½ teaspoon baking powder
¾ teaspoon baking soda
½ teaspoon salt
½ cup butter or soft shortening
1½ cups sugar
2 eggs
1 teaspoon vanilla
¼ cup buttermilk

Lemon Butter Frosting:
½ cup butter
1 pound powdered sugar
½ teaspoon salt
3 teaspoons lemon juice
1 teaspoon grated lemon rind

Cake: Break bananas into chunks. Beat on low speed until mashed. Sift together next 4 ingredients. In a large mixer bowl beat butter, sugar, eggs and vanilla. Add flour mixture alternately with buttermilk and mashed bananas. Blend about 2 minutes. Pour batter into three 8″ or two 9″ prepared pans. Bake in a 350° oven, 30 to 35 minutes.

Lemon Butter Frosting: Beat all ingredients together until a good spreading consistency, adding water if necessary. Fill and top cake with frosting. (35 minutes preparation time. Not suitable for freezing.)

Mrs. Sam Johnson, *wife of Representative (Texas)*

Biscotti Cookies

10 eggs
2 cups sugar
3 sticks margarine, melted
2 Tablespoons almond flavoring

8 cups flour
8 teaspoons baking powder
½ pound toasted almonds (slices)

Beat eggs and sugar. Add melted margarine. Add dry ingredients. Knead until smooth. Refrigerate dough for several hours. Shape into loaves, 8″ long and 3″ wide. Bake at 375° for approximately 20 minutes. Remove from oven and cut loaves into diagonal slices. Place slices flat side down on baking sheet and return to oven to dry and brown (approximately 20 minutes). These cookies can be frozen but will also keep well in an airtight container for several weeks. Recipe can be halved. Makes 5 to 6 dozen. (40 minutes preparation time. Suitable for freezing.)

Mrs. Thomas W. Ewing, *wife of Representative (Illinois)*

Oranges a la Rogers
SERVES 8

4 oranges (preferably Florida
   navel oranges)
1 cinnamon stick

8 Tablespoons Kirsch
4 teaspoons sugar

Peel oranges. Put oranges on their side and slice across the orange into thin slices about ¼″ thick. Spread half of the orange slices on a dessert plate. Grate cinnamon stick lightly over orange slices (not too much). Pour ½ tablespoon of Kirsch on orange slices. Sprinkle with about ½ teaspoon of sugar. Repeat for each orange. (15 minutes preparation time. Not suitable for freezing.)

Paul Rogers, *former Representative (Florida)*

White Chocolate Brownies

1 cup unsalted butter
10 ounces white chocolate, broken
   in small pieces
1¼ cups sugar
4 large eggs

1 Tablespoon vanilla
2 cups unbleached all-purpose flour
½ teaspoon salt
1 cup coarsely chopped pecans

Preheat oven to 325°. Line an 11″ × 9″ pan with aluminum foil leaving a little overhang around the edges of the pan, and butter the foil. No aluminum foil necessary if disposable aluminum pan is used, which I find easier. Heat the butter and chocolate, stirring frequently, in a large saucepan over low heat until melted and smooth. Remove from heat. Using a wooden spoon, stir the sugar into the melted chocolate, then stir in the eggs and vanilla. (The mixture will look curdled.) Add the flour, salt and chopped pecans and quickly stir just until mixed. Pour batter into the pan. Bake the brownies until the top is lightly golden but the center is somewhat soft when pressed lightly, 30 to 35 minutes. Let cool to room temperature. Refrigerate the brownies at least 3 hours. Using the foil, lift the brownies from the pan. Cut into 20 to 25 squares, although larger portions are usually requested! (45 minutes preparation time. Suitable for freezing.)

John F. Tierney

John Tierney, *Representative (Massachusetts)*

Grandma Cockrum's Seven Minute Icing

2 egg whites
1½ cups sugar
dash of salt

¼ teaspoon cream of tartar
⅓ cup cold water
1 teaspoon vanilla

Combine ingredients, except vanilla, in the top of a double boiler away from the stove. Beat 30 seconds. Put top pan of ingredients over bottom pan of gently boiling water. Continue beating over water until mixture forms peaks (approximately 5 minutes). Remove from heat. Add 1 teaspoon vanilla and beat until it's of spreading consistency (approximately 1 minute). Add food coloring if desired. Makes enough icing to ice one 9″ two-layer cake. (15 minutes preparation time. Not suitable for freezing.)

Gina Costello Keen

Gina Costello-Keen, *daughter of Representative Jerry F. Costello (Illinois)*

RED CLOVER
(TRIFOLIUM PRATENSE)

VERMONT

A symbol of fertility and domestic virtue, it was considered good luck to give a woman clover as a gift. Clover flowers were used medicinally to treat coughs, purify the blood, and improve the texture of finger and toe nails. A poultice of clover flowers was believed to cure athlete's foot.

Pineapple Pudding Cake
SERVES 12

1 box of yellow cake mix
2 boxes of vanilla pudding
(cooked not instant)
1 #2 can of crushed pineapple

½ cup sugar
1 large container of Cool Whip
coconut
pecans (sliced)

Bake cake according to directions on box. While cake is baking cook pudding and start cooling. Cook pineapple (do not drain) with sugar until it comes to a boil. Let pineapple mixture cool. When the cake is done, poke holes in the cake. Pour the cooled pineapple mixture over the cake. Spread the cooled pudding over the cake. Spread most of the large container of Cool Whip over the cake. Sprinkle coconut and pecans on top of the Cool Whip. Refrigerate. Use a 13″ × 9″ baking dish or pan. (20 minutes preparation time. Suitable for freezing.)

Mrs. Thomas W. Ewing, wife of Representative (Illinois)

Apple Pie
SERVES 8

6 cups sliced apples
1¼ cups sugar
3 Tablespoons flour
1 teaspoon cinnamon
¼ teaspoon nutmeg

Topping:
½ cup brown sugar
¾ cup flour
⅓ cup margarine
9″ unbaked pastry shell

Mix all ingredients for apple mixture in large mixing bowl. Set aside. For topping: Mix brown sugar and flour in small mixing bowl. Using a fork or pastry blender, cut margarine into sugar and flour until well-mixed and crumbly. Place apple mixture into unbaked pastry shell. Top with crumb topping and press topping firmly into apples. Bake for 50 minutes in a preheated 400° oven. (25 minutes preparation time. Not suitable for freezing.)

Thomas W. Ewing, *Representative (Illinois)*

My Mom's Pumpkin Pie

1½ cups canned pumpkin
¾ cup sugar
½ teaspoon salt
1-1¼ teaspoons cinnamon
½-1 teaspoon ginger
¼-½ teaspoon nutmeg

¼-½ teaspoon cloves
3 slightly beaten eggs
1¼ cups milk
1 6-ounce can evaporated milk
1 unbaked 9" pie shell (crimp the edges to hold batter in)

Combine first 7 ingredients; blend in eggs, milk and evaporated milk. Pour batter into crimp-edged pie shell. Bake in hot 450° oven for 10 minutes. Lower oven to 325° and bake for additional 55 minutes or until knife inserted in center comes out clean. Cool. (15 minutes preparation time. Suitable for freezing.)

Mrs. F. James Sensenbrenner, Jr., *wife of Representative (Wisconsin)*

Texas Pralines

1 box (1 pound) light brown sugar
½ stick margarine
¼ cup water
2 Tablespoons light Karo syrup

2 cups pecans (halves or broken pieces)
dash salt
1 teaspoon vanilla extract

Place all ingredients in a heavy, medium-sized saucepan. Over medium-high heat, bring mixture to 240° on a candy thermometer. Stir only occasionally. Remove from heat, and add vanilla. Stir mixture with a wooden spoon until it begins to thicken and lose its gloss (usually around 7 to 8 minutes). Using 2 tablespoons and working quickly, drop candy onto foil. If mixture becomes too thick, stir in a few drops of hot water. The pralines will be set in a few minutes. Remove from foil and store in an airtight container. Makes about 25 pralines. We have given these pralines at Christmas for many years...a family tradition! (15 minutes preparation time. Not suitable for freezing.)

Jim Turner, *Representative (Texas)*

Sour Orange Meringue Pie

Filling:

⅓ cup plus 1⅓ Tablespoons cornstarch

⅓ cup flour

2 cups sugar

½ teaspoon salt

2 cups boiling water

4 egg yolks

2 Tablespoons butter or margarine

1½ teaspoons grated orange rind

⅔ cup plus 1 Tablespoon sour orange juice (Sour oranges can be obtained at orange groves. Have a friend who lives in Florida get some and send them to you. The juice can be frozen indefinitely.)

Meringue:

4 egg whites

½ teaspoon vanilla

¼ teaspoon cream of tartar

6 Tablespoons sugar

1 baked 9″ or 10″ pie shell

Filling: Mix cornstarch, flour, sugar and salt in the top of a double boiler. Add boiling water gradually, stirring constantly to prevent lumping. Place over direct heat and cook, stirring constantly, until thickened throughout. Cook, uncovered, over simmering water about 10 minutes, until clear and thick. Stir 2 or 3 times. Stir a small amount of hot mixture into the egg yolks. Combine this with the remaining hot mixture. Continue cooking over simmering water about 5 minutes, stirring constantly. Remove from heat. Add butter, orange rind and sour orange juice. Blend thoroughly. Cool for about 5 minutes. Pour into baked pie shell. Set aside to cool.

Meringue: Beat egg whites with vanilla and cream of tartar until soft peaks form. (Whites will whip fluffier at room temperature.) Add sugar, 1 tablespoon at a time, beating until the sugar is dissolved between each addition. Beat until the meringue is stiff and glossy. Spread on pie sealing to the edges of the pastry. Swirl knife across the top of the meringue to form peaks. Bake at 350° for 12 to 15 minutes or until peaks are golden brown. Allow the pie to cool before serving. A sharp knife, warmed in a glass of water will facilitate cutting. (Not suitable for freezing.)

Lynn Staton

Mrs. Mick Staton, *wife of former Representative (West Virginia)*

Apple Tart Pizza
S E R V E S   8

Pastry:
1½ cups all-purpose flour
1 Tablespoon sugar
¼ teaspoon salt (optional)
½ cup butter
6 Tablespoons cold water

Filling:
3 red delicious apples
2 Tablespoons sugar
½ teaspoon cinnamon
1 Tablespoon butter, cut into 12 pieces

In food processor (see note) combine flour, sugar, salt and butter. Process with an on-off motion until mixture resembles coarse crumbs. With processor on, gradually add water, and process with an on-off motion 10 times. On a clean work surface, shape mixture into a 5″ wide flat circle. Wrap and refrigerate for 20 minutes. Preheat oven to 425°F. On a well-floured surface, roll pastry into a 16″ wide circle (do not worry if the edges are rough). Fold pastry in half to transfer to a 14″ pizza pan. Pastry will hang over edge. Refrigerate. Cut each apple in quarters; remove core and seeds. Use a food processor (see note below) fitted with a slicing blade to slice apples. Remove pastry from refrigerator and arrange apples over pastry in a circular motif. Mix sugar and cinnamon, and sprinkle over apples. Dab with butter pieces. Fold pastry edges up over apples (about ½″ to 1″ around the edges). Bake for 20 to 25 minutes in a 425° oven, until crust is golden. Top with ice cream and serve like pizza slices.

Note: If you do not have a food processor, make pastry in a bowl. Combine dry ingredients, and cut in butter with 2 knives. Add water until pastry forms. Cut each apple quarter in 6 slices. (30 minutes preparation time. Not suitable for freezing.)

Adam Smith, *Representative (Washington)*

"Cherry Berries On A Cloud"

SERVES 8 TO 10

6 egg whites

½ teaspoon cream of tartar

¼ teaspoon salt

1¾ cups sugar

2 cups chilled whipping cream

2 3-ounce packages cream cheese, softened

1 cup sugar

1 teaspoon vanilla

2 cups miniature marshmallows

Cherry-Berry Topping:

1 21-ounce can cherry pie filling

1 teaspoon lemon juice

2 cups sliced fresh strawberries or 1 16-ounce package frozen strawberries, thawed

Heat oven to 275°. Butter (heavily) a 13″ × 9″ × 2″ pan. In large mixing bowl, beat egg whites, cream of tartar and salt until foamy. Beat in 1¾ cups sugar, 1 tablespoon at a time and continue beating until stiff and glossy (do not under-beat). Spread in pan. Bake for 1 hour. Turn off oven. Leave in oven with door closed for 12 hours or longer. In chilled bowl, beat whipping cream until stiff. Blend cream cheese, 1 cup sugar and vanilla. Gently fold whipped cream and marshmallows into cream cheese mixture. Spread over meringue. Chill for 12 to 24 hours. Cut into serving pieces. Top with cherry-berry topping.

Cherry-Berry Topping: Stir together cherry pie filling, lemon juice and sliced fresh strawberries or frozen strawberries. (2 hours preparation time. Not suitable for freezing.)

Mrs. John Tanner, *wife of Representative (Tennessee)*

Vanilla Fudge
SERVES 25 TO 35

2 cups sugar
1 cup heavy cream
¼ cup butter
¼ cup light corn syrup

½ teaspoon salt
1 cup miniature marshmallows
1 Tablespoon vanilla extract
½ cup chopped walnuts or pecans,
    if desired

Combine sugar, cream, butter, corn syrup and salt in large, heavy saucepan. Bring to gentle boil over low heat. Cook, stirring constantly, until mixture reaches the soft ball stage (238° to 240°F). Remove from heat, stirring in marshmallows and vanilla. Stir until marshmallows melt and candy starts to lose its gloss. Stir in nuts, if desired. Stir until candy starts to set. (DO NOT USE MIXER. STIR BY HAND.) Pour into buttered 8″ square pan. Cool. Makes 25 to 35 pieces. (Note: Do not attempt to double the recipe. The fudge will become too grainy.) (45 minutes preparation time. Suitable for freezing.)

John T. Doolittle, Representative (California)

Ricotta Cheese Pie

Crust:
1¼ cups graham cracker crumbs
¼ cup sugar
6 Tablespoons melted butter

Filling:
2½ cups (1¼ pounds) ricotta cheese
¾ cup sugar

1 cup toasted ground almonds
½ cup semi-sweet chocolate chips
    (well chilled and ground in the blender)
1½ cups Cool Whip
1 teaspoon almond extract

Press crust into a 9″ pie pan. Bake 10 minutes at 350° and cool. Beat cheese and sugar thoroughly. Stir in nuts and chocolate. Fold in the remaining ingredients. Spoon into the pie shell and refrigerate overnight.

Mrs. Joe Knollenberg, wife of Representative (Michigan)

Dipped Gingersnaps

2 cups sugar
1½ cups vegetable oil
2 eggs
½ cup molasses
4 cups flour
4 teaspoons baking soda
1 Tablespoon ground ginger
2 teaspoons ground cinnamon

1 teaspoon salt
additional sugar
2 12-ounce packages vanilla baking chips
¼ cup shortening
(I prefer Borden's Eagle Brand Candy
   Coating in place of chips and
   shortening if you can find it.)

In a mixing bowl, combine sugar and oil; mix well. Add eggs, 1 at a time, beating well after each addition. Stir in molasses. Combine dry ingredients; gradually add to creamed mixture and mix well. Shape into ¾" balls and roll in sugar. Place 2" apart on ungreased baking sheets. Bake at 350° for 10 to 12 minutes or until cookie springs back when touched lightly. Remove to wire racks to cool. Melt chips with shortening in a small saucepan over low heat. (Candy coating can be melted in microwave.) Dip the cookies halfway; shake off excess. Place on waxed paper-lined baking sheets to harden. Yield: About 12+ dozen. (30 minutes preparation time. Suitable for freezing.)

Julia H. Doolittle

Mrs. John T. Doolittle, *wife of Representative (California)*

Old-Fashioned Lemon Meringue Pie

1 cup sugar
4 Tablespoons flour
2 eggs, separated
juice and grated rind of 1 lemon

1 cup cold water
2 Tablespoons butter
1 pie shell, baked

Mix together in top of double boiler: sugar, flour, egg yolks (well beaten) and cold water. Cook over boiling water, stirring until thick. Stir in lemon juice, rind and butter. Pour into baked crust. Top with meringue made from 2 egg whites, beaten until stiff with 2½ tablespoons sugar. Brown lightly in hot oven (400°) for 7 to 10 minutes.

Nancy Black

Nancy Black, *daughter of former Representative L. H. Fountain (North Carolina)*

Key Lime Pie

8 large eggs, lightly beaten
2 cups sugar
⅔ cup Key lime juice
¼ cup grated lime rind
1 cup unsalted butter or margarine,
 softened

dash of salt
2 cups whipping cream
¼ cup sifted powdered sugar
2 teaspoons vanilla extract

Garnish: lime twists

Crust:
2½ cups graham cracker crumbs
½ cup firmly packed light brown sugar
⅔ cup unsalted butter, melted

Crust: Combine all ingredients; press into two 9″ pie plates. Bake at 375° for 6 to 8 minutes. Cool. Yield: Two 9″ pie crusts.

Combine first 5 ingredients in top of a double boiler; bring water to a boil. Reduce heat to low; cook, whisking constantly, until thickened. Add butter; whisk constantly until butter melts and mixture thickens. Pour into graham cracker crusts. Bake at 300° for 20 minutes or until set; cool. Cover and chill at least 8 hours. Beat whipping cream at high speed with an electric mixer until foamy. Gradually add powdered sugar, beating until soft peaks form. Stir in vanilla, and spread over filling. Chill. Garnish just before serving, if desired. Yield: Two 9″ pies. (Not suitable for freezing.)

Mary Hayworth

Mrs. J. D. Hayworth, *wife of Representative (Arizona)*

F L O W E R I N G   D O G W O O D
(C O R N U S   F L O R I D A)

VIRGINIA

Flowering dogwood is one of about 18 species of dogwoods native to the United States. It is truly a plant for all seasons. Masses of white, pink or red flowers bloom in the spring to be replaced by a crop of beautiful red berries during the late summer and early fall. The leaves turn a brilliant shade of crimson for several weeks during the late fall, providing dazzling color as the seasons change.

Chocolate Birthday Cake

Cake:
1½ cups sugar
1 cup Crisco
2 eggs
3 Tablespoons cocoa
3 Tablespoons red food coloring
2¼ cups cake flour
1 cup buttermilk
1 teaspoon baking soda
1 teaspoon white vinegar

Frosting:
1 cup milk
5 Tablespoons flour
1 cup butter
1 cup sugar
1 teaspoon vanilla

Cake: Mix sugar in Crisco. Add eggs 1 at a time. Then stir in cocoa and food coloring. Sift in flour and add buttermilk. Dissolve baking soda in vinegar and add to mixture. Pour mixture into two 8″ cake pans and bake for 30 minutes at 325°.

Frosting: Cook milk and flour together over low heat until warm and remove. In a separate bowl cream butter. Add milk mixture to butter and then mix in sugar and vanilla. Frost cooled cakes and then refrigerate cake before serving.

Marianne Gingrich

Mrs. Newt Gingrich, *wife of The Speaker of The House (Georgia)*

Kendel's Cookies

1 12-ounce package Nestle's chocolate mint chips
1 12-ounce package Nestle's butterscotch chips
1 16-ounce package Chinese noodles (chow mein)

Place chocolate and butterscotch chips in microwave safe bowl. Melt chips. (No more than 2 minutes.) Gradually add noodles to the mixture. Drop onto coated paper plates or wax paper. Place in freezer/refrigerator. Keep refrigerated and enjoy! Makes 36 cookies. (15 minutes preparation time. Suitable for freezing.)

Kendel & Ehrlich

Mrs. Robert L. Ehrlich, Jr., *wife of Representative (Maryland)*

Date Nut Sponge Cake

SERVES 14

5 egg yolks
5 egg whites
1 cup flour, sifted 2 times
1 cup sugar, sifted through fine sifter
¼ teaspoon salt
1 Tablespoon lemon juice or vinegar
grated rind of ½ lemon
2 10-ounce containers of chopped and sugared dates
16 ounces chopped pecans

Sift sugar through fine sifter one time before measuring. Sift flour one time before measuring. Separate yolks and whites of eggs (they will beat easily if at room temperature). Beat egg whites until stiff but not dry and beat in gradually 1 tablespoon of sugar for each egg white using sugar called for in recipe; set aside. It is unnecessary to wash beater before beating yolks. Add liquid to egg yolks and beat until lemon-colored and so thick that beater turns with difficulty. Add lemon rind. Beat in remaining sugar. Combine yolks and whites and fold together with spoon until mixture is even. Mix and sift remaining dry ingredients. Add dates/nuts and fold into egg mixture. Do not beat after adding flour, to avoid breaking air bubbles.

To fill pans and bake: Pour into 2 unbuttered 9" loaf pans or 1 tube pan. Cut through mixture several times to break large air bubbles. Bake 1 hour or more in moderately slow oven (325°). Invert on wire cooling rack and let stand until cold. Loosen with a spatula or knife. (45 minutes preparation time. Not suitable for freezing.)

Ann K. Chapman

Mrs. Oscar Chapman, *wife of former Representative (Colorado)*

Chocolate Mousse Cake

1½ cups softened butter

1 cup sugar

6 eggs

6 squares (1 ounce each) unsweetened baking chocolate, melted and at room temperature

2 packages unfilled lady finger cookies

½ pint whipping cream

1-3 Tablespoons sifted confectioners' (powdered) sugar

½ Tablespoon vanilla

In a large bowl, cream butter with electric mixer. Slowly add sugar and beat until fluffy. Add eggs one at a time, beating well after each. Pour in chocolate and mix well. Refrigerate while pan is prepared. Separate lady fingers (top from bottom), leaving them connected at the sides. Line a 10″ spring form pan with the lady fingers, sides and bottom. Pour filling into pan and return to refrigerator. Pour chilled cream into chilled small bowl. With mixer running slowly, add 1 to 3 tablespoons powdered sugar and ½ teaspoon vanilla. Whip until soft peaks form. Spread whipped cream on mousse cake and refrigerate for 2 hours. Remove from spring form pan and garnish. (45 minutes preparation time. Not suitable for freezing.)

Janis H. Battle

Mrs. Laurie C. Battle, *wife of former Representative (Alabama)*

Chocolate Chiffon Pie
SERVES 6 TO 8

6 Tablespoons cocoa
½ cup water
¾ cup sugar
3 slightly beaten egg yolks
¼ teaspoon salt
1 Tablespoon gelatin

¼ cup cold water
1 teaspoon vanilla
3 egg whites
¼ cup sugar
baked pie shell or graham cracker crust

Mix cocoa and water in top of double boiler. When dissolved, add sugar, 3 egg yolks and salt. Cook until the consistency of soft custard. Add gelatin softened in cold water. Stir until dissolved; then add vanilla. Cool. When mixture begins to thicken, fold in egg whites beaten with sugar until stiff, but not dry. Pour into baked pie shell or graham cracker shell. (20 minutes preparation time. Not suitable for freezing.)

Faith Hendricks Battle

Faith Battle, *daughter-in-law of former Representative Laurie C. Battle (Alabama)*

Cream Cheese Pound Cake
SERVES 24

3 sticks real butter, softened
8 ounces cream cheese, softened
3 cups sugar
½ teaspoon salt

1 Tablespoon almond extract
1 teaspoon vanilla extract
6 large eggs
3 cups flour

Cream butter, cream cheese and sugar in large mixing bowl. Add salt, almond and vanilla extracts. Add eggs, one at a time. Stir in flour, then beat for 2 to 3 minutes. Put batter in a well-greased tube pan, and bake at 325° for approximately 1 hour. Do not over-cook. Batter may also be split into 3 loaves and then frozen in aluminum foil after cooking. (15 minutes preparation time. Suitable for freezing.)

Elizabeth Atkins

Elizabeth Atkins, *daughter of Representative John Tanner (Tennessee)*

Delicious Black-Bottomed Pie

SERVES 8

½ cup sugar
1 Tablespoon cornstarch
2 cups milk, scalded
4 beaten egg yolks
1 teaspoon vanilla
1 6-ounce package semi-sweet
  chocolate pieces
1 baked 9" pie shell

1 Tablespoon (1 envelope) unflavored
  gelatin
¼ cup cold water
4 egg whites
½ cup sugar
1 cup heavy cream, whipped
chocolate decorettes

Combine sugar and cornstarch. Slowly add scalded milk to the beaten egg yolks. Stir in sugar mixture. Cook and stir in top of double boiler until the custard coats a spoon. Add vanilla. To 1 cup of the custard, add the chocolate pieces. Stir until the chocolate is melted. Pour in bottom of cooled, baked pie shell. Chill. Soften gelatin in cold water; add to remaining hot custard. Stir until dissolved. Chill until slightly thick. Beat egg whites, adding sugar gradually until mixture stands in stiff peaks. Fold in custard-gelatin mixture. Pour over chocolate layer and chill until set. Garnish with whipped cream and chocolate decorettes. (20 minutes preparation time. Not suitable for freezing.)

Joseph Pitts, *Representative (Pennsylvania)*

Baked Pears With Brie

SERVES 4

⅓ cup raisins
¼ cup hazelnuts
2 teaspoons honey

2 ounces peeled Brie cheese
4 pears, peeled, halved and cored
1 cup apple juice or sweet cider

Preheat oven to 350°F. Combine raisins and hazelnuts in a food processor or blender and process until finely chopped. With the motor running, add honey and cheese. Continue to process until a soft ball forms. Spoon cheese mixture into cavities of pears and set them in an oven-proof casserole. Pour juice around them and bake until pears are tender, about 35 minutes. Serve hot as a dessert, breakfast, or snack. (45 minutes preparation time. Not suitable for freezing.)

Mrs. Charles Rangel, *wife of Representative (New York)*

Newt's Fruit

SERVES 6 TO 8

1 medium size can of peaches
1 can of pears
1 can of chunk pineapple in light syrup
½ cup sugar
1 heaping Tablespoon cornstarch
1 heaping Tablespoon butter or
  margarine

1 Tablespoon vanilla
1 Tablespoon white vinegar
1 pinch of salt
2 bananas
maraschino cherries, halved (optional)

Drain peaches, pears and chunk pineapple <u>very well</u> and reserve liquid. Cut the fruit into bite-size pieces. Make a syrup using 1 cup of the reserved fruit juice, sugar and cornstarch. Cook over the stove, stirring constantly, until thick. Remove from stove and stir in margarine, vanilla, white vinegar and salt. Pour the syrup over the fruit while it is still hot. Stir the fruit well and refrigerate overnight. When ready to serve, slice the bananas over the fruit and stir again. Top with maraschino cherries if desired.

Marianne Gingrich

Mrs. Newt Gingrich, *wife of The Speaker of The House (Georgia)*

Bourbon Balls

2½ cups crushed vanilla wafers
1 cup finely chopped pecans
1 cup powdered sugar
1½ Tablespoons cocoa

2 Tablespoons light corn syrup
½ cup bourbon
¼ cup sifted powdered sugar for dusting

Combine wafer crumbs and pecans. Sift powdered sugar and cocoa together and add to crumb mixture. Stir corn syrup into bourbon and then into crumb mixture. Mix well and roll into small balls. Roll balls in the sifted powdered sugar. Set aside in a closed container to ripen for a few days. Note: Orange juice may be substituted for the bourbon. (30 minutes preparation time. Not suitable for freezing.)

Lucy Foley

Mrs. John R. Foley, *wife of former Representative (Maryland)*

Momo's Brownies

4 eggs, slightly beaten
2 cups sugar
½ cup melted butter
4 squares Bakers chocolate
1 cup flour

1 cup chopped nuts (pecans or
    walnuts are best)
2 teaspoons vanilla
powdered sugar

Beat eggs. Mix in sugar. In small bowl or saucepan melt butter and chocolate together. Add to eggs and sugar. Add flour. Stir well. Add nuts and vanilla. Bake at 350° in a greased and floured 9″ × 13″ pan for 20 to 30 minutes. Do not bake longer. Sift powdered sugar on top while still warm. Makes 1½ dozen brownies. (20 minutes preparation time. Suitable for freezing.)

Mrs. Lloyd Doggett, *wife of Representative (Texas)*

Outrageous Cookies

1 cup margarine
1 cup sugar
⅔ cup brown sugar
1 teaspoon vanilla
2 eggs
1 cup peanut butter

2 cups flour
1 cup oatmeal (quick)
2 teaspoons baking soda
½ teaspoon salt
1 package chocolate chips

Cream margarine, sugar, vanilla and eggs. Add peanut butter. Stir in flour, oatmeal, baking soda and salt. Add chocolate chips. Bake for 10 to 12 minutes. Makes 4 dozen. "Super Good!" (10 minutes preparation time. Suitable for freezing.)

Mrs. John Thune, *wife of Representative (South Dakota)*

Angel Lemon Pie

SERVES 6

3 eggs, separated
2 lemons (juice of)
¾ cup sugar

6 Tablespoons sugar
1 pre-baked pie shell

Beat egg yolks slightly and mix in lemon juice and ¾ cup sugar. Cook 1 minute. Beat egg whites. Take half of beaten egg whites and mix in to thicken. Pour mixture into pre-baked pie shell. Add 6 tablespoons of sugar to the remaining beaten egg whites. Spread this meringue on top of lemon mixture. Bake at 350° until done. (Not suitable for freezing.)

Cindy Stenholm

Mrs. Charles Stenholm, *wife of Representative (Texas)*

Cathy's Sandtarts

1 cup of butter (do not substitute)
4 Tablespoons of sugar
1 teaspoon vanilla
2 cups flour
2 cups chopped pecans
1 cup powdered sugar
3 dozen chocolate kisses (optional)

Beat butter until smooth. Add sugar and stir. Add flour, pecans and vanilla and mix well. Shape into small balls and place on ungreased cookie sheet. Bake at 325° for 20 to 30 minutes, until lightly browned. Roll in powdered sugar while still warm. We also love to put a chocolate kiss in the middle of each before baking. Makes 3 dozen cookies. (45 minutes preparation time. Suitable for freezing.)

Libby Doggett

Mrs. Lloyd Doggett, *wife of Representative (Texas)*

Dana's Fab Flan

SERVES 8

WESTERN RHODODENDRON
(RHODODENDRON SP.)
SPECIES SENT: RHODODENDRON
MACROPHYLLUM

WASHINGTON

Members of the heath family, rhododendrons grow on acidic soils in forests of the Cascades from British Columbia to northern California and east to Oregon. The striking flower stalks, which sometimes reach six feet in height, bloom from May to June.

4 eggs
4 egg yolks
¾ cup sugar
1 14-ounce can sweetened condensed milk
2 cups whole milk
1 Tablespoon vanilla extract
¾ cup of sugar for caramel topping

Preheat oven to 325°. In a medium-size bowl use an electric mixer to beat the eggs and egg yolks. Add the sugar and beat for another minute. Add both kinds of milk and vanilla extract. Beat until frothy; set aside. To make the caramel topping, pour the ¾ cup of sugar into a small Teflon skillet and place over a medium flame. Cook until the sugar dissolves and starts to turn brown. Remove from heat and pour into a 9" round pan. Swirl around until the bottom of the pan is coated. Pour the egg and milk mixture into the caramel coated pan. Place the pan in a large baking dish. Pour water into the baking dish halfway up the side of the flan pan (this is a water bath). Place in preheated oven. Bake for 1 to 1½ hours. Check to see if done by inserting a knife in the center, it should come out clean. Remove the flan from the oven and take the pan out of the baking dish. Cool. Cover with plastic wrap and refrigerate for at least 4 hours. To serve: run knife along the sides and invert the flan onto a plate. The caramel syrup will cover the flan. (20 minutes preparation time. Not suitable for freezing.)

Nancy B. Aiken

Nancy B. Aiken, *daughter of former Representative William S. Broomfield (Michigan)*

Blitz Torte

Torte:
½ cup butter
½ cup sugar
⅛ teaspoon salt
4 egg yolks, lightly beaten
1 teaspoon vanilla
3 Tablespoons milk
1 cup sifted cake flour
1 teaspoon baking powder
4 egg whites
¾ cup sugar
½ cup sliced blanched almonds
1 Tablespoon sugar
½ teaspoon cinnamon

Cream Filling:
⅓ cup sugar
3 Tablespoons cornstarch
¼ teaspoon salt
2 egg yolks
2 Tablespoons butter
2 cups milk, scalded
1 teaspoon vanilla

Torte: Cream butter. Beat in sugar and salt, then egg yolks, vanilla, milk and flour (sifted with baking powder). Spread mixture in 2 round 9″ greased cake pans. Beat egg whites until very light. Add ¾ cup sugar gradually and spread on unbaked mixture in both pans. Sprinkle with almonds, 1 tablespoon sugar and cinnamon and bake at 350° about 30 minutes. Cool and put together with cream filling.

Cream Filling: Combine sugar, cornstarch, salt and egg yolks; beat thoroughly. Add butter and enough milk to make a smooth paste. Add paste to remaining hot milk and cook over boiling water, stirring constantly until mixture is thickened. Cool and add vanilla. Makes one 9″ two-layer cake. Serve garnished with whipped cream.

Claudia Fox Cannon

Mrs. Chris Cannon, *wife of Representative (Utah)*

Baked Apples with Raspberries and Grand Marnier

SERVES 4

4 golden delicious apples, cored and left whole
¼ cup raisins
2 cups dry white wine
½ cup Grand Marnier
⅓ cup sugar
24 raspberries
4 sprigs fresh mint

Preheat oven to 350°. Place apples in baking dish large enough to hold them snugly. Divide raisins evenly among apples to fill each core hole. Pour wine and half Grand Marnier over apples; sprinkle sugar evenly over top. Bake 1 hour or until tender. Baste regularly to achieve a golden brown glaze. Remove from oven. Pour over the apples remaining Grand Marnier; let cool. To serve, place 1 apple on plate and spoon sauce over apple. Garnish with raspberries and mint sprigs. (1 hour preparation time.)

Mrs. Joyce Hubbard

Mrs. Joyce Hubbard, *member of Congressional Club (Kentucky)*

Tapas Sesame Peanut Fingers

6 slices white toast, crust removed
1 cup peanut butter
½ cup butter or margarine
½ cup brown sugar
¼ teaspoon cinnamon
1 cup sesame seeds

Blend together peanut butter, butter, brown sugar and cinnamon. Melt in a saucepan over low heat or in microwave for 1½ minutes until smooth. Cut toast into ½″ strips. Dip toast strips into peanut mixture until coated. Place on waxed paper. Let cool for a couple of minutes; then roll in sesame seeds. Place in refrigerator to finish chilling. Makes 2 dozen. (20 minutes preparation time. Not suitable for freezing.)

Phil English

Phil English, *Representative (Pennsylvania)*

Swedish Tea Ring

SERVES 10

2 yeast cakes
¼ cup luke warm water
¼ cup shortening
½ cup sugar
1 teaspoon salt
2 eggs, beaten
1 cup milk, scalded
1 teaspoon grated lemon rind

5 cups sifted flour
melted butter
brown sugar
cinnamon
1 cup confectioners' sugar
2 Tablespoons warm milk
½ teaspoon vanilla
chopped pecans

Soften yeast in luke warm water. Add shortening, sugar and salt to scalded milk; cool to luke warm. Add softened yeast, eggs, lemon rind and enough flour to make a soft dough. Turn out on lightly floured board and knead until satiny. Place in greased bowl, cover and let rise until doubled in bulk. Shape into 2 rectangular sheets about ¼" thick. Brush with melted butter and sprinkle with brown sugar and cinnamon. Roll like a jelly roll and then shape into a ring. Place on a greased baking sheet and cut with scissors at 1" intervals almost through the ring. Turn slices slightly. Cover and let rise until doubled in bulk. Bake in moderate oven (375°F) for 25 to 30 minutes. While warm, spread with icing made from 1 cup confectioners' sugar, 2 tablespoons warm milk and ½ teaspoon vanilla. Sprinkle with chopped pecans. (6 hours preparation time. Suitable for freezing.)

Gene Green, *Representative (Texas)*

Chocolate Bundt Cake

1 package chocolate cake mix (without pudding in mix)
¾ cup water
¾ cup vegetable oil
4 eggs
1 3¾-ounce package instant chocolate pudding mix
½ cup sour cream
1 6-ounce package chocolate chips
powdered sugar

Combine cake mix, water, oil, eggs, instant pudding mix and sour cream in a large mixing bowl. Beat on medium speed of an electric mixer for 10 minutes. Fold in chocolate chips and pour into greased bundt pan. Bake at 350° for 50 to 60 minutes. Cool for 20 minutes and remove cake from pan. Sprinkle with powdered sugar. (Suitable for freezing.)

Jim Slattery, *former Representative (Kansas)*

BIG RHODODENDRON
(RHODODENDRON SP.)
SPECIES SENT:
RHODODENDRON MACROPHYLLUM

WEST VIRGINIA

There are approximately 800 species of rhododendrons worldwide. They are evergreen, semi-evergreen, or deciduous shrubs. Found primarily in temperate regions of the Northern Hemisphere, they are found on all continents except Africa and South America. They are most abundant in the Himalayas, southeast Asia, and the mountains of Malaysia.

Grasshopper Pie
SERVES 8

14-16 Oreo or Hydrox cookies
2 Tablespoons butter, melted
24 large marshmallows
½ cup milk

4 Tablespoons green creme de menthe
2 Tablespoons white creme de cacao
1 cup whipping cream

Remove white centers from cookies and roll cookies to a fine crumb. Mix creme center mixture back into cookie crumbs, blending well. Add butter and mix until well-blended. Butter a 9″ pie pan and press cookie mixture on bottom and sides of pan. Melt marshmallows and milk over low heat. Cool. Stir creme de menthe and creme de cacao into marshmallow mixture. Whip cream and fold into mixture. Pour into cookie crumb pie shell and chill or freeze for several hours before serving. Take pie out of freezer about 10 minutes before serving. You can make it even fancier by decorating with a few chocolate curls or saving a few cookie crumbs to sprinkle on top. A few days aging even improves it.

Mrs. Scott McInnis, *wife of Representative (Colorado)*

Key Lime Pie
SERVES 6

4 eggs, separated
½ cup lime juice
1 14-ounce can sweetened
    condensed milk

½ teaspoon cream of tartar
⅓ cup sugar
1 8″ pie shell

Beat egg yolks until light and thick. Blend in lime juice, then milk; stirring until mixture thickens. If desired, add a few drops of green food coloring. Pour mixture into baked 8″ pie shell. Beat egg whites with cream of tartar until stiff. Gradually beat in sugar. Beat until glossy peaks form. Spread egg whites over surface of pie to edge of crust. Bake in a 350° oven until golden brown, about 20 minutes. Chill before serving. (40 minutes preparation time. Not suitable for freezing.)

Mrs. Paul Gillmor, *wife of Representative (Ohio)*

Strawberry Freeze
SERVES 12

1 cup flour
½ cup margarine, melted
¼ cup brown sugar
½ cup nuts, chopped
2 egg whites, unbeaten
¾ cup sugar

2 teaspoons lemon juice
1 10-ounce package frozen
   strawberries (thawed), or 2 cups
   fresh berries (sliced)
½ pint whipping cream

Mix the flour, margarine, brown sugar and chopped nuts together. Spread in a 13″ × 9″ pan. Bake for 15 to 20 minutes at 350°, stirring often to make crumbs. Leave half the crumbs in pan, take out the rest for topping. Cool. Using largest electric mixer bowl, beat for 20 minutes the egg whites, sugar, lemon juice and strawberries. Scrape the sides of the bowl and clean beaters occasionally. In separate bowl, whip the whipping cream and fold in the other mixture. Spread carefully over the crumbs and top with reserved crumbs. Freeze. Cut in squares to serve. Keeps well. (1 hour preparation time. Suitable for freezing.)

Peggy Soderberg

Mrs. William Soderberg, *daughter of former Representative Robert A. Grant (Indiana)*

Easy Peanut Butter Cookies
SERVES 10

1 14-ounce can Eagle Brand
   condensed milk
¾ cup peanut butter

2 cups biscuit baking mix
1 teaspoon vanilla extract
granulated sugar

Preheat oven to 375°. In large mixer bowl, beat Eagle Brand condensed milk and peanut butter until smooth. Add biscuit mix and vanilla. Mix well. Shape into 1″ balls. Roll in sugar. Place 2″ apart on ungreased baking sheets. Flatten with fork. Bake 6 to 8 minutes or until lightly browned. Do not over-bake. Cool. Store tightly covered at room temperature. (10 minutes preparation time. Suitable for freezing.)

Marie Porter Royce

Mrs. Edward Royce, *wife of Representative (California)*

Et Cetera

Et Cetera

INTERNATIONAL DOLL MUSEUM

Friendships in Washington are one of our most precious commodities. Every year the members of the Congressional Club host the wives of the diplomatic corps at a very special luncheon. We have the honor on this occasion to show off our International Doll Museum.

Mrs. John C. Kunkel of Pennsylvania, President of the Congressional Club in 1966, asked the foreign embassies to donate a doll from their countries dressed in native costumes. This provided the opportunity for greatly needed redecorating and expansion of the board room. Now the room could provide the adaptability for meetings, lessons and bridge, plus house our beautiful Doll Museum in specially designed cabinets that line the walls.

In her dedication address, Mrs. Kunkel said, "This Doll Museum is dedicated to friendship and understanding among people from every country in the world. It will be a permanent reminder of the esteem in which the members of The Congressional Club hold the representatives of foreign nations serving in Washington."

Popovers
SERVES 6

2 eggs
1 cup milk
1 cup flour, sifted
¼ teaspoon salt
1 Tablespoon melted butter

Beat the eggs slightly, add the milk. Combine this slowly to the sifted flour and salt. Mix until there are no lumps. Add the butter. Pour the batter into hot greased popover pans until about half full. Bake for 30 minutes in hot oven (450°), then reduce the temperature to moderate (350°) for 15 minutes longer. (10 minutes preparation time. Not suitable for freezing.)

Mrs. John Sparkman, *wife of former Senator (Alabama)*

Carmie's Fruit Dip

1 pint sour cream
4 Tablespoons brown sugar
4 Tablespoons Kahlúa
Fresh fruit

Add brown sugar and Kahlúa to sour cream, refrigerate at least 4 hours or more. Serve with fresh fruit. (Not suitable for freezing.)

Tish Traficant

Mrs. James Traficant, wife of *Representative (Ohio)*

Eagle River Inn Honey Granola

2½ cups Quaker Quick Oats
½ cup brown sugar
½ cup raw sunflower seeds
⅓ cup honey
⅓ cup melted butter
¼ cup bran

1 teaspoon cinnamon
1 teaspoon vanilla extract
½ cup raisins
½ cup chopped dates
½ cup dried apricots or dried cranberries

Combine oats, brown sugar, sunflower seeds, honey, butter, bran, cinnamon and vanilla. Mix well and bake in a lightly greased 9″ × 13″ × 2″ pan for 20 to 25 minutes at 325°, stirring occasionally, until light brown. Remove from oven and stir in the dried fruit. Spread mixture onto a cookie sheet to cool. Store in the refrigerator in an airtight container. Makes 4½ cups. (15 minutes preparation time. Not suitable for freezing.)

Stephanie A Blatnik

Stephanie Blatnik, *daughter of former Representative John A. Blatnik (Minnesota)*

Breaded Dandelions
SERVES 4

¼ cup milk
1 Tablespoon baking powder
½ cup flour
2 Tablespoons powdered milk

1 egg
pinch of salt
16 large dandelion blossoms

Mix all ingredients, except blossoms. Wash blossoms lightly. Drain. Do not let wilt. Dip into batter. Fry in hot deep fat until golden brown. (Not suitable for freezing.)

Mrs. Ron Lewis, *wife of Representative (Kentucky)*

Tomato Dressing

1 cup sugar
1 Tablespoon salt
1 teaspoon pepper
¾ cup vinegar

1 cup salad oil
1 can tomato soup
2-3 cloves garlic, whole

In a large glass jar combine all ingredients and shake well. Refrigerate overnight. Before serving, remove garlic. Will keep for several weeks in the refrigerator. Wonderful on fresh tomatoes. Makes 4 cups. (10 minutes preparation time. Not suitable for freezing.)

Melanie Broyhill, *daughter-in-law of former Senator James T. Broyhill (North Carolina)*

Watermelon Jelly

4 cups seeded, diced watermelon
3½ cups sugar
2 Tablespoons lemon juice
½ of a 6-ounce foil pouch package liquid fruit pectin

Prepare 4 half-pint jelly jars and lids by boiling and keeping hot in water. Place diced watermelon in a blender container. Cover and blend until smooth. Should make 2 cups pureé. In a Dutch oven combine pureé, sugar and lemon juice. Bring the mixture to a full rolling boil over high heat, stirring constantly with a long-handled wooden spoon. Stir in the pectin all at once. Return to a full rolling boil. Boil hard for 1 minute, stirring constantly. Remove from heat; skim off foam. Ladle jelly into clean hot half-pint jars. Adjust lids. Allow to cool completely. This is great with cream cheese and English muffins or bagels. Wonderful Christmas gifts! Makes 4 half pints. (60 minutes preparation time. Not suitable for freezing.)

Jeff Sessions, *Representative (Alabama)*

Easy Hollandaise Sauce in Microwave
SERVES 2

¼ cup butter
¼ cup half and half (or light cream)
2 egg yolks, slightly beaten
1 Tablespoon lemon juice

½ teaspoon dry mustard
¼ teaspoon salt
dash of Tabasco

Melt butter for 1 minute (medium high in microwave). Stir in the rest of the ingredients and cook for 1 minute, stirring every 15 seconds. Remove from microwave and stir briskly with a whisk. Very easy and delicious. (5 minutes preparation time. Suitable for freezing.)

Diane Lewis Nagle, *member of the Congressional Club (Iowa)*

Muesli

SERVES 8

4 cups uncooked quick oatmeal
½ cup plain wheat germ
½ cup sweetened wheat germ
½ cup raisins

½ cup pecans or almonds
12 chopped dried apricot halves
1 cup confectioners sugar
1 Tablespoon grated orange peel

Spread 4 cups uncooked quick oatmeal on baking sheet. Bake for 30 minutes at 250°. Cool. In a large bowl mix the toasted oats and other ingredients well. Refrigerate. Serve with milk or yogurt. (30 minutes preparation time. Suitable for freezing.)

David Minge, *Representative (Minnesota)*

All Purpose Hot Sauce

1 Tablespoon corn oil
1 cup chopped onion (large)
½ chopped green pepper
1 garlic clove, minced
7 ounces whole kernel corn, drained
4-ounce can roasted peeled green
　chilies (I remove seeds)

16-ounce can tomatoes, chopped
½ cup stuffed green olives
3 Tablespoons hot chili sauce
1 Tablespoon chili powder
1 teaspoon salt
1 teaspoon pepper

In skillet heat oil; add onion, green pepper and garlic. Cook slowly, stirring often until contents are wilted. Add remaining ingredients and heat, stirring to mix. Serve hot or cold as a relish for vegetables or meat. Makes 1½ pints. Store in the refrigerator. (20 minutes preparation time. Not suitable for freezing.)

Mrs. Donald Matthews, *wife of former Representative (Florida)*

WOOD VIOLET
(VIOLA PEDATA)

WISCONSIN

Members of the violet family (Violaceae), the genus Viola includes some 500 species, of which twenty occur in the United States. Violets spread by creeping underground rhizomes. The flowers form capsules that dry and break to project the seeds into the air.

Jeanne's Spaghetti Sauce
SERVES 6

2 small or medium onions
1¼-1½ pounds ground beef
4 8-ounce cans tomato paste
2 cans of water for each can of paste
⅓ cup sugar
½ teaspoon fennel seed
½ teaspoon oregano

½ teaspoon garlic salt
¼ teaspoon Italian seasoning
½ Tablespoon garlic powder
½ teaspoon celery salt
½ teaspoon pepper
salt to taste

Sauté onions until clear. Brown and drain ground beef. Add tomato paste and water. Add spices according to your taste. Add onions, meat and sugar. Let simmer for 1 to 4 hours. (1 hour 30 minutes minimum preparation time. Suitable for freezing.)

Evelyn Madigan

Mrs. Edward Madigan, *wife of former Representative and former Cabinet Secretary (Illinois)*

Fig Jam

3 cups mashed figs (use very ripe figs)
3 cups sugar
1 6-ounce package strawberry Jell-O

Combine figs, sugar, and Jell-O. Let the mixture stand to blend for 30 minutes. Bring to boiling point (not to a fast rolling boil.) Cook and stir for 5 minutes. Pour into sterilized jars and seal.

We grow figs on the family farm in South Carolina and love to make this jam during the hot, lazy days of late summer. The Jell-O helps to make the jam a bright red which makes it a perfect gift for friends at Christmas. The sweet taste of this jam is enjoyed by children and adults alike! Will keep more than 1 year, unfrozen, in sterilized jars. (1 hour preparation time. Suitable for freezing.)

Jenny Sanford

Mrs. Marshall (Mark) Sanford, wife of *Representative (South Carolina)*

Cranberry Strawberry Relish

1 12-ounce package frozen strawberries
½ cup sugar

1 12-ounce package fresh cranberries
½ cup chopped pecans, optional

Drain 1 12-ounce package frozen strawberries (thawed). Save juice and add water to make 1 cup. Add ½ cup sugar to the liquid and bring to a boil. Add 1 12-ounce package cranberries. Cook until the berries pop. Stir in the strawberries and refrigerate 3 hours. Chopped pecans may be added if desired.

Suzie Brewster

Mrs. Bill Brewster, *wife of former Representative (Oklahoma)*

Brandied Cranberries
SERVES 8

4 cups fresh cranberries, cleaned
2¼ cups granulated sugar
½ cup brandy
½ cup granulated sugar

Place cranberries on 13″ × 9″ shallow pan. Sprinkle sugar over cranberries. Do not stir. Cover tightly with aluminum foil. Bake for 1 hour at 350°, if using a metal pan, or 325°, if using a glass pan. Remove from oven and stir gently. Let cool. Pour brandy over cranberries and sprinkle with remaining sugar. Stir gently. Refrigerate. (1 hour preparation time. Not suitable for freezing.)

June Harvey

Mrs. James Harvey, *wife of former Representative (Michigan)*

White Barbecue Sauce for Grilled Chicken

3 cups Hellmann's mayonnaise
1 cup lemon juice
½ cup sugar
½ cup vinegar

½ cup Worcestershire sauce
8 teaspoons salt
¼ cup pepper

Mix all ingredients with a wire whisk. Marinate chicken breasts for 30 minutes. Baste chicken with sauce while grilling.

Candace Bevill

Candace Bevill, *stepdaughter of Representative Spencer Bachus (Alabama)*

My Mother's Chili Sauce

1 large can tomatoes, crushed
1 large onion, chopped
1 large green pepper, chopped
½ cup brown sugar
⅓ cup cider vinegar
salt and pepper to taste

Combine ingredients in saucepan. Bring to boil. Reduce heat and simmer for 45 minutes. Adjust seasonings. Sauce will keep in refrigerator for weeks. Serve with meat loaf or roast beef. (Not suitable for freezing.)

John J. Rhodes

John J. Rhodes, *former Representative (Arizona)*

"Puppy" Chow

1½ sticks margarine
¾ cup creamy peanut butter
12 ounce bag chocolate chips
1 box Wheat Chex
powdered sugar

On top of double boiler, melt margarine, peanut butter and chocolate chips. Pour over box of Wheat Chex. Cool until hardened. Sprinkle with powdered sugar. This children's recipe is a healthy snack easily made. Stephanie Lampson won "First Prize" in a newspaper recipe contest with this recipe.

Stephanie Lampson

Stephanie Lampson, *daughter of Representative Nicholas V. Lampson (Texas)*

Ice Box Bran Muffins

2 cups boiling water
2 cups Nabisco 100% Bran cereal
4 cups Kelloggs All Bran
1 cup shortening
4 eggs, beaten

1 quart buttermilk
5 cups flour
5 teaspoons baking soda
1 teaspoon salt

Pour boiling water over Nabisco cereal. Cool. Cream shortening and sugar. Add eggs, buttermilk and soaked cereal. Sift together flour, baking soda and salt. Add to mixture and beat. Add All Bran and fold in until moistened. Store in 4 quart jars. Will keep up to 6 weeks. Bake 20 minutes at 375° in greased muffin pans. (20 minutes preparation time. Not suitable for freezing.) Makes 5 dozen.

Alice Baesler

Mrs. Scotty Baesler, *wife of Representative (Kentucky)*

Sourdough Bread
SERVES 24

Starter:
1 package yeast
1 cup warm water
3 Tablespoons instant potatoes

Feeder for sourdough bread:
1 cup hot water
¾ cup sugar
3 Tablespoons instant potatoes

Sourdough bread:
6 cups bread flour
½ cup sugar
1 teaspoon salt

1 cup starter
½ cup canola oil
1½ cups hot water

Starter: Combine starter ingredients and let this set at room temperature for 6 to 8 hours. Store in refrigerator 3 to 5 days, then feed.

Feeder: Mix feeder ingredients and add to starter every 3 to 5 days, whether you use starter or not. Let stand 10 to 12 hours after feeding and use 1 cup per recipe.

Sourdough bread: Mix ingredients and feeder portion together well. Let stand all day. Punch down and divide into 3 parts. Knead on a well floured surface. Put into 3 well greased loaf pans and let stand 10 to 12 hours. In the morning, bake at 350° for about 30 minutes. Dough can be formed into rolls or into miniature individual loaves. This is a great product to share with family and friends. (Suitable for freezing.)

Bob Etheridge, *Representative (North Carolina)*

Angel Biscuits

1 package dry yeast
¼ cup warm water
2 Tablespoons sugar
⅔ cup salad oil
2 cups buttermilk

5 cups flour
1 teaspoon salt
5 teaspoons baking powder
½ teaspoon baking soda

Mix sugar, yeast and warm water in a bowl. Mix flour, baking soda, salt and baking powder together in a large bowl. In another large bowl, combine the buttermilk, oil and yeast mixture. Combine the dry and liquid ingredients and mix well. Turn out mixture on a floured board and knead gently until easy to handle. Use only as much of the dough that is needed at a time. Roll out and cut in a shape desired for rolls. Bake at 350° until brown. Save remaining dough in a plastic bag and place in the refrigerator. Use only the amount needed and the rest will last several days. Makes 2 dozen. (15 minutes preparation time. Not suitable for freezing.)

Dawn Gibbons

Mrs. Jim Gibbons, *wife of Representative (Nevada)*

Cinnamon Buns

1 package of ready to bake biscuits
1 stick butter or margarine

1 cup sugar
1 heaping Tablespoon cinnamon

Preheat oven according to biscuit package instructions. Melt butter in bowl. Mix sugar and cinnamon together. Dip biscuits in butter. Then coat on all sides with sugar and cinnamon mixture. Place on ungreased cookie sheet close together. Follow baking instructions on biscuit package and serve hot from oven.

Richard H. Bryan

Richard H. Bryan, *Senator (Nevada)*

Blueberry Gingerbread
SERVES 12

½ cup cooking oil
1 cup sugar
3 Tablespoons molasses
1 egg
2 cups flour
1 teaspoon baking soda
½ teaspoon ginger

1 teaspoon cinnamon
½ teaspoon nutmeg
1 cup buttermilk (or ¾ cup milk mixed with 1 teaspoon vinegar)
1 cup fresh or frozen blueberries (fresh New Jersey blues are best!)
2 Tablespoons sugar

Beat together oil, sugar and molasses with an electric mixer. Beat in egg. Combine the flour, spices and baking soda. Toss the blueberries with 2 tablespoons of the flour mixture. Save. Add remaining flour to wet ingredients alternating with buttermilk, beating each time. Stir in blueberries by hand. Pour into a greased and floured or sprayed 12″ × 7″ baking dish. Sprinkle top with sugar. Bake in 350° oven for 35 to 40 minutes. Top will be golden and cake will not stick to testing toothpick. Cut into serving squares. Serve as is or top with whipped cream or ice cream. Powdered sugar can also be sprinkled on top. (20 minutes preparation time. Suitable for freezing.)

Marie Smith

Mrs. Chris Smith, *wife of Representative (New Jersey)*

Food Processor Mayonnaise

1 extra-large egg
½ teaspoon salt
½ teaspoon dry mustard

¼ teaspoon paprika
2 Tablespoons lemon juice
1 cup canola oil

Put egg, seasonings, lemon juice and 1 tablespoon oil in the processor. Process until well blended. Add oil in a steady stream while processing until it is thick and blended.

Lou Bevill

Mrs. Tom Bevill, *wife of former Representative (Alabama)*

Delicious Broccoli Cornbread
SERVES 14

4 eggs, well beaten
1 onion, chopped
1 cup cottage cheese (8 ounces)

2 boxes Jiffy cornbread mix
1 box frozen broccoli
1 stick margarine

Mix first 4 ingredients and let sit for 5 minutes. Steam broccoli until tender, drain and cool. Melt 1 stick margarine in 9″ × 13″ pan. Pour ¾ or more of melted margarine into cornbread mix, add broccoli and mix well. Bake in a 400° oven for 25 minutes. (30 minutes preparation time. Suitable for freezing.)

Ed Bethune

Ed Bethune, *former Representative (Arkansas)*

Poppy Seed Bread
SERVES 20

3 beaten eggs
2½ cups sugar
1½ cups milk
1¼ cups cooking oil
1 Tablespoon poppy seeds

1½ teaspoons baking powder
1½ teaspoons salt
1½ teaspoons vanilla
1½ teaspoons almond extract
3 cups flour

Frosting:
2 Tablespoons soft margarine
2 cups powdered sugar

1 teaspoon vanilla
1 teaspoon almond extract

Cream together the eggs and sugar. Blend in milk, oil, poppy seeds, baking powder, salt, vanilla and almond extract. Gradually add the flour. Batter will be runny. Pour into 2 large, greased and floured loaf pans or several smaller loaf pans. Bake at 325° for 40 minutes to 1 hour (depending on loaf sizes) or until done in the middle. Cool in pan for 5 minutes. Tip: Do not over-beat batter. Frosting: Add enough hot water to frosting ingredients and beat until thin consistency. Pour or spread over hot poppy seed bread. (60 minutes preparation time. Suitable for freezing.)

Leslie Howell Sandlin

Mrs. Max Sandlin, *wife of Representative (Texas)*

Russian Black Bread

(This recipe is a modification of a recipe from the book A La Russe by Darra Goldstein and from advice of Russian grandmothers.)

Starter—4 days before baking bread: Mix 1 cup dark rye flour and 1 cup flat beer, set aside. Stir every day.

2 Tablespoons or packages
  active dry yeast
2 cups flat beer, ale or Kvass
  (a Russian fermented drink)
3-3½ cups dark rye flour
3 cups white flour
2 Tablespoons cooking oil
4 Tablespoons butter

4 Tablespoons honey
1 teaspoon black pepper
2 Tablespoons instant coffee
3-4 Tablespoons dark powdered
  chocolate
2½ Tablespoons salt
3 teaspoons powdered coriander

If you are using a bread maker, follow directions for putting in ingredients. If not, mix the yeast with some of the beer to soften. Add to starter, rye and white flours, oil, spices, salt and beer. Hold back some of the white flour to test for the thickness of the dough. Melt the butter, honey and coffee flakes so they are smooth. Knead together, adding more white flour until the dough is of a sticky consistency. Shape into a ball and place in a greased bowl. Cover and let rise, about 2 hours. The dough should double. Divide the dough into 2 or 3 parts, knead into ball and let rise again, until double in size, about 1 to 2 hours. Put on baking sheets in oven at 350° for 50 minutes to 1 hour. To make a hard crust place dough in oven heated to 400° and reduce temperature to 350°. Makes 2 loaves.

Tom and Susanne Campbell, *Representative and Mrs. (California)*

White Bread
2 LOAVES

2⅓ cups water
5½ Tablespoons butter
2 packages yeast

1 Tablespoon salt
3 Tablespoons sugar
5-6 cups unbleached bread flour

Place water and butter in pan and heat until warm on wrist. Place yeast, sugar, salt and 2 cups flour in a large bowl. Add water and butter. Mix with electric beater until smooth. Add 1 cup flour and beat with mixer. Add 1 cup flour and mix with spoon. When thick, place on floured cloth and knead in another cup of flour. Add more flour until dough is smooth. Knead 5 minutes or so, until you can put a hole in the dough that will not fill in. Cover with plastic wrap and tea towel for 30 minutes. Punch dough down and place in 2 greased bread pans. Let rise in a warm place until it doubles in size or the way you like it. Bake in a 425° oven for 30 to 35 minutes. Remove from pans, cool and enjoy. (2½ hours preparation time. Suitable for freezing.)

Frances S Minshall

Mrs. William E. Minshall, *wife of former Representative (Ohio)*

Pumpkin Bread
SERVES 12

1 cup salad oil
4 eggs
2 cups canned pumpkin
⅔ cup water
3½ cups all purpose flour

2 teaspoons baking soda
2 teaspoons salt
1½ teaspoons cinnamon
1½ cups sugar
1½ cups chopped walnuts
1 cup chopped dates

Mix first 4 ingredients with electric mixer. Sift dry ingredients. Reserve ¼ cup dry ingredients and mix with nuts and dates. Add flour mixture to pumpkin mixture. Stir in floured nuts and dates. Grease and flour 2 loaf pans 9″ × 5″ × 3″. Fill pans ½ full. Bake at 350° for 50 to 60 minutes. (60 minutes preparation time. Suitable for freezing.)

Virginia Lipscomb

Mrs. Glenard Lipscomb, *wife of former Representative (California)*

Date and Nut Bread

1 pound dates, chopped
2 teaspoons baking soda
1 pint boiling water
3 Tablespoons butter
1½ cups sugar

2 eggs, beaten
½ teaspoon salt
3 cups flour
1 cup nuts, chopped
1 Tablespoon vanilla

Sprinkle baking soda over chopped dates. Pour in boiling water and stir. Add butter, sugar and eggs to mixture. Add salt, flour, nuts and vanilla. Pour batter into 4 greased (7½″ × 3½″ × 2″) pans. Bake 45 minutes at 350° or until toothpick comes out clean. Makes 4 medium sized bread pans. (15 minutes preparation time. Suitable for freezing.)

Carol Paul

Mrs. Ron Paul, *wife of Representative (Texas)*

Dick's African Camp Bread
SERVES 10 TO 12

¼ cup pure maple syrup
1 stick margarine
½ cup brown sugar
1 cup Cream of Wheat
1 cup Quick Mother's Oats
2 Tablespoons salt
1 5-ounce can evaporated milk

1 cup low-fat cottage cheese
2 cups whole wheat flour
1 cup boiling water
5 Tablespoons yeast, in 1 (additional) cup of warm water
4 cups white flour
1 cup raisins

Combine first 10 ingredients and stir until cool, (or mix in bread machine). Then add yeast in 1 cup warm water and white flour. Place in greased bowl in warm place for 60 to 90 minutes. Punch down and knead in raisins. Turn into well greased 12″ Dutch oven and let rise 45 to 60 minutes. Cook for 1 hour in covered Dutch oven over "camp fire", using 17 glowing white charcoal briquettes under the pot and 12 glowing white briquettes on lid, turning pot every 15 minutes. Can also be cooked in a conventional oven at 350° for 50 to 60 minutes in the Dutch oven or in 2 good sized conventional bread baking pans. (4 hours preparation time. Suitable for freezing.)

Dick Schulze

Dick Schulze, *former Representative (Pennsylvania)*

Biscuits

SERVES 6

4 teaspoons baking powder
1 teaspoon salt
7 Tablespoons margarine
2 cups flour
¾-1 cup flour additional while kneading

Combine dry ingredients, cut in margarine thoroughly, add milk. Stir until soft and sticky. Knead 10 times. Cut or shape as desired. Bake 10 minutes at 450°. (10 minutes preparation time. Suitable for freezing.)

Neal Smith, *former Representative (Iowa)*

Poppy Seed Bread

2¼ cups sugar
1½ cups oil
1½ cups milk
1½ teaspoons butter extract
1½ teaspoons vanilla extract
1 Tablespoon almond extract

3 eggs
1½ Tablespoons poppy seeds
3 cups flour
1½ teaspoons salt
1½ teaspoons baking powder

Glaze:
¼ cup orange juice
¾ cup powdered sugar

½ teaspoon almond extract
½ teaspoon vanilla extract

Mix first 8 ingredients. Add dry ingredients and mix well. Pour into 3 small greased and floured loaf pans or 2 larger bread pans. Bake at 350° for 45 minutes. After baking, punch holes with a long fork into bread and pour glaze into holes. Makes 2 large or 3 small loaves. (15 minutes preparation time. Suitable for freezing.)

Ernest Istook, *Representative (Oklahoma)*

Dentist's Dream French Toast

6 slices white bread
5 large eggs
¼ cup heavy cream
1 Tablespoon sugar
¼ teaspoon cinnamon
1 capful vanilla
4 Tablespoons butter

Combine eggs, cream, sugar, cinnamon and vanilla in a bowl. Melt butter in large frying pan as needed. Soak slices of bread in mixture and fry on each side until lightly browned. Sprinkle lightly with powdered sugar if desired, and dig in — then call the dentist!! (Not suitable for freezing.)

Joseph P. Kennedy II, *Representative (Massachusetts)*

Grandma Miedema's Banana Bread
SERVES 6 TO 8

5 Tablespoons milk
1 teaspoon vinegar
1 teaspoon baking soda
1½ cups sugar
2 eggs

2 sticks real butter
2 cups flour
3 mashed bananas
½ cup pecans or walnuts

Mix first 3 ingredients in a bowl. Let sit for 15 minutes (no longer, no shorter). Mix in a bowl remaining ingredients, and then add the 3 from the first bowl. Grease a loaf air pan with butter, no flour, and cook at 350° for 1 hour and 15 minutes. (1 hour 15 minutes preparation time. Suitable for freezing.)

Lori Costello, *daughter-in-law of Representative Jerry F. Costello (Illinois)*

Banana Nut Bread

4 eggs
3½ cups flour
3 cups white sugar
2 teaspoons baking soda
1½ teaspoons salt

1 teaspoon cinnamon
1 teaspoon nutmeg
1 cup oil
⅔ cup water
2 cups mashed, ripe bananas

Combine all ingredients in a large bowl. Mix well, but do not beat. Put into 3 greased bread pans. Bake 1 hour at 350°. Makes 3 bread pans. (60 minutes preparation time. Suitable for freezing.)

Mrs. Ernest Istook, *wife of Representative (Oklahoma)*

Shawna Bread
SERVES 6

1 loaf French bread
Swiss cheese slices
½ pound margarine or butter
2 Tablespoons grated onion

1 teaspoon mustard
2 teaspoons lemon juice
1 teaspoon Beau Monde seasoning

Slice loaf of bread. Place Swiss cheese slices between bread slices. Mix other ingredients and spread over top. Make an aluminum foil "boat" and put the loaf inside. (This catches the butter that drips from the bread.) Place on baking sheet. Bake at 350° for 20 to 25 minutes. (25 minutes preparation time. Not suitable for freezing.)

Sharon VanderSchel

Sharon VanderSchel, *daughter of former Representative Neal Smith (Iowa)*

Aunt Deda's Homemade Biscuits
SERVES 4 TO 6

2 cups Gold Medal self-rising flour
2 level Tablespoons Crisco shortening
3 Tablespoons Crisco shortening, melted
buttermilk

Crumble 2 cups Gold Medal self-rising flour with 2 level tablespoons Crisco shortening. Add buttermilk to moisten. Form into loose ball. Lay ball of dough on floured surface. Pat down gently with heavily floured hands. DO NOT ROLL OUT. Cut biscuits. Place in a greased 13″ × 9″ glass baking dish. Brush melted Crisco on top of biscuits. Bake at 400° for 40 to 45 minutes. Brown, if necessary, using broiler for only a few seconds. (45 minutes preparation time. Not suitable for freezing.)

Jerry J. Costello

Jerry Costello, *Representative (Illinois)*

Cranberry-Walnut-Orange Muffins

3 cups all purpose flour
1 Tablespoon baking powder
½ teaspoon baking soda
½ teaspoon salt
10 Tablespoons unsalted butter, softened
1 cup minus 1 Tablespoon granulated sugar
1 Tablespoon grated orange zest
1½ cups coarsely chopped fresh, frozen, or dried cranberries
2 large eggs
1½ cups low-fat buttermilk
1 cup coarsely chopped, lightly toasted walnuts
vegetable cooking spray or unsalted butter for muffin tins

Adjust oven rack to lower middle position and preheat oven to 375°. Mix flour, baking powder, baking soda and salt in a medium bowl; set aside. Beat butter and sugar with electric mixer at medium speed until light and fluffy. Add eggs, one at a time, beating well after each addition. Add orange zest. Beat in ½ of the dry ingredients. Beat in ½ of the buttermilk. Beat in ½ of the remaining flour, all of the remaining buttermilk, and lastly, all of the remaining flour. Do not over-mix. Fold in cranberries and toasted walnuts. Spray 12-cup muffin tin with cooking spray or coat lightly with butter. Fill tins about ⅔ full. Bake until muffins are golden brown, 25 to 30 minutes. Cool slightly on wire rack for 5 minutes. Remove muffins from tin and serve warm or store. Makes 1 dozen large muffins.

Eulada P. Watt

Mrs. Melvin Watt, *wife of Representative (North Carolina)*

AMERICAN BEAUTY ROSE
(ROSA SP.)

DISTRICT OF COLUMBIA

In the language of flowers, roses can have a number of different meanings depending on their color. Red roses say "I love you" and symbolize respect and courage. White roses can symbolize reverence and humility, innocence and purity, or secrecy and silence. Red and white roses together signify unity.

Dilly Cheese Bread
SERVES 4 TO 6

2 cups Bisquick
1½ cups grated sharp cheddar cheese
1 Tablespoon sugar
1¼ cups milk
2 eggs, beaten slightly
1 Tablespoon oil
½ teaspoon dill
½ teaspoon dry mustard

Lightly grease a 9″ × 5″ loaf pan or a 6-cup Bundt pan. Combine Bisquick, cheese and sugar in large bowl. Combine remaining ingredients in second bowl and mix well. Stir wet mixture into dry mixture, blending well. Beat slightly to remove lumps. Bake 45 to 50 minutes at 350° until golden. (15 minutes preparation time. Suitable for freezing.)

Colleen Nunn

Mrs. Sam Nunn, *wife of former Senator (Georgia)*

Lampson Family Homemade Bread

6 cups flour
2 packages yeast
½ cup sugar

warm water
1 Tablespoon salt
vegetable oil

Dissolve 2 packages dry yeast in a cup of warm (not hot) water with 1 teaspoon of sugar. Mix flour, salt and sugar then add yeast (after it begins to ferment). Gradually add more water until all the flour is absorbed. Put about 1 Tablespoon vegetable oil on your hands and the dough and begin to knead. Knead about 10 minutes or until shiny and pliable. Add about 2 Tablespoons more oil and swirl dough in bowl to coat bread and bowl. Cover with cloth or Saran wrap and let rise in warm area until doubled. Punch down and gently knead. Let rise. After doubling, put in bread pans and let rise. Bake in 350° oven until golden brown (25 to 35 minutes).

Hillary Lampson

Hillary Lampson Shanning, *daughter of Representative Nicholas V. Lampson (Texas)*

Miracle Whip Cheese Rolls
SERVES 24

2 packages brown and serve rolls
1 cup Parmesan cheese
3 Tablespoons Miracle Whip
1 stick butter

Punch hole in center of roll with finger. Melt 1 stick of butter, and mix with cheese and Miracle Whip. Use a spoon to pour the mixture inside the hole. Spread the remainder on top of the rolls. Bake per instructions for brown and serve rolls. Wonderful with any meal, especially ham. (Suitable for freezing.)

Mrs. John J. Duncan, Jr., *wife of Representative (Tennessee)*

Biscuits

4 cups self-rising flour
3 heaping Tablespoons sugar
1 Tablespoon baking soda

½ cup butter flavored Crisco
1½ cups buttermilk

Preheat oven to 400°. In a large bowl, mix all dry ingredients. Cut in Crisco until mixture is crumbly. Slowly add buttermilk until dough holds together. Remove dough to a floured board and knead 6 to 8 minutes. Let stand 10 minutes. Roll dough to ½" thickness. Cut with biscuit cutter that has been dipped in flour. Place biscuits close together for soft sides, 1" apart for crusty sides, on an ungreased cookie sheet. Bake 10 to 12 minutes until golden brown. Makes 24 biscuits. (25 minutes preparation time. Not suitable for freezing.)

Ike Skelton, *Representative (Missouri)*

Poppy Seed Bread

3 cups all-purpose flour

1½ teaspoons baking powder

1½ teaspoons salt

2¼ cups sugar

3 eggs

1½ cups milk

1½ cups vegetable oil

1½ Tablespoons poppy seeds

2 teaspoons vanilla

2 teaspoons almond flavoring

Glaze:

¾ cup sugar

¼ cup orange juice

1½ teaspoons vanilla

½ teaspoon almond flavoring

Preheat oven to 350°. Mix together all ingredients. Beat 2 minutes. Bake for 45 to 60 minutes, or until toothpick comes out clean. Makes three 4″ × 8″ loaves.

Glaze: Mix together and pour over hot bread. Let stand for 30 minutes, and remove bread from pan. (45 minutes preparation time. Suitable for freezing.)

Robba Addison Moran

Mrs. Jerry Moran, *wife of Representative (Kansas)*

Bread Maker Oatmeal Bread

1   ¼-ounce package active dry yeast
1   cup quick-cooking oats
3   cups bread flour
1   teaspoon salt
½   cup light molasses
1   Tablespoon vegetable oil
1¼ cups plus 1 Tablespoon warm water

Place ingredients in order into bread maker machine pan. Select "white bread" setting.
Bake according to machine directions. Delicious served with honey. Makes 1 loaf,
approximately 1½ pounds. (Suitable for freezing.)

David King, *former Representative (Utah)*

Honey Oatmeal Bread

2½ cups boiling water
1¼ cups oatmeal
2½ Tablespoons butter
2   packages yeast, dissolved in 1¼ cups of warm water
1   Tablespoon salt
¾   cup honey
7½-8 cups flour

Combine boiling water, oatmeal and butter. Let stand 30 minutes. Add salt and honey.
Soak yeast 5 minutes and add to oatmeal. Add flour and knead until dough is stiff and
shiny (10 to 15 minutes). Put into a greased bowl and let rise for 1½ hours. Punch
down and let rise another hour. Form into 3 loaves and let rise ½ hour. Bake at 350°
for approximately 1 hour. Recipe doubles well. (Suitable for freezing.)

Mrs. Scott McInnis, *wife of Representative (Colorado)*

Corn Bread
SERVES 8

1 cup cornmeal
½ teaspoon salt
1 cup low-fat sour cream
2 eggs
1 small can chili peppers (green),
   drained

⅔ cup buttermilk
½ teaspoon baking soda
⅓ cup shortening
1 cup grated sharp cheese

Drain and chop chilies. Mix other ingredients, except cheese, and pour ½ of the mixture into a hot skillet. Sprinkle cheese and green chilies over it. Pour the remaining mixture over it and bake at 375° for 30 to 40 minutes. This is best made in an iron skillet. (60 minutes preparation time. Suitable for freezing.)

Jim Bunning

Jim Bunning, *Representative (Kentucky)*

Crawfish Corn Bread

1 cup self-rising cornmeal
⅓ cup cooking oil
1 teaspoon salt
1 can cream style corn
2 eggs
½ pound grated sharp cheddar cheese

2 chopped jalapeno peppers
1 cup chopped onions
1 pound crawfish (you may wish
   to substitute shrimp, sausage
   or ground meat cooked)

Mix all ingredients, except crawfish, in order given. Blend until dry ingredients are moist. Add crawfish. At this point, it may be done 2 different ways. You may fry by dropping by the spoonful into hot oil and frying until crisp, or you may pour into well greased 9″ × 12″ baking dish. Bake for 30 minutes at 375°. Cut into small bite size squares. (Not suitable for freezing.)

Lois Breaux

Mrs. John Breaux, *wife of Senator (Louisiana)*

Shaker Lemon Blueberry Bread

1½ cups blueberries
1 Tablespoon flour
½ cup sugar
2 cups sifted flour
1½ teaspoons baking powder
½ teaspoon baking soda

1 teaspoon grated lemon rind
½ cup chopped nuts
1 egg, beaten
¾ cup orange juice
2 Tablespoons oil

Toss blueberries with 1 Tablespoon flour. Set aside. In large mixing bowl sift together 2 cups flour, baking powder, baking soda, salt and sugar. Add berries, lemon rind and nuts. Set aside. In another bowl mix egg, orange juice and oil. Combine with first mixture until just moistened. Pour batter into greased and floured 9″ × 5″ loaf pan. Bake in a 350° oven for 50 minutes or until golden brown. Makes 1 loaf of bread. (1 hour 30 minutes preparation time. Not suitable for freezing.)

Rob Portman, *Representative (Ohio)*

Pineapple Bread
SERVES 6

4 eggs, slightly beaten
1 cup sugar
¼ cup butter, melted
2 Tablespoons flour
1 20-ounce can crushed pineapple with juice
2 slices white bread without crusts, cut into cubes

Combine eggs, sugar, butter, flour and pineapple. Mix in bread cubes. Pour into 1½-quart greased casserole dish. Bake 1 hour at 350° until brown and bubbly. (1 hour 20 minutes preparation time. Not suitable for freezing.)

Mrs. Robert Ehrlich, Jr., *wife of Representative (Maryland)*

Hallah Bread

6 cups unbleached flour
2 packages dry yeast
½ cup sugar
2 cups warm water

½ cup vegetable oil
3 eggs beaten (reserve small portion)
1 teaspoon salt

Make a well in middle of flour, stir dry yeast into well, mixing with a small portion of the flour. Using a wire whip, slowly stir in ¾ cup of the warm water, making a thin paste. Add oil, eggs and salt. Beat in balance of water. From the beginning, stir in a circular motion in the center of the well, taking more flour from the sides with each stir. Dough should be stiff. More flour can be added to make handling easier. Place dough on floured board and knead well (about 5 minutes or more). Return to bowl, cover and let rise 1 hour. Dough will more than double. Punch down, place on floured board and divide into 6 parts. Shape into 6 cylinders about 18" long. Place on lightly greased baking sheet and braid into 2 long loaves of bread, tucking ends under. Cover with cloth and let rise 1 hour or until double in size. Brush with remaining portion of eggs and bake at 350° until golden brown (about 30 to 40 minutes). This recipe makes 2 beautiful, delicious loaves of bread that can be served immediately, kept for several days, or frozen to use later. I have been making it for my family and friends for years. It has never failed for me. I try to keep some made and frozen to have on hand in case of an emergency like a death in a family or unexpected company. I hope you enjoy it as much as the Jenkins clan has. (40 minutes preparation time. Suitable for freezing.)

Kathryn M. Jenkins

Mrs. William L. Jenkins, *wife of Representative (Tennessee)*

1998 First Lady's Luncheon

1998 First Lady's Luncheon

Menu

Chef Gordon Marr
Washington Hilton Hotel

Sweet Potato Soup with Chilies

Marinated Sliced Grilled Chicken

with

Phyllo Flower of Caramelized Onion and Gorgonzola

Peach and Berry Crisp

Sweet Potato Soup with Chilies
8 TO 10 SERVINGS

2 ounces butter

4 ounces diced onion

2 ounces diced celery

16 ounces peeled and diced sweet potato

1 quart canned vegetable stock

6 ounces honey

8 ounces heavy cream

2-3 Tablespoons chipotle in adobo sauce, puréed (may be purchased at many South American stores)

salt and pepper to taste

Garnish

fried corn tortillas   cinnamon-flavored sour cream

In a large pot, sauté the onions and celery in the butter until translucent. Add sweet potatoes and continue to cook for 5 minutes. Add the stock. Bring to a boil and simmer until potatoes are soft (30-40 minutes). Add honey, chipotle peppers, heavy cream and seasonings. Purée in food processor. Adjust seasonings to taste. Return to pot and heat for service. Garnish with strips of fried corn tortillas and cinnamon-flavored sour cream.

Marinated Sliced Grilled Chicken with Phyllo Flower of Caramelized Onion and Gorgonzola

12 SERVINGS

Sliced grilled marinated chicken on bed of assorted greens, roasted tomato, grilled red and yellow pepper slices, mushroom with herb vinaigrette dressing.

1 package phyllo sheets	3 ripened tomatoes, diced in 3/8" cubes
1 stick melted butter	8 ounces heavy cream
2 pounds thinly sliced white onions	3 eggs
1/2 ounce olive oil	12 ounces gorgonzola, cut in 1/2" pieces
2 Tablespoons balsamic vinegar	salt and pepper to taste
2 pounds destemmed leaf spinach	2 jumbo 12-section muffin molds

In a sauté pan, sauté onions and garlic in olive oil until brown. Deglaze the pan with vinegar. Remove from heat and add spinach and tomatoes. In a bowl, mix heavy cream and eggs. With the phyllo sheets and melted butter, create 12 6"x 6" squares. Lightly brush one sheet with butter. Repeat for a total of 6 layers. Place each square in muffin mold, alternating so that only 6 of the 12 sections have the phyllo in them. Gently push square to bottom and pull up sides to create flower effect. Place in 400° oven until just brown. Combine onion mixture with cheese. Fold in cream mixture. Season to taste. Divide mixture into the phyllo-lined muffin cups. Bake immediately at 275° approximately one hour until firm to the touch. Place warm phyllo cup on plate with chilled chicken and greens to serve.

Peach and Berry Crisp

SERVES 8

3 pounds fresh peaches or 2 pounds of frozen peaches
 Frozen: drain very well after defrosting
 Fresh: peel and remove stone; slice 1/2 inch thick

granulated sugar	1 cup all-purpose flour
1 pint fresh raspberries	1 teaspoon cinnamon
1 pint fresh blueberries	1 cup brown sugar
1 pint fresh blackberries	1 stick butter
2/3 cup granulated sugar	

Toss peaches with granulated sugar. Quantity will vary depending on ripeness of peaches. Place peach mixture in ramekins. Sprinkle fresh berries on top of peach mixture (choose any one or all three varieties). Mix the 2/3 cup granulated sugar, flour, cinnamon, brown sugar and butter in a bowl with your fingers until the mixture develops the consistency of crumbs. Sprinkle 2 Tablespoons of crumbs on top of each ramekin. Bake at 375° until top is golden and peaches are soft (approximately 35-45 minutes). Serve with vanilla ice cream.

Friends of the Congressional Club

Diamond Chef Sponsors

Federal Express Corporation

Massachusetts Mutual Life Insurance Company

National Restaurant Association

Oxxford Clothes

PricewaterhouseCoopers LLP

Doyle Cloud's Key Lime Pie

1-9" Keebler graham cracker pie crust
14 ounces condensed sweetened milk (fat free)
3 egg yolks (whites are not used)
1/2 cup Nellie & Joe's key lime juice

Combine condensed milk, egg yolks and lime juice.
Blend until smooth. Pour filling into pie crust and bake at 350 degrees
for ten minutes. Allow to stand for ten minutes before refrigerating.
Just before serving, top with fresh whipped cream and garnish with lime
slices. (Use Cool Whip if you want to stay slim.)

A. Doyle Cloud, Jr.
Corporate Vice President
Government Affairs
FDX Corporation
Memphis, Tennessee

Fresh Seafood Stew

Whether it's called cioppino, bouillabaisse, or another regional name, these simple one pot meals began as peasant fare, the day's catch with a few local vegetables thrown into a single pot together, but have now ascended to fine dining menus throughout the world. This very flavorful variation uses a modern day kitchen staple, canned tuna, to replace fish stock and add complexity to the flavor.

1 Tablespoon olive oil	4-6 garlic cloves, chopped
1 medium onion, diced	1/2 cup fresh fennel, chopped
1 green or red pepper, diced	1 bay leaf
2 medium tomatoes	1 - 8 ounce can tuna in spring water
(4 plum tomatoes), diced	1/4 cup fresh basil

Any combination of seafood including mussels, cherrystone or little neck clams in shell, scallops, shrimp, lobster or any fish such as cod/scrod, haddock, bass, blackfish, swordfish, shark, tuna, halibut.

In your favorite pot heat oil, then add garlic, fennel, onion and green pepper and sauté for three minutes, tossing throughout. Add tomatoes and bay leaf and toss for 2 minutes more. Add tuna and its water, then fill can with water again to remove all tuna bits and add. Simmer for 5 minutes. At this point begin adding seafood in the order of its required cooking time: add any mollusks in the shell; add sturdy diced fish like sword, tuna or shark; add diced white fish like cod or scrod; add shrimp, scallops or any cooked meat like lobster last. When clams or mussels are open and fish is cooked, stir in fresh basil then ladle into soup bowls.

Note: The fresh fish ingredients and portions are purposely vague, as there is no right or wrong. Simply add your own catch of the day, or whatever the fish market recommended, to create a unique dish every time.

OUR FAVORITE THING TO MAKE

FOR DINNER IS *Reservations.*

WITH OVER 500,000

RESTAURANTS NATIONWIDE—

Take a break

Let us wait on you

NATIONAL RESTAURANT ASSOCIATION ®

Summer Dinner for Eight

MENU

Kentucky Bibb Lettuce with Ches' Mayonnaise
Grilled Alaska Salmon
New England Blueberry Pudding

Kentucky Bibb Lettuce with Ches' Mayonnaise

Separate, wash and compose one head of bibb lettuce for each person. In a blender, combine 1/4 cup Major Grey's chutney with 1/4 cup Worcestershire sauce until smooth. Mix with 2 cups good mayonnaise. Drizzle on lettuce.

Grilled Alaska Salmon

Marinate 1 1/2 inch thick salmon steaks in 2 1/2 cups light vegetable oil, 2 cups bourbon, and 1/2 cup soy sauce for 3 hours. Grill steaks over very hot charcoal fire 7 minutes on each side or until medium rare. Do not over-cook. Serve immediately.

New England Blueberry Pudding

Pick over and wash 3 pints blueberries. In a saucepan, combine berries with 1 cup sugar and cook slowly over low heat until berries give up juices yet retain their shape. Line a 1 1/2 quart mold with overlapped day-old, crustless, sliced white bread. Fill mold with blueberry compote and top with more overlapped bread slices. Weight the top of mold and refrigerate overnight. Invert pudding on serving plate and garnish with fluted whipped cream and berries. Pass additional whipped cream.

Oxxford Clothes

Country Retreat Dinner

Hors d'Oeuvres

Charleston Chile-Pickled Shrimp
Pulled BBQ Spiced Rub Pork on Corn Crisp
Shiitake Mushroom Caps with Pickled Shad and Scallop Mousse

Preserved Duck and Foie Gras with Red-Eye Gravy over Creamy Grits

Low Country's Crab and Sweet Potato Gratin

Red Snapper Fillet with Spicy Lentils,
Roasted Cipolline Onions, and Pecan Wild Rice Cake

Stewed Squab with Herbed Biscuit Dumplings

Persimmon-Peach Tart with Pumpkin Seed Brittle,
Buttermilk Ice Cream and Brandied Caramel Sauce

Bourbon Pecan Truffles
Plantation Hickory Coffee

Executive Chef Michael Lemon
FLIK International Corp. at PricewaterhouseCoopers LLP

PRICEWATERHOUSECOOPERS 🅟

Gold Chefs

American General Corporation

Anheuser-Busch Companies, Inc.

Baker Hostetler LLP and the Chubb Corporation

Bell Atlantic

Bob Evans Farms, Inc.

The Bond Market Association

B.P. Exploration and Oil, Inc.

Bristol-Myers Squibb Company

Compaq Computer Corporation

Continental Airlines, Inc.

Davis and Harman

Golden Rule Insurance Co.

Houston Industries, Inc.

M&M/Mars, Inc. and Uncle Ben's, Inc.

Marriott International, Inc.

National Association of Broadcasters

National Food Processors Association

Schering-Plough Corporation

Todhunter International, Inc.

Union Pacific

UST Public Affairs, Inc.

Van Scoyoc Associates, Inc.

Silver Chefs

Association for Advanced Life Underwriters
Coors Brewing Company
Fluor Corporation
General Mills, Inc.
Grocery Manufacturers of America
United Parcel Service

Bronze Chefs

Ann Hand Collection
The Boeing Company
ENRON Corporation
Gottehrer and Company
Health Insurance Association of America
Hotel Employees and Restaurant Employees International Union
Kessler and Associates, Inc.
Motion Picture Association of America, Inc.
Proctor and Gamble Manufacturing Company
Shell Oil Company
TECO Energy, Inc.
Wendy's International, Inc.
Winston and Strawn

Other Contributors

The Advocacy Group
Downey, Chandler, Inc.
Pennzoil Company
Vinson and Elkins

A Special Acknowledgement

The Congressional Club extends its grateful appreciation to the contributors of the photos which grace the pages of this cookbook and made its theme possible.

The floral pattern printed in pink on the covers and endsheets, and on the pages preceeding chapter titles, appears through the courtesy of the Society of American Florists.

Jessie Harris photographed the beautiful flowers which appear at random throughout the book and on every chapter title page, as well as a number of the state flowers.

Flo Oxley, Senior Botanist at the National Wildflower Research Center, researched the information pertaining to the state flowers and gathered many of the photos.

Index to State Flowers

**State wildflowers

State Flower Photo Credits

Alabama	National Wildflower Research Center
Alaska	Bennie Bengston
Arizona	Russ Finlay
Arkansas	Jessie Harris
California	W.D. Bransford
Colorado	Holmes O. Miller
Connecticut	Jessie Harris
Delaware	Jessie Harris
Florida	Florida Citrus Commission
Georgia	Campbell & Lynn Loughmiller
Hawaii	Rodney G. Engard
Idaho	Idaho Dept. of Commerce
Illinois	George H. Bruso
Indiana	Carolyn Harstad
Iowa	USDA Natural Resources Conservation Service, Plant Materials Center, Bismark, ND
Kansas	Robert C. Duncan
Kentucky	Jessie Harris
Louisiana	Campbell & Lynn Loughmiller
Maine	Albert F. W. Vick, Jr.
Maryland	W.D. Bransford
Massachusetts	Jessie Harris
Michigan	Jessie Harris
Minnesota	Doug Sherman
Mississippi	Keep Mississippi Beautiful
Missouri	Jessie Harris
Montana	W.D. Bransford
Nebraska	Jessie Harris
Nevada	Jessie Harris
New Hampshire	Jessie Harris
New Jersey	Doug Sherman
New Mexico	Edith Bettinger
New York	M.W. Carlton
North Carolina	W.D. Bransford
North Dakota	USDA Natural Resources Conservation Service, Plant Materials Center, Bismark, ND
Ohio	Jessie Harris
Oklahoma	Robert L. Stone
Oregon	W.D. Bransford
Pennsylvania	Jessie Harris
Rhode Island	Phyllis Weyand
South Carolina	National Park Service
South Dakota	Doug Sherman
Tennessee	Jessie Harris
Texas	Doug Sherman
Utah	W.D. Bransford
Vermont	Phyllis Weyand
Virginia	W.D. Bransford
Washington	Doug Sherman
West Virginia	W.D. Bransford
Wisconsin	Julia Sanders
Wyoming	Lela Jane Tinstman
Dist. of Columbia	Jessie Harris

Index to Contributors

Doolittle, Mrs. John T., Wife of Representative
(California), 252, 356
Duncan, Mrs. John J., Jr., Wife of Representative (Tennessee), 397

E

Edwards, Chet, Representative (Texas), 317
Edwards, Mrs. Chet, Wife of Representative (Texas), 77
Ehrlich, Robert L., Jr., Representative (Maryland), 173
Ehrlich, Mrs. Robert L., Jr., Wife of Representative
(Maryland), 358, 401
English, Glenn, former Representative (Oklahoma), 289
English, Mrs. Glenn, Wife of former Representative
(Oklahoma), 165
English, Phil, Representative (Pennsylvania), 368
English, Mrs. Philip, Wife of Representative
(Pennsylvania), 119, 238
Ensign, John E., Representative (Nevada), 89
Ensign, Mrs. John, Wife of Representative (Nevada), 170
Enzi, Mrs. Mike, Wife of Senator (Wyoming), 191
Esch, Emily, Daughter of former Representative Marvin Esch
(Michigan), 288
Esch, Mrs. Marvin, Wife of former Representative (Michigan), 251
Etheridge, Bob, Representative (North Carolina), 384
Etheridge, Mrs. Bob, Wife of Representative (North Carolina), 261
Everett, Terry, Representative (Alabama), 163
Everett, Mrs. Terry, Wife of Representative (Alabama), 143, 163
Ewing, Thomas W., Representative (Illinois), 350
Ewing, Mrs. Thomas W., Wife of Representative (Illinois), 348, 350

F

Fawell, Harris, Representative (Illinois), 284
Fawell, Mrs. Harris, Wife of Representative (Illinois), 113
Flippo, Ronnie G., former Representative (Alabama), 100
Flippo, Mrs. Ronnie G., Wife of former Representative
(Alabama), 234
Foley, John R., former Representative (Maryland), 135
Foley, Mrs. John R., Wife of former Representative (Maryland), 363
Foley, Lydia, Daugher-in-law of former Representative John R.
Foley (Maryland), 169
Foran, Lynn, Daughter of Representative David L. Hobson
(Ohio), 200
Fountain, Mrs. L. H., Wife of former Representative (North
Carolina), 61
Frist, Bill, Senator (Tennessee), 31
Frist, Mrs. Bill, Wife of Senator (Tennessee), 85, 285
Fuqua, Don, former Representative (Florida), 263
Fuqua, Mrs. Don, Wife of former Representative (Florida), 159

G

Gallegly, Elton, Representative (California), 191
Gallegly, Mrs. Elton, Wife of Representative (California), 172
Gavin, Kristy, Daughter of Senator Jon Kyl (Arizona), 121
Gekas, George W., Representative (Pennsylvania), 86
Gekas, Mrs. George, Wife of Representative
(Pennsylvania), 263, 286

Giaimo, Robert N., former Representative (Connecticut), 9
Giaimo, Mrs. Robert, Wife of former Representative
(Connecticut), 232
Gibbons, Jim and Jimmy, Representative and Son (Nevada), 316
Gibbons, Mrs. Jim, Wife of Representative (Nevada), 256, 385
Gillmor, Paul, Representative (Ohio), 85
Gillmor, Mrs. Paul, Wife of Representative (Ohio), 93, 371
Gilman, Ben, Representative (New York), 332
Gilman, Mrs. Ben, Wife of Representative (New York), 332
Gingrich, Mrs. Newt, Wife of The Speaker of The House
(Georgia), 358, 363
Goode, Virgil, Jr., Representative (Virginia), 19
Goode, Mrs. Virgil, Jr., Wife of Representative (Virginia), 345
Goss, Porter, Representative (Florida), 346
Goss, Mrs. Porter, Wife of Representative (Florida), 67, 178
Grant, Mrs. George, Wife of former Representative (Alabama), 259
Grant, Mrs. Robert, Wife of former Representative (Indiana), 4
Grassley, Mrs. Charles, Wife of Senator (Iowa), 150, 151
Grassley, Chuck, Senator (Iowa), 91
Green, Angela, Daughter of Representative Gene Green (Texas), 18
Green, Gene, Representative (Texas), 369
Green, Mrs. Gene, Wife of Representative (Texas), 68, 285
Greigg, Stanley, former Representative (Iowa), 250
Greigg, Mrs. Stanley, Wife of former Representative (Iowa), 70

H

Hagan, Mrs. G. Elliott, Wife of former Representative
(Georgia), 344
Hall, Ralph and Mary Ellen, Representative and Mrs. (Texas), 268
Hall, Tony, Representative (Ohio), 214
Hall, Mrs. Tony, Wife of Representative (Ohio), 27, 148
Hamilton, Lee H., Representative (Indiana), 343
Hamilton, Mrs. Lee H., Wife of Representative
(Indiana), 121, 329
Hammerschmidt, Mrs. John, Wife of former Representative
(Arkansas), 14
Hanley, Mrs. James, Wife of former Representative
(New York), 109
Hansen, Mrs. George, Wife of former Representative (Idaho), 283
Hard, Kyle, Daughter of former Senator and former Cabinet
Secretary Richard Schweiker (Pennsylvania), 224
Harris, Mrs. Claude, Jr., Wife of former Representative
(Alabama), 342
Harvey, Mrs. James, Wife of former Representative
(Michigan), 381
Hastings, Doc, Representative (Washington), 237
Hastings, Mrs. Doc, Wife of Representative
(Washington), 268, 274
Hatfield, Mrs. Mark, Wife of former Senator (Oregon), 157
Hayworth, J.D., Representative (Arizona), 108
Hayworth, Mrs. J.D., Wife of Representative (Arizona), 107, 357
Hefner, Shelly, Daughter of Representative Bill Hefner
(North Carolina), 233
Hefner, W.G. (Bill), Representative (North Carolina), 341
Hefner, Mrs. W.G. (Bill), Wife of Representative
(North Carolina), 319
Herger, Mrs. Wally, Wife of Representative (California), 94
Hinojosa, Ruben, Representative (Texas), 229

Hinojosa, Mrs. Ruben, Wife of Representative (Texas), 249, 274

Hobson, David, Representative (Ohio), 210

Hobson, Mrs. David, Wife of Representative (Ohio), 61, 251

Hochbrueckner, Mrs. George, Wife of former Representative (New York), 198

Hollings, Mrs. Ernest F., Wife of Senator (South Carolina), 106, 278

Horn, Steve, Representative (California), 17

Horn, Mrs. Steve, Wife of Representative (California), 94, 122

Howard-Lazzaro, Mrs. James J., Wife of former Representative (New Jersey), 122

Howell, Mrs. Evan, Wife of former Representative (Illinois), 139

Hubbard, Mrs. Joyce, Member of the Congressional Club (Kentucky), 368

Hubbard, Krista, Daughter of former Representative Carroll Hubbard (Kentucky), 301

Hunter, Mrs. Duncan, Wife of Representative (California), 87

I

Ichord, Mrs. Richard, Wife of former Representative (Missouri), 284

Inhofe, Mrs. James, Wife of Senator (Oklahoma), 243, 276

Ireland, Andy, former Representative (Florida), 184

Ireland, Mrs. Andy, Wife of former Representative (Florida), 48

Istook, Ernest, Representative (Oklahoma), 391

Istook, Mrs. Ernest, Wife of Representative (Oklahoma), 63, 393

J

Jacobs, Andrew, Jr., former Representative (Indiana), 264

Jacobs, Mrs. Andrew, Jr., Wife of former Representative (Indiana), 142

Jenkins, Bill, Representative (Tennessee), 314

Jenkins, Mrs. William L. "Bill," Wife of Representative (Tennessee), 312, 402

Johnson, Sam, Representative (Texas), 295

Johnson, Mrs. Sam, Wife of Representative (Texas) 93, 347

Johnston, Mrs. J. Bennett, Wife of former Senator (Louisiana), 258

K

Karsten, Mrs. Frank, Wife of former Representative (Missouri), 205

Kastens, Theana Yatron, Daughter of former Representative Gus Yatron (Pennsylvania), 20

Kemp, Mrs. Jack, Wife of former Representative and former Cabinet Secretary (New York), 215

Kempthorne, Dirk, Senator (Idaho), 211

Kempthorne, Mrs, Dirk, Wife of Senator (Idaho), 250, 329

Kennedy, Joseph P., II, Representative (Massachusetts), 392

Kerns, Lori, Daughter of former Representative John T. Myers (Indiana), 29

Kildee, Dale E., Representative (Michigan), 235

Kildee, Mrs. Dale E., Wife of Representative (Michigan), 211, 326

Kind, Ron, Representative (Wisconsin), 204

Kind, Mrs. Ron, Wife of Representative (Wisconsin), 65, 326

King, David, former Representative (Utah), 399

King, Mrs. David, Wife of former Representative (Utah), 206

Kingston, Jack, Representative (Georgia), 23

Kingston, Mrs. Jack, Wife of Representative (Georgia), 24

Kleppe, Mrs. Tom, Wife of former Representative (North Dakota), 198

Klink, Ron, Representative (Pennsylvania), 158

Klink, Mrs. Ron, Wife of Representative (Pennsylvania), 289

Knollenberg, Joe, Representative (Michigan), 240

Knollenberg, Mrs. Joe, Wife of Representative (Michigan), 111, 355

Kornegay, Horace R., former Representative (North Carolina), 149

Kornegay, Mrs. Horace R., Wife of former Representative (North Carolina), 75

Kyl, Mrs. John, Wife of former Representative (Iowa), 297

Kyl, Jon, Senator (Arizona), 156

Kyl, Mrs. Jon, Wife of Senator (Arizona), 244, 281

L

LaFalce, Mrs. John, Wife of Representative (New York), 39

Lamb, Sandra, Daughter of former Representative Harold Lovre (South Dakota), 171

Lampson, Mrs. Nicholas V., Wife of Representative (Texas), 179

Lampson, Stephanie, Daughter of Representative Nicholas V. Lampson (Texas), 383

Lancaster, Mrs. Martin, Wife of former Representative (North Carolina), 219

Latham, Tom, Representative (Iowa), 156

Latham, Mrs. Tom, Wife of Representative (Iowa), 62

Laughlin, Ginger, Member of Congressional Club (Texas), 207

Laughlin, Mary, Daughter of former Representative Greg Laughlin (Texas), 190

Laxalt, Paul, former Senator (Nevada), 29

Laxalt, Mrs. Paul, Wife of former Senator (Nevada), 277

LaRocco, Larry, former Representative (Idaho), 101

LaRocco, Mrs. Larry, Wife of former Representative (Idaho), 118

Leach, Mrs. Jim, Wife of Representative (Iowa), 269

Leath, Alta, Member of Congressional Club (Texas), 110

Lent, Mrs. Norman, Wife of former Representative (New York), 102

Lewis, Ron, Representative (Kentucky), 293

Lewis, Mrs. Ron, Wife of Representative (Kentucky) 308, 377

Linder, John, Representative (Georgia), 98

Linder, Mrs. John, Wife of Representative (Georgia), 98, 123

Lipscomb, Mrs. Glenard, Wife of former Representative (California), 389

Livingston, Bob and Bonnie, Representative and Mrs. (Louisiana), 123

Livingston, Jeanne, Daughter-in-law of Representative Bob Livingston (Louisiana), 120

Livingston, Susan, Daughter of Representative Bob Livingston (Louisiana), 334

Lloyd, Mrs. Jim, Wife of former Representative (California), 249

Long, Mrs. Edward V., Wife of former Representative (Missouri), 321

Lott, Diane, Daughter-in-law of Senator Trent Lott (Mississippi), 30

Lott, Trent, Senator (Mississippi), 236

Lott, Mrs. Trent, Wife of Senator (Mississippi), 188, 253

Lott, Tyler, Daughter of Senator Trent Lott (Mississippi), 3

M

Mackie, Mrs. John, Wife of former Representative (Michigan), 309

Madigan, Mrs. Edward, Wife of former Representative and former Cabinet Secretary (Illinois), 380

Manzullo, Donald, Representative (Illinois), 21

Manzullo, Mrs. Donald, Wife of Representative (Illinois), 74

Marr, Gordon, Chef, Washington Hilton Hotel, 405, 406

Marshall, Mrs. Thurgood, Wife of former U.S. Supreme Court Justice, 215

Mascara, Mrs. Frank, Wife of Representative (Pennsylvania), 279, 287

Mathews, Dorothy, Daughter of former Representative Claude A. Fuller (Arkansas), 69

Matthews, Mrs. Donald, Wife of former Representative (Florida), 379

McClory, Mrs. Robert, Wife of former Representative (Illinois), 257

McCrery, James, Representative (Louisiana), 124

McCrery, Mrs. James Hawkins, Wife of Representative (Louisiana), 10, 176

McDade, Mrs. Tess, Member of Congressional Club (Pennsylvania), 152

McEwen, Bob, former Representative (Ohio), 106

McEwen, Mrs. Bob, Wife of former Representative (Ohio), 60

McInnis, Scott, Representative (Colorado), 147

McInnis, Mrs. Scott, Wife of Representative (Colorado), 371, 399

McIntosh, David, Representative (Indiana), 172

McIntosh, Mrs. David, Wife of Representative (Indiana), 174, 245

McIntyre, Mike and Dee, Representative and Wife (North Carolina), 167

Mica, Dan, former Representative (Florida), 273

Mica, Mrs. Daniel, Wife of former Representative (Florida), 77

Mica, John L., Representative (Florida), 124

Mica, Mrs. John, Wife of Representative (Florida), 309

Miller, Ann, Daughter of former Representative Edward V. Long (Missouri), 310

Miller, Dan, Representative (Florida), 236

Miller, Mrs. Dan, Wife of Representative (Florida), 18, 190

Miller, Nancy, Daughter-in-law of former Senator Jack Miller (Iowa), 213

Mineta, Norman, former Representative (California), 53

Mineta, Mrs. Norman, Wife of former Representative (California), 21

Minge, David, Representative (Minnesota), 379

Minge, Mrs. David, Wife of Representative (Minnesota), 51

Minshall, Mrs. William E., Wife of former Representative (Ohio), 389

Moeller, Mrs. Walter, Wife of former Representative (Ohio), 310

Moore, W. Henson, former Representative (Louisiana), 125

Moore, Mrs. Henson, Wife of former Representative (Louisiana), 311

Moorhead, Mrs. Carlos, Wife of former Representative (California), 311

Moran, Jerry, Representative (Kansas), 330

Moran, Mrs. Jerry, Wife of Representative (Kansas), 147, 398

Morgan, Margaret Anne, Daughter of former Senator Robert Burren Morgan (North Carolina), 3

Morgan, Mrs. Robert, Wife of former Senator (North Carolina), 313

Morse, Janeen, Daughter of former Representative Walter H. Moeller (Ohio), 78

Murtha, Mrs. John, Wife of Representative (Pennsylvania), 69, 108

Muth, Victoria, Daughter of former Representative J. Glenn Beall, Jr. (Maryland), 127

Myers, Carol, Daughter of former Representative John T. Myers (Indiana), 45

Myers, John, former Representative (Indiana), 2

Myers, Mrs. John, Wife of former Representative (Indiana), 318

N

Nagle, Diane Lewis, Member of the Congressional Club, (Iowa), 378

Nedzi, Mrs. Lucien N., Wife of former Representative (Michigan), 78

Neumann, Mark W., Representative (Wisconsin), 337

Neumann, Mrs. Mark W., Wife of Representative (Wisconsin), 127, 337

Norwood, Charlie, Representative (Georgia), 213

Norwood, Mrs. Charlie, Wife of Representative (Georgia), 26, 28

Norwood, Tolise, Daughter of former Representative E.C. "Took" Gathings (Arkansas), 336

Nowak, Henry and Rose, former Representative and Mrs. (New York), 54

Nunn, Sam, former Senator (Georgia), 264

Nunn, Mrs. Sam, Wife of former Senator (Georgia), 396

Nunner, Susan, Daughter of Representative David Hobson (Ohio), 67

Nye, Mrs. Gerald, Wife of former Senator (North Dakota), 22

O

O'Neal, Mary Hamilton, Daughter of former Representative Emmet O'Neal (Kentucky), 323

Orton, William, former Representative (Utah), 340

Orton, Mrs. William, Wife of former Representative (Utah), 339

Oxley, Mrs. Michael, Wife of Representative (Ohio), 134

P

Packard, Mrs. Ron, Wife of Representative (California), 54

Pallone, Frank, Jr., Representative (New Jersey), 318

Pallone, Mrs. Frank, Jr., Wife of Representative (New Jersey), 231, 336

Parris, Stan, former Representative (Virginia), 1

Parris, Mrs. Stan, Wife of former Representative (Virginia), 2

Patterson, Sally, Member of Congressional Club (California), 12

Paul, Ron, Representative (Texas), 12

Paul, Mrs. Ron, Wife of Representative (Texas), 319, 390

Payton, Angelique, Daughter-in-law of Representative Elton Gallegly (California), 248

Pitts, Joseph, Representative (Pennsylvania), 362

Pitts, Mrs. Joseph, Wife of Representative (Pennsylvania) 90, 91

Portman, Rob, Representative (Ohio), 401

Portman, Mrs. Rob, Wife of Representative (Ohio), 38, 320

Poshard, Glenn, Representative (Illinois), 322

Poshard, Mrs. Glenn, Wife of Representative (Illinois), 327

Poston, Jackie, Daughter of former Representative Wylie Chalmers (Ohio), 269

Powell, Mrs. Walter, Wife of former Representative (Ohio), 261

Pressler, Mrs. Larry, Wife of former Senator (South Dakota), 130

Price, Georgeanne, Daughter of former Representative William L. Jenkins (Tennessee), 169

Prouty, Mrs. Winston, Wife of former Senator (Vermont), 184

Puckett, Kimberly, Daughter of former Representative George E. Sangmeister (Illinois), 126

Q

Quinlivan, Margaret, Daughter of former Representative John R. Foley (Maryland), 79

R

Rangel, Charles B., Representative (New York), 182

Rangel, Mrs. Charles, Wife of Representative (New York), 233, 362

Reeves, Mary, Daughter of former Senator Robert B. Morgan (North Carolina), 126

Regula, Ralph, Representative (Ohio), 265

Regula, Mrs. Ralph, Wife of Representative (Ohio), 128, 303

Reich, Elizabeth, Daughter of former Representative John J. Rhodes (Arizona), 181

Reyes, Silvestre, Representative (Texas), 52

Reyes, Mrs. Silvestre, Wife of Representative (Texas), 246, 306

Rhodes, Adeline, Daughter-in-law of former Representative John J. Rhodes III (Arizona), 5

Rhodes, Chris, Daughter-in-law of former Representative John J. Rhodes (Arizona), 180

Rhodes, Jay, former Representative (Arizona), 83

Rhodes, Mrs. John (Jay), III, Wife of former Representative (Arizona), 42

Rhodes, John J., former Representative (Arizona), 382

Rhodes, Mrs. John J., Wife of former Representative (Arizona), 80

Rhodes, Stacey, Daughter-in-law of former Representative John J. Rhodes III (Arizona), 4

Rice, Cynthia, Daughter of former Representative Laurie C. Battle (Alabama), 195

Riley, Bob, Representative (Alabama), 30

Riley, Mrs. Bob, Wife of Representative (Alabama), 210, 300

Roberts, Mrs. Pat, Wife of Senator (Kansas), 84, 136

Roemer, Mrs. Tim, Wife of Representative (Indiana), 262

Rogan, James, Representative (California), 313

Rogan, Mrs. James, Wife of Representative (California), 306

Rogers, Paul, former Representative (Florida), 348

Rogers, Mrs. Paul, Wife of former Representative (Florida), 189

Rose, Charlie, former Representative (North Carolina), 47

Rose, Mrs. Charlie, Wife of former Representative (North Carolina), 283

Rousselot, Mrs. John, Wife of former Representative (California), 44

Rowland, Mrs. Roy, Wife of former Representative (Georgia), 161, 305

Royce, Edward R., Representative (California), 299

Royce, Mrs. Edward, Wife of Representative (California), 80, 372

S

Sabo, Martin, Representative (Minnesota), 266

Sabo, Mrs. Martin, Wife of Representative (Minnesota), 187, 298

Sanders, Annie Laurie Rankin, Daughter of former Representative John E. Rankin (Mississippi), 245

Sandlin, Max, Representative (Texas), 239

Sandlin, Mrs. Max, Wife of Representative (Texas), 23, 387

Sanford, Marshall (Mark), Representative (South Carolina), 59

Sanford, Marshall (Mark) and Jenny, Representative and Mrs. (South Carolina), 237, 380

Sangmeister, Mrs. George, Wife of former Representative (Illinois), 128

Sangmeister, Gina, Daughter-in-law of former Representative George Sangmeister (Illinois), 241

Sarpalius, Mrs. Bill, Wife of former Representative (Texas), 162

Sawyer, Mrs. Harold, Wife of former Representative (Michigan), 157

Schulze, Dick, former Representative (Pennsylvania), 390

Schulze, Mrs. Dick, Wife of former Representative (Pennsylvania), 246

Schweiker, Kathleen, Daughter-in-law of former Senator and former Cabinet Secretary Richard Schweiker (Pennsylvania), 88

Schweiker, Richard S., former Senator and former Cabinet Secretary (Pennsylvania), 167

Schweiker, Mrs. Richard S., Wife of former Senator and former Cabinet Secretary (Pennsylvania), 278

Schwengel, Mrs. Fred, Wife of former Representative (Iowa), 280

Sensenbrenner, Mrs. F. James, Wife of Representative (Wisconsin), 196, 351

Sessions, Jeff, Representative (Alabama), 378

Sessions, Mrs. Jeff, Wife of Representative (Alabama), 34, 105

Shadegg, John, Representative (Arizona), 280

Shadegg, Mrs. John, Wife of Representative (Arizona), 151

Shanning, Hillary, Daughter of Representative Nicholas V. Lampson (Texas), 396

Shaw, E. Clay, Representative (Florida), 6

Shaw, Mrs. Clay, Wife of Representative (Florida), 81, 219

Shelton, Lani, Daughter of former Senator and former Cabinet Secretary Richard Schweiker (Pennsylvania), 129

Shepard, Jan, Daughter of former Senator John Sparkman (Alabama), 81

Shepard, Julia Ann, Daughter of former Senator John Sparkman (Alabama), 33

Shepherdson, Beth, Daughter of Senator John Breaux (Louisiana), 155

Sherer, Tara, Daughter of former Representative William L. Dickinson (Alabama), 164

Shimkus, John, Representative (Illinois), 145

Shimkus, Mrs. John, Wife of Representative (Illinois), 50, 146

Sikorski, Gerry, former Representative (Minnesota), 323

Sikorski, Mrs. Gerry, Wife of former Representative (Minnesota), 129

Skelton, Anita, Daughter-in-law of Representative Ike Skelton (Missouri), 270

Skelton, Caroline, Daughter-in-law of Representative Ike Skelton (Missouri), 225

Skelton, Ike, Representative (Missouri), 397

Skelton, Mrs. Ike, Wife of Representative (Missouri), 177, 254

Skelton, Elena, Daughter-in-law of Representative Ike Skelton (Missouri), 5

Slattery, Jim, former Representative (Kansas), 370

Slattery, Mrs. Jim, Wife of former Representative (Kansas), 56

Smith, Adam, Representative (Washington), 353

Smith, Mrs. Adam, Wife of Representative (Washington), 176, 220

Smith, Chris, Representative (New Jersey), 177

Smith, Mrs. Chris, Wife of Representative (New Jersey), 386

Smith, Neal, former Representative (Iowa), 391

Smith, Mrs. Neal, Wife of former Representative (Iowa), 38

Smith, Nick, Representative (Michigan), 135

Smith, Mrs. Nick, Wife of Representative (Michigan), 141, 292

Smith, Robert C., Senator (New Hampshire), 296

Smith, Mrs. Robert, Wife of Senator (New Hampshire), 260

Snowbarger, Vince, Representative (Kansas), 186

Snowbarger, Mrs. Vince, Wife of Representative (Kansas), 43, 257

Soderberg, Peggy, Daughter of former Representative Robert A. Grant (Indiana), 372

Solomon, Jerry, Representative (New York), 178

Solomon, Mrs. Jerry, Wife of Representative (New York) 175, 230

Sparkman, Mrs. John, Wife of former Senator (Alabama), 375

Staton, Cynthia, Daughter of former Representative Mick Staton (West Virginia), 345

Staton, Mrs. Mick, Wife of former Representative (West Virginia), 352

Stenholm, Mrs. Charles, Wife of Representative (Texas), 62, 365

Stevens, Ted, Senator (Alaska), 166

Stevens, Mrs. Ted, Wife of Senator (Alaska), 165

Strickland, Ted, Representative (Ohio), 83

Strickland, Mrs. Ted, Wife of Representative (Ohio), 275, 276

Sununu, Mrs. John E., Wife of Representative (New Hampshire), 292

Swift, Al, former Representative (Washington), 266

Swift, Mrs. Al, Wife of former Representative (Washington), 230

Symms, Steve, former Senator (Idaho), 222

Symms, Mrs. Steve, Wife of former Senator (Idaho), 221

T

Talent, James M., Representative (Missouri), 238

Talent, Mrs. James M., Wife of Representative (Missouri), 331, 335

Tanner, John, Representative (Tennessee), 99

Tanner, Mrs. John, Wife of Representative (Tennessee), 64, 354

Tauke, Tom, former Representative (Iowa), 205

Tauke, Mrs. Tom, Wife of former Representative (Iowa), 304

Tauzin, Mrs. Billy, Wife of Representative (Louisiana), 31

Tauzin, W.J. Billy, Representative (Louisiana), 185

Teague, Mrs. Olin, Wife of former Representative (Texas), 132

Terry, Mrs. John, Wife of former Representative (New York), 100

Thompson, Jean, Daughter of former Representative John H. Terry (New York), 6

Thune, John, Representative (South Dakota), 144

Thune, Mrs. John, Wife of Representative (South Dakota), 144, 364

Tiahrt, Todd, Representative (Kansas), 131

Tiahrt, Mrs. Todd, Wife of Representative (Kansas), 63, 296

Tierney, John, Representative (Massachusetts), 349

Tierney, Mrs. John, Wife of Representative (Massachusetts), 8

Traficant, Mrs. James, Wife of Representative (Ohio), 376

Turner, Jim, Representative (Texas), 351

Turner, Mrs. Jim, Wife of Representative (Texas), 33, 131

U

Udall, "Mo", former Representative (Arizona), 209

Udall, Mrs. Morris, Wife of former Representative (Arizona), 10

Upton, Fred, Representative (Michigan), 242

Upton, Mrs. Fred, Wife of Representative (Michigan), 182

V

Valentine, Mrs. Tim, Wife of former Representative (North Carolina), 258

Vander Jagt, Mrs. Guy, Wife of former Representative (Michigan), 183

VanderSchel, Sharon, Daughter of former Representative Neal Smith (Iowa), 394

Vanik, Charles, former Representative (Ohio), 103

Vanik, Mrs. Charles, Wife of former Representative (Ohio), 179

W

Wagner, Anne, Daughter of former Representative Laurie C. Battle (Alabama), 328

Walsh, Mrs. James, Wife of Representative (New York), 150, 221

Wamp, Zach, Representative (Tennessee), 103

Wamp, Mrs. Zach, Wife of Representative (Tennessee), 294

Waters, Kathleen, Daughter of former Representative John Foley (Maryland), 307

Watkins, Wes, Representative (Oklahoma), 299

Watkins, Mrs. Wes, Wife of Representative (Oklahoma), 298

Watt, Melvin L., Representative (North Carolina), 223

Watt, Mrs. Melvin, Wife of Representative (North Carolina), 295, 395

Waxman, Mrs. Henry, Wife of Representative (California), 58, 133

Weldon, Mrs. Dave, Wife of Representative (Florida), 242, 287

White, Kylene, Daughter of former Representative Richard H. Ichord (Missouri), 47

Wicker, Roger, Representative (Mississippi), 13

Wicker, Mrs. Roger, Wife of Representative (Mississippi), 32, 325

Williams, Pat, former Representative (Montana), 294

Williams, Mrs. Pat, Wife of former Representative (Montana), 302

Wilson, Mrs. Bob, Wife of former Representative (California), 188

Wolf, Frank R., Representative (Virginia), 324

Wolf, Mrs. Frank, Wife of Representative (Virginia), 82

Wylie, Mrs. Marjorie, Wife of former Representative (Ohio), 137

Y

Yates, Rebecca, Daughter of former Representative Wilbur D. Mills (Arkansas), 171

Z

Zeliff, Mrs. Bill, Wife of former Representative (New Hampshire), 8